The Essence of the new Testament:

A *Survey*

The Essence of the new Testament: *A Survey*

Elmer L. Towns
Ben Gutierrez
Editors

Nashville, Tennessee

Published by B&H Publishing Group
Nashville, Tennessee

Dewey Decimal Classification: 225.076
Subject Heading: BIBLE. O.T—STUDY \ BIBLE. N.T.—HISTORY OF
BIBLICAL EVENTS

Image credits are on pages 367–68. At time of publication, all efforts had been
made to determine proper credit. Please contact B&H if any are inaccurate.

Printed in the United States of America

5 6 7 8 9 10 11 12 • 18 17 16 15 14

SB

Dedicated to

Andreas J. Köstenberger

*for his influence in the lives of
several contributing authors of this work.*

Table of Contents

MAPS

Abbreviations

AB	Anchor Bible
BECNT	Baker Evangelical Commentary on the New Testament
BKC	*Bible Knowledge Commentary*
BKCNT	*Bible Knowledge Commentary: New Testament*
EBC	*The Expositor's Bible Commentary*
HNTC	Holman New Testament Commentary
ICC	International Critical Commentary
ISBE	*International Standard Bible Encyclopedia*
IVP	InterVarsity Press
NAC	New American Commentary
NICNT	New International Commentary on the New Testament
NIGTC	New International Greek Testament Commentary
NIVAC	New International Application Commentary
NT	New Testament
NTC	New Testament Commentary (Baker Academic)
PNTC	Pelican New Testament Commentaries
TNTC	Tyndale New Testament Commentary
VT	*Vetus Testamentum*
WBC	Word Biblical Commentary
WEC	Wycliffe Exegetical Commentary
ZECNT	Zondervan Exegetical Commentary on the New Testament
ZIBBC	Zondervan Illustrated Background Commentary

Contributors

GENERAL EDITORS AND AUTHORS

Elmer Towns (D.Min., Fuller Theological Seminary) is cofounder of Liberty University, Distinguished Professor of Systematic Theology, and Dean of the School of Religion at Liberty University and Liberty Baptist Theological Seminary. He is the author of more than 170 books, has contributed articles to more than 10 encyclopedias, and has published widely both popular and scholarly articles. *Ephesians, Colossians, 1 Timothy, 2 Timothy*, and *James*.

Ben Gutierrez (Ph.D., Regent University) is Professor of Religion and Administrative Dean for Undergraduate Programs at Liberty University. He is the coauthor of *Learn How to Read New Testament Greek Workbook and Ministry Is: How to Serve Jesus with Passion and Confidence* (B&H Academic). *Philippians*.

CONTRIBUTORS

James A. Borland (Th.D., Grace Theological Seminary) is Professor of New Testament and Theology at Liberty University. He is a past president and secretary treasurer of the Evangelical Theological Society. *Mark, Luke, Galatians, and Philemon*.

Wayne A. Brindle (Th.D., Dallas Theological Seminary) is Professor of Biblical Studies and Greek at Liberty University. He served as Associate Editor for *The Popular Bible Prophecy Commentary* and *The Popular Encyclopedia of Bible Prophecy* (Harvest House). *Romans, 1 Thessalonians, 2 Thessalonians, Titus, 1 Peter, 2 Peter*, and *Jude*.

David A. Croteau (Ph.D., Southeastern Baptist Theological Seminary) is Associate Professor of Biblical Studies at Liberty University. *How We Got the New Testament* and *Interpreting the New Testament*.

Edward E. Hindson (D.Litt. et Phil., University of South Africa); FIBA (Cambridge University) is Distinguished Professor of Religion and Biblical Studies at Liberty University in Virginia. He is a gold medallion author of more than 40 books, including five study Bibles and numerous commentaries. *Revelation* and *editorial assistance*.

Gaylen P. Leverett (Ph.D., The Southeastern Baptist Theological Seminary) is Associate Professor of Theology and Faculty Chaplain at Liberty University. *The History Between the Testaments, The Essence of the Synoptic Problem*, and *Matthew*.

Donald R. Love III (Th.M. Southeastern Baptist Theological Seminary) is Assistant Professor of Biblical Studies at Liberty University. *John, Hebrews, 1 John, 2 John,* and *3 John*.

Michael J. Smith (Ph.D., Dallas Theological Seminary) is Associate Professor of Biblical Studies at Liberty University. He has contributed scholarly articles to academic journals. *Acts, 1 Corinthians*, and *2 Corinthians*.

PREFACE

Y ou are about to study the most influential book ever written, the New Testament. Of course that claim includes the Old Testament because it is the foundation upon which the New Testament rests. These two books comprise the Bible, God's message to the world.

The New Testament's influence is illustrated by the many people throughout history who have read its message of salvation from sin and freedom in Christ Jesus, have believed the promises of God, and have had their lives changed.

It is also illustrated by nations and empires that have been founded upon and influenced by the Bible. Their laws have been based on Judeo-Christian values, and their citizens have attempted to live by the Protestant/Puritan ethic. Following the principles of God's Word has made them a great nation.

The Old Testament tells of God's creation of the universe, including planet Earth. It tells how God created the first man in His image and gave him life, liberty, and fellowship with Himself. It shows that man's task was to worship God, obey Him, and serve Him in a beautiful environment. It also speaks of the origin of sin that has had a devastating impact on the entire human race. Then the Bible tells the story of God's plan of salvation, how people must please God by their lives and worship Him.

God chose one man, Abraham, and one group of people, the Jews, to fulfill His plan of redemption for all. God gave them principles for living, the Ten Commandments, and the land we know as Palestine. God gave them kings and rulers, and prophets as His messengers, to guide them to worship Him, to gain victory over their enemies, and to embrace His plan on how to glorify Him in their lives.

The Jews, the nation called Israel, failed to obey God and follow Him. In 586 BC Nebuchadnezzar destroyed Jerusalem, their capital, and burned the temple, then took the rest of the population into captivity in Babylon—all as a sign of God's judgment for their sin. Seventy years later some of the Jews returned to the Promised Land, and in succeeding years a few other Jews returned.

Prophets delivered God's message to the Jews scattered among the nations and those in the Promised Land. The last prophet who delivered a message from God to His people was Malachi whose ministry concludes the Old Testament. Then followed approximately 400 years of silence, called "silent" because God was not speaking through prophets.

The New Testament begins with four biographies of God's Son, called "Gospels," each emphasizing a different aspect of Jesus' life. A virgin gave birth and called her Son "Jesus," as an angel had directed her. Jesus was reared in Nazareth of Galilee and "increased in wisdom and stature, and in favor with God and with people" (Luke 2:52). At age 30 He began preaching the message of God's kingdom and performing miracles to show that He was the Messiah. The people heard Him gladly, but the Jewish religious and political leaders rejected Him and plotted to kill Him. He was crucified by Roman soldiers but died as the Lamb of God for the sins of the world (John 1:29). Three days later He arose from the dead and spent 40 days preparing His disciples for a worldwide ministry, preaching the message of His death and resurrection as the basis of salvation for as many as would believe.

The book of Acts (the second section of the New Testament) tells the story of the beginning and growth of groups of believers called the church. The church was victorious wherever it went because many gladly began following Jesus, but at the same time there was persecution from the Jewish establishment and later from the Roman authorities. The power of the church came from their prayers to God when they asked Him to use their preaching to change lives. The Holy Spirit worked in hearts to spread the message, and the church carried out the commission given them by Jesus, "But you will receive power when the Holy Spirit has come upon you, and you will be My witnesses in Jerusalem, in all Judea and Samaria, and to the end of the earth" (Acts 1:8). The book of Acts gives the history of the early church from Pentecost to Paul's imprisonment in Rome (approximately AD 62).

Simon Peter, the leader of the Twelve, preached on Pentecost when the New Testament church was introduced to the world. He also preached the gospel to Cornelius, a Roman army officer, marking the introduction of the gospel to Gentiles.

Paul, the other leader in spreading the gospel, was a Jew born in Tarsus (Turkey) who originally had a high position among the Jewish establishment in Jerusalem. After his conversion Paul carried the gospel to modern-day Turkey, Greece, and several islands in the Mediterranean Sea, and ultimately to Rome, Italy.

New churches were planted wherever the message was preached, and they grew in size and influence. Because of the diverse backgrounds of new believers, and the influence of sin in their lives, problems arose in those churches.

Paul had to (re)visit these churches to clear up doctrinal or lifestyle problems; but he also began writing letters to address a variety of important issues. These letters became the basis to teaching doctrinal beliefs and church practices. The letters of Paul make up the third section of the New Testament

The fourth section of the New Testament is called General Letters or Epistles. These include a letter to the Hebrews in Jerusalem, a letter from James the half brother of Jesus, and letters from the apostles Peter, John, and Jude. These were written to solve specific problems among churches and/or believers.

The last or fifth section of the New Testament is the book of Revelation, written by John the apostle when Jesus appeared to him and said, "Therefore write what you have seen, what is, and what will take place after this" (Rev 1:19). John sums up God's message in the Scriptures by describing the state of Christianity that was symbolically represented in seven churches in and around Ephesus in western Turkey. He then describes the events of the last days, including the coming of Jesus Christ at the end of time. He concludes with a brief description of heaven and life in eternity.

Also included in this survey of the New Testament are four important preliminary chapters that provide a background for your study. The first chapter explains "How We Got the New Testament." Chapter 2 is "Interpreting the New Testament." You will need this orientation to help you clearly understand the message of each of the 27 books that appear in sequence. Chapter 3, "The History Between the Testaments," gives an in-depth account of the historical events leading up to the birth of Jesus. Finally, chapter 4, "The Essence of the Synoptic Problem," examines the issues surrounding the similarities and differences among what we call the "Synoptic Gospels"—Mathew, Mark, and Luke.

This New Testament survey is the result of a team of writers who have taught this course at Liberty University and other educational institutions. This book represents the overflow of our academic studies, our experiences with students like you, and our passion to know God and His Word. We want you to study the New Testament so you will learn about God and in that experience find God's will for your life. Our prayer is that you enjoy studying the New Testament and that, in your research, you reach out to touch God. But more importantly, we pray that, in return, God may touch you.

Elmer L. Towns   Ben Gutierrez
General Editor   General Editor

Chapter 1

HOW WE GOT THE NEW TESTAMENT

The history of how the New Testament was **written**, **copied**, and **translated** is an important topic that impacts the foundation of the faith of Christianity. This chapter answers the following questions: How did we get the New Testament? Who decided which books would be included? Why were some ancient texts not included? Why are there so many translations?

THE WRITING OF THE NEW TESTAMENT

The New Testament consists of **27 books** that were written between about AD 45 to approximately AD 100. Some authors penned their books themselves while others typically dictated the contents of a letter or narrative to an assistant or a scribe. This assistant would write down what was spoken, and the author would then check the document for accuracy. Apparently, Paul handwrote some of his first letters (Gal 6:11) and dictated his later ones, adding his handwritten salutation to authenticate them (Col 4:18; 2 Thess 3:17; see also 1 Pet 4:12). The books of the New Testament were written on **leather scrolls** and **papyrus sheets**.[1] These books were circulated independently at first, not as a collection. Perhaps itinerant preachers such as the apostle Matthew stayed in the home of a rich believer who had a library and slave to serve as his personal scribe. Matthew may have allowed a scribe to copy his Gospel. Hence, the Gospel of Matthew was circulated widely as he traveled from church to church. Paul instructed that some of his letters be circulated (Col 4:16). We don't know if the actual letter (called an **autograph**) was circulated to various churches or if copies were made by

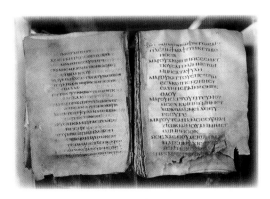

Oldest complete Coptic Psalter.

1

scribes to be circulated. In any case copies were eventually gathered into collections. Apparently, there were collections of Paul's letters (cf. 1 Pet 3:16). They were copied into codices, which are similar to modern-day books, with the pages sewn together to form a binding. In this form the documents were easier to read. Leather or scrolls were harder to use because the entire book had to be unrolled to find a passage. Also, papyrus sheets cracked if rolled into a scroll; hence, the flat papyrus pages were sewn into a book. In Latin the codex collection was called *Ta Bibla*, the words we use to designate our Bible. But the codex form forced decisions to be made, none more important than this: Which books would be included?

THE CANON

Setting the Table for the New Testament

Several factors need to be considered when addressing the formation of the canon. *Canon* refers to a permanent list of **authoritative books** recognized as Scripture.[2] The formation of the Old Testament canon, which will not be discussed here in any detail, gave the church the idea of forming the New Testament. Some scholars place the gathering of the 39 books of the Old Testament to Ezra. Remember, the first five books of the Old Testament had been gathered into the Pentateuch. Other scholars say the Old Testament was gathered into a canon when the Septuagint was translated from Hebrew into Greek. Therefore, the concept of a canon would have been familiar to the writers of the New Testament and Jewish Christians in general.

God "inbreathed" the writings of Scripture so that the writers wrote the Word of God without error. God chose **three languages** for His self-revelation. First, the Old Testament is written in Hebrew, a language structure that reflected the Jew. Of all the Semitic languages, it is simple, solitary, and straightforward. **Hebrew** is as beautiful in its descriptive words as it is ingenious in its idiomatic expressions. Some parts of Daniel and Ezra were written in another Semitic language, **Aramaic**. The New Testament was written in **Greek.**

The Greek of the New Testament was different from the classical Greek of the philosophers. However, the archaeological excavations have uncovered thousands of parchments of "common language Greek," verifying that God chose the language of common people (*Koine* Greek) in which to communicate His revelation. God chose an expressive language to communicate the minute colors and interpretations of His doctrine. Still others feel that God prepared Greeks with their intricate language, allowed them to conquer the world, used them to influence their tongue as the universal "trade language," and then inspired men of God to write the New Testament in **common Greek** for the common people who were part of the new formation of the church. This made the Word of God immediately accessible to everyone. If the Bible had been written in literary Greek or "a special language of the Holy Ghost," Christianity would have had a language barrier to reach the common people.

We do not have the original manuscripts or "autographs" of any book of the Bible. These were lost, mostly during the persecution of the early church. Roman emperors felt that if they could destroy the church's literature, they could eliminate Christianity. Others were lost due to wear and tear. The fact that some early churches did not keep these autographs but made copies and used them demonstrates that they were more concerned with the message than the vehicle of the message. God in His wisdom **allowed the autographs to vanish**. Like the relics from the Holy Land, they would have been venerated and worshipped. Surely "bibliolatry" (worship of the Bible) would have replaced the worship of God.

While some may have difficulty with the idea of not having the original manuscripts, scholars who work with the nonbiblical documents of antiquity usually likewise do not have access to those originals. When considering the manuscript evidence, it should be remembered that there are close to **5,000 Greek manuscripts** and an additional 13,000 manuscript copies of portions of the New Testament. This does not include 8,000 copies of the Latin Vulgate and more than 1,000 copies of other early versions of the Bible. These figures take on even more significance when compared to the similar statistics of other early writings.[3]

Greek Papyrus.

Motivators for a Canon

Some writers have supposed that Christians didn't discuss a canon for New Testament books until several centuries after the life of Jesus. However, because of the presence of the **heretic Marcion** (died c. 160), this is unlikely. Marcion was a church bishop who had a negative view of the God presented in the Old Testament. He rejected the Old Testament and had a severely shortened New Testament canon, consisting of only the Gospel of Luke and 10 of Paul's letters. However, even these were edited to remove as much Jewish influence as possible. The church excommunicated Marcion and swiftly rejected his teachings and canon.

Another heretical movement, **Gnosticism**, developed in the second century. In general this group believed that salvation was found in attaining "special knowledge." The Gnostics had their own set of writings defending their beliefs and practices. Included in their writings are false Gospels (for example, the Gospel of Thomas). The Gnostics and Marcion raised the question as to which books were genuine and authoritative for Christians.[4] Metzger concludes, "All in all, the role played by Gnostics in the development of the canon was chiefly that of provoking a reaction among members of the Great Church so as to ascertain still more clearly which books and epistles conveyed the true teaching of the Gospels."[5]

The Main Criteria for Canonicity

The process in which the canon was formed is rather complicated. However, some offer the following **three tests** for a book to be considered part of the canon: (1) apostolicity, (2) rule of faith, and (3) consensus.[6] There are also other lists that determine canonicity.

The test of apostolicity means that a book must be **written by an apostle** or one connected to an apostle. When applied to the New Testament, most books automatically meet this requirement (those written by Matthew, John, Paul, and Peter). Mark and Luke were both associates of Paul. James was a half brother of Jesus, and Jude is either an apostle or the half brother of Jesus. The only book that has much difficulty with this criterion is Hebrews. Many in the early church believed that Paul wrote Hebrews, but many New Testament scholars today suggest it was written by Luke. If we don't know who wrote the book, how can we connect it to the canon? Hebrews 13:23a says, "Be aware that our brother Timothy has been released." Whoever the author of Hebrews was, this reference places him within the Pauline circle.[7]

The rule of faith refers to the conformity between the book and orthodoxy. "Orthodoxy" refers to "right doctrine." Therefore, the document had to be **consistent with Christian truth** as the standard that was recognized throughout Christian churches (e.g., in Corinth, Ephesus, Philippi, etc.). If a document supported heretical teachings, it was rejected.

Finally, consensus refers to the widespread and continuous use of a document by the churches.[8] At first complete agreement was lacking not because a particular book was questioned but because not all books were universally known. However, the books that were included had **widespread acceptance**. Because the Holy Spirit breathed His life into a book by the process of inspiration (2 Tim 3:16), the Holy Spirit who indwelt individual believers (1 Cor 6:19–20) and the Holy Spirit who indwelt churches (1 Cor 3:16) yielded a unified consensus that a book was authoritative from God.

Applying these criteria to the books contained within the New Testament, and to those that were left out, shows the consistency of the canon as it was handed down. Some "Gospels" have been found in recent years and have raised quite a stir, such as the Gospel of Thomas and the Gospel of Judas. Why aren't these "Gospels" considered authoritative for Christians? First, these Gospels cannot be definitively linked to apostles, even though apostles are named in the titles.[9] Second, some heretical teachings in each document contradict the teachings of Scripture.[10] Third, none of these documents was used universally or continuously by the church.[11] Therefore, they each fail at all three criteria.[12]

Fragment of an Exodus passage from the Septuagint, the Greek translation of the Hebrew Scriptures.

The Logical Argument

The *a priori* **argument** states that God would guard the gathering of the books into the canon because He had originally written each book. The argument is based on the following premise. (1) God had a message He wanted to reveal to man. (2) God chose a multiple number of authors who would write the message for others to understand. (3) God knew that His revelation would be attacked from without. (4) God knew that the recipients of His revelation were not scholars but average people in average circumstances. (5) Therefore, God could be expected personally to guarantee the contents (revelation), the accuracy of the words (inspiration), and the compilation of the different messages from all His messengers into one coherent unit (canon). In this way the message would be transmitted to future generations (inerrancy) so there would be no corruption, alteration, deletion, and/or addition to the Word of God.[13]

THE BIBLE IN TRANSLATION[14]

Early Translations of Scripture

The Old Testament was originally written in Hebrew (with some Aramaic) and the New Testament in Greek. The Old Testament was translated into Greek by Jewish scholars about 200 years before the birth of Jesus. This translation became known as the **Septuagint**, abbreviated as LXX. At times the LXX is a fairly literal translation, but at other times it substantially deviates from the Hebrew text.[15] Also prior to the writing of the New Testament, the Old Testament was translated into Aramaic, the primary language of Israel. At first these translations were done in the synagogue so the congregation could understand the Scripture when the Hebrew text was read aloud. The synagogue leader would verbally translate the Hebrew text into Aramaic, and eventually these translations were written down. The translations were known as Targums.

The entire Bible (Old and New Testaments) was **translated into many languages** early in church history. There were many Latin translations of Scripture, and these were used throughout the churches. In the late fourth century, Pope Damascus commissioned Jerome to create a standard Latin version for the church from the existing translations. The product was the Vulgate. It was quickly accepted and became the standard text throughout the church for the next 1,000 years. The Bible was also translated into Syriac beginning in the second century. A standard Syriac version, called the Peshitta, was completed in the fifth century. Translations were also done into Coptic, Georgian, Armenian, Gothic, and Ethiopic. The goal was to **make Scripture accessible** to Christians who did not know Hebrew and/or Greek.

The Bible Translated into English

Some parts of the Bible were translated into English in the seventh through tenth centuries. **John Wycliffe** began an ambitious translation project in the fourteenth century. He translated all four Gospels, maybe even the entire New Testament. His associates completed the translation of the rest of Scripture. This translation was based on the Latin Vulgate, not the Hebrew and Greek. It was so literal that it was difficult to understand at times. Wycliffe died of a stroke and shortly afterward was declared a heretic by the Roman Catholic Church.[16] The church declared anyone in possession of this translation a heretic as well.

The sixteenth century saw a proliferation of translations into English. With the rediscovery of Hebrew and Greek in the European renaissance and the invention of the printing press, translating the Bible into the languages of the laity became a priority for men like **William Tyndale** (1494–1536). Tyndale completed his translation of the New Testament in 1526. Since the English Bible was forbidden in England, it was printed in Germany and smuggled into England. He continued the task by translating the Pentateuch (the first five books of the Old Testament) and other Old Testament books while

William Tyndale.

continually revising his New Testament translation. He was eventually put on trial and found guilty of heresy. He was executed by being strangled and burned at the stake. Tyndale's translation is far superior to Wycliffe's. His desire to see the common man understand the Bible is evident in his translation.

Many more versions were produced following Tyndale. The Coverdale Bible (1535) was the first complete Bible printed in English. This was essentially a revision of Tyndale's translation. The first Bible published with the approval of the king of England was Matthew's Bible (1537).[17] The Great Bible (1539) was the first authorized translation and was the official Bible of England for about 20 years.

The **Geneva Bible** (first printed in Geneva, Switzerland, in 1560) was a significant achievement for Bible translation in English. This translation was completed by a group of scholars, not one man. The Old Testament was translated from the Hebrew text, unlike most of the translations before it. Also, many consider it the first "study Bible," since it contained annotations, introductions to the books of the Bible, as well as maps and cross-references. Finally, it was the first English Bible translation to use both **chapters and verse numbers**. It quickly replaced the Great Bible in the churches.

The **King James Version** (1611), also known as the Authorized Version, was in part motivated by King James I of England's lack of appreciation for the notes that accompanied the Geneva Bible. About 50 scholars were assembled, and translation began in 1607. The rules and principles they used to guide their translation were published as an 11-page preface.[18] The translators argued that students of Scripture should study a variety of translations and look at the alternate translations provided in the margins of the KJV.[19] This translation was an excellent work of scholarship. Soon after publication it became the standard translation used in England. It was the dominant English translation used for over four centuries.

There has been a tradition of English translations that are **revisions** in the KJV tradition. The English Revised Version (ERV) completed the New Testament in 1881 and the Old Testament in 1885. The main advancements from the KJV to the ERV were: (1) the ERV updated words since the English language had changed significantly in the previous 250 years; and (2) many manuscripts older than the ones used by the KJV translators had been discovered, and these were used by the translators of the ERV.[20] The ERV committee was composed of scholars in England and America. The American representatives had a significantly weaker influence on the committee and published their own revision of the KJV in 1901: the American Standard Version (ASV). The ASV was revised in 1952 in the form of the Revised Standard Version (RSV).[21]

Modern Translations in English

Many translations have appeared on the American scene in recent years. The following is a summary of a selection of the more popular translations and their origin. Some of these translations are considered **essentially literal**, which is a translation philosophy that understands the relationship between the modern reader and the message of the text to be the same as that between the original reader and the message of the text. This philosophy emphasizes the importance of translating every word, using the same (or similar) grammatical structures as the original, preserving idioms, and maintaining consistency in translating words from the original languages. Other translations are in the **functional or dynamic equivalence** category, which attempts to render the ancient text in such a way as to have the same impact on the contemporary reader that it had on the ancient reader. This philosophy emphasizes that the translation should be easy to read and have contemporary English grammar. Many translations fall between these philosophies.

Essentially Literal Translations

Four popular essentially literal translations have recently been published. The most literal is the New American Standard Version (NASB: 1971, 1995). The NASB is a revision of the ASV prepared by a committee of conservative evangelicals. The New King James Version (NKJV: 1982) is an update in grammar and style from the KJV. The translators made significant changes by removing the historic second-person pronouns (such as "thee" and "thou"). They also changed verbs by removing the "eth" me, euen thine owne ſelfe beſides:

20 Yea, brother, let mee haue ioy of thee in the Lord : refreſh my bowles in the Lord.

21 Hauing confidence in thy obedience, I wrote vnto thee, knowing that thou wilt also doe more then I ſay.

22 But withall prepare mee also a lodging : for I truſt that through your prayers I ſhall be giuen vnto you.

23 There ſalute thee Epaphras, my fellow priſoner in Chriſt Ieſus :

24 Marcus, Ariſtarchus, Demas, Lucas, my fellow labourers.

25 The grace of our Lord Ieſus Chriſt be with your ſpirit. Amen.

¶ written from Rome to Philemon, by Oneſimus a ſeruant.

¶ THE EPISTLE OF PAVL
the Apoſtle to the Hebrewes.

CHAP. I.

1 Chriſt in theſe laſt times comming to vs from the Father, 4 is preferred aboue the Angels, both in Perſon and Office.

God who at ſundry times, and in diuers manners, ſpake in time paſt vnto the Fathers by the Prophets,

2 Hath in theſe laſt dayes ſpoken vnto vs by his Sonne, whom he hath appointed heire of all things, by whom alſo he made the worlds,

3 *Who being the brightneſſe of his glory, and the expreſſe image of his perſon, and vpholding all things by the word of his power, when hee had by himſelfe purged our ſinnes, ſate downe on the right hand of the Maieſtie on high,

4 Being made ſo much better then the Angels, as hee hath by inheritance obtained a more excellent Name then they.

5 For vnto which of the Angels ſaid he at any time, Thou art my ſonne, this day haue I begotten thee : And againe, I will be to him a Father, and he ſhall be to me a Sonne.

6 And againe, when he bringeth in the firſt begotten into the world, hee ſaith, And let all the Angels of God worſhip him.

7 And of the Angels he ſaith : who

* Wiſd. 7. 16.

maketh his Angels ſpirits, and his miniſters a flame of fire.

8 But vnto the Sonne, he ſaith, Thy throne, O God, is for euer and euer : a ſcepter of †righteouſneſſe is the ſcepter of thy kingdome.

9 Thou haſt loued righteouſneſſe, and hated iniquitie, therefore God, euen thy God hath anointed thee with the oyle of gladneſſe aboue thy fellowes.

10 And, *thou Lord in the beginning haſt layed the foundation of the earth : and the heauens are the workes of thine hands.

11 They ſhall periſh, but thou remaineſt : and they all ſhal waxe old as doth a garment.

12 And as a veſture ſhalt thou fold them vp, and they ſhall be changed, but thou art the ſame, and thy yeeres ſhall not faile :

13 But to which of the Angels ſaid hee at any time, * Sit on my right hand, vntill I make thine enemies thy footſtoole :

14 Are they not all miniſtring ſpirits, ſent foorth to miniſter for them, who ſhall be heires of ſaluation :

CHAP. II.

1 Wee ought to bee obedient to Chriſt Ieſus, 5 and that becauſe he vouchſafed to take our nature vpon him, 14 as it was neceſſarie.

Therefore we ought to giue the more earneſt heede to the things which we haue heard, leſt at any time we ſhould †let them ſlip.

2 For

† Gr. righteneſſe, or ſtraightnes.

*Pſa. 102. 7. eſa. 34. 4.

*Pſal. 110. 1. matth. 22. 44.

† Gr. run out as leaking veſſels.

Original page from a KJV 1611 Bible.

from the end (so "believeth" became "believes"). The style and literary quality of the KJV was retained. The translators also used the same Greek text (the Majority Text) in translation as the KJV, as opposed to other modern translations.

The English Standard Version (ESV: 2001, 2007, 2011) is a revision of the RSV. The translators of the ESV sought to update the language of the RSV while "correcting" some of the translations they believed were of a liberal bent. The Holman Christian Standard Bible (HCSB: 2004, 2009) is a fresh translation from the Hebrew and Greek, not a revision of a previous version. Two factors motivated the HCSB translation: (1) Bible translations must keep pace with the **rapidly changing English language**, and (2) significant advances in biblical research (such as the discovery of the Dead Sea Scrolls) have given modern translators more information for more accurate translations. The HCSB translation represents a high-quality, accurate translation for today's reader.

Functional Equivalent Translations and Attempts at Balance

One popular contemporary translation follows the functional equivalence philosophy: the New Living Translation (NLT: 1996, 2004, 2007).[22] Kenneth Taylor paraphrased The Living Bible (LB: 1971) from the ASV.[23] His translation was a best seller in the 1970s. Tyndale House Publishers, started by Taylor, decided to revise The Living Bible in 1989. The second edition firmly moved the NLT away from the paraphrase and into the functional equivalence category in its translation philosophy.

The Bible that has succeeded in replacing the KJV from being the standard English translation is the New International Version (NIV: 1978, 1984, 2011). The NIV translators were a group of approximately 100 scholars who held to a high view of Scripture and were committed to the authority and infallibility of the Bible. The committee planned a revision that was eventually published as the TNIV (2005). In 2009, the publisher announced that the 1984 NIV and the 2005 TNIV would no longer be published. Instead, an updated NIV would be released in 2011. The 2011 NIV has made many changes from the 1984 NIV but remains about 95 percent the same. Changes were made for one of three reasons: (1) changes in the English language, (2) progress in scholarship, (3) a concern for clarity.[24] The translators sought to strike a balance between an essentially literal and a functional equivalence philosophy. The NIV has been the top-selling Bible translation for over two decades.

The New Revised Standard Version (NRSV: 1989) was another revision from the RSV. This was one of the first major translations to incorporate gender-neutral language into their translation philosophy. The **gender-neutral issue** in Bible translation is a dialogue over how to approach the issue of the gender of certain words. Translators disagree over whether certain words and phrases in Hebrew and Greek were originally gender specific or more universal. For example, Matt 4:19 reads in the KJV, "I will make you fishers of men," but in the NRSV, "I will make you fish for people."

The New English Translation (NET: 2001, 2003, 2005) is another fresh translation from the Hebrew and Greek. The goal of this unique translation was to provide a digital translation that could be obtained for free on the Internet. The NET

Bible contains over 60,000 translators' notes, which often contain discussions on the Hebrew or Greek text. While the main translation is balanced and gender neutral, the footnotes contain more literal alternative translations.[25]

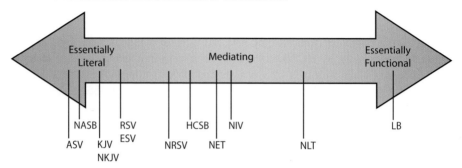

CONCLUSION

The New Testament that Christians use today has a long, rich history. The original copies were written almost 2,000 years ago and were copied for over 1,000 years by hand. The dialogue over the Old Testament canon set the table for the dialogue over the New Testament canon. The heretic Marcion and Gnosticism motivated the early church to discuss which books were authoritative and which books were not. All the books in the New Testament can be connected to an apostle, have content consistent with sound doctrine, have apostolic authority, and were used widely throughout the early church. The New Testament was translated into many languages early in church history. Wycliffe and Tyndale were early translators of the Bible into English, culminating in the King James Version. Many contemporary versions now exist for the edification of the body of Christ. With the King James translators, we urge you to compare several versions of Scripture as you show yourself to be a diligent student of God's Word, always remembering that the original intent of the biblical author is the key to interpreting the text.

For Further Reading

Bruce, F. F. *The Canon of Scripture*. Downers Grove: IVP, 1988.

Carson, D. A. *The Inclusive-Language Debate: A Plea for Realism*. Grand Rapids: Baker, 1998.

Fee, Gordon D., and Mark L. Strauss. *How to Choose a Translation for All Its Worth: A Guide to Understanding and Using Bible Versions*. Grand Rapids: Zondervan, 2007.

Köstenberger, Andreas J., and David A. Croteau. "A Short History of Bible Translation." In *Which Bible Translation Should I Use? A Comparison of 4 Major Recent Versions*, ed. Andreas J. Köstenberger and David A. Croteau. Nashville: B&H Academic, 2012.

Köstenberger, Andreas J., and Michael J. Kruger. *The Heresy of Orthodoxy: How Contemporary Culture's Fascination with Diversity Has Reshaped Our Understanding of Early Christianity*. Wheaton: Crossway, 2010.

Metzger, Bruce M. *The Bible in Translation: Ancient and English Versions*. Grand Rapids: Baker, 2001.

———. *The Canon of the New Testament*. New York: Oxford University Press, 1987.

Metzger, Bruce M., and Bart D. Ehrman. *The Text of the New Testament: Its Transmission, Corruption, and Restoration*. 4th ed. New York: Oxford University Press, 2005.

Study Questions

1. What is the definition of the word *canon*?
2. How did Marcion and Gnosticism contribute to the development of the canon?
3. What are the three main tests a book had to pass when being considered for inclusion into the canon?
4. How has understanding the process of canonization increased your trust in the Bible?
5. Who were some of the earliest Christians to translate the Bible into English?
6. What are the differences between the major translation philosophies?
7. What translation do you use most often? What translation philosophy does it use?

ENDNOTES

1. Papyrus is a thick paper material that comes from the center tissue of the papyrus plant (2 John 12; 3 John 13).

2. Cf. James Barr, *Holy Scripture: Canon, Authority, Criticism* (Philadelphia: Westminster, 1983), 71.

3. Josh McDowell, *Evidence That Demands a Verdict* (San Bernardino, CA: Campus Crusade for Christ International, 1972), 48.

4. Cf. F. F. Bruce, *The Canon of Scripture* (Downers Grove: IVP, 1988), 153.

5. Bruce M. Metzger, *The Canon of the New Testament* (New York: Oxford University Press, 1987), 90.

6. Other possible criteria included the age, adaptability, and inspiration of the book. See also Elmer L. Towns, *Theology for Today* (Fort Worth, TX: Harcourt Custom Publishers, 2001), 79.

7. For more on the authorship of Hebrews, see the chapter on Hebrews.

8. Also referred to as universality or catholicity.

9. See Andreas J. Köstenberger and Michael J. Kruger, *The Heresy of Orthodoxy: How Contemporary Culture's Fascination with Diversity Has Reshaped Our Understanding of Early Christianity* (Wheaton: Crossway, 2010), esp. 151ff.

10. For example, v. 114 (probably added at a later date) in the Gospel of Thomas is an affront to New Testament teaching on women and salvation (cf. Gal 3:28). Also, the entire story line of the Gospel of Judas contradicts the Gospels and Acts, especially with regard to Judas's death (cf. Matt 27:5 and Acts 1:18 with the claim that the disciples stoned Judas).

11. See Nicholas Perrin, *Thomas: The Other Gospel* (Louisville: Westminster, 2007).

12. Similarly, if another of Paul's or Peter's letters were found, these might be helpful for understanding the New Testament, but they would not be considered part of the canon.

13. Towns, *Theology for Today*, 80.

14. The discussion below is based upon Andreas J. Köstenberger and David A. Croteau, "A Short History of Bible Translation," in *Which Bible Translation Should I Use? A Comparison of 4 Major Recent Versions*, ed. Andreas J. Köstenberger and David A. Croteau (Nashville: B&H Academic, 2012).

15. It should be noted that there wasn't an official "Septuagint" but many versions, or "Septuagints," because many variations existed among the manuscripts.

16. This was not necessarily just because of his translation but because of his views on predestination, authority, wealth and possessions, the Lord's Supper, and the papacy.

17. It was edited by John Rogers, who wrote under a false name.

18. Unfortunately, most modern editions of the King James Version do not contain this preface. Those who want to appreciate the fullness of the King James Version should by all means read the preface.

19. The preface can be found at http://www.ccel.org/bible/kjv/preface/pref1.htm.

20. The KJV was translated from copies of the Old Testament and New Testament books. These copies, or manuscripts, have a wide range of dates, some being just several hundred years removed from the writing of the New Testament.

21. When multiple dates are listed for translations, the first refers to the original publication date and all following dates refer to revisions.

22. See http://www.nltblog.com/index.php/2008/08/nlt-1-on-july-cba-bestseller-list.

23. A paraphrase seeks to reword the message of Scripture in the same language. Some scholars would consider paraphrases as "translations."

24. See http://www.niv-cbt.org/niv-2011-overview/translators-notes.

25. It can be downloaded for free from www.bible.org.

Chapter 2

INTERPRETING THE NEW TESTAMENT

After finishing a meal at a Chinese restaurant, a seven-year-old daughter opened her fortune cookie and read: "Keep your feet on the ground even though friends flatter you." She inquisitively asked what it meant. Her father explained that the phrase, "Keep your feet on the ground" is an expression (really, an idiom) that means to have a realistic understanding of your own ideas, actions, and decisions. She looked at him, more puzzled than ever, and said, "But I still have to keep my feet *on the ground*, right?" She didn't understand how idioms worked. She still assumed a more *literal* meaning existed. People can misunderstand the Bible in the same manner. An example is John 17:12 where Judas is called "the son of destruction." Does that mean Judas's father was named "Destruction"? No, this is an **idiom** in the New Testament that refers to someone's character or destiny.[1] So John 17:12 means that Judas is destined for destruction. When we read the Bible we must ask: what did the original author intend to communicate?

THE IMPORTANCE OF CORRECT INTERPRETATION

Much of the Bible can be interpreted literally without any problem. However, the approach described in this chapter, the **grammatical-historical approach**, is a much better way to approach Scripture. That is, readers of Scripture must understand the grammar and the historical setting of the passage in order to understand correctly and apply any passage with confidence.[2]

In 2 Tim 2:15, the apostle Paul said, "Be diligent to present yourself approved to God, a worker who doesn't need to be ashamed, correctly teaching the word of truth." Paul commands Timothy to "be diligent," a word that refers to **examining thoroughly** all you do. Timothy is commanded to be diligent in his handling and teaching of Scripture. Skeptics have said, "You can make the Bible say anything you want it to say." Is this the principle for interpreting the Bible? No! Then what are the steps for understanding the Bible? How can Christians apply a passage to their lives today from a book that was completed almost 2,000 years ago? These questions, and others, will be answered in this chapter.

One mandatory concept that needs to be grasped is that the Bible cannot be read properly without being interpreted. Every word that is read is assigned a definition. Every sentence is understood in relationship to the sentences surrounding it. These decisions on meaning, usually taking place subconsciously, are in fact interpretations because people filter what they read through their **presuppositions**. Every reader is influenced by his or her worldview, doctrines, traditions, upbringing, and culture. People don't just read it and understand it, because when a statement is read, it is interpreted. The question is not whether Christians should interpret the Bible (because all people do); the question is whether Christians interpret the Bible correctly.

CONCEPTS FOR INTERPRETATION

Two universal concepts to keep in mind when reading your Bible are: (1) context and (2) the rule of interpretation. With these two concepts in your "interpretive toolbox," you will safeguard yourself against wayward or even heretical interpretations.

Context

There are **two types of context** when interpreting Scripture: (1) the literary context, which refers to the surrounding words, sentences, and paragraphs; and (2) the historical context, which refers to the culture and historical setting of the original author and audience. For example, the **literary context** of John 3:16 is: (1) the paragraph (John 3:16–21), (2) the discourse (John 3:1–21), (3) the section of the Gospel of John it is in (John 1:19–4:54), and (4) the entire Gospel of John. You could picture it like this:

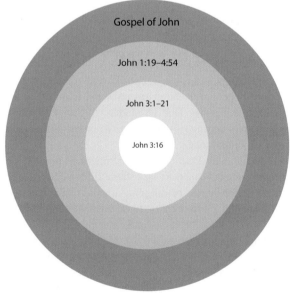

The **historical context** includes the culture, language, customs, time period, situation, and the covenant of the original author and readers. Many additional resources are available to help you understand the historical context.[3]

The refrain "**context is king**" should be repeated until it echoes in your mind. No principle of interpreting Scripture is more important than context. The majority of errors in interpretation can be resolved through studying the context more carefully. The old adage that "you can make the Bible say anything you want it to say" is true only if you ignore literary context. The most common way this is done is through proof texting.

Inappropriate proof texting is a plague that hinders good interpretation. Proof texting refers to quoting a verse of Scripture without regard for the literary context. Sometimes **proof texting** is done correctly. For example, if a preacher were to state that "everyone who believes in Jesus will have eternal life, like it says in John 3:16," he would be proof texting John 3:16. Since the statement is correct, this is an example of appropriate proof texting. This practice becomes dangerous if someone doesn't know the literary context of that passage. But suppose a football player said, "I know that God will help me be the greatest football player ever because Phil 4:13 says that 'I am able to do all things through Him who strengthens me.'" The context of Philippians is one of being strengthened through persecution. In Phil 1:27–29, Paul says:

> Just one thing: Live your life in a manner worthy of the gospel of Christ. Then, whether I come and see you or am absent, I will hear about you that you are standing firm in one spirit, with one mind, working side by side for the faith that comes from the gospel, not being frightened in any way *by your opponents*. This is a sign of destruction for them, but of your deliverance—and this is from God. For it has been given to you on Christ's behalf not only to believe in Him, but *also to suffer for Him*.[4]

These verses depict the Philippians facing persecution. This should come as no surprise since Paul was arrested and beaten while in Philippi (see Acts 16) and was in prison while writing this letter. While many small indicators further this argument, in the verse immediately before 4:13, Paul describes some of the suffering he has been through. After 4:13, Paul mentions his "hardship." All of these contextual clues indicate that Paul was not making a blanket statement that God will help Christians do anything they want to do.

The Analogy of Faith

A popular confession of faith summarizes this concept well: "The infallible rule of interpretation is that the Scripture interprets itself: and therefore, when there is a question about the true and full sense of any Scripture (which is not manifold, but one), it must be searched and known by other places that speak more clearly."[5] The first statement explains that Scripture should be used to interpret Scripture. **Scripture will never contradict Scripture**. Also, every text has only one correct interpretation but many applications. When a verse is unclear, one should seek to understand that verse by studying the verses on the same topic that are clearer. For example, Heb 6:1–6 is often cited as a passage that demonstrates people can be saved and subsequently lose their salvation. These verses are hard to interpret by themselves: Are they describing Christians or just those who appear to be Christians? The descriptions seem so positive (they were enlightened, tasted the heavenly gift, were companions with the Holy Spirit, etc.), but the text never explicitly says they are in fact Christians. Since this is an unclear passage, a **comparison with other passages** that address this topic will be necessary for clarity. Reading John 6:39; 10:28–29; and 1 John 2:19, passages that are much clearer on the issue, will help to clarify the meaning of Heb 6:1–6.

CONSIDERATIONS IN INTERPRETATION

Interpreting a passage of Scripture involves a **conscientious reading** of the text. Careful readers of Scripture will want to read the passage over and over again, meticulously figuring out how every sentence and paragraph add to the meaning of the passage they are studying. Skimming over the passage will enforce the readers' prior beliefs about the passage. But when they engage in a deeper examination, diligently studying God's Word, they will truly be able to understand His Word and know God more intimately.

Observing the Parts of a Passage

Both the details of the passage and the big picture need to be analyzed. The process starts with **observation**. Write down as many observations about the passage as possible. Howard Hendricks has said, "A pen is a mental crowbar."[6] Conscientious readers will discover that there are too many observations to remember without writing them down. Therefore, write them down so you can sift through them later. You need to complete this simple step, observation, before you can interpret or apply the passage. The great English pastor and author, John Stott, said:

> To search for [a passage's] contemporary message without first wrestling with its original meaning is to attempt a forbidden shortcut. It dishonours God (disregarding his chosen way of revealing himself in particular historical cultural contexts), it misuses his Word (treating it like an almanac or book of magic spells) and it misleads his people (confusing them about how to interpret Scripture).[7]

What are some ways careful observers of Scripture should read Scripture? Here is a road map to reading sentences and paragraphs.

The Place of Observation in Interpretation

John Stott's quote emphasizes the importance of understanding the meaning of the passage for the original audience before understanding the contemporary meaning. **Three key concepts** are observation, interpretation, and application. The order for these concepts is of utmost importance. If readers change the order, they are in danger of misinterpreting a passage. First, **observe** the passage using some of the categories discussed below. Second, **interpret** the passage, which means to figure out what the passage meant to the original audience. Third, **apply** the passage to a contemporary situation.

Observing Sentences

There is a difference between a "sentence" and a "verse." Some verses will have multiple sentences. Some sentences will span multiple verses. Here are **seven things** to look for when reading sentences. This is not an exhaustive list but a way to get started reading sentences more attentively.[8]

1. Repetition: One way an author emphasizes an important point is by repeating a word or phrase several times. For example, John 1:9–10 says, "The true light, who gives light to everyone, was coming into the world. He was in the world, and the world was created through Him, yet the world did not recognize Him." John used the word "world" four times in two verses. So, in observing this text, write down: "The word 'world' is used four times in two verses." Don't be concerned yet about the reason or implication of this observation; just make the observation.

2. Contrasts: The use of the words "but," "rather," and "however" signifies a contrast. Paul says in Rom 6:14, "For sin will not rule over you, because you are not under law but under grace." When you see the word "but," make sure to write down the two items being contrasted. In Rom 6:14, "not under law" and "under grace" are being contrasted.

3. Comparisons and Metaphors: Luke's description of Jesus in Luke 22:44 is a good example: "Being in anguish, He prayed more fervently, and His sweat became like drops of blood falling to the ground." Sermons have been preached describing the process of hematohidrosis in relationship to this verse. Without denying the medical condition of small blood vessels rupturing near sweat glands and blood coming out through the sweat glands, recognize that Luke 22:44 only says that Jesus' sweat was "like" drops of blood.[9] This means there was a relationship between His sweat and drops of blood. It appears more likely that the relationship was that of the size of the sweat drops, not the color.[10]

4. Cause and Effect: Study Rom 12:2 and try to figure out the cause-and-effect relationships: "Do not be conformed to this age, but be transformed by the renewing of your mind, so that you may discern what is the good, pleasing, and perfect will of God." The first cause is a renewed mind, and the effect is transformation. The second cause is transformation, and the effect is the ability to discern the will of God.

5. Conjunctions: Romans 12:1 begins, "Therefore, brothers, by the mercies of God, I urge you to present your bodies as a living sacrifice." This verse begins with "therefore," which should cause an observant reader to ask, "Why does the author say 'therefore'?"[11] It refers to the foundation on the basis of which Paul is going to teach in Romans 12–16, which is all of Romans 1–11.

6. Verbs: Verbs are where the action takes place. This is true in the entire New Testament but especially in the epistles. Beyond simply noting the verb, also try to decide if the verb is active or passive. An active verb occurs when the subject of the sentence is doing the action. In the sentence "I hit the ball," the subject ("I") is doing the action ("hit"). Therefore, "hit" is an active verb. In the sentence "I was hit by the ball," the subject ("I") did not do the action of hitting but received the action. When the subject receives the action, it is a passive verb. Look at Eph 1:11: "In him we have obtained an inheritance, having been predestined according to the purpose of him who works all things according to the counsel of his will" (ESV). "Having been predestined" is passive. Christians were passive in receiving the action of predestination. The active verb has as its subject the One who "works all things." God is the active agent, and Christians are passive. Remember, all you are doing is making observations. Don't prematurely jump into application or theology. People must train themselves to make observations and allow the text to speak for itself.

7. Pronouns: Sometimes it is difficult to decipher all the pronouns in a biblical text, and many times readers take them for granted. Always write down to whom or to what the pronoun is referring. Read through Phil 1:27–30 and identify to whom all the pronouns refer:

> Just one thing: Live your life in a manner worthy of the gospel of Christ. Then, whether **I** come and see **you** or am absent, **I** will hear about **you** that **you** are standing firm in one spirit, with one mind, working side by side for the faith that comes from the gospel, not being frightened in any way by **your** opponents. This is a sign of destruction for **them**, but of **your** deliverance—and this is from God. For it has been given to **you** on Christ's behalf not only to believe in **Him**, but also to suffer for **Him**, having the same struggle that **you** saw **I** had and now hear that **I** have.

Here are the pronouns in each verse and their definitions:

Verse	Definition
verse 27	I = Paul
	you = the Philippians
	I = Paul
	you = the Philippians
	you = the Philippians
verse 28	your = the Philippians
	them = the opponents
	your = the Philippians
verse 29	you = the Philippians
	Him = Christ
	Him = Christ
verse 30	you = the Philippians
	I = Paul
	I = Paul

While this passage was a rather simple one, some passages in the New Testament are more confusing.[12]

Observing Paragraphs

There are five items to look for when observing paragraphs. These can be a little more difficult because you have to take into consideration a larger section of material.

1. General to Specific: Sometimes a biblical author will introduce something using "general" terms, and then he will provide a specific example. For example, Paul exhorts his audience in Eph 4:1, "Therefore I, the prisoner for the Lord, urge you to walk worthy of the calling you have received." This is a generic principle they are to follow. However, in the following verse he provides four specific examples: be humble, gentle, patient, and accepting one another in love. These four are specific ways in which to live obediently to the general command.

2. Dialogue: In John 21:15, Jesus asks Peter a question. The dialogue goes back and forth between Jesus and Peter (John 21:15–19). It's important to recognize who is speaking. The author chose to portray the events using dialogue. Many times John the Baptist is saying something, but some teachers credit Jesus with the words (cf. John 3:27–30). Make sure to note who is speaking!

3. Question and Answer: In Rom 6:1, Paul says: "What should we say then? Should we continue in sin so that grace may multiply?" Paul expected his readers to think about this question. So he asked a question, then provided the answer in the next verse: "Absolutely not!"

4. Means: An important element in many passages is the communication of how something is accomplished. When doing this, an author is providing the means. In Eph 2:13, Paul says: "But now in Christ Jesus, you who were far away have been brought near by the blood of the Messiah." The means or instrument that brought those who were separated from God near to God is "the blood of the Messiah." Matthew describes Jesus driving out demons in Matt 8:16 by saying He drove them out "with a word." The "word" of Jesus was the instrument or means that drove out the demons.

5. Purpose: Purpose statements are vitally important to understanding passages in the New Testament. Ephesians 2:8–9 is one the best-known passages in the New Testament: "For you are saved by grace through faith, and this is not from yourselves; it is God's gift—not from works, so that no one can boast." However, Paul gives a purpose for the salvation brought by God's grace in verse 10 (italics added): "For we are His creation—created in Christ Jesus for good works, which God prepared ahead of time *so that* we should walk in them." The purpose is that those who have received the grace of God are to walk in the good works God prepared for them to do. The words "so that" communicate the concept of purpose in this verse.

INTERPRETATION AND GENRE

Before skilled readers can interpret a text, they must consider the **rules of interpretation** that apply to that text. These rules will be known by understanding the genre of the passage being read. When those rules are taken into consideration, it is possible to find the abiding theological principle underlying the passage with confidence. This will significantly aid the process of applying the text to a person's life.

Considering Genre

What is genre? Genre refers to a **type of literature**. People encounter different genres (types of literature) every day. They have been trained to interpret them or can logically deduct how to use them. For example, the way people read a newspaper depends on the section they are reading. If they are in the sports section, they assume they are being given facts about sporting events. If they were reading the front page of a newspaper and saw a story of a cat talking to a dog, they would understandably be puzzled. But if they were to read a story about a cat talking to a dog in the comics section, they would know that reality is suspended for this genre of literature and won't stop and say to themselves, "Wait! This is impossible! Cats and dogs don't talk!" They don't do that because they understand how the genre of comics works. Unfortunately, the Bible is written in ancient genres with which most people today are unfamiliar. Therefore, becoming familiar with these ancient genres and the rules of interpreting them will greatly aid in reading them correctly.[13]

The Gospel Genre

The first four books in the New Testament are Gospels: Matthew, Mark, Luke, and John. Gospels must be approached differently from letters and poetry because they have different rules for interpreting them. The four Gospels are **biographies** of the life of Jesus of Nazareth. However, they are ancient, not modern biographies. What's the difference?

First, ancient biographies did not give many details about someone's entire life. For example, if someone wrote a biography on the life of Brad Pitt, it would probably include some information about his birth in Oklahoma and being raised in Missouri. But if this book skipped over much of his childhood and early adult years, even skipping over his marriage to Jennifer Aniston, and instead focused on his relationship with Angelina Jolie, it would be considered (by modern standards) to be an inadequate account of his life. Ancient biographies often purposely **focused on one period** of a person's life rather than covering a person's entire life span equally. Comparing the four Gospels, notice how Jesus' birth is discussed by only two (Matthew and Luke) and His childhood by only one Gospel (Luke), but **His adult life** following 30 years of age is the focal point of all four Gospels, particularly the last week of His life.

Second, ancient biographies were **not necessarily chronological**. If the afore-mentioned biography of Brad Pitt discussed his movies out of order (not chronologically), this would, again, be considered problematic by modern-day standards. However, while ancient biographies could be chronological, they weren't required to be. Luke says that he wrote "in orderly sequence" (Luke 1:3), whereby the word "orderly" could refer to chronological, geographical, or logical order.[14]

Asking the **right questions** of the passage being read is one of the keys to good interpretation. There are two primary questions to ask when reading the Gospels: (1) What does this story communicate about Jesus? (2) What is the primary point of the passage? When trying to answer those questions, keep in mind the following considerations.

1. Historical Context: When a person reads the Gospel of John, there are two settings to consider: **the original, historical setting** of Jesus and the setting of the church when John wrote (c. AD 90). So when Jesus is speaking to His disciples, crowds, or Pharisees, remember that none of them is around today. Recognize that the original audience of Jesus' words does not exist anymore. For example, when Jesus washes the feet of His disciples, those in the original setting knew that foot washing was done only by Gentile slaves. Feet were always washed by an inferior. Jesus was turning cultural norms upside down. This original context at the time when Jesus' words were spoken is not necessarily the same context as that of the audience of John's Gospel when he wrote the Gospel about 50 years later.

2. Literary Context: The literary context, which is the immediate and larger context of the passage, trumps all other factors in interpretation. Sometimes readers get concerned with comparing the Gospels to one another. While it's not wrong to compare the Gospels, make sure that you allow Matthew's message to speak for itself and that your presumptions don't smother Matthew's meaning by comparing it to Mark's.

One way to emphasize the literary context is to read **the stories before and after the passage** under examination to see if a similar theme is present. For example, John 2:1–11 appears to present Jesus as offering something superior than Judaism, whether a superior law or a superior purification. John 2:12–25 presents Jesus as the new center of worship. Connecting these stories together shows that John is trying to prove to his audience that what Jesus was offering is superior to what Judaism was offering.

Another way of emphasizing literary context is to examine how **characters** develop in the story or how someone's perception of Jesus grows (or doesn't grow). Tracing the character of Peter through Mark's Gospel will lead to the discovery that at times Peter's understanding seems to grow and develop (cf. Mark 8:29) and at other times his understanding is deficient (cf. Mark 8:32–33).

Authors may use different **literary devices**: dialogue, repetition, irony, misunderstanding, contrast, and symbols. **Irony** is a subtle contrast between what is stated and what is suggested. For example, it is ironic in Matt 16:2–3 that the Pharisees and Sadducees know how to interpret the sky, but they don't know how to interpret "the signs of the times" (Matt 16:3), something that is much more important. Misunderstanding is highlighted frequently in Mark's and John's Gospels. In reading John 3:1–10, Nicodemus is not grasping what Jesus is trying to communicate. Note the **contrast** in John 3 and 4; there are differences between wealthy Nicodemus and an unnamed poor woman. A final literary device is the use of symbolic language. When Jesus says, "I am the true vine" (John 15:1), He doesn't mean that He is a plant with a long stem that creeps along the ground. He is using **symbolic language** to express the intimate relationship He has with the Father.

3. Description Versus Prescription: Apart from context the difference between description and prescription may be the most important principle for interpreting the Gospels. Everything in the Gospels is describing something. The author could be describing the geographic setting for one of Jesus' messages (cf. Mark 6:39) or describing words Jesus said. However, a command given by Jesus to someone in the Gospels is not directly a command for Christians today. In Matt 8:1–4, Jesus healed a man who had a skin disease. Then Jesus gave him a command in verse 4: "See that you don't tell anyone; but go, show yourself to the priest, and offer the gift that Moses prescribed, as a testimony to them." If everything described in the Gospels is automatically a command (i.e., a prescription) for Christians today, then: (1) Never tell anyone if you've been healed of an illness. (2) Go show yourself to the priest (which might be the modern-day pastor). (3) Obey Moses' commands in Leviticus 14, which includes bringing two clean birds, two male lambs, and one ewe lamb to the "priest." This is an example where a command (**a prescription**) in the Gospels does not equal a direct command today. Remember that all of Jesus' commands in the Gospels were given to people living under the old covenant (cf. Heb 8:6–8). Even so, Matthew wrote these words in the AD 60s for the early church, which was under the new covenant. The Gospels are relevant for Christians today, but remembering the original setting of Jesus' life and the setting of the church helps the reader understand how to balance description and prescription.

At the same time, just because "description does not equal prescription,"[15] this does not mean that something described is never commanded. If a descriptive element is repeated over and over again and is always portrayed positively, then it may take on some prescriptive force.[16] There are three parts to deciding if a description is a command for Christians today. First, look in the passage for clues as to what the author is trying to communicate by including the story in his narrative. Second, examine the entire book for positive and negative connotations. Third, analyze the specific context in the book that includes the story.[17]

Historical Narrative

The historical narrative of the Acts of the Apostles is similar to the genre of Gospels, but there are some additional factors to consider. Acts was written about **a transition period** from Judaism under the old covenant to the church age under the new covenant. For example, Christians in Acts are struggling with the concept of how the Gentiles relate to the church between Acts 8 and 15. Many of the stories included in Acts are told by Luke not because they are normative but because they are **not normative**. He doesn't include the mundane, ordinary stories that occurred during this time but the stories that were extraordinary.

When applying the principles of description versus prescription to Acts, many themes could be considered commands for Christians today. The most prominent theme is that of mission. Acts 13 describes Paul and Barnabas's first missionary journey as they were sent out by the church at Antioch. The majority of the following chapters continue to describe the **missionary activity** of Paul. The theme of Paul intentionally going out and spreading the gospel is repeated frequently. Therefore, a discerning reader should see that Luke is trying to communicate the necessity of the church's being involved in missionary activity.

Parables

A parable, as used in the New Testament, is a story that has two levels of meaning. Some of the details in the story represent commonplace realities outside the basic story. One of the keys to interpreting parables is knowing how to **avoid allegorizing** the passage when interpreting those details. To do this, six principles should be taken into consideration.

First, there is **one main point** for every major character or group of characters. In the story of the good Samaritan (Luke 10:25–37), many details are given in the story: a man going to Jericho from Jerusalem, robbers, a priest, a Levite, a Samaritan, a beast, and an innkeeper. How many of these are major characters? The second principle will help with this question: there are one, two, or three main points but no more. The good Samaritan, the man going to Jericho, and the priest/Levite (combined as a group: Jewish leaders) make up the three major characters or groups.

Third, always remember to **consider the context**. When studying the parable of the Prodigal Son, ignoring the opening verses (Luke 15:1–2) will cause the parable to have less of an impact on the reader: "All the tax collectors and sinners were approaching to listen to Him. And the Pharisees and scribes were complaining, 'This man welcomes sinners and eats with them!'" In this parable, the tax collectors and sinner will relate to the prodigal son, and the Pharisees and scribes will relate to the older son. The introduction gives hints as to the meaning of the parable for the original audience.[18]

Fourth, beyond the major characters and groups, all the **other details** are simply props used to carry the story. Make sure you identify relevant and irrelevant details. Anything that is not a major character or group is irrelevant with regard to interpretation, like the beast or the innkeeper. They are useful for telling the parable but not for interpreting it.

Fifth, the main points must have been **intelligible to the original audience**. This principle prevents readers from thinking the prodigal son represents the Southern Baptist Convention between the years 1970 and 1980 and the older son the United Methodists. There is no way Jesus' original audience could have understood this interpretation, nor could Luke's original audience have done so. If an interpretation would have been impossible for the original readers to grasp, then it is almost certainly wrong.

Finally, a warning: it is best to base doctrine on clear, more straightforward passages than on parables.[19] Parables can be used to support doctrine, but a parable should not be the foundational passage for a specific doctrine. The symbolic language employed in parables makes their use in developing doctrine unwise.

Letters

Letters in the New Testament were intended to be **authoritative substitutes** for the authors who were unable to be present and speak to the recipients face-to-face. When the church at Galatia received a letter from Paul, they arguably viewed that letter as words from Paul the apostle himself. Since they didn't have text-messaging, e-mails, or cell phones, it was much more difficult to communicate from a long distance back then compared to today. Therefore, letters provided an opportunity to communicate without being present personally.

The main principle to remember when interpreting letters is that they are occasional. This means that the author is **addressing a particular issue** or situation when he writes the letter. For example, when Paul writes Philippians, he is addressing the concern the Philippians had when they heard that Paul was in prison and that Epaphroditus, whom they had sent to minister to Paul, was sick. This was the occasion for Paul's writing Philippians and should be kept in mind when interpreting the letter.

Since the letters were written to address different situations, sometimes they seem to contradict one another. However, a better perspective would be that the author is seeking to address the situations individually. For example, the church at Galatia struggled with some form of legalism. Therefore, Paul emphasized their freedom in Christ (cf. Gal 2:4; 5:1,13). The Corinthians were basking in their freedom. Therefore, Paul emphasized obedience to temper their immoral extremes.

	Galatians	1 Corinthians
Problem	Struggled with legalism	Basking in freedom
Solution	Emphasized freedom in Christ	Emphasized obedience

PRINCIPLES AND APPLICATION

To apply a passage of Scripture properly, it must be interpreted correctly. Once it has been carefully read, as many observations as possible have been noted, and the context and genre have been taken into consideration, then the passage is ready to be interpreted. The key here is to restate the text in terms that are less temporal. The following example may help.

The **underlying principle** to Phil 4:13 is not a blanket statement that God will empower Christians to do anything they set out to accomplish. Instead, within this context of trials and hardships, Christians can know that God will enable them to persevere through difficult times and they need to rely on Him for their material and physical needs. Richard Melick says: "Many who misapply this verse step out of God's will for their lives. They hope to cover their actions by a blanket promise of power, but power comes in the will of God."[20]

If a group of Christians are ministering faithfully in the inner city and struggling to meet their needs, they must remember to trust God and rely on His strength to sustain them. Dishonesty is not the answer. Self-sufficiency is not the answer. Throwing themselves by faith upon the mercies of God is the answer.

CONCLUSION

Correctly interpreting Scripture is important for a vital relationship with God and true doctrine. Several universal concepts in interpreting Scripture must be considered when reading a passage. Make sure you know the context of the passage and use the clear passages to help you understand the ambiguous ones. Close observation of the sentences and paragraphs is a sure foundation to a good interpretation. Correctly identifying the genre and the rules of interpreting the passage will safeguard against correctable mistakes. Once you discover an abiding theological principle that underlies your passage, you are ready to begin the process of applying the principle. Finally, be encouraged that the more people read Scripture, the better they will become at interpreting it. The more skillful one is in interpreting God's Word, the more intimate one's relationship can be with one's Creator through the living pages of God's Word. "For the word of God is living and effective and sharper than any double-edged sword, penetrating as far as the separation of soul and spirit, joints and marrow. It is able to judge the ideas and thoughts of the heart" (Heb 4:12).

For Further Reading

Blomberg, Craig L. *Interpreting the Parables*. Downers Grove: IVP, 1990.

Duvall, J. Scott, and J. Daniel Hays. *Grasping God's Word: A Hands-on Approach to Reaching, Interpreting, and Applying the Bible*. Grand Rapids: Zondervan, 2001.

Fee, Gordon D., and Douglas Stuart. *How to Read the Bible for All Its Worth: A Guide to Understanding the Bible*. Grand Rapids: Zondervan, 1982.

Hendricks, Howard G., and William D. Hendricks. *Living by the Book Workbook: The Art and Science of Reading the Bible*. New ed. Chicago: Moody, 2007.

Köstenberger, Andreas J., and Richard D. Patterson. *Invitation to Biblical Interpretation: Exploring the Hermeneutical Triad of History, Literature, and Theology*. Grand Rapids: Kregel, 2011.

McQuilkin, Robertson. *Understanding and Applying the Bible*. Rev. and exp. ed. Chicago: Moody, 2009.

Plummer, Robert. *40 Questions About Interpreting the Bible*. 40 Questions and Answers Series. Grand Rapids: Kregel, 2010.

Sproul, R. C. *Knowing Scripture*. Rev. ed. Downers Grove: IVP, 2009.

Zuck, Roy B. *Basic Bible Interpretation: A Practical Guide to Discovering Biblical Truth*. Colorado Springs: David C. Cook, 1991.

Study Questions

1. What are the two universal concepts to keep in mind when reading your Bible, and how are they defined?
2. What are some different things to look for when observing sentences?
3. What is detrimental about reading the Bible superficially?
4. What is the definition of *genre*?
5. What does the phrase "description versus prescription" mean?
6. What are some principles for interpreting parables?
7. How can you apply some of these concepts to your own study of Scripture?

ENDNOTES

1. This kind of idiom is called a "Semitism."

2. For a recent helpful treatment, see Andreas J. Köstenberger and Richard D. Patterson, *Invitation to Biblical Interpretation: Exploring the Hermeneutical Triad of History, Literature, and Theology* (Grand Rapids: Kregel, 2011).

3. Three of the best resources are Clinton Arnold, ed., *Zondervan Illustrated Bible Backgrounds Commentary: New Testament*, 4 vols. (Grand Rapids: Zondervan, 2002); Craig S. Keener, *The IVP Bible Background Commentary: New Testament* (Downers Grove: IVP, 1994); and Everett Ferguson, *Backgrounds of Early Christianity*, 3rd ed. (Grand Rapids: Eerdmans, 2003).

4. Emphasis added.

5. *The Westminster Confession of Faith*, chap. 1, IX.

6. J. Scott Duvall and J. Daniel Hays, *Grasping God's Word: A Hands-on Approach to Reaching, Interpreting, and Applying the Bible* (Grand Rapids: Zondervan, 2001), 58.

7. John Stott, *Between Two Worlds: The Challenge of Preaching Today* (Grand Rapids: Eerdmans, 1982), 221.

8. In the following Scripture passages, emphasis was added to indicate the words on which the interpreter should focus.

9. Cf. Mark Strauss, "Luke," in *Zondervan Illustrated Bible Backgrounds Commentary*, vol. 1 (Grand Rapids: Zondervan, 2002), 485, who says, "Luke does not say that Jesus sweated blood, but that his sweat was like (*hōsei*) drops of blood—that is, it fell profusely."

10. Note the translation of the NKJV and NLT. For other examples of comparisons, see Acts 2:2; 1 Pet 5:8; and Rev 2:18.

11. Or, as has been said: What's the "therefore" there for?

12. For example, Acts 5:11–14.

13. For understanding the prophetic genre, see the chapter on Revelation.

14. Robert H. Stein, *Luke*, NAC 24 (Nashville: B&H, 2001), 65. The Gospels of both Luke and John appear to be in chronological order, but even they could have exceptions.

15. For the entire discussion on description versus prescription, see Gordon D. Fee and Douglas Stuart, *How to Read the Bible for All Its Worth: A Guide to Understanding the Bible* (Grand Rapids: Zondervan, 1982), 107; Duvall and Hays, *Grasping God's Word*, 263–69.

16. An example of this will be shown in the chapter on Acts.

17. See example under "Historical Narrative."

18. Craig L. Blomberg, *Interpreting the Parables* (Downers Grove: IVP, 1990), 174–75.

19. See Robertson McQuilkin, *Understanding and Applying the Bible*, rev. and exp. ed. (Chicago: Moody, 2009), 218–21.

20. Richard R. Melick, *Philippians, Colossians, Philemon*, NAC 32 (Nashville: B&H, 2001), 154–55.

Chapter 3

THE HISTORY BETWEEN THE TESTAMENTS

The history of the Jewish people between the Old and New Testaments covers a period of approximately **400 years**. This period is sometimes called **the "silent years"** because, as Josephus the historian remarked, "the succession of prophets" had been interrupted.[1] The Old Testament had ended with Malachi, and there was no sure word from heaven. God seemed silent. But that did not mean God was not at work in the world. He was preparing the world for the coming of Christ.

Much of this history did not go well for the Jews. Their troubles began even when prophets like Jeremiah, Ezekiel, and Daniel were still speaking. The political oppression of the Jewish people extending from the biblical period through the "silent years" can be divided into four eras: the Babylonian, the Medo-Persian, the Grecian, and the Roman. In between the Grecian and the Roman eras, the Jews won for themselves nearly a century of self-rule under a family of Jewish priests called the Hasmoneans. In each of these periods, God was at work preparing the Jews and the rest of the world for Christ.

THE BABYLONIAN CAPTIVITY (605–535 BC)[2]

After a series of attacks, Jerusalem finally fell to Nebuchadnezzer's forces in 586 BC. The **temple was destroyed**, and the Jews were taken captive to Babylon. There the Jews learned to preserve their identity without a temple by gathering around their

religious teachers. Most scholars believe that Jews developed the habit of regularly meeting for prayer and study at this time. Eventually the study and prayer groups were called "synagogues" (literally, "gatherings"). This development in Jewish culture helped pave the way for Christians to form similar groups. The New Testament word *ekklēsia* (translated "church" in most English Bibles today) literally means "congregation" or "assembly."

The Cyrus Cylinder, inscribed with the famous Edict of Cyrus the Great in 538 BC.

THE MEDO-PERSIAN PERIOD (537–331 BC)

The Medo-Persian domination of Jerusalem began when **Cyrus** defeated the Babylonians in 539 BC. Almost immediately Cyrus reversed the grievous Babylonian policy that displaced subjugated peoples from their ancestral homes. Cyrus believed his conquered peoples would be more manageable and more profitably taxed if they were happily returned to their temples and cities to prosper in their native lands.

The providential hand of God was seen in Cyrus's proclamation that all captives could return to their homes. This meant the Jews could return to their homeland. Zerubbabel, the political leader, and Joshua, the high priest, led the first band of captives back to Jerusalem (Ezra 2:2), bringing back the temple furniture with them (Ezra 5:14–15; 520 BC). Immediately they set up an altar for burnt offerings, kept the Feast of Tabernacles, and took steps to **rebuild the temple** (Ezra 3:2–8). The temple was finished in 516 BC with the encouragement and motivation of the prophets Haggai and Zechariah.

In 458 BC, Ezra led a group of captives back from Persia to Jerusalem who instituted moral reforms among the people. Nehemiah was appointed governor of Jerusalem and Judea in 445 BC and received a decree from King Artaxerxes I to **rebuild the walls**. This was accomplished in 52 days (Neh 6:15), and dedication ensued (Neh 12:27). Ezra led the people in a solemn assembly of fasting, confession of sin, and recommitment to the nation's covenant with God. Old Testament law was made central to Jewish life. Sabbath worship was stressed, non-Israelites were expelled, and the priesthood was carefully regulated.

THE SAMARITANS

In 722 BC, the Assyrians conquered the northern kingdom of Israel, removed the Jewish tribes from those lands, and replaced them with Gentiles from other countries. Some of the Jews who remained in the land and those who returned later intermarried with these Gentiles. This new people group mixed Jewish and pagan religions together (2 Kgs 17:24,32–33; Ezra 4:10). During this time the Samaritans emerged with a **rival religion** that represented a divergent form from traditional Judaism. Ezra and Nehemiah kept Jerusalem free from their influence, which explains the obvious tension that existed between Jews and Samaritans in the New Testament (see John 4:1–26).

During this time **Aramaic** increasingly replaced Hebrew as the common language of the region. Ezra began the habit of reading the Scripture first in Hebrew before giving an understandable translation in Aramaic (Neh 8:8). This practice was repeated so broadly by later generations that the Aramaic translations became more or less standardized. These translations were called "Targums." The Targums characteristically avoided descriptions of God as if He had body parts. Phrases like "the hand of the Lord" or "the eyes of the Lord" were replaced by references to the Lord's "work" or "knowledge." God was seen as Spirit, Creator, Provider, and Sustainer. The teaching of the synagogues during New Testament times can in part be traced in these Targums.

Samaritans of the twentieth century celebrating their Passover on Mount Gerizim.

THE GRECIAN PERIOD (331–164 BC)

The Grecian period of domination began when Alexander the Great expanded his empire and its culture across the land of Israel beginning around 331 BC. Alexander conquered the Persian Empire and forever changed the cultural face of the Middle East. This shift toward Greek culture is called "**Hellenization**." Upon Alexander's death in 323, his vast empire was divided among his generals. Ptolemy I (323–285 BC) inherited Egypt and soon gained control of Israel. For over a century the descendants of Ptolemy in Egypt ruled the Jewish lands with a measure of respect for the Jewish faith.

The Jewish community in and around Jerusalem faced a new threat with the coming of Alexander and **Greek culture**. Would the Jewish community become engulfed by Greek traditions? Would the idolatry of the Greeks make inroads among the Jews? Egypt became Hellenized. Its great port city Alexandria became a cultural center of Hellenization. The threat to Jews at this time did not come from armies but through culture's influence on Israel's way of life and religion. In response the Jews retreated into their synagogues and remained isolated from the world.

At this time the Hebrew Bible began to be translated into Greek. There was much controversy over this move. Some Jews thought it was a transgression to translate the pure Word of God written in the Hebrew language, the language of God, into a pagan language. But Jews scattered over the Mediterranean world couldn't speak or read Hebrew. The new translation was greeted with pragmatic enthusiasm. The oldest translations of the books of the Hebrew Bible into Greek are collectively known as the **Septuagint**.[3] According to tradition a Greek translation was requested by Ptolemy II Philadelphus (285–246 BC). Exactly how much of the Old Testament was translated at that time is debated among scholars today. The most ancient traditions say only that "the divine Law"—that is, the five books of Moses—was translated at first.[4] The differences in translational methods used for each biblical book of the Septuagint suggest that the entire Old Testament was not all translated at the same time by the same people. However, long before the time of the New Testament, the entire Old Testament was available in Greek translation. About 80 percent of the New Testament's quotations of the Old Testament come from the old Greek translations we know now as the Septuagint.

For generations the Ptolemies of Egypt were challenged for their right to govern Israel by the Syrian fragment of Alexander's empire to Israel's north. This Syrian branch of the empire was led by the descendants of Seleucus I, another of Alexander's generals. In 198 BC the **Seleucids** won the upper hand when a Seleucid king named Antiochus III defeated Ptolemy V at the headwaters of the Jordan River. The Syrians far exceeded the Egyptian Ptolemies in their zeal to force the Jews to adopt Hellenistic culture and religion. Hardly any Jewish custom went unchallenged. The Aaronic and Zadokite priests were replaced. Money taken from the temple helped finance "advances" in Hellenistic culture. A gymnasium was built. Jewish boys were expected to compete like Greeks in the nude. Soon circumcision was outlawed, along with Sabbath observance, Jewish festivals, Jewish Scripture, and the Jewish diet. It literally became a capital offence to practice the Jewish religion. Many were crucified or otherwise tortured to death.

Alexander the Great fighting Darius III at the Battle of Issus in 333 BC.

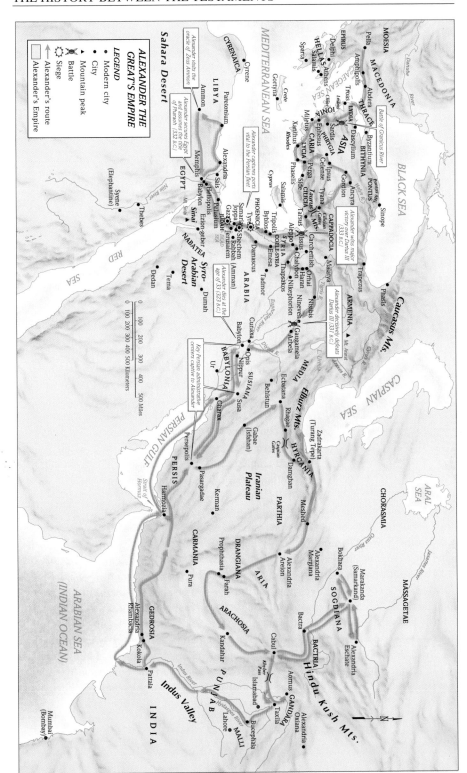

ALEXANDER THE
GREAT'S EMPIRE

LEGEND
• Modern city
• City
▲ Mountain peak
⚔ Battle
☼ Siege
↑ Alexander's route
☐ Alexander's Empire

Alexander visits the
oracle of Zeus Ammon

Alexander secures Egypt
and assumes the title
of Pharaoh (332 B.C.)

Alexander captures ports
vital to the Persian fleet

Battle of Granicus River

Alexander wins major
victory over Darius III
(333 B.C.)

Alexander decisively defeats
Darius III (331 B.C.)

Alexander dies at the
age of 33 (323 B.C.)

Key Persian administrative
centers captive to Alexander

At this time Jewish culture began to divide among those who were compliant and those who resisted. Members of the latter faction were called the "**Hasidim**" ("pious ones"). Those opposed to Hellenism were called "**zealots**." The turmoil came to a head when Antiochus IV Epiphanes stormed Jerusalem, murdered many of its citizens, offered a sow on the temple's altar, and erected an idol to the Olympian Zeus. Jews were ordered to offer sacrifices to the Grecian gods. Many Jews resisted unto death.

THE MACCABEAN REVOLT
AND JEWISH INDEPENDENCE (164–63 BC)

A few months after Antiochus Epiphanes desecrated the temple, an agent was sent to Modein, a small village northwest of Jerusalem, to force its citizens to offer a pagan sacrifice. An aged man named Mattathias from the priestly Hasmonean family refused. When a bystander volunteered to offer the sacrifice, Mattathias killed the turncoat as

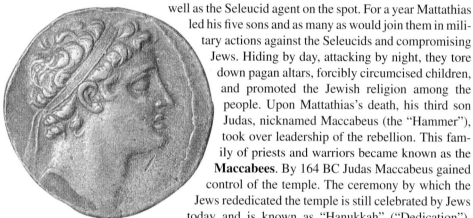

well as the Seleucid agent on the spot. For a year Mattathias led his five sons and as many as would join them in military actions against the Seleucids and compromising Jews. Hiding by day, attacking by night, they tore down pagan altars, forcibly circumcised children, and promoted the Jewish religion among the people. Upon Mattathias's death, his third son Judas, nicknamed Maccabeus (the "Hammer"), took over leadership of the rebellion. This family of priests and warriors became known as the **Maccabees**. By 164 BC Judas Maccabeus gained control of the temple. The ceremony by which the Jews rededicated the temple is still celebrated by Jews today and is known as "Hanukkah" ("Dedication"). Political freedom took longer for the Jews, but it eventually came.

Coin bearing the image of Antiochus IV Epiphanes.

An idea of the Hasmonean family's impact on Israel can be gained from even a brief list of the high points of their history. Judas's brother, Jonathan, was given the office of high priest, a title his family kept until the Roman occupation of Jerusalem in 63 BC. Because the Hasmoneans were not descendants of the line of Zadok, religious opposition to the family began to grow. At this time the **Essenes** separated from the temple,[5] and the **Pharisees** and **Sadducees** also became distinct religious groups. Jonathan's brother Simon gained full release from paying Syrian taxes in 142 BC. This fully established the Hasmonean-Maccabean period of Jewish self-rule (142–63 BC).[6] Simon's son John Hyrcanus (134–104 BC) expanded Israel's territory into Samaria to the north and Idumea to the south. Hyrcanus forced both circumcision and the Jewish law upon the Idumeans. In 108 BC, Hyrcanus destroyed the Samaritan **temple**. At this time some discontent with the Hasmoneans began to grow among the Jews. A Pharisee's challenge against Hyrcanus's right to be high priest led Hyrcanus to shift his allegiance from the Pharisees to the Sadducees. Opposition from the Pharisees intensified more as the Hasmonean priests began to adopt Hellenistic attitudes.

Aristobulus I (104–103 BC), the first openly to call himself king, assumed the title Philhellene ("Lover of Greek things"). His brother Alexander Janneaus (103–67 BC), though living the private life of a debauched Asian tyrant, successfully expanded Israel's borders westward to the Mediterranean and eastward to the other side of the Jordan. He is infamously remembered for crucifying in one day 800 Pharisees as their wives and children were killed before their eyes. Alexander's widow Salome Alexandra (76–67 BC) reigned with some success as she shifted her support back to the Pharisees. Her two sons, however, fought each other so ruthlessly for political control that the entire nation was destabilized. The **civil war** between Aristobulus II and Hyrcanus II weakened Israel to such an extent that the Roman general Pompey had little trouble when he invaded Israel and added it to Rome's expanding empire in 63 BC. The peoples whom the Hasmoneans had recently conquered were willing to accept Rome's version of justice in place of the harsh rule of the Hasmoneans.

THE ROMAN PERIOD (63 BC–AD 134)

When **Pompey captured Jerusalem,** he appointed Hyrcanus II as high priest. A wealthy Idumean named Antipater, whose support Pompey enjoyed during the hostilities, was appointed governor over Judea. Soon Antipater's two sons also became regional rulers: Phasael over Judea and Herod over Galilee. When the Parthians invaded Syria and stormed Jerusalem in 40 BC, Phasael was killed, but Herod escaped to Rome. There the Roman Senate declared Herod "king of the Jews." This title, however, only gave Herod Rome's permission to militarily win the kingdom for himself. With the troops Rome supplied, Herod conquered Jerusalem to become "Herod the Great," king of the Jews (37–4 BC). This is the Herod responsible for the great landscaping and architectural project that transformed the Jewish temple into a marvel of

---

Chart of Herod's Descendants

Upon Herod's death his kingdom was divided among his **three sons.** **Archelaus** was made ruler of Judea and Samaria (4 BC–AD 6). Banished to Gaul for mismanagement, his territory was placed under a series of Roman governors, including Pontius Pilate, until AD 41. **Herod Philip** was made tetrarch of the northern stretches of his father's realm (4 BC–AD 34). **Herod Antipas** reigned as tetrarch over Galilee, Perea, and the land east of the Jordan (4 BC–AD 39). Antipas is infamous for putting John the Baptist to death (Matt 14:1–12).

Herod Agrippa I was the third generation to rule. Eventually he ruled the same land as his grandfather. Herod Agrippa I is the Herod who killed James and imprisoned Peter (Acts 12:1–3). In AD 44, he was struck with a painful death, according to Acts 12:20–23, for unwisely receiving the praise that should go to God alone.[7] He left a son, **Herod Agrippa II,** who became king of Judea in AD 50. Paul's defense before King Agrippa II is recorded in Acts 26.

the ancient world. For this reason the temple which stood in Jesus' day is sometimes called "Herod's temple."

POLITICAL OPPRESSION CREATED A LONGING FOR THE MESSIAH

The restrictive policies of foreign domination, as well as the disappointing outcome of Jewish self-government, each in its own way, worked together to increase among the Jews a general longing for perfect justice and the coming of their promised Messiah. The developing economies of a succession of empires lured Jews to foreign markets or otherwise displaced them as refugees away from their homeland. The **synagogues** these Jews established abroad took the Scriptures far beyond the borders of ancient Israel. Eventually, these synagogues became the launching pads for churches as Paul preached Christ in them "to the Jews first and also to the Greeks." In God's time, according to Paul, "when the time came to completion, God sent His Son" (Gal 4:4) into the world that was already prepared for Him.

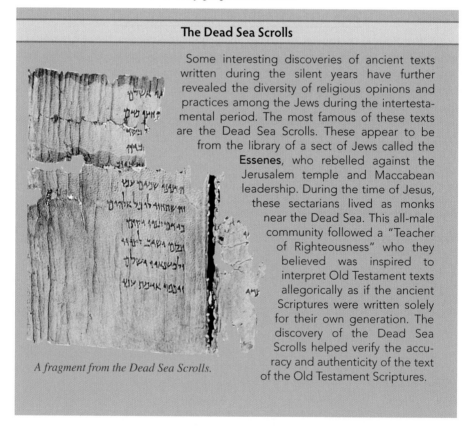

The Dead Sea Scrolls

Some interesting discoveries of ancient texts written during the silent years have further revealed the diversity of religious opinions and practices among the Jews during the intertestamental period. The most famous of these texts are the Dead Sea Scrolls. These appear to be from the library of a sect of Jews called the **Essenes**, who rebelled against the Jerusalem temple and Maccabean leadership. During the time of Jesus, these sectarians lived as monks near the Dead Sea. This all-male community followed a "Teacher of Righteousness" who they believed was inspired to interpret Old Testament texts allegorically as if the ancient Scriptures were written solely for their own generation. The discovery of the Dead Sea Scrolls helped verify the accuracy and authenticity of the text of the Old Testament Scriptures.

A fragment from the Dead Sea Scrolls.

For Further Reading

Bruce, F. F. *New Testament History.* New York: Doubleday, 1969.

Jeffers, J. S. *The Greco-Roman World of the New Testament Era.* Downers Grove: IVP, 1999.

Metzger, Bruce M. *The New Testament: Its Background, Growth, and Content.* 3rd ed. Rev. and enl. Nashville: Abingdon, 2003.

Price, Randall. *Secrets of the Dead Sea Scrolls.* Eugene, OR: Harvest House, 1996.

Richardson, Peter. *Herod: King of the Jews and Friend of the Romans.* Columbia: University of South Carolina Press, 1996.

Russell, D. S. *Between the Testaments.* London: SCM Press, 1960.

Scott, J. Julius, Jr. *Jewish Backgrounds of the New Testament.* Grand Rapids: Baker, 1995.

Tenney, Merrill. *New Testament Times.* Grand Rapids: Eerdmans, 1995.

Vanderkam, J. C. *The Dead Sea Scrolls Today.* Grand Rapids: Eerdmans, 1994.

ENDNOTES

1. Josephus, *Against Apion*, 1.8.

2. Though Jerusalem fatally fell to Babylon in 586 BC, deportations from Jerusalem to Babylon began as early as 605. This makes the captivity of Israel in Babylon roughly compatible to Jeremiah's round prediction of 70 years, shortened a little because of God's mercy (Jer 29:10; cf. 2 Chr 36:15–23).

3. The oldest traditions say that 72 scribes originally worked to translate the "divine law" into Greek. The Latin word for "70" is *septuaginta.* Eventually the entire Old Testament in Greek was called the Septuagint. The oldest accounts of the translation are in the Letter of Aristeas and the Fragments of Aristobulus. A masterful review of all the current state of scholarly opinion can be found in Jennifer M. Dines, *The Septuagint* (London: T&T Clark, 2005).

4. See Philo, *Life of Moses*, 2.57; Josephus, *Antiquities of the Jews*, proem, 3.

5. See sidebar. The Essenes eventually settled in a community near the Dead Sea. The Dead Sea Scrolls are believed to be part of their library.

6. For ease of reference, historians often separate the military process of winning Jewish independence from the period of Jewish self-rule under the Hasmonean priests. The struggle for independence is called the Maccabean period (167–142 BC). The period of self-rule is called the Hasmonean period (142–63 BC).

7. Josephus's account is similar: see his *Antiquities of the Jews*, 19.8.2.

Chapter 4

THE ESSENCE OF THE SYNOPTIC PROBLEM

The story of Jesus' life and ministry is told and retold in the Gospels, the first four books of the New Testament. The **differences in detail** in some episodes of Jesus' life often raise interpretive questions. Take the story of Jesus' healing blind Bartimaeus, for example. Matthew and Mark both report this miracle; Matthew says that Jesus healed two blind men, while Mark only mentions Bartimaeus (Matt 20:29–34; Mark 10:46–52). Luke, like Mark, mentions only one blind man but does not name him (Luke 18:35–43). Luke also seems to differ from both Matthew and Mark regarding the place of the healing. Luke says it occurred as Jesus "drew near Jericho" while Matthew and Mark say it happened as Jesus was "leaving Jericho." These differences can be puzzling. We may ask, "Did Jesus heal one or two blind men here?" and "Was Jesus going into Jericho or leaving the city when He performed this miracle?" There can be a precise reconciliation of these details, but distinctions such as these lead us to be cautious about pressing the Gospels for precision when one account doesn't give all the facts.[1] Questions such as this are part of what commentators often call "**the Synoptic problem**."

IN HOW MANY WAYS CAN THE TRUTH BE TOLD?

God often repeats His lessons to us in different words and **from different perspectives**. In the Bible we have two accounts of Adam's creation (Gen 1:27; 2:7), two versions of the Ten Commandments (Exodus 20; Deuteronomy 5), and two accounts of the lives of kings of Israel (1 Samuel–2 Kings; 1–2 Chronicles). Old Testament prophets often addressed the same themes, but each gave God's message through different words. Each message emphasized what God had placed on each prophet's heart at the time. If we want to know what God has revealed about any particular matter, we must read all the related passages in light of one another. It is not surprising that God would, in a similar way, give His church four inspired accounts of Jesus' earthly life and teaching. These are the Gospels according to Matthew, Mark, Luke, and John.

As we would expect, these Gospels **include many similarities**. Each tells us that John the Baptist foretold the coming of Jesus, that Jesus was baptized by John at the beginning of His public ministry, and that the Holy Spirit descended upon Jesus in the form of a dove. Each presents Jesus as an itinerant preacher who healed the sick, cast out demons, and miraculously fed the hungry crowds who came to hear Him. Each tells us that Jesus called some special disciples whom He selected to travel with Him. Each tells us that when Peter confessed Jesus as the Christ, Jesus began to move toward Jerusalem under the expressed conviction that He must die there and rise again. Each tells us that Jesus was betrayed by Judas Iscariot during Passover week, that Jesus was condemned to crucifixion under Pontius Pilate, that He was buried in the tomb of Joseph of Arimathea, and that His tomb was discovered empty by some of His female followers on the third day.

On the other hand, each Gospel tells us some things that the other Gospels do not mention. Only Matthew tells us about the wise men who followed the star. Only Luke tells us about the angel who announced Jesus' birth to the shepherds. Only Luke tells us about Jesus commissioning 70 evangelists and of the parable of the Good Samaritan (Luke 10:1–37). Only Mark quotes Jesus explicitly saying, "The Sabbath was made for

The green waters of the Jordan River as it meanders through Israel.

man and not man for the Sabbath" (Mark 2:27), and that Jesus "made all foods clean" (Mark 7:17–23). Only John records Jesus' conversation with Nicodemus explaining the "new birth" (John 3). Without the **unique contributions** of each of the evangelists, our understanding of the life and ministry of Jesus would be incomplete.

IS THERE A PROBLEM WITH THE SYNOPTIC GOSPELS?

Because Matthew, Mark, and Luke have more stories in common with one another than they have in common with the Gospel of John, these three have often been studied together. Since the time of J. J. Griesbach (d. 1812), these three Gospels have been compared by arranging their contents in three parallel columns—an arrangement called a "synopsis." This is why these three Gospels are called "**Synoptic Gospels**." The story lines of each of the Synoptic Gospels are similar but not always identical. As mentioned above, the details are different in the several accounts of the healing of blind Bartimaeus. Other differences may be noticed. Both Matthew and Luke describe Jesus' three temptations by Satan after His baptism, but they each give the temptations in a different order (Matt 4:1–11; Luke 4:1–13). Commentators still struggle with the puzzle over whether Jesus sent out His apostles with instructions to carry a "walking stick" (Mark 6:8), to carry "no walking stick" (Luke 9:3), or not to carry an "extra" one (as Matt 10:10 may suggest).

Mount of Beatitudes as viewed from the Sea of Galilee.

Even the wording of Jesus' teaching in the Synoptic Gospels is seldom identical. In Matthew's Sermon on the Mount (Matthew 5–7), Jesus ascends a mountain, sits, and, after His disciples gather, begins the beatitudes with, "The poor in spirit are blessed, for the kingdom of heaven is theirs." Luke, on the other hand, describes a scene in which Jesus, having come down from a mountain, stands on a level area and begins the beatitudes with different wording: "Blessed be ye poor: for yours is the kingdom of God" (Luke 6:17,20 KJV). These differences invite a **variety of explanations**. On the one hand, these two accounts could be seen as precise descriptions of two separate sermons given at different times and places. On the other hand, the distinctions could be due to the insightful and inspired reporting of Matthew and Luke, each summarizing and dramatizing the essence of Jesus' teaching in harmony with their own distinctive emphases. Mark, on the other hand, included no version of this sermon or of the beatitudes. This omission is also one of the reasons some people think there is a "Synoptic Problem."

Because of **differences** such as this, questions have arisen about what the inspired authors of each Gospel really intended to convey about the life of Jesus. Should we think that each of the evangelists intended to give a purely objective and precise account of each of the sayings and deeds of Jesus? Or should we read these Gospels with more attention to their broad themes rather than to their precise details? The whole question boils down to finding out what the evangelists intended their reports to be. Did they intend to summarize the essence of Jesus' life and teaching? Or did they intend for each quotation and story to be a precise repetition of Jesus' exact words and deeds? An accurate reading of these Gospels depends on a correct answer to these questions.

WHAT DID THE EVANGELIST INTEND TO SAY?

There are good reasons for thinking that all of the Gospels were **intended primarily to summarize** the essence of Jesus' life. This would mean that a selection was made from Jesus' teachings and deeds by each evangelist and that each edited these together to emphasize his own distinctive and inspired theme. John's Gospel clearly states that the miracles he reported are only a small selection of the many miracles Jesus did and that a comprehensive account would be impossible (John 21:25). John also explains that his selection was compiled to help people believe that Jesus is the Son of God so they may have life in His name (John 20:30–31). The selections made by the synoptic evangelists were no doubt made for related, but perhaps not identical, purposes. What we have in each Gospel is therefore **not a comprehensive account** of Jesus' life (which would be impossible) but thematically purposed presentations of the sayings and deeds of Jesus. The differences in wording and detail between the Synoptic Gospels may therefore be seen as windows into these particular themes.

Matthew's Gospel regularly avoids the phrase "kingdom of God" (used in five verses) and mostly uses instead the phrase "kingdom of heaven" (33 verses). This pattern supports the ancient theory that Matthew's Gospel was initially written for Christians who were still affected by a Jewish culture which refrained from speaking the word "God" for fear of breaking the third commandment. Luke's Gospel, on the other hand, traditionally believed to be written for Gentiles, never uses the phrase "kingdom of heaven" but uses "kingdom of God" (32 verses). Mark's peculiar habit of explaining Jewish terms and customs (7:1–4; 14:12; 15:42) agrees with the ancient tradition that Mark's Gospel was composed in Rome for readers who needed cross-cultural commentary.

Mark Explains Jewish Customs for Non-Jews (Mark 7:1–4)

The Pharisees and some of the scribes who had come from Jerusalem gathered around Him. They observed that some of His disciples were eating their bread with unclean—that is, unwashed—hands. (For the Pharisees, in fact all the Jews, will not eat unless they wash their hands ritually, keeping the tradition of the elders. When they come from the marketplace, they do not eat unless they have washed. And there are many other customs they have received and keep, like the washing of cups, jugs, copper utensils, and dining couches.)

DID THE SYNOPTIC EVANGELISTS SHARE
THE SAME WRITTEN OR ORAL SOURCES?

Another question related to the Synoptic Gospels concerns the manner in which these Gospels were written. Does the similarity between these Gospels suggest that they each used the same sources? Could one evangelist have borrowed and edited the words of another? The information used by scholars to address this question is drawn from both external and internal evidence. External evidence comes from ancient traditions regarding the original authors and audiences of the Gospels. This **external evidence** has produced the longest held view about how these Gospels were composed. The strongest stripe in this evidence is its basic uniformity. With few exceptions, the ancient traditions agree that Matthew was written first and that all three Synoptic Gospels were written independently of one another. In modern times, however, a second line of evidence called "internal evidence" has been used to challenge the traditions. Internal evidence is based on the wording of the Gospels themselves. Unfortunately, the reviews of the **internal evidence** have not led to uniform conclusions about how the evangelists composed their Gospels. The development of theories of composition and the influence which these theories have on our interpretations will be discussed below. But first, a theological comment is in order.

CAN GOD USE THE EDITING PROCESSES OF PEOPLE
TO PRODUCE HIS INSPIRED WORD?

We who take seriously the inspiration of Scripture may prefer to avoid questions such as this. After all, the **inspired wording** of the books is what really counts—not the literary processes by which that wording took shape. While this is certainly true, we must also recognize that the unique contribution of each evangelist can be better understood if we can identify more precisely the specific Spirit-led motivations of each. The idea that these Gospels are the products of an editing process is not really in conflict with the doctrine of divine inspiration. Luke even told us that he knew and used the accounts of many "eyewitnesses" who had "undertaken to compile a narrative about the events that have been fulfilled among us" (Luke 1:1). Since Luke combined already existing accounts with his own knowledge to help him compose his Gospel, it is possible that Matthew or Mark did the same.

The doctrine of inspiration affirms the accuracy of the written Word of God. The **literary processes** by which God worked through human authors to produce His written word may have been complex. Certainly the evangelists would have combined their own memories with other written and oral accounts to produce with God's help the inspired texts we have today. What the book of Hebrews says of the Old Testament should inform us about the New Testament as well: "Long ago God spoke to the fathers by the prophets at different times and in different ways" (Heb 1:1).

WHAT DOES THE EXTERNAL EVIDENCE SUGGEST?

The earliest explanation we have regarding the origin of the Synoptic Gospels comes from the bishop of Hierapolis in Asia Minor named **Papias** who may have written as early as AD 95–110. The books Papias himself wrote have been lost. Thankfully, some of his comments were preserved by the church historian Eusebius (253–339). In Papias we have the oldest surviving witness and possibly the original source from which grew most of the ancient testimony. This tradition held that Matthew's Gospel was written first and that the other Synoptic Gospels were written independently. Papias's quote is found in Eusebius's *Church History*, 3.39.15–16a:

> "Mark, having become the interpreter of Peter, wrote down accurately, though not in order, whatsoever he remembered of the things said or done by Christ. For he neither heard the Lord nor followed him, but afterward, as I said, he followed Peter, who adapted his teaching to the needs of his hearers, but with no intention of giving a connected account of the Lord's discourses, so that Mark committed no error while he thus wrote some things as he remembered them. For he was careful of one thing, not to omit any of the things which he had heard, and not to state any of them falsely." These things are related by Papias concerning Mark. But concerning Matthew he writes as follows: "So then Matthew wrote the oracles in the Hebrew language, and every one interpreted them as he was able."

One can see from this quote how a belief that Matthew's Gospel was written first could have arisen. The quote by itself, however, only affirms that while others made use of Matthew's Gospel, Mark's Gospel was gathered directly from the sermons of Peter and was therefore not directly dependent on Matthew's. Papias says nothing here about Luke's Gospel. Whatever Papias said about Luke can only be guessed based on the sayings of men who were influenced by him. This quote, as we have it, does not rule out the possibility that Luke used either Matthew's Gospel or Mark's or both.

Another interesting detail in Papias's comment concerns the idea that Matthew originally wrote in the "**Hebrew language**." Some modern scholars have begun to challenge this translation of Papias's words. This is because Papias's Greek terms, if translated as part of the vocabulary of formal speech-making (rhetoric) in antiquity, would only convey that Matthew wrote the oracles in the "Hebraic style" and that everyone "explained" them as he was able. This notwithstanding, many important ancient witnesses, apparently influenced by Papias, claimed that Matthew originally wrote in Hebrew. Grammatical specialists today, however, usually conclude that our Gospel of Matthew was originally written in Greek. It does not read like a translation. If the specialists are correct, then the most we should conclude from Papias is that Matthew wrote something—perhaps some basic notes—in Hebrew and that other writers may have used these notes to compose other accounts in other languages. If this much is accurate, then Matthew himself may also have used the Hebrew notes to help him compose the Gospel we now have in Greek.

About 100 years after Papias, **Irenaeus of Lyons** (115–200) held that Matthew's (Hebrew) Gospel was written while both Peter and Paul preached in Rome and that Mark did not complete his Gospel until after Peter had died. Thus Irenaeus implied that Matthew was written first (in Hebrew). Irenaeus also added that Luke's Gospel was based on Paul's preaching in Rome during the same period (*Against Heresies*, 3.1.1; 3.14.1). Perhaps a few years later, **Clement of Alexandria** (150–215) wrote that both Matthew and Luke were written before Mark and no literary dependence between the three is implied (Eusebius, *Church History*, 6.14.6). **Origen** (185–253), in agreement with all known witnesses, also places Matthew as first written (in Hebrew). In disagreement with Clement, however, Origen seems to place Mark's Gospel (based on Peter's sermons) as written second, followed by Luke (based on Paul's sermons). Origen also adds the fresh insights that Matthew was written for Jewish converts and that Luke was written for Gentile converts (Eusebius, *Church History*, 6.25.4–6). While there apparently is some development in the traditions cited here, two common opinions seem to extend from Papias's early writing: (1) Matthew was written first (in Hebrew); (2) Matthew, Mark, and Luke were written independently of one another. As we will see below, scholars who analyze the internal evidence of the Gospels have often challenged both of these points.

WHAT HAS THE INTERNAL EVIDENCE LED SCHOLARS TO CONCLUDE?

In his work *On the Harmony of the Gospels*, **Augustine** (354–430) accepted only half of the traditional consensus. With those already cited above, Augustine agreed that Matthew wrote first (even in Hebrew), but unlike his predecessors Augustine concluded by comparing the Gospels together that Mark and Luke did not ignore what Matthew had written but that they used the preceding work as the Holy Spirit led each to follow the divinely appointed theme of their Gospels (1.2). The simplest summary of Augustine's theory of dependence is that Matthew wrote first to portray the kingly position of Jesus; Mark abbreviated Matthew with the same theme; and Luke, writing third, composed his Gospel with the theme of Christ's priesthood (1.1).

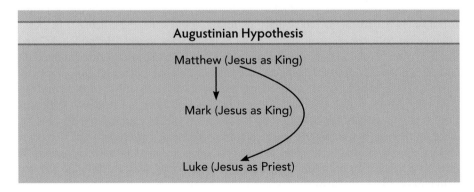

Augustinian Hypothesis

Matthew (Jesus as King)

Mark (Jesus as King)

Luke (Jesus as Priest)

In time many other **theories of interdependence** have arisen. After the Enlightenment, Christian studies of the New Testament began to revisit historical issues long considered settled. Many new theories about the interdependence of the Synoptic Gospels arose. **Griesbach** (mentioned above) carefully analyzed his synopsis and concluded that Matthew probably wrote first, that Luke used Matthew, and that Mark used both.[2] Another idea later connected to this hypothesis supports other elements of the ancient tradition. This idea explains that Mark's Gospel resembles Matthew's and Luke's so much because Peter's sermons in Rome were based on the Gospels of Matthew and Luke. Since, as tradition says, Mark wrote his Gospel based on Peter's sermons, Mark's Gospel would naturally resemble Matthew's and Luke's.[3] One line of internal evidence for this idea is taken from the places where Mark's Gospel appears to conflate the wording of Matthew and Luke (see graphic below).

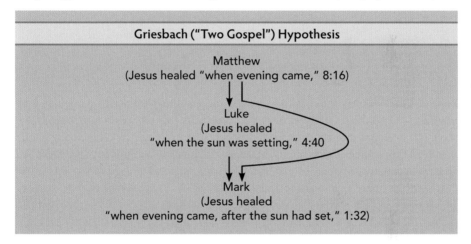

The hypotheses of Augustine and Griesbach both maintained the ancient tradition that Matthew's Gospel was written first. They only departed from tradition by denying the independent composition of the Synoptic Gospels. Nor did Griesbach think a Hebrew original for Matthew was essential. Beginning in the 1800s, new theories arose to challenge Matthean priority.

The **"two-source" theory** holds that Matthew and Luke both made independent use of two sources. One of these sources is believed to be Mark's Gospel. The other source supposedly contained the 250 or so verses that Matthew and Luke share but which Mark omits. An early form of this theory held that the version of Mark used by Matthew and Luke was earlier and slightly different from the one we have now. The introduction of this **"Proto-Mark"** helped explain the few occasions when Matthew and Luke agree with each other but do not agree with the current Mark.[4] The other source from which Matthew and Luke supposedly drew some 250 verses would eventually be called **"Q"** (*Quelle* is German for "source"). A serious weakness in this theory is that no manuscript containing "Q" has ever been discovered. Arguments supporting this theory are too numerous and complex to list here, but chief among them are the following: (1) Matthew repeats nearly all of Mark, and Luke repeats nearly half of Mark. (2) It is not likely that Mark used Matthew or Luke because Mark omits so many important things they contain. (3) The conclusion that neither Matthew nor Luke depended on each other is deduced from the fact that when both Matthew and Luke make editorial changes to Mark, they do not end up with exactly the same words. Had one depended on the other, we should expect them to change Mark's words in the same way far more than they do.

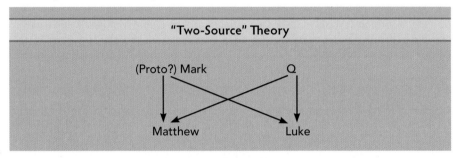

"Two-Source" Theory

(Proto?) Mark   Q

Matthew   Luke

In time, this "two-source" theory was adopted and expanded particularly by scholars at Oxford University in England. Eventually this school of thought held that the literary relationship between the Gospels is best explained by recognizing a total of at least four sources. Accordingly, Matthew and Luke, in addition to using Mark and Q, each had a private source of material. The material peculiar to Matthew was called "M," and the material peculiar to Luke was called "L." This theory may be graphed as follows:

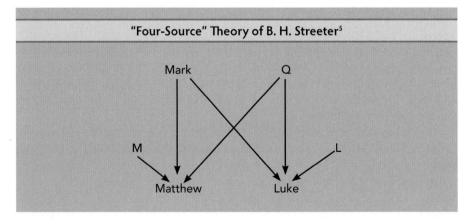

"Four-Source" Theory of B. H. Streeter[5]

Mark   Q

M   L

Matthew   Luke

While some form of the "two-source" or "four-source" theory currently guides the majority of both conservative and critical scholars today, a renewed interest in the "Griesbach hypothesis" (see above) developed late in the twentieth century.[6] Another challenge to the "Oxford school" comes from those who agree upon internal evidence that Matthew and Luke used Mark but who do not think a document called Q was necessary. This theory holds that the non-Markan material held in common by Matthew and Luke can be satisfactorily explained by Luke's use of Matthew.[7] This theory may be charted as follows:

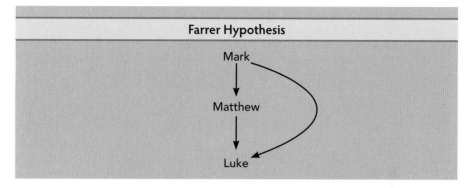

WHAT EFFECT ON INTERPRETATION SHOULD THESE THEORIES HAVE?

Many commentaries on the Synoptic Gospels presuppose one of the theories described above. Commentators who hold to one of these theories usually use the slight difference in wording between the Gospels to highlight the new emphasis intended by each evangelist who edited an older source. This style of interpretation that speculates why a later writer edited (or "redacted") an earlier source in a particular way is called "**redaction criticism.**" It must be pointed out that redaction criticism can only be as accurate as the theory of interdependence it presupposes. We must remember that each suggestion of interdependence between the Gospels is **only a theory** of synoptic composition. We should be careful not to embrace dogmatically the results of redaction criticism, for we may end up with false doctrines. We need to know how to let speculation be speculation and how to let the clear Word of God as it stands speak its clearest message.

Commentators who hold that the Gospels were **written independently** by the designated writers tend to use cross-references between the Gospels only to illumine a biblical theme. In the studies that follow, we will accept the Gospels as divinely inspired accounts that tell the story that "when the time came to completion, God sent His Son, born of a woman . . . to redeem those under the law" (Gal 4:4–5 NKJV).

For Further Reading

Linnemann, Eta. *Is There a Synoptic Problem? Rethinking the Literary Dependence of the First Three Gospels*. Translated by Robert W. Yarbrough. Grand Rapids: Baker: 1992.

Stein, Robert H. *Studying the Synoptic Gospels: Origin and Interpretation*. 2nd ed. Grand Rapids: Baker, 2001.

Streeter, B. H. *The Four Gospels: A Study of Origins, Treating of the Manuscript Tradition, Sources, Authorship & Dates*. London: MacMillan, 1924.

Thomas, Robert L., ed. *Three Views on the Origins of the Synoptic Gospels*. Grand Rapids: Zondervan, 2002.

ENDNOTES

1. These distinctions can be reconciled. Nothing in Luke's account prevents the "certain blind man" from being Mark's Bartimaeus. Nothing in Mark or Luke rules out Matthew's claim that Jesus healed two blind men. Furthermore, during Jesus' life, the ancient city called Jericho lay in ruins about two miles north of a newer "Jericho" recently rebuilt by Herod the Great. Jesus could have healed these men leaving one Jericho while approaching the other. See A. T. Robertson, *Word Pictures in the New Testament* (Nashville: Broadman, 1930), 1.163.

2. The "Griesbach hypothesis" has most recently been defended by William R. Farmer in *The Synoptic Problem: A Critical Analysis* (New York: Macmillan, 1964; 2nd ed., Dillsboro, NC: Western North Carolina Press, 1976). Contra, see Robert H. Stein, *The Synoptic Problem: An Introduction* (Grand Rapids: Baker, 1987).

3. David Alan Black, *Why Four Gospels? The Historical Origins of the Gospels* (Grand Rapids: Kregel, 2001).

4. Early originators of the "two-source" theory include Hermann Weisse (1801–66) and Heinrich J. Holtzmann (1832–1910).

5. Originally published as *The Four Gospels: A Study of Origins, Treating of the Manuscript Tradition, Sources, Authorship & Dates* (London: MacMillan, 1924).

6. Farmer, *Synoptic Problem*.

7. Austin M. Farrer, "On Dispensing with Q," in *Studies in the Gospels: Essays in the Memory of R. H. Lightfoot* (Oxford: Blackwell, 1955), 55–88.

Chapter 5

MATTHEW
The Kingdom of Heaven

Matthew's Gospel deserves its privileged place as the first book in the New Testament. It is the most Jewish of all the Gospels. Its many quotations and subtle allusions to Old Testament texts and themes make it an excellent bridge between the Old and New Testaments. Matthew was also placed first before the other Gospels when the New Testament began to be bound together into one book. Of the four Gospels, Matthew's most likely reflects the style of teaching Jewish Christians used before the Gospel was written and distributed.

Key Facts	
Author:	Matthew (also called Levi)
Recipient:	Written initially for Jewish Christians
Where Written:	Unknown
Date:	AD 60–65
Key Word:	Kingdom (Gk. *basileia*)
Key Verse:	"Where is He who has been born King of the Jews? For we saw His star in the east and have come to worship Him" (2:2).

AUTHOR

The titles in every ancient manuscript of this book describe it as the Gospel "according to Matthew." According to all three Synoptic Gospels, Matthew (or "Levi," as he is called in Mark and Luke) was collecting taxes near Capernaum when he answered Jesus' call, "Follow Me!" (Matt 9:9–13; Mark 2:13–17; Luke 5:27–31). All three Gospels say that Matthew immediately began to follow Jesus and that Jesus had supper with Matthew and other tax collectors and sinners that same evening. Note the **three lines of evidence** that point to Matthew as the author of the first Gospel.

The first line of evidence points out that only Matthew makes a clear connection between this *tax collector* and the *disciple* with the same name. Mark and Luke call the tax collector "Levi" instead of "Matthew." While Mark and Luke list Matthew among the disciples (Mark 3:18; Luke 6:15), only Matthew's list calls him "Matthew the tax collector" (Matt 10:3). This clarity is consistent with the tradition that Matthew is the Gospel's author.

The second line of argument is seen in Matthew's *description of the supper*. Luke implies a lavish setting and calls this meal a "grand banquet." Matthew, perhaps to avoid boasting, simply says, "While He [Jesus] was reclining at the table in the house, many tax collectors and sinners came as guests to eat with Jesus and His disciples" (Matt 9:10). Such a modest report would be expected of the evangelist who recorded Jesus' warning against boasting over the gifts one gives (Matt 6:1–4).

Reconstruction of a typical first-century synagogue.

The third line of argument is based on the possible meaning of the phrase "*in the house*" in 9:10. The rules of Greek grammar allow this phrase to be translated "in my house." If this translation carries the intended meaning, then this phrase would be the strongest piece of evidence inside the first Gospel that Matthew was its author.[1]

Additional internal evidence also points to Matthew as the author. This Gospel contains many parables and stories that emphasize the details of **financial transactions** (17:24–27; 18:23–35; 20:1–16; 26:15; 27:3–10; 28:11–15). This is what we should expect from a Gospel written by one who handled money. As a tax collector Matthew would have had the literary skills and writing tools necessary to take notes on Jesus' words and deeds during his travels with Jesus. Matthew's place of business near Capernaum would have required him to be fluent in Hebrew, Aramaic, Latin, and Greek. His linguistic skill is apparent in the way Matthew translates his quotes of the Old Testament into Greek. Matthew often uses the standard readings of the Septuagint (e.g., 3:16; 17:11; 26:3–4,64; 27:35). At other times he appears to translate the Hebrew into Greek personally (22:7; 24:21,29,31; 26:28).

Finally, all the **external sources** agree that Matthew is the author of the Gospel that bears his name. After this the history of Matthew's further ministry is difficult to trace. Some reports say that he traveled to serve in the region just south of the Caspian Sea. Others say he reached as far as Parthia or the Persians. In any case the Gospel he left behind still reaches out to the entire world today.

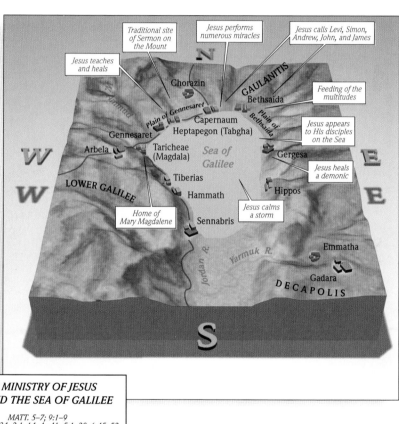

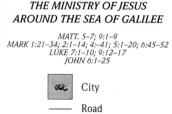

THE MINISTRY OF JESUS AROUND THE SEA OF GALILEE

MATT. 5–7; 9:1–9
MARK 1:21–34; 2:1–14; 4:–41; 5:1–20; 6:45–52
LUKE 7:1–10; 9:12–17
JOHN 6:1–25

City

—— Road

RECIPIENTS

Matthew's Gospel names no audience for its message other than that which is implied in its Great Commission. Its message was ultimately intended to go to "all nations" (28:19). Manuscript evidence, the sermons, letters, and commentaries of early Christians, and even the habits of worship in the early church point to the fact that Matthew's Gospel was the most popularly quoted of the four Gospels in the first several centuries of Christian history. Even today the Sermon on the Mount (chaps. 5–7) and especially Matthew's version of the Lord's Prayer (6:9–13) are among the most recognizable passages in the entire Bible.

Matthew originally crafted this Gospel for a group of Christians who were already familiar with the Old Testament. Both church tradition (external evidence) and the contents of the Gospel itself (internal evidence) suggest that this Gospel was originally

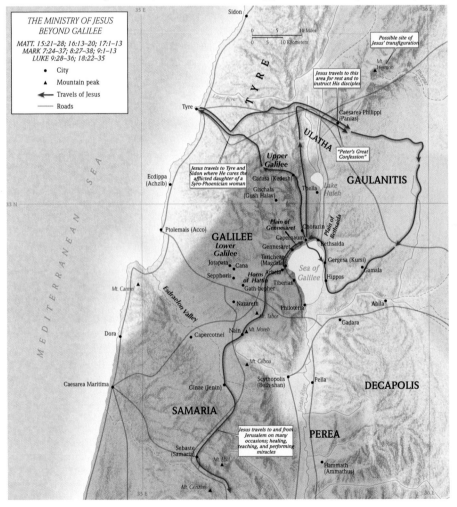

written for **Jewish Christians** who were given the responsibility to share its message with the world

Matthew and his Gospel were originally oriented to the Hebrew people according to Papias.[2] Also, Irenaeus, Origen, and Eusebius explicitly state that Matthew first wrote in the Hebrew language (or in Aramaic, another Semitic language often referred to as Hebrew) for the Hebrews among whom he ministered.[3] Some of the earliest quotations and allusions to Matthew's Gospel come to us from **Syria**, a region rich in Jewish culture that also became the hub of early Christian missionary work (Acts 11:19–26; 13:1–3). References to Matthew in the *Didache* (first or early second century) suggest an early Syrian readership for Matthew. Ignatius, a church leader in Antioch of Syria, also shows a familiarity with Matthew's Gospel. These facts suggest that Matthew could have written his Gospel when he was located in Syria.

Internal evidence also suggests that the Gospel was written for **Jewish converts** to Christianity. Only Matthew's Gospel explicitly restricts the early mission of Jesus and the 12 apostles "to the lost sheep of the house of Israel" (10:6; 15:24). Although Matthew's Gospel hints at a future time when Gentiles would be gathered into the kingdom of heaven with Abraham, Isaac, and Jacob (8:11–12) and records Jesus' Great Commission to make disciples of "all nations" (28:19), the emphasis on Jesus' initial ministry in Matthew's Gospel was primarily to the Jews.

Reconstruction of Herod's temple (20 BC–AD 70) at Jerusalem as viewed from the southeast.

As would be expected for a Jewish audience, Matthew refers to **Jewish practices** without taking time to explain them as other Gospel writers do (Mark 7:3; John 19:40). He more often describes Jesus as "Son of David" (1:1,20; 9:27; 12:23; 15:22; 20:30–31; 21:9,15; 22:45). He reverently avoids using God's name according to the custom of his people. This is most evident in his unique use of the phrase "kingdom of heaven" (33 times) where the other Gospels use "kingdom of God."

Finally, Matthew's rich and varied use of the Old Testament would be persuasive among people who already believed the Old Testament was God's inspired word. Depending on how one counts, the Gospel of Matthew includes between 60 and 100 quotations and allusions to Old Testament texts. Some of these texts so clearly predict the details of the Messiah's life that almost anyone should be able to recognize them. Other connections between the Old Testament and the life of Jesus are more subtle and best understood by people who are already familiar with the Old Testament.

OCCASION AND DATE

According to Neciphorus Callistus (fourteenth century), Matthew wrote within 15 years after Christ's ascension (AD 45–48). However, there is no evidence he had any

Sea of Galilee at Nof Ginnosar looking across the Sea to the Mount of Beatitudes.

proof for this early date. Irenaeus (late second century) and Eusebius (fourth century) cite **Papias** (early second century) as a source for their dating of Matthew. Irenaeus tells us *when* Matthew wrote, and Eusebius tells us *why*. However, both of them described only that Matthew wrote "in Hebrew" (which also could mean Aramaic). If the New Testament's Greek Gospel according to Matthew is based on this Semitic text, the comments of Irenaeus and Eusebius suggest a date as early as AD 60–65.

According to **Eusebius**, "Matthew, who had at first preached to the Hebrews, when he was about to go to other peoples, committed his Gospel to writing in his native tongue, and thus compensated those whom he was obliged to leave for the loss of his presence."[4] If Eusebius is correct, Matthew wrote in Hebrew or Aramaic at a time when he departed from the Jewish people to a broader area of ministry. Scant reports in church traditions make it difficult to date Matthew's departure for the mission field. Irenaeus's comment is more relevant to the date.

According to **Irenaeus**, Matthew wrote while Peter and Paul were preaching in Rome and before any of the other Gospels were written. Here is the entire passage:

> Matthew also issued a written Gospel among the Hebrews in their own dialect, while Peter and Paul were preaching at Rome, and laying the foundations of the Church. After their departure, Mark, the disciple and interpreter of Peter, did also hand down to us in writing what had been preached by Peter. Luke also, the companion of Paul, recorded in a book the Gospel preached by him. Afterwards, John, the disciple of the Lord, who also had leaned upon His breast, did himself publish a Gospel during his residence at Ephesus in Asia.[5]

If Irenaeus's report is accurate, Matthew's Gospel—or at least its Semitic basis— was written before the deaths of Peter and Paul while they both were in Rome. The book of Acts closes with Paul as a prisoner in Rome in the early 60s, but there is no mention in Acts of Peter's presence in Rome (by AD 62). According to Irenaeus, Matthew had not yet written his Gospel at that time.

Other traditions say that Nero, in response to the great fire of Rome in the year 64, executed many Christians in Rome in an effort to blame Christians for the great fire.[6] Perhaps Peter and Paul were martyred in Rome soon after that fire. In any case Eusebius reports that both apostles died under Nero.[7] This would date their deaths between AD 64 and 68, the year Nero himself died. All of this together implies that Matthew originally wrote the Semitic basis for the Greek Gospel sometime before the mid-60s. The years 60–65 are a good estimate. This also means that the Greek Gospel of Matthew in the New Testament could have been written by Matthew using his own Semitic text soon afterward.

GENRE AND STRUCTURE

The word **gospel** (Greek *euangelion*) was used by Christians to refer to the message of Jesus Christ and to the four Gospels in the New Testament. The word *gospel*, that is, "good news," was used to describe the announcement of important events. It literally means "good announcement." English translators chose to represent this word with the Old English term *godspell*, which literally meant "God's story" or "good story." Today the term is most popularly explained as the "good news." The Gospels tell us about the life, deeds, teaching, death, and current position of Jesus and what this can mean for us today, tomorrow, and into eternity. The Gospels are declarations of what is true—specifically, the truth about Jesus as well as the truth Jesus told.

The word **kingdom** is important in Matthew's Gospel.[8] Over one-third of the New Testament's use of the word *kingdom* appears in the Gospel of Matthew (55 out of 162 times). Today we think of kingdoms in terms of the land over which a king reigns. In the Bible, and especially in Matthew, the focus is not so much on land as it is on the authority of the king. When Jesus preached about the kingdom of heaven, His emphasis was not geographical but relational. This emphasis is crucial for a proper understanding of the phrase "kingdom of heaven" in Matthew's Gospel.

Tradition indicates that Matthew taught his Gospel **orally** before he wrote it down into a book. Then, as Matthew transferred his teaching to written form, the several lines of thought around which Matthew organized his sermons about Jesus began to appear side by side in the written text. Scholars sometimes argue over which organizing principle Matthew intended to emphasize, but Matthew more likely intended us to notice all of them. For this reason a fair analysis of the structure of Matthew's Gospel must recognize this multifaceted characteristic.

The simplest outline of Matthew's Gospel divides the book into **three parts**. Each new part is introduced by a transitional phrase that describes what readers should expect to see next.

Part 1:	"The Person of Jesus" (which introduces Jesus, 1:1–4:16)
Transition Phrase:	"From then on Jesus began to preach, 'Repent, because the kingdom of heaven has come near!'" (4:17).
Part 2:	"The Proclamation of Jesus" (which begins with His teaching, 4:17–16:20)
Transition Phrase:	"From then on Jesus began to point out to His disciples that He must go to Jerusalem and suffer many things from the elders, chief priests, and scribes, be killed, and be raised the third day" (16:21).
Part 3:	"The Passion and Authority of Jesus" (Jesus' death and resurrected life, 16:21–28:20)

Another outline is clearly visible in Matthew's Gospel. This outline organizes Jesus' teaching into **five sermons**. Each of these sermons is preceded by a set of stories about Jesus and is concluded with a transitional phrase (repeated five times), which prepares readers for the next section. This analysis results in the following seven-part outline:

Introduction: "The Birth of the Son of God" (chaps. 1–2)

First narrative section (chaps. 3–4)

"Sermon on the Mount" (chaps. 5–7)

| Transition: | "When Jesus had finished this sermon, the crowds were astonished at His teaching" (7:28). |

Second narrative section (8:1–9:35)

"Sermon on the Sending of the Twelve" (9:36–10:42)

| Transition: | "When Jesus had finished giving orders to His 12 disciples, He moved on from there to teach and preach in their towns" (11:1). |

Third narrative section (11:2–12:50)

"Parables of the Kingdom" (13:1–52)

| Transition: | "When Jesus had finished these parables, He left there" (13:53). |

Fourth narrative section (13:54–17:21)

"Sermon on Church Administration" (17:22–18:35)

| Transition: | "When Jesus had finished this instruction, He departed from Galilee and went to the region of Judea across the Jordan" (19:1). |

Fifth narrative section (19:2–22:46)

"Sermon on the End Times" (23:1–25:46)

| Transition: | "When Jesus had finished saying all this, He told His disciples, 'You know that the Passover takes place after two days, and the Son of Man will be handed over to be crucified'" (26:1–2). |

| Conclusion: | Last Supper, Trial, Death, Resurrection/ Appearances, Great Commission (26:3–28:20) |

Finally, the Gospel may be outlined simply on the basis of the **locations** of Jesus' ministry.

Pre-Galilean Life and Ministry (1:10–4:11)

Transition: "When He heard that John had been arrested, He withdrew into Galilee" (4:12).

Galilean Ministry (4:13–13:58)

Transition: "When Jesus heard about it [i.e., about Herod's murder of John the Baptist], He withdrew from there by boat to a remote place to be alone. When the crowds heard this, they followed Him on foot from the towns" (14:13).

Ministry Expanded Beyond Galilee (14:14–18:35)

Transition: "When Jesus had finished this instruction, He departed from Galilee and went to the region of Judea across the Jordan" (19:1).

Final Ministry on the Way to Judea and in Jerusalem (19:2–28:20)

Outline

I. The Person of the King (Matthew 1:1–4:16)
II. The Proclamation of the King (Matthew 4:17–16:20)
III. The Passion and Authority of the King (Matthew 16:21–28:20)

MESSAGE

The Person of the King

Matthew's Gospel opens with the **genealogy** of Jesus traced all the way back through King David to Abraham, the forefather of the Jewish people. This emphasizes Jesus' Jewish identity and position as the royal "Son of David." This kingly emphasis is sustained throughout the book. Many other descriptions of Jesus are also concentrated in the opening chapters.

- 1:21: "He will save His people from their sins."
- 1:23: He is "Immanuel," which is translated "God is with us."
- 2:2: He is "King of the Jews."
- 2:4: He is "Messiah."
- 2:6: He is "leader" and "shepherd" of Israel.
- 2:15: He is God's "Son" (see chart).

In Matthew's Gospel, Jesus' power and authority exceed the prophets and kings of Israel's past. He is greater than the prophet Jonah (12:41) and greater than King Solomon (12:42). Finally, Jesus' ability to drive out demons and heal the sick demonstrates that wherever Jesus is, there the kingdom of God is present (12:28).

The Power of the King

Matthew specifically reports no fewer than **21 miracles**. Summary statements also show that Jesus performed far more miracles than the ones Matthew describes in detail (8:16). Five of the healing miracles specifically described by Matthew included the casting out of demons (8:32; 9:32; 12:22; 15:28; 17:18). Others mention specific diseases (8:14; 9:2,18,20,27; 12:9; 20:30). Jesus also miraculously fed thousands of people with a few loaves and fish—not once but twice (14:13; 15:22). He calmed a raging storm at sea (8:23), raised the dead (9:25), walked on water (14:25), and miraculously directed Peter to find money in a fish's mouth so they could pay the temple tax (17:24). The power of Jesus in Matthew's Gospel extends far beyond that of ordinary kings. Jesus is shown to have power over all demons, disease, death, hunger, the weather, and even over the basic elements of the earth.

MIRACLES OF JESUS			
Miracle	Bible Passage		
Water Turned to Wine				John 2:1
Many Healings	Matt 4:23	Mark 1:32	
Healing of a Leper	Matt 8:1	Mark 1:40	Luke 5:12
Healing of a Roman Centurion's Servant	Matt 8:5		Luke 7:1
Healing of Peter's Mother-in-law	Matt 8:14	Mark 1:29	Luke 4:38
Calming of the Storm at Sea	Matt 8:23	Mark 4:35	Luke 8:22
Healing of the Wild Men of Gadara	Matt 8:28	Mark 5:1	Luke 8:26
Healing of a Lame Man	Matt 9:1	Mark 2:1	Luke 5:18
Healing of a Woman with a Hemorrhage	Matt 9:20	Mark 5:25	Luke 8:43
Raising of Jairus's Daughter	Matt 9:23	Mark 5:22	Luke 8:41
Healing of Two Blind Men	Matt 9:27		
Healing of a Demon-Possessed Man	Matt 9:32		
Healing of Man with a Withered Hand	Matt 12:10	Mark 3:1	Luke 6:6
Feeding of 5,000 People	Matt 14:15	Mark 6:35	Luke 9:12	John 6:1

MIRACLES OF JESUS (continued)			
Miracle	*Bible Passage*		
Walking on the Sea	Matt 14:22	Mark 6:47		John 6:16
Healing of the Syrophoenician's Daughter	Matt 15:21	Mark 7:24		
Feeding of 4,000 People	Matt 15:32	Mark 8:1		
Healing of an Epileptic Boy	Matt 17:14	Mark 9:14	Luke 9:37	
Healing of Two Blind Men at Jericho	Matt 20:30			
Healing of a Man with an Unclean Spirit		Mark 1:23		
Healing of a Deaf, Speechless Man		Mark 7:31		
Healing of a Blind Man at Bethesda		Mark 8:22		
Healing of Blind Bartimaeus		Mark 10:46	Luke 18:35	
A Miraculous Catch of Fish			Luke 5:4	John 21:1
Raising of a Widow's Son			Luke 7:11	
Healing of a Stooped Woman			Luke 13:11	
Healing of a Man with the Dropsy			Luke 14:1	
Healing of Ten Lepers			Luke 17:11	
Healing of Malchus's Ear			Luke 22:50	
Healing of a Royal Official's Son				John 4:46
Healing of a Lame Man at Bethesda				John 5:1
Healing of a Blind Man				John 9:1
Raising Lazarus				John 11:38

According to one summary of Jesus' miracles (4:23–25), the great crowds who gathered to hear Jesus preach were attracted to Him not only for His words but also for His miraculous works.

The Proclamation of the King

Most commentators recognize that Matthew arranged Jesus' sermons so readers could better follow what Jesus said about specific subjects. Matthew's Gospel describes **five extended teachings**. The most broadly recognized outline for Jesus' teaching in Matthew's Gospel lists five major discourses.

CHAPTER	DISCOURSE	THEME
5–7	Sermon on the Mount	The Righteousness of the Kingdom of Heaven
9:36–10:42	Sending of the Twelve	Announcing to Israel the Kingdom of Heaven
13	Parables of the Kingdom	Principles of the Kingdom of Heaven
17:22–18:35	Sermon on Church Administration	Applying Kingdom Principles to the Church
23:1–25:46	Sermon on the End Times	God's Judgment When His Kingdom Comes

Greek Highlight

Blessed. Greek μακάριος **(makarios).** This term occurs 30 times in the Gospels, all but two on the lips of Jesus (Luke 1:45; 11:27). The OT Hebrew term ashrey stands behind the NT usage of makarios. Both terms are normally translated "blessed" or "happy." Makarios has two main nuances in the NT. It predominately refers to God's blessing upon His people, and secondarily to God's people blessing Him. In the latter sense, makarios is basically synonymous with praise. When a person is blessed by God, he is approved by God. The opposite of makarios is "woe" (ouai), the status of one who is not approved by God and is thus the object of impending judgment (Matt 23:13–32; Luke 6:24–36). In spite of being a tax collector (Matt 9:9), Matthew himself became a recipient of ultimate blessing from God of both salvation and direct mentorship from Jesus Himself and thus remained sensitive to his obligation to bless the Lord for having received true life-change from God. Having himself once put the acquisition of money before the cultivation of spirituality, Matthew often highlights the benefit of receiving the blessing of God above pursuing earthy possessions and following faulty human perspectives (Matt 5:21–48; 6:19–21; 9:12–13; 16:26).

The Sermon on the Mount

The Sermon on the Mount contrasts the **righteousness** of the kingdom of heaven with the righteousness of the scribes and Pharisees. According to Jesus, true righteousness cannot be defined by following lists of things to do or not do (5:20). We must not only avoid murder, adultery,and breaking oaths. We must also avoid the causes of these sins: hatred, lust, and the desire to manipulate the truth (5:21–26,28–30,33–37). Since God designed marriage to be permanent, we should not seek legal loopholes for divorce (5:31–32; cf. 19:8–12). The heart of God and the spirit of the law are more important than the letter of the law. Early in Jesus' ministry, the message of the kingdom of heaven was directed to the nation of Israel. Later, after His rejection by the leaders of Israel, Jesus announced that He would gather all nations into His kingdom.[9]

Sea of Galilee from the Church of the Beatitudes, built on the site where Jesus is thought to have taught the Sermon on the Mount. This church, built in 1938, is an octagonal structure, representing the eight beatitudes.

The Sending of the Twelve

Jesus' instructions to the 12 apostles helped them speak to Israel, but many of these principles are still applicable today. We should pray that God will send more laborers into the harvest (9:38). Faithful preaching will encounter persecution (9:16–23), even from family members (9:34–36). Cooperation with missionaries is like cooperating with Jesus (10:42). Matthew also emphasized the uniqueness of Jesus in contrast to John the Baptist who was sent to prepare the way for the true Messiah (Matt 11:1–15).

View of the Kidron Valley to the northeast toward the Mount of Olives.

The Parables of the Kingdom

The parables of the kingdom relay many important principles. "The Sower" teaches that certain differences between people will produce different responses when the Gospel is preached (13:1–9,18–23). "Wheat and Tares" and "The Net" show that some people will be included and some rejected when the kingdom comes. "The Hidden Treasure" and "The Pearl" show that the kingdom is more valuable than all other possessions (13:44–46). Altogether there are **40 parables** recorded in Matthew's Gospel. Tasker notes that they represent a significant and pivotal change in Jesus' message.[10]

The Sermon on Church Administration

Jesus applied the principles of the kingdom to the church. He spoke about the church in Matthew's Gospel as something that was yet to be built (16:18). In His **"Great Prediction,"** Jesus promised to continue to build His church (Gk. *ekklesia*) so that even the "gates of Hades" could not stand against it. This Gospel shows that many principles of the kingdom apply to the church. This especially shows the need to practice both forgiveness and church discipline (18:11–35).

The Sermon on the End Times

Finally, the Sermon on the End Times (Olivet Discourse) in Matthew's Gospel describes the events that will lead up to the judgment of the world. When Jesus returns to judge the world, He will say to those He recognizes as "righteous": "Come, you who are blessed by My Father, inherit the kingdom prepared for you from the foundation of the world" (25:34). But to the "wicked" Jesus will say, "Depart from Me, you who are cursed, into the eternal fire prepared for the Devil and his angels!" (25:41). Many other passages in Matthew carry this same message.[11]

The Passion and Authority of the King

Soon after Peter confessed that Jesus was "the Messiah, the Son of the living God!" (16:16), Jesus began to talk about His own coming **death and resurrection**: "From then on Jesus began to point out to His disciples that He must go to Jerusalem and suffer many things from the elders, chief priests, and scribes, be killed, and be raised the third day" (16:21; cf. 20:18–19). On the way to Jerusalem, Jesus explained that His death would be a "*ransom*"—a payment so others could be free (20:28). When Jesus established the Lord's Supper, He further taught that His blood would be "shed for many for the *forgiveness* of sins" (26:28). After His death and resurrection Jesus appeared to His disciples to announce His royal authority. On His **Great Commission**, Jesus announced: "All authority has been given to Me in heaven and on earth" (28:18). He also promised to be with the disciples until "the end of the age" as they go to "make disciples of all nations, baptizing them in the name of the Father and of the Son and of the Holy Spirit" (28:19–20).

CONCLUSION

Matthew's message is about King Jesus and the kingdom of heaven. This Gospel describes the powerful and victorious role of King Jesus as well as the standards, blessings, and ultimate triumph of the kingdom of God. Matthew tells that Jesus bought us with the sacrifice of His own life and His victory over death. Now Jesus expects His followers to **proclaim the gospel** to the end of the age. Jesus will one day establish His kingdom with the truth He taught His followers to pray, "Your kingdom come. Your will be done on earth as it is in heaven" (6:10).

For Further Reading

Blomberg, Craig. *Matthew*. NAC. Nashville: B&H, 1992.
Hindson, Edward, and James Borland. *Matthew: The King Is Coming*. Chattanooga: AMG Publishers, 2006.
Keener, Craig S. *A Commentary on the Gospel of Matthew*. Grand Rapids: Eerdmans, 1999.
MacArthur, John, Jr. *Matthew*. NTC, 4 vols. Chicago: Moody Press, 1987–89.
Turner, David L. *Matthew*. BECNT. Grand Rapids: Baker, 2008.
Walvoord, John F. *Matthew: Thy Kingdom Come*. Chicago, Moody Press, 1974.

Study Questions

1. What evidence in the Gospel itself and in the testimony of ancient Christians demonstrates that Matthew the tax collector is the author of this Gospel?
2. For whom was this Gospel initially written, and why do we think so?
3. Why is Matthew's Gospel so naturally divided into more than one outline?
4. What was the major theme in Matthew's Gospel, and how is that theme presented?
5. What evidence do we have that the message of Matthew's Gospel was ultimately intended for the whole world?

ENDNOTES

1. B. F. C. Atkinson, "The Gospel According to Matthew," in the *New Bible Commentary* (Grand Rapids: Eerdmans, 1953), 771. In Greek, the definite article most often translated as "the" can be translated as a possessive pronoun "his/her/my" when the context suggests that it should be. Most commentators, however, follow the traditional translation "in the house" and conclude that the author left the house unspecified.

2. Eusebius, *Church History*, 3.39.16.

3. Irenaeus, *Against Heresies*, 3.1.1; Eusebius, *Church History*, 3.24.6. Eusebius in the same work also cites Origen to the same effect (6.25.4).

4. Eusebius, *Church History*, 3.24.6.

5. Irenaeus, *Against Heresies*, 3.1.1.

6. Tacitus, *Annals*, 15.44.

7. Eusebius, *Church History*, 2.25.5.

8. See, e.g., 3:2; 4:17,23; 5:3,10,19; 6:33; 10:7; 13:11; 16:19; 18:1,4; 21:43–45; 24:44; 26:29.

9. See detailed comments on the Sermon on the Mount in E. Hindson and J. Borland, *Matthew: The King Is Coming* (Chattanooga: AMG Publishers, 2006), 47–86.

10. R. V. G. Tasker, *The Gospel According to St. Matthew*, TNTC (Grand Rapids: Eerdmans, 1961), 134–35

11. Matthew uses a lesson on the judgment of the world to conclude each of the five major "sermons" in this Gospel: 7:21–27; 10:32–42; 13:47–50; 18:23–35; 25:31–46.

Chapter 6

MARK
The Divine Servant

In the Roman Empire slaves were everywhere. The Gospel of Mark presents Jesus as "the Son of God" and the **perfect slave** (or servant) of God. A slave's birth is unimportant, so Mark does not include the birth of Christ. A slave is expected to rush from task to task and to do any job immediately, so the key word in Mark is "**immediately**" (Gr. *eutheos*). The narrative is action packed. Jesus' actions and achievements are relived. His words and works are rehearsed. Mark reads like a Greek drama. Jesus, the chief character, is a wonderful man who had supernatural powers to heal the sick and raise the dead. He is actually the Savior-King. But Jewish officials feel threatened by Him and plot His death. The Jews persuade the Roman procurator Pilate to crucify Jesus. He lies dead in a borrowed tomb for three days. But then He supernaturally rises from the dead, appears to many eyewitnesses, and ascends to heaven after leaving a final commission: "Go into all the world and preach the gospel to the whole creation. Whoever believes and is baptized will be saved, but whoever does not believe will be condemned" (16:15–16).

Key Facts	
Author:	John Mark
Recipient:	Roman Christians
Where Written:	Rome
Date:	AD 65
Key Word:	Immediately (*eutheōs*)
Key Verse:	"For even the Son of Man did not come to be served, but to serve, and to give His life—a ransom for many" (10:45).

AUTHOR

The testimony to Mark's authorship of the Gospel that bears his name is **early and undisputed**. In the early second century, both Papias and Justin Martyr say that the second Gospel was written by Mark and that he received his information from Peter.[1] The Greek title *Kata Markon*, "according to Mark," appears in the earliest manuscripts. It is hard to believe that anyone would ascribe this Gospel to such a minor character as John Mark if he were not the actual author. John was his Jewish name while Mark was his Roman name.

Greek Highlight

Slave. Greek δοῦλος (*doulos*). Several Greek words in the NT convey the idea of one person being the servant of another. By far the most common is *doulos*, best conveyed by the English word *slave*. Other types of servants had various responsibilities, privileges, and rights, but under Roman law, the *doulos* had no rights. He belonged completely to his master and had only those responsibilities and privileges granted by his master. In the NT, *doulos* is normally used literally (Mark 8:9; 14:47; Luke 17:7–10; John 13:16; Eph 6:5–9; Phlm 16), but a figurative meaning describing someone who serves God and His people is also common (Mark 10:44; Acts 2:18; 4:29; Rom 1:1; 2 Cor 4:5; 1 Pet 2:16; Rev 2:20). Paul has two significant uses of *doulos*, one about Christ and the other about Christians: (1) Phil 2:6 refers to Jesus' condescension in the incarnation, and (2) Rom 6:16–18 refers to being slaves of righteousness instead of *slaves* of sin. The use of this word in the Bible is a vivid reminder of how Christianity engaged relevant social terms to convey spiritual truths in an understandable way. Being a slave of Christ also expresses the level of consecration each believer must devote towards his or her Savior and Lord Jesus Christ.

Mark lived in Jerusalem during the time of Jesus, and it is thought that the upper room was in his mother Mary's house. The early church often met there, so Mark was well acquainted with the **apostles**. Mark was probably at the house in AD 44 when an angel released Peter from the deadly threat of Herod Agrippa I (Acts 12:12). Mark was also a cousin of Barnabas (Col 4:10) and assisted Paul and Barnabas on their first missionary journey until he left them midway and returned to Jerusalem (Acts 13:5,13).

Paul refused to allow Mark on the next journey, so **Barnabas** took Mark with him to Cyprus in about AD 50. Ten years later, however, Mark was with **Paul** in Rome as a "co-worker" (Col 4:10; Phlm 24), so his initial failure was not final. Mark also served alongside **Peter** in Babylon (Rome?) for a while. Just as Timothy was Paul's son in the faith, Peter called Mark his "son" (1 Pet 5:13). In his final epistle Paul asked for Mark to join him in Rome, noting that Mark was "useful to me in the ministry" (2 Tim 4:11).

One unique story in the Gospel may point to Mark himself. After the soldiers arrested Jesus in the garden of Gethsemane and the disciples had fled, the guards laid hold on a **young man**, but he left the linen cloth about his body and fled away naked (Mark

14:51–52). Why tell this story? Who was this individual? Many Bible interpreters think it was Mark. Mark may have wanted to tell us that he was also there on that dreadful night.

RECIPIENTS

There are several indications that Mark wrote his Gospel with a **Gentile Roman audience** in mind. First, Mark is the only Gospel writer to mention that Simon the Cyrenian, the man who carried Jesus' cross, was the father of Alexander and Rufus (15:21). But why include the names of the sons of this little-known character? In Rom 16:13, Paul greeted a Roman Christian named Rufus. It is hard to imagine any other reason for Mark to include this reference unless he was writing to believers in Rome who knew this man.

Second, Mark uses **Latinisms** 12 times in his Gospel. None of the other Gospels do this. Mark's Gospel was written in Greek, but Mark takes certain Latin words and turns them into Greek. Examples are *spekoulatora* for executioner (6:27), *kenson* for taxes (12:14), *quadrans* for the value of the widow's two coins (12:42), *praetorium* for the governor's residence (15:16), and *centurion* for a leader of 100 (15:39).

Third, Mark **translates Semitic words** he uses such as *Boanerges* (3:17), *talitha koum* (5:41), *corban* (7:11), *Ephphatha* (7:34), *Bartimaeus* (10:46), *Abba* (14:36), *Golgotha* (15:22), and Jesus' words on the cross *Eloi, Eloi, lemá sabachtháni*, "My God, My God, why have You forsaken Me?" (15:34).

Fourth, Mark assumes that his readers know about the baptism of John the Baptist and the baptism of the Holy Spirit (1:5,8). Roman readers did not need to have these issues explained.

A panoramic view of the ruins of the Roman Forum.

Fifth, there is only one quote from the Old Testament (1:2–3) and a marked absence of references to the law of Moses. This shows that Mark does not presume his readers have much of a biblical background. Also, Mark regularly **explains Jewish customs and geography** for his Gentile readers. Mark explains that the Jews will not eat unless they first wash their hands (7:2–4), that the Mount of Olives is "across from the temple complex" (13:3), and that the Jews sacrifice the Passover lamb "on the first day of Unleavened Bread" (14:12).

Sixth, Jesus' prohibition of preaching to the Samaritans and Gentiles is purposely omitted by Mark (cp. Mark 6:7–11 with Matt 10:5–6).

But Mark's Gospel is also meant for **other people** beyond the Romans—both geographically and in terms of time. Hints of this are sprinkled throughout Mark— *everyone* is looking for Jesus (1:37); Christ died a ransom for *many* (10:45); the temple is to be a house of prayer for *all nations* (11:17); God will give His vineyard to *others*

(12:9); the gospel is to be preached to *all nations* (13:10); and the gospel is to be preached to *the whole creation* (16:15).

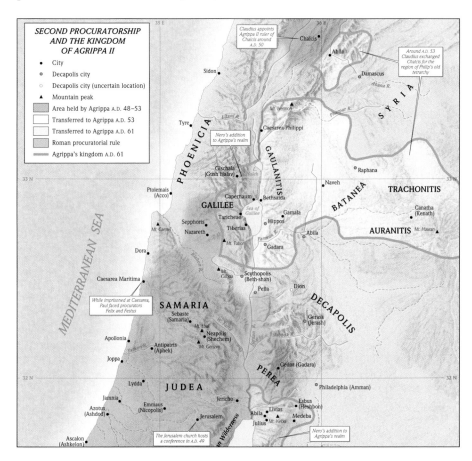

OCCASION AND DATE

Mark was a close **disciple of Peter**. As Mark accompanied Peter, he heard Peter tell and retell the stories about Jesus everywhere they went. After relating the story of the transfiguration, Peter expressed a desire for believers to "be able to recall these things at any time" (2 Pet 1:15). The context of that statement is this. Peter says, "I will soon lay aside my tent, as our Lord Jesus Christ has also shown me. And I will also make every effort that you may be able to recall these things at any time after my departure" (2 Pet 1:14–15). These words may indicate Peter's desire to leave behind a **written record** of Jesus' words and deeds. Peter penned that statement in his final epistle, dated about AD 64–65, shortly before his martyrdom.

Irenaeus, an early church father around AD 180, said that after Peter's departure (Gk. *exodus*), Mark, the disciple and interpreter of Peter, handed down in writing what

Peter had preached.[2] If that statement is true, this would date Mark's Gospel sometime around AD 65 but probably before the Jewish temple was destroyed in AD 70. Others have dated Luke's Gospel about AD 60, before the concluding events he recorded in the book of Acts (AD 62). Matthew may have been the first Gospel written. It is fittingly placed at the beginning of the New Testament. Jesus appeared and ministered to the Jewish people first. Later the good news spread to other nations and peoples.

An overview of the third-century synagogue at Capernaum.

But some scholars today insist that Mark must have been the first Gospel written because Matthew and Luke share **large literary connections** with Mark. Their opinion is that Matthew and Luke depended much on Mark for his order of events and selection of words.[3] This, however, would reduce those two brilliant writers almost to plagiarists. Perhaps a better solution is to note that Mark follows the outline of Peter's typical preaching as seen, for example, in his message to Cornelius and his household (Acts 10:34–43). Long before any Gospel accounts were written down, there was a spoken presentation of the message. This oral tradition assumed a set format that was repeated over and over again, though with some variation. The three Synoptic Gospels—Matthew, Mark, and Luke—view Christ in a similar manner and have many verbal correspondences, not because they copy one another but because this was the way Christ's life was regularly told in the early church. Matthew, another eyewitness, adds details of his own that present Christ as King of the Jews in fulfillment of Old Testament prophecy. Luke portrays Christ as the perfect Son of Man and includes facts gleaned from many early followers of Christ and apparently from other brief written episodes (Luke 1:1).

Mark never formally states his purpose for writing his Gospel. But as one evaluates the contents of his book, one gathers the **reasons** Christ came to earth. Jesus came to preach (1:38), to call sinners to repentance (2:17), and to give His life a ransom for many (10:45). But Mark also addressed some immediate practical concerns. Mark's readers faced persecution and even martyrdom. His Gospel would strengthen and guide Roman believers through the trials of Nero's terrible persecutions. Being Jesus' disciple was costly. Jesus experienced rejection, suffering, and eventual martyrdom, yet God was behind all His afflictions, and Jesus emerged as Victor over death. Mark was interested in transformation, not just information.

Mark's theological purpose was to explain the most significant life in all of human history. Who was Jesus? He was the Son of God (1:1,11; 14:61; 15:39), Son of Man (2:10; 8:31; 13:26), Messiah (8:29), and Lord (1:3; 7:28). With Peter and the other apostles passing off the scene, it was imperative to have an **authentic written record** of the good news found in Jesus Christ.

GENRE AND STRUCTURE

The Gospel genre is unique. Gospels are not biographies that just recount a person's background, family history, and career. Mark's Gospel contains **no genealogy** or birth narrative of Jesus. Romans were interested in power not pedigree. Mark's King is a Savior-King who conquered demons, disease, and death. A Gospel is a unique blend of narrative, poetry, and proverb. It is filled with figures of speech and paints life situations one can relive as though one were there.

In a brief prologue of just 13 verses, Mark introduces Jesus Christ, the main character, to his audience. Matthew takes 76 verses, and Luke uses 183 before getting to the same point in their narratives. Mark weaves in both **expectation**, "Prepare the way for the Lord" (Mark 1:3), and **conflict** as Christ is immediately "tempted by Satan" (1:13). This is followed by a large section (1:14–8:30), which serves to complicate the plot as in a Greek tragedy. Mark wrote about success but also hostility. Opposition and conflict grew. Withdrawal from public sight was sometimes required. This culminated in a crisis moment when Peter and the disciples recognized Jesus as the Messiah (8:29–30).

Mark's drama follows (8:31–15:47) where the final outcome of the plot unfolds. Christ announces His coming death on three separate occasions (8:31; 9:31; 10:33) and prepares His disciples for His departure. He dies. But in the epilogue (16:1–20), the dramatic counterpart to the necessity of His death, Christ rises from the dead. This is the Gospel of Mark—the good news about Jesus Christ. But interestingly, Mark's first words are "The beginning of the gospel of Jesus Christ, the Son of God" (1:1). Then Mark describes three years of ministry. Those three years that Mark chronicles were indeed just the beginning. When Peter and the other apostles saw Jesus ascend into heaven, they soon realized that what they had witnessed for three years was really just "the beginning" of the good news.

MESSAGE

Jesus the Divine Servant Son of God

Mark's goal is to present Jesus as the divine Servant Son of God. He dispenses with any mention of Jesus' birth and childhood and rushes immediately to Jesus' miraculous works. Though Mark includes many teachings and several sermons of Christ, he focuses on what makes Jesus so unique. Mark only includes **four parables** Jesus told but recounts nearly **20 miracles**. All of Jesus' activity in Mark focuses on His Galilean ministry until the final week in Jerusalem. About 93 percent of Mark's account, which represents the basic oral preaching of the Gospel story, is also contained in parts of Matthew and Luke. By contrast, John, writing later than the three Synoptics, has only 8 percent of the material included in Mark.

The synagogue at the site of ancient Capernaum.

Mark's first chapter portrays Jesus' long Sabbath-day ministry in **Capernaum**, His adopted hometown on the northern edge of the Sea of Galilee. First, Jesus came "preaching" (1:14). Jesus was first and foremost a preacher of the good news. Second, Jesus called four disciples to accompany Him in full-time ministry (1:16–20). John tells us that Andrew, Peter, James, and John had already been following Christ for about six months, prior to John the Baptist's imprisonment but on an itinerant basis.[4] Their lives would radically change from this moment. Third, Jesus cast out a demon from a man in the synagogue in the middle of His sermon (1:23–26). Fourth, Jesus healed Peter's mother-in-law (1:29–31). Finally, way into the night, Jesus continued to heal all who came to the door of Peter's home (1:32–34).

The next paragraph is a significant commentary on **Jesus' prayer life**, which describes an event that happened the next day: "Very early in the morning, while it was still dark, He got up, went out, and made His way to a deserted place. And He was praying there" (1:35). Jesus' prayer life was successful because He got up early enough, went far enough away, and stayed long enough to pray. The phrase "was praying" is in a verb tense that portrays continued action in past time. Jesus' prayer life was planned, private, and prolonged.

Action Packed

Throughout his Gospel, Mark presents more *works* of Jesus and fewer of His *words*. Mark's writing is action packed, forceful, fresh, vivid, dramatic, realistic, graphic, simple, direct, swift, rough, brief, and to the point. Mark uses the historical

A view of the Temple Mount area from the Mount of Olives.

present tense more than 150 times in 673 verses and is fond of using the imperfect tense as well. The latter describes continuous action in the past. The historical present is like saying, "Here He comes; He is looking at the blind man; He touches him; the blind man sees; he bows before Jesus and thanks Him." It records the events as occurring before our very eyes. It has the **eyewitness quality** of an on-the-spot reporter. We relive the stories through Peter's eyes and Mark's vivid retelling.

Attention to Detail

Another characteristic of Mark is his *attention to detail*. This can be seen in his treatment of the demoniac in 5:1–20. Mark uses 20 verses to recount this story while Luke has only 14 and Matthew but 7. Similarly, the story of the woman who touched Jesus' garment occupies just 3 verses in Matthew, 6 in Luke, but 10 in Mark.

Yet Mark's Gospel is still the **most concise**, containing only 673 verses, compared to Matthew's 1,068 and Luke's 1,147. Why is this so? Mark's emphasis is different. Matthew and Luke record many of Jesus' words. Sixty percent of Matthew is Jesus' words. For Luke, the figure is 51 percent, but for Mark it is just under 42 percent. Mark's emphasis is on Jesus' mighty works.

As one might expect, **Peter** figures more prominently in Mark's account than he does in either Matthew or Luke. Peter's name appears in a number of places in Mark but is absent from the other Gospels. Three notable places where this occurs are 1:36 where Peter leads the contingency looking for Jesus only to find Him in private prayer, 11:21 where Peter comments about the withered fig tree, and 13:3 where Peter heads the list of the four fishermen disciples who ask Jesus about His predicted destruction of the Jewish temple. Modesty may have kept Mark from mentioning Peter's walking on the water in 6:50–51 (cf. Matt 14:28–31), Peter's asking about the parable in 7:17 (cf. Matt 15:15), and where Peter and John were the two disciples Jesus sent into Jerusalem to prepare the room for the Passover in 14:13 (cf. Luke 22:8). On occasion Mark's use of "they" may be a recounting of a story in which Peter said "we."[5]

Jesus' mighty works in Mark include at least 18 separate miracles, as well as places where Mark says He healed the multitudes as in 1:32–34; 3:10–12; and 6:53–56. Two of Jesus' miracles are recorded in Mark and nowhere else. One is the restoring of speech and hearing to a deaf and dumb man in the Decapolis (7:32–35); the other is the healing of a blind man at Bethsaida (8:22–26). Mark included many miracles Jesus performed to show that Jesus was indeed the Son of God.

Mark purposely records fewer of Jesus' teachings than the other three Gospels. He recounts four parables in chap. 4, including the unique one about the mysterious and miraculous way seeds sprout and grow (4:26–29). Mark also presents Jesus' **Olivet Discourse** (13:1–36). A red-letter New Testament will reveal that Jesus spoke in no fewer than 279 verses in Mark. Sometimes these were words spoken to a sick person or warnings to His disciples about the leaven of the Sadducees or Pharisees, but all of Jesus' words are instructive. Sometimes Jesus asked rhetorical questions to spur the minds of His disciples or other listeners.

Mark includes more **personal details** about Jesus than any other Gospel. Mark is the only writer who mentions that Jesus was a carpenter (6:3). This helps us understand what Jesus was doing during His early adulthood. Mark shows Jesus' full humanity as well as His deity. Jesus got tired and hungry, just as we do (4:38; 6:31; 11:12). He experienced great heaviness of heart and sorrow as He prayed in the garden of Gethsemane the night before His crucifixion where He would take God's punishment upon Himself for the sins of the whole world (14:33–36). Mark notes Jesus' anger and sorrow at the hardness of people's hearts in a synagogue (3:5) and how He rebuked His disciples for turning little children away from Him (10:14). Jesus was also compassionate toward a leprous man (1:41) and toward a huge crowd of people who were like sheep without a shepherd (6:34). Jesus had compassion on the crowd of about 4,000 men and their families who had not eaten for several days as they listened to Him (8:2). He then miraculously fed them all with plenty to spare.

The Last 12 Verses of Mark

The ending of Mark's Gospel, 16:9–20, has been a matter of dispute among scholars.[6] The large majority of all Greek manuscripts of Mark include these last 12 verses. However, these verses are missing in two prominent early manuscripts dating to the fourth century. The problem then carries over into Bible translation. A quick look at 16:9–20 in one's Bible will reveal where the translators stood on this **textual problem**. The King James Version considered these verses to be genuine.[7] Some modern translators indicate that this passage on Christ's resurrection appearances, the Great Commission, and His ascension should not be included. For example, the New American Standard Version brackets vv. 9–20. A note in the *ESV Study Bible* says, "In summary, vv. 9–20 should be read with caution. As in many translations, the editors of the *ESV* have placed the section within brackets, showing their doubts as to whether it was originally part of what Mark wrote, but also recognizing its long history of acceptance by many in the church."[8] The *NLT Study Bible* says, "Nearly all scholars agree that Mark did not write the 'shorter' and 'longer' endings. . . . Many scholars conclude that the original ending was accidentally torn off and lost, or was never finished."[9]

It is amazing that a passage of this magnitude (12 verses), if not inspired by God, could insert itself into our Bibles from the earliest of times. Most of the material found in this passage is also contained in either Matthew or Luke. Some of the vocabulary of vv. 9–20 is not found elsewhere in Mark. But the same could be said for almost any section of the book. Almost every paragraph presents a few unique words. But it would be puzzling for Mark to record the angels' prediction that the disciples would see Jesus in Galilee and then not note its fulfillment. It would also be strange for Mark to end on a note of fear. Verse 8 concludes, "So they went out and started running from the tomb, because trembling and astonishment overwhelmed them. And they said nothing to anyone, since they were afraid." Does Mark begin his Gospel so boldly and then end with women who are fleeing and afraid?

CONCLUSION

Mark has been called a **passion story** with a long introduction. Christ's passion includes His entrance into Jerusalem; His cleansing of the temple; His answering His opponents' questions; the last supper; His agony in the garden; His arrest, trial, and crucifixion; His burial and resurrection; His postresurrection appearances; and His ascension. Chapters 11–16 make up the passion narrative. Chapters 1–10 lead up to Christ's passion and point to it. Mark 8:31 says, "Then He began to teach them that the Son of Man must suffer many things, and be rejected by the elders, the chief priests, and the scribes, be killed, and rise after three days." Jesus repeated this dire prediction in 9:31 and 10:33. Then six chapters (11–16), are devoted to that last fateful week in the Savior's life. Just before Mark tells the story of the passion, he pens his key verse, 10:45, emphasizing that Jesus came to serve and to give His life a ransom for many.

Christ died for our sins, but He also rose from the dead to provide eternal salvation for all who will trust Him. Mark ends his Gospel with a challenge, an invitation, and a warning. The *challenge* is: "Go into all the world and preach the gospel to the whole creation" (16:15). The *invitation* is: "Whoever believes and is baptized will be saved" (16:16a). The *warning* is: "but whoever does not believe will be condemned" (16:16b). We will do well to heed the challenge, accept the invitation, and announce the warning.

Gordon's Calvary is one of two sites considered to be the possible location of Jesus' crucifixion.

For Further Reading

Black, David Alan, ed. *Perspectives on the Ending of Mark: 4 Views*. Nashville: B&H, 2008.

Brooks, James A. *Mark*. NAC 23. Nashville: B&H, 1991.

Evans, Craig A. *Mark 8:27–16:20*. WBC, 34B. Nashville: Thomas Nelson, 2001.

France, R. T. *The Gospel of Mark: A Commentary on the Greek Text*. NIGTC. Grand Rapids: Eerdmans, 2002.

Lane, William. *The Gospel According to Mark*. NICNT. Grand Rapids: Eerdmans, 1974.

Study Questions

1. Who was John Mark, and how did he come to be the author of this Gospel? Explain Mark's relationship to Peter and how that may have influenced what he wrote.
2. What is the key verse of Mark's Gospel, and what does it tell us of the message Mark tries to get across to his readers?
3. Were Roman Christians the original recipients of Mark's Gospel? What are some indications that this might be the case?
4. What are some of the unique features found in the Gospel of Mark?
5. What are some of the issues discussed regarding the dating of Mark's Gospel and the "Synoptic problem"? How does the concept of an often-repeated oral tradition enter into this equation?

ENDNOTES

1. Eusebius, *Ecclesiastical History* 3.39, cites Papias; Justin Martyr, *Dialogue with Trypho*, chap. 56.

2. Irenaeus, *Against Heresies*, 3.1.1.

3. Robert H. Stein, *Luke*, NAC 24 (Nashville: B&H, 1992), 27–30; R. T. France, *The Gospel of Mark* (Grand Rapids: Eerdmans, 2002), 35–45.

4. Compare Mark 1:14 with John 3:24. All the material in John up to that point occurred *before* John was placed in prison. Jesus had called at least 6 of the 12 disciples before John was arrested by Herod Antipas. This calling in Mark 1:14 was a second calling to a permanent full-time following and took place "after John was arrested."

5. See, e.g., 1:21,29; 5:1,38; 6:53–54; 8:22; 9:14,30.

6. The issue is debated in David Alan Black, ed., *Perspectives on the Ending of Mark: 4 Views* (Nashville: B&H, 2008). David Alan Black and Maurice Robinson argue that the verses are genuine. Daniel Wallace and Keith Elliott contend that they are not.

7. This is true of the NKJV as well.

8. *ESV Study Bible* (Wheaton: Crossway, 2008), 1933.

9. *NLT Study Bible* (Carol Stream, IL: Tyndale House, 2008), 1693.

Chapter 7

LUKE
The Son of Man

Luke was a **medical doctor**, a missionary, an evangelist, a historian, a researcher, and the writer of the third Gospel. His account of Jesus' life and ministry emphasizes that He is the perfect Son of God and the Savior of all mankind. Luke countenances no prejudice. Jesus loves all, mingles with all, died for all, and calls all to be saved. Luke is the **longest book** in the New Testament and gives us the fullest picture of the life of Christ. Luke begins by explaining how the angel Gabriel predicted Jesus' coming to Mary, and he concludes with a glimpse of Jesus ascending back to heaven after His resurrection from the dead.

The first chapter pictures Zechariah the priest coming out of the temple speechless and unable to give the customary blessing to the people. The last chapter shows Jesus, our great high priest, giving His disciples a parting blessing, "And while He was blessing them, He left them and was carried up into heaven" (24:51). Jesus had completed His earthly ministry and was stepping into His heavenly high-priestly ministry of interceding for all believers at the right hand of God the Father.

Key Facts	
Author:	Luke
Recipient:	Theophilus
Where Written:	Caesarea?
Date:	AD 60
Key Word:	People (Gk. *laos*)
Key Verse:	"For the Son of Man has come to seek and to save the lost" (19:10).

AUTHOR

Luke, the author of the Gospel that bears his name, is mentioned by name only three times in the New Testament.[1] He **joined Paul** at Troas on his second missionary journey as part of the missionary team. Luke writes, "God had called us to evangelize them" (Acts 16:10). After the church was founded in Philippi, Luke remained there to shepherd the new congregation when Paul left for Thessalonica, Athens, and Corinth. Luke also accompanied Paul on the final part of his third missionary journey from Philippi back to Jerusalem (Acts 20:1–21:17) and on his trip to Rome (Acts 27–28). Luke remained with Paul at Rome and is mentioned in two of Paul's prison epistles.[2] Paul called Luke "the dearly loved physician" (Col 4:14) and also distinguished him from those who were "of the circumcision" or Jewish (Col 4:11). Luke may have been Jewish, but he was probably a **Gentile**. He wrote in polished Greek. Tradition says Luke was from Syrian Antioch and also a brother of Titus.[3] The latter may explain why Luke does not mention Titus in Acts. In 2 Tim 4:11, Paul wrote, "Only Luke is with me." Luke was the only one with Paul during his final Roman imprisonment before Paul was beheaded.

Two types of evidence point to Luke as the author of the third Gospel. The **external evidence** consists of the comments made by early church fathers and other documentation. By AD 200, Irenaeus, Clement of Alexandria, Tertullian, and the Muratorian Canon unequivocally name Luke as the author of this Gospel.[4] The Muratorian Canon

View overlooking Bethlehem, birthplace of King David and Jesus, Son of David.

is a list of canonical books. It says simply that the third Gospel was written by Luke the physician.

One piece of **internal evidence** is that Luke and Acts have a common author.[5] Both are addressed to the same individual, Theophilus (Luke 1:3; Acts 1:1). The author of Acts says, "I wrote the first narrative, Theophilus, about all that Jesus began to do and teach" (Acts 1:1). This is a reference to the Gospel account. Whoever penned Acts also wrote Luke.

The second key from internal evidence for Luke's authorship flows from the book of Acts back to the Gospel of Luke. Three passages in Acts repeatedly use the first-person plural "**we**" when describing the action.[6] This means the author was a participant in those sections, all of which were on Paul's missionary journeys. The author distinguishes himself from others in the story. For example, he names Sopater, Aristarchus, Secundus, Gaius, Timothy, Tychicus, and Trophimus and then says, "These men went on ahead and waited for us at Troas" (Acts 20:5). By this process of elimination, only Luke and Titus are left as possibilities for writing Acts. No one ever asserts that Titus wrote Acts, but the early church unanimously names Luke.

Paul called Luke "the dearly loved physician" (Col 4:14), and there seems to be an interest in **sickness and healing** in the third Gospel. Mark says Peter's mother-in-law had a fever (1:30), but Luke notes it was "a high fever" (Gk. *megalo*; 4:38). Mark says a man had "a serious skin disease" (1:40), but Luke adds that this disease was "all over him" (5:12). Mark tells of a man with a paralyzed hand (3:1), but Luke observes that his right hand was paralyzed (6:6). Mark reports that Peter cut off a man's ear (14:47), but only Luke adds that Jesus touched his ear and healed him (22:51). Luke has five healings in his account that neither Matthew nor Mark mention. But none of this evidence proves conclusively that a doctor penned the third Gospel.[7]

RECIPIENT

The recipient of the Gospel of Luke was the "most honorable **Theophilus**" (Luke 1:3). The term "most honorable" is found thrice elsewhere by Luke in addresses to the Roman officials Felix and Festus. Both are called "most excellent" (Acts 23:26; 24:3; 26:25). Theophilus may have been a Roman official or a nobleman, who may have recently become a Christian.

Luke says he wants Theophilus to "know the certainty of the things about which you have been instructed" (Luke 1:4). Luke takes care to frame his message in ways that would appeal to Theophilus and other **Gentile readers**. Here are some examples. Whereas Mark quotes Jesus using the Semitic phrase "*Talitha koum!*" (Mark 5:41) when He raised Jairus's daughter, in Luke He says, "Child, get up!" (Luke 8:54). Jesus says no one covers a lamp with a "basket" (Gk. *modion*, Mark 4:21; Matt 5:15), but Luke uses a different Greek word for "basket" (Gk. *skeuei,* 8:16). The word "lawyer" (Gk. *nomikos*) is used six times in Luke but only once in the other two Synoptics. Instead, Matthew and Mark use the Hebrew term "scribe" (Gk. *grammateus*) 46 times to Luke's 15 times.

Luke explains Jewish customs such as the Passover and unleavened bread to his Gentile readers (22:1,7). The genealogy of Jesus in Luke 3:23–38 extends back to the first man, Adam, whereas Matthew traces it only to Abraham, the progenitor of the Hebrew nation (1:1–16). Luke's readers are seemingly unfamiliar with Palestinian geography because he describes Nazareth (1:26), and later Capernaum (4:31), as "a town in Galilee." The conclusion is that Luke's primary recipient (Theophilus) and others beyond him were Gentiles with largely Greek backgrounds.

A fourth-century AD synagogue built on the foundation of a first-century AD synagogue in Capernaum.

OCCASION AND DATE

The occasion for the Gospel of Luke was that Theophilus, and other new believers like him, needed a clear account of the life and ministry of Jesus as an aid to confirmation in their faith. However, the precise dating of Luke's writing is difficult to determine. Some conservative evangelicals argue for a date around AD 60, and others posit a date in the mid-60s or even after the year 70.[8] **Two issues** are involved in this determination: (1) Did Luke use Mark as a primary source for writing his Gospel? If so, then Luke could not be written before Mark. Many hold that Mark was penned around AD 65 or a little later, although Robert Gundry argues that "no compelling reasons exist to deny an early date in the period AD 45–70 . . . and—if Luke's gospel reflects Mark—Mark still earlier in the fifties or late forties."[9] (2) Does Acts 28 leave Paul in Roman bonds because the outcome of his first Roman trial was unknown when Acts was published in AD 62? Or did Luke purposely end Acts at this point? Acts was not meant to be a biography of either Peter or Paul. If Acts was simply an account of the spread of Christianity from Jerusalem to Rome, we should not expect to know the outcome of Paul's trial. On the other hand, reporting Paul's exoneration would be in keeping with the mission of Acts to show Christianity as no threat to the Roman Empire.

The idea of **Markan priority** is a complicated issue. Most liberal scholars and some evangelicals as well are convinced of this thesis. However, it is unnecessary to make Matthew and Luke subservient and indebted to a written form of Mark. The oral preaching of the Jesus story had already taken on a set form of expression for several decades as seen in Peter's and Paul's sermon outlines in Acts 2, 10, and 13. The fact that Matthew, Mark, and Luke each tell of Jesus' great Galilean ministry in a particular order and use some of the same vocabulary can easily be attributed to the widespread existence of the oral communication of the gospel.

Another factor in the dating is when Luke might have met Theophilus and others like him who needed such a Gospel account. Luke journeyed with Paul through **Greece** and **Asia Minor** on the second and third missionary journeys from AD 50 to 57. They visited Philippi, Thessalonica, Athens, Corinth, Troas, and Ephesus. This is where people like Theophilus heard the gospel and joined these thriving churches. The need was present in the mid-50s.

The question was when would Luke be able to write? Paul's detention in Caesarea from AD 58 to 60 gave Luke the opportunity to **research and interview** early

The Sea of Galilee as viewed from the northwest.

eyewitnesses, even some of the apostles, deacons, and other early Christians in Israel. He had access to the people he needed to receive first-hand information.

In addition, Luke was with Paul during his two-year house arrest in **Rome**. This would have been an ideal time to compose the book of Acts. Acts ends with Paul still in custody, which may indicate that the outcome of his trial was not known when Acts was published. Since Acts was the sequel to Luke, it makes sense to date Luke around AD 60, if the latter scenario is true.

GENRE AND STRUCTURE

Luke penned a **formal literary introduction** noting his purpose in writing, his methodology, and the attempts others had made in such writing. Luke's purpose was to give "an orderly sequence" of the events about Christ's birth, life, and sacrificial death followed by His resurrection and ascension back to heaven. He wanted Theophilus and other readers to "know the certainty of the things about which you have been instructed" (1:4). First, Luke gathered his information from competent, reliable, first-hand sources—"the original eyewitnesses and servants of the word" (1:2). Luke knew the facts both as an inquirer and as an observer. Second, he recorded his message accurately (*akribōs* speaks of precision and accuracy). Third, the length of his search took him back to the beginning of things, so only Luke gives the account of the angel Gabriel speaking to Zechariah and Mary. His material is primarily **chronological** but always planned and logical. Fourth, Luke's use of *anōthen* (literally, "from above"), suggests that he probably was aware of divine inspiration. Luke's Greek style has been called "the most refined in the New Testament."[10]

The Gospel of Luke is the **longest** book in the New Testament with 1,151 verses. Matthew is next with 1,071, followed by Acts with 1,007. Luke's orderly narrative begins with Gabriel's predictions of the birth of John the Baptist to Zechariah and of the birth of Jesus to Mary. These events call forth poetic responses by both Mary (1:46–55) and Zechariah (1:68–79).

Following his prologue (1:1–4) and the preparations for the arrival of God's Son (1:4–2:52), Luke tells of the public presentation of Christ with His baptism by John the Baptist, followed by His temptations in the wilderness (3:1–4:13). A longer section recounts Jesus' preaching ministry, healings and other miracles, and the calling of the Twelve (4:14–9:50). Luke then covers the Perean ministry of Christ, that is, His work on the eastern side of the Jordan River (9:51–19:27). The final sections of Luke show Jesus' offer of the kingdom to the Jews, their rejection of Him, His crucifixion, burial, and the events at Jesus' tomb on resurrection morning (19:28–24:12). The final few paragraphs recount several postresurrection appearances, Jesus' Great Commission, and His ascension back to heaven (24:13–53).

Outline

I. Prologue (Luke 1:1–4)
II. Christ's Presentation, Baptism, and Temptation (Luke 1:5–4:13)
III. Christ's Preaching and Miracles (Luke 4:14–9:50)
IV. Christ's Perean Ministry and Parables (Luke 9:51–19:27)
V. Christ's Passion, Resurrection, and Ascension (Luke 19:28–24:53)

MESSAGE

The Comprehensive Gospel

Luke's is the most **comprehensive** Gospel. His message can be seen in what interests him and in how he presents it. It records events prior to Matthew's story of Mary and Joseph, reaching back to Gabriel's announcements to Zechariah and Mary. Its conclusion also extends beyond the other Gospels clear to the ascension of Christ and the disciples' worship in the temple after this.[11]

The Universal Gospel

Luke's is also the most **universal** Gospel. Men of every nationality are to see Jesus as the universal Savior of all peoples. The good news about Jesus is for the whole world. Twice Jesus is referred to as Savior in Luke (1:47; 2:11) but not at all in the other Synoptics. The Greek word *euangelizō,*

Cameo of Augustus Caesar.

"I preach the gospel," is found 10 times in Luke and 15 times in Acts. Matthew uses it once and the other Gospels not at all. Jesus came to announce the good news to all. The Jews are not favored over the Samaritans in Luke. Jesus rebukes James and John for wanting to call down fire on the Samaritans (9:54); the "good Samaritan" outclassed the Jewish priest and Levite (10:33); and the only leper out of 10 who returned to give Jesus thanks was a Samaritan (17:6).

The Historical Gospel

Luke references more **historical events** in the Roman Empire during the life of Jesus than the other Gospels. "Caesar Augustus" issued the census proclamation "while

Quirinius was governing Syria" (2:1–2); Jesus began ministry in the fifteenth year of Tiberius Caesar's reign when Pontius Pilate governed Judea (3:1); Annas and Caiaphas were high priests at the time (3:2); and Pilate slaughtered some Galileans along with their sacrifices (13:1). Luke even records that Jesus referred to Herod Antipas as "that fox" (13:32). Luke's account is not literary fantasy; it is historically grounded.

Greco-Roman arches in the ruins of Gerasa (modern Jerash, Jordan), a city in the Decapolis.

The Individual Gospel

Another Lukan emphasis is on the **individual person**. Whereas Matthew's parables are about the kingdom, Luke's 19 peculiar parables are about individuals. The lost sheep and the lost shekel, the good Samaritan, the prodigal son, the Pharisee and the tax collector in the temple, the dishonest manager, and the 10 servants who received some money to invest portray individuals for whom Christ came. Luke's narratives also portray more individuals than the other Gospels, including Zechariah and Elizabeth, Anna and Simeon, Mary and Martha, Cleopas and his friend, as well as Zacchaeus, Mary Magdalene, Simon the Cyrenian, Joseph of Arimathea, the widow of Nain, the three hesitant disciples, the women who helped Jesus financially, and a host of others. Luke sees supreme value in each person's soul before God.

The Lowly Gospel

Throughout his Gospel, Luke demonstrates Jesus' special love for the *downtrodden*, the *sinner*, and the *outcast*. Luke tells us that at Nain the dead man was a widow's *only* son (7:12), that Jairus lost his *only* daughter (8:42), and that the boy the disciples would not cure of demon possession was the *only* son of his father (9:38). Jesus took **pity** on the unlovely. He forgave the dying thief (23:42–43), accepted an immoral woman (7:36–50), and made a point of going to Zacchaeus's home (19:5). To summarize Luke's Gospel: "All the tax collectors and sinners were approaching to listen to Him. And the Pharisees and scribes were complaining, 'This man welcomes sinners and eats with them!'" (15:1–2).

The Forgiving Gospel

Forgiveness is also prominent in Luke's Gospel. Jesus told the paralyzed man, "Friend, your sins are forgiven you" (5:20). Both debtors in Jesus' story to Simon were forgiven, and the sinful woman in Simon's house heard Jesus say, "Your sins are forgiven" (7:48). We are to forgive (6:37) and to pray for forgiveness (11:4). Jesus said if your brother "sins against you seven times in a day, and comes back to you seven times, saying, 'I repent,' you must forgive him" (17:4). Jesus' first words from the cross were "Father, forgive them, because they do not know what they are doing" (23:34). Many other times in Luke, the word *forgive* is not found, but it is experienced. Think of Zacchaeus and the criminal on the cross. Luke's Gospel practically ends with this command from Jesus that "repentance for forgiveness of sins would be proclaimed in His name to all nations, beginning at Jerusalem" (24:47). Luke wants all people to know that forgiveness of sins is possible through Christ.

Greek Highlight

Repent. Greek μετανοέω (metanoeō). The Greek verb for repent (*metanoeo*) and the related noun for repentance (*metanoia*) signify a change of mind (*meta*, meaning after or change; and *nous*, meaning mind). More than just an intellectual change of mind is in view; rather, both terms refer to a change in one's way of thinking that results in different beliefs and a change in the direction of one's life. The verb *pisteuo* (meaning *believe*—see comments on *pisteuo* in Gospel of John) is much more common than *metanoeo*, though both words refer to concepts foundational to salvation (15:7,10; Matt 4:17; John 3:16). *Repent* and *believe* may be understood as opposite sides of the same coin. *Repent* means to turn from one's allegiance to sin and unbelief, whereas *believe* means to place one's trust in Christ. Thus, when one is mentioned the other is implied.

The Prayerful Gospel

Also, Luke's is the most *prayerful* Gospel. Luke shows **Jesus at prayer** more than any other Gospel writer—11 times. Seven of these prayer times are unique to Luke. Jesus prayed at His baptism (3:21), all night before selecting the 12 apostles (6:12), over the fish and loaves before feeding 5,000 (9:16), just before announcing His coming death to the Twelve (9:18), at His transfiguration (9:29), when the 70 returned from their mission (10:21–22), when the Twelve saw Jesus praying before asking Him to teach them how to pray (11:1), in Gethsemane before His arrest (22:41–42); and twice on the cross He prayed, "Father, forgive them, because they do not know what they are doing" (23:34); and He prayed when He "called out with a loud voice, 'Father, into Your hands I entrust My spirit'" (23:46).

In addition to Christ's own prayer life, Luke records three of Jesus' unique **parables on prayer**: the friend who arrives at midnight (11:5–13), the persistent widow (18:1–8), and the Pharisee and the publican praying in the temple (18:9–14). Furthermore, Jesus exhorts His followers to pray for their enemies (6:28), for workers to be sent into God's harvest field (10:2), and for needed things (11:9–13). He instructed them to pray "always and not become discouraged" (18:1) and to avoid temptation (22:40,46). W. Graham Scroggie has noted that Jesus taught prayer "by exhortation, illustration, and demonstration."[12]

The Lord's Prayer in three of many languages displayed at Christ's Church in Jerusalem.

A model of the temple built by Herod the Great with the surrounding courts.

The Worshipful Gospel

Luke also places special emphasis on **worship**. Worship is praising and glorifying God. It is magnifying God's greatness and rejoicing in it. Luke is filled with worship.

Only Luke records the great worship hymns expressed by Gabriel, Mary, Zechariah, the angels before the shepherds, and Simeon.[13] Glorifying, praising, and blessing God occur more in Luke than in the other Synoptics combined. In addition, joy and rejoicing, exulting, and laughter abound in Luke. Luke ends with the disciples returning to Jerusalem "with great joy. And they were continually in the temple complex praising and blessing God" (24:52–53).[14]

The Women's Gospel

Luke also stresses the **role of women** more than the other Gospels. He mentions women 43 times compared to Matthew's 30 and Mark and John's 19. Jesus lifts women up socially and spiritually. Mary sat at Jesus' feet, having "made the right choice" (10:42). Women supported Jesus and His disciples "from their possessions" (8:3). Women lingered at the cross and arrived first at Christ's tomb. What matchless pictures we have of Elizabeth, Mary, Anna, Joanna, Susanna, Mary and Martha, the sinful woman in Simon's house, the widow of Nain, and Mary Magdalene. Who can forget Jesus' parables of the woman sweeping to find her coin (15:8–10) and the persistent widow before the unjust judge (18:2–8)? Women were disrespected among the Gentiles but ennobled by Jesus. Luke portrays this for all time, for all to see.

The Holy Spirit Gospel

One of the most distinctive emphases in Luke's Gospel is on the **Holy Spirit**. Luke references the Holy Spirit in the life of Jesus more than any of the other Gospels, including John in his Upper Room Discourse.[15] Luke continues this trend in the book of Acts with more than 70 mentions of the Holy Spirit. One cannot read Luke without noticing how Jesus was filled with the Holy Spirit, led by the Spirit, spoke by the Spirit, and worked miracles by the Spirit. Mary conceived Christ by the Holy Spirit (1:35), and Elizabeth was filled with the Holy Spirit (1:41).

The Parable Gospel

Finally, Luke includes the most **unique parables**. Of the 23 parables Luke records, 19 are peculiar to Luke, and 16 of these parables are included in Luke 9:51–19:28, commonly referred to as Christ's Perean ministry. Included are such well-known parables as the good Samaritan; the rich fool; the sensible manager; the large banquet; the lost sheep, the lost shekel, and lost (prodigal) son; the persistent widow; the Pharisee and the publican; and the journeying nobleman who entrusted each of his 10 slaves with one *mina* (a coin worth about 100 days' wages). The story of the rich man and Lazarus is sometimes thought to be a parable (16:19–31). However, this is a true story about two individuals.[16] Jesus gives a brief glimpse into the afterlife of an unsaved man. He was tormented in hell and feared greatly that his unsaved relatives would suffer the same fate.

THE PARABLES OF JESUS	
Parable	*Reference*
1. The speck and the log	Matt 7:1–6; Luke 6:37–43
2. The two houses	Matt 7:24–27; Luke 6:47–49
3. Children in the marketplace	Matt 11:16–19; Luke 7:32
4. The two debtors	Luke 7:42
5. The unclean spirit	Matt 12:43–45; Luke 11:24–26
6. The rich man's meditation	Luke 12:16–21
7. The barren fig tree	Luke 13:6–9
8. The sower	Matt 13:3–8; Mark 4:3–8; Luke 8:5–8
9. The tares	Matt 13:24–30
10. The seed	Mark 4:20
11. The grain of mustard seed	Matt 13:31–32; Mark 4:31–32; Luke 13:19
12. The leaven	Matt 13:33; Luke 13:21
13. The lamp	Matt 5:15; Mark 4:21; Luke 8:16; 11:33
14. The dragnet	Matt 13:47–48
15. The hidden treasure	Matt 13:44
16. The pearl of great value	Matt 13:45–46
17. The householder	Matt 13:52
18. The marriage	Matt 9:15; Mark 2:19–20; Luke 5:34–35
19. The patched garment	Matt 9:16; Mark 2:21; Luke 5:36
20. The wine bottles	Matt 9:17; Mark 2:22; Luke 5:37
21. The harvest	Matt 9:37; Luke 10:2
22. The opponent	Matt 5:25; Luke 12:58
23. Two insolvent debtors	Matt 18:23–35
24. The good Samaritan	Luke 10:30–37
25. The three loaves	Luke 11:5–8
26. The good shepherd	John 10:1–16
27. The narrow gate	Matt 7:14; Luke 13:24
28. The guests	Luke 14:7–11
29. The marriage supper	Matt 22:2–9; Luke 14:16–23
30. The wedding clothes	Matt 22:10–14
31. The tower	Luke 14:28–30
32. The king going to war	Luke 14:31
33. The lost sheep	Matt 18:12–13; Luke 15:4–7

THE PARABLES OF JESUS (continued)	
Parable	*Reference*
34. The lost coin	Luke 15:8–9
35. The prodigal son	Luke 15:11–32
36. The unjust steward	Luke 16:1–9
37. The rich man and Lazarus	Luke 16:19–31
38. The slave's duty	Luke 17:7–10
39. Laborers in the vineyard	Matt 20:1–16
40. The talents	Matt 25:14–30; Luke 19:11–27
41. The importunate widow	Luke 18:2–5
42. The Pharisee and tax-gatherer	Luke 18:10–14
43. The two sons	Matt 21:28
44. The wicked vine-growers	Matt 21:33–43; Mark 12:1–9; Luke 20:9–15
45. The fig tree	Matt 24:32; Mark 13:28; Luke 21:29–30
46. The watching slave	Matt 24:43; Luke 12:39
47. The man on a journey	Mark 13:34
48. Character of two slaves	Matt 24:45–51; Luke 12:42–46
49. The ten virgins	Matt 25:1–12
50. The watching slaves	Luke 12:36–38
51. The vine and branches	John 15:1–6

CONCLUSION

Luke was educated as a doctor, served as an evangelist and missionary with the apostle Paul, pastored the church at Philippi, researched about Jesus, and wrote the Gospel that bears his name as well as the book of Acts. Luke may have written his Gospel as early as AD 58–60 when Paul was confined by the Roman governors Felix and Festus in a cell in Caesarea. That was when Luke had time and access to research about Jesus' birth, life and ministry, death and resurrection. Luke's writing style is sophisticated and polished.

Luke's aim is to ground Theophilus, a Gentile convert, in the true **historical account** of Christ as Savior. He presents Jesus as the Son of God in His perfect humanity. Luke's Gospel is the most comprehensive, universal, and individualistic of the Gospel records. Luke emphasizes forgiveness, worship, prayer, Christ's sympathetic nature, and Jesus' respect for women. Luke includes more about the Holy Spirit and Christ's unique parables than the other Gospels. The Gospel of Luke is the longest book in the New Testament and certainly demands our careful reading and studying.

For Further Reading

Bock, Darrell L. *Luke*. IVP New Testament Commentary. Downers Grove: IVP, 1994.

Card, Michael. *Luke: The Gospel of Amazement*. Downers Grove: IVP, 2011.

Garland, David E. *Luke*. ZECNT. Grand Rapids: Zondervan, 2011.

Marshall, I. Howard. *The Gospel of Luke*. NIGTC. Grand Rapids: Eerdmans, 1978.

Morris, Leon. *The Gospel According to Luke: An Introduction and Commentary*. Grand Rapids: Eerdmans, 2002.

Stein, Robert. *Luke*. NAC. Nashville: B&H, 1992.

Study Questions

1. Who was Luke, what can be known about him, and why did he write his Gospel?
2. Explain how Luke can be characterized as comprehensive, universal, historical, and individualistic.
3. How do the following carry out the theme of Luke: forgiveness, sympathy, prayer, worship, and the Holy Spirit?
4. What characterizes the unique parables found in Luke?

ENDNOTES

1. Colossians 4:14; 2 Tim 4:11; and Phlm 24.

2. Colossians and Philemon. But Luke is absent in Philippians, so he may have left for a while.

3. At Acts 11:27, Codex D inserts, "And there was great rejoicing; and when we were gathered together one of them named Agabus stood up." The "we" would indicate Luke as an early Hellenist convert at Antioch. See Doremus Almy Hayes, *The Synoptic Gospels and the Book of Acts* (New York: Methodist Book Concern, 1919), 193; and John Dickie, "Christian," *ISBE*, ed. James Orr (Grand Rapids: Eerdmans, 1939), 1.622.

4. See Irenaeus, *Against Heresies*, 3.1.1; 3.14.1; Clement of Alexandria, *Stromata*, 1.26; Tertullian, Against *Marcion*, 4.5.3.

5. Robert H. Stein, *Luke*, NAC 24 (Nashville: B&H, 1992), 21–22, summarizes nine points that demonstrate a common author for Luke and Acts.

6. Acts 16:10–17; 20:5–21:18; 27:1–28:16.

7. William Kirk Hobart, *The Medical Language of St. Luke* (Dublin: Hodges, Figgis & Co., 1882), claimed the use of medical language in Luke-Acts pointed to Lukan authorship, but H. J. Cadbury, *The Style and Literary Method of Luke* (Cambridge: Harvard University Press, 1920), sought to refute those claims.

8. Stein, *Luke*, 24–26, likes a post-AD 70 date; D. Edmond Hiebert, *An Introduction to the New Testament: The Gospels and Acts* (Chicago: Moody, 1975), 135–39, advocates a date of AD 66 or early 67; Henry C. Thiessen, *Introduction to the New Testament* (Grand Rapids: Eerdmans, 1943), 156–58; and Robert G. Gromacki, *New Testament Survey* (Grand Rapids: Baker, 1974), 111, hold to a date around AD 60.

9. Robert H. Gundry, *A Survey of the New Testament*, rev. ed. (Grand Rapids: Zondervan, 1981), 79.

10. Ibid., 91.

11. Mark 16:19 also mentions Christ's ascension.

12. W. Graham Scroggie, *A Guide to the Gospels* (London: Pickering & Inglis, n.d.), 370.

13. These are commonly called *Ave Maria, Magnificat, Benedictus, Gloria in Excelsis,* and *Nunc Dimittis.*

14. Majority manuscripts have both "praising and blessing."

15. Luke 17; John 15; Matthew 12; Mark 6.

16. See James A. Borland, "Luke," in *Liberty Commentary on the New Testament*, ed. Jerry Falwell (Lynchburg, VA: Liberty, 1978), 158.

Chapter 8

JOHN
Believe and Live

The Gospel of John is an **eyewitness account** of Jesus' life and teachings written by someone so close to Jesus that he can confidently call himself "the beloved disciple." Through his time spent with Jesus, he became convinced that Jesus was the Messiah whom the Old Testament had predicted. Rather than focusing on what was already written, this disciple focuses on events, discourses, and signs not found in the other Gospels. What emerges is a fresh presentation of Jesus as the Messiah, which **fills in the gaps** left by the Synoptic writers and invites its readers to believe that Jesus is the Messiah, the Son of God, and by believing have life in His name.

Key Facts	
Author:	John, "the beloved disciple"
Recipient:	Greek-Speaking Jews Living Outside of Israel
Where Written:	Ephesus
Date:	AD 90
Key Word:	Believe (pisteuō)
Key Verse:	"Jesus performed many other signs in the presence of His disciples that are not written in this book. But these are written so that you may believe Jesus is the Messiah, the Son of God, and by believing you may have life in His name" (20:30–31).

AUTHOR

The writer of the Gospel only identifies himself as "the disciple Jesus loved" (21:20). Therefore, any argument from internal evidence needs to be established by a process of elimination. Internally, it can be determined that the writer was: (1) an apostle (1:14; 2:11; 19:35), (2) one of the Twelve (13:25),[1] and (3) not anyone who is listed with or interacted with the beloved disciple.[2] This narrows the possibilities to Matthew, Simon the Zealot, James the son of Alphaeus, and John the Son of Zebedee. Which of these four were close enough to Jesus to consider himself "*the* disciple Jesus loved"?

While Jesus called 11 of the 12 disciples His friends,[3] the Gospels as a whole seem to indicate that Peter, James, and John were His closest friends. This closeness is illustrated by their exclusive witness to important events in Jesus' life and in their role as prayer partners in the hours preceding His arrest (Matt 17:1; 26:27; Mark 9:2; 14:33). Likewise, the Fourth Gospel presents the **beloved disciple** in close relationship with Jesus and Peter (John 20:2; 21:7,20). Consequently, Peter can be ruled out as the beloved disciple. James, too, can be ruled out because he was martyred by the time the Fourth Gospel was written.[4] Therefore, of these three John rises to the top of the list as the most likely candidate for "beloved disciple." Johannine authorship is in line with the external evidence of church tradition that holds that the author of the Fourth Gospel is John, the son of Zebedee.[5]

The question which remains is, why does John choose to call himself "the disciple Jesus loved" rather than by his name or some other title? Since the Baptist's name appears 21 times in the Fourth Gospel,[6] John would certainly have been faced with the decision as to how he was going to alleviate any confusion caused by two Johns in one Gospel. He could have called himself John the disciple, John the apostle, John the son of Zebedee, etc. Instead, he avoids these titles in favor of one that focuses on the **intimacy** of his relationship with Jesus—he was "the disciple Jesus loved." With this title in place, he can refer to John the Baptist as simply "John" without the qualifier "the Baptist."

RECIPIENTS

Unlike Luke, John does not directly identify his audience. However, he seems to assume that his audience has familiarity with Jewish traditions and certain aspects of Jesus' life.[7] At other times he seems to explain things a Hebrew-speaking Jew living in Israel would know.[8] With these facts in view, John's original audience seems to have consisted of **Greek-speaking Jews** who were living outside of Israel.

OCCASION AND DATE

John was probably written after the Synoptic Gospels and before 1–3 John and Revelation. This dates the Fourth Gospel to sometime after AD 70 and before AD 90.[9] John makes his purpose in writing clear: he hopes that by telling his audience about Jesus' signs, which were performed in the presence of His disciples, they might believe that Jesus is the Messiah, the Son of God, and by believing have life in His name (20:30–31).

MESSAGE

The Book of Signs (John 1:1–12:50)

Prologue: Pre-existence of "the Word" (John 1:1–18)

Referring to creation in the beginning, John says "the Word" existed before creation and was the agent through whom the world was made. What does this have to do with Jesus? John explains that the **Word is Jesus**, "the one and only Son from the Father, full of grace and truth," who "took on flesh" and "pitched His tent" among us (1:14, author's translation). Ironically, though the world was created by Him, "His own" did not receive Him. But to those who did receive Him by believing on His name, He gave the right to become children of God (1:11–12). This birth as a child of God was a new birth unlike the natural birth of every human; it was not dependent on the will and flesh of mankind but on the will of God (1:13).

Another important feature of John's prologue is the **comparison** of Jesus with two other prophets. First, it compares Jesus with *John the Baptist*. The Baptist was "sent from God" to "testify about the light" (1:6–7). He was not the light, only one who testifies about it (1:8). In other words, the Baptist's testimony is forward looking to the Son; mankind would need to receive the Son if they wanted to become God's children. Next John compares Jesus to *Moses*. God's grace came through Moses (through the Giving of the law). Nevertheless, just as the Baptist was inferior to Jesus, so Moses was inferior; for while the Law came through Moses, grace and truth came through Jesus, the Son (1:17). Through these comparisons John shows Jesus' ministry as linked to yet superior to those of John the Baptist and Moses.

Early Professions (1:19–51)

In the last half of chap. 1, Jesus' identity is further revealed through the **professions** of John the Baptist and Jesus' disciples (1:19–51). Collectively the confessions of Jesus' first disciples make clear that they saw Jesus as the Messiah, the Son of God, the Lamb of God, and the King of Israel that was predicted by the law of Moses, the prophets, and John the Baptist. As such, these witnesses identify Jesus as the fulfill-ment of the prophetic expectations of the Old Testament. Though some of these titles are simply titles concerning Jesus' humanity, others carry heavy messianic overtones. As a prophet, the Baptist may have fully understood his profession that Jesus was the Passover Lamb (cf. 1:29).[10] The disciples' professions, however, are somewhat pre-mature because they have not yet sat under the teachings of Jesus and or experienced the Holy Spirit's illumination. Though they make these professions early on, they will only later understand the full implications of the titles as we understand them today.

When referring to Himself, Jesus uses the title "the Son of Man" (1:51). While this title was used in Ezekiel to describe God's messenger, it was not as politically charged or as clearly defined as the other titles bestowed on Jesus. His choice of this title could therefore mean His hearers would need to listen to His message before com-ing to know who He was.[11] Though "**Son of Man**" may sound like an earthly title, heavenly things are in store for His disciples. Jesus predicts that the disciples "will see heaven opened and the angels of God ascending and descending on the Son of Man" (1:51). This statement seems to be tied to the account of Jacob's ladder in Gen 28:12. Just as God supernaturally revealed Himself to Jacob/Israel, He will now reveal Himself through the Son.

Khirbet Cana in the Asochis Valley. Cana was where Jesus performed His first sign (miracle).

The Cana Cycle (John 2:1–4:54)

The Cana Cycle is a **unified narrative** that traces Jesus' early ministry geographically from Cana (2:1) to Cana (4:54). John uses Jesus' two signs in Cana to bookend this section as a literary unit. The first sign takes place at the *wedding at Cana* where Jesus turns water into wine (2:1–12). As a result, Jesus shows Himself to be the one who is ushering in a new and different age flowing with new wine. This abundant provision of wine fits well with the Jewish expectation that wine would flow freely in the messianic kingdom (Amos 9:13–14). Through this event in Nathaniel's hometown, Jesus' glory is first revealed, and His disciples first believe (2:11; 21:2).

Next is *the temple clearing* (2:12–23). When visiting Jerusalem at the Passover, Jesus became unsettled because His Father's house was used as a marketplace, so He made a whip, turned over the moneychangers' tables, and drove everyone out (2:12–16). The Jewish leaders, however, asked Him for a sign to prove His authority to cleanse the temple. Ironically, the **temple cleansing** itself may have been a sign; if so, they missed it. Jesus responds to this request by challenging them to "destroy this sanctuary," so that He could "raise it up in three days" (2:19). The Jewish leaders do not realize that Jesus is talking about His body as a temple and treat Him like an arrogant carpenter. They reason that the temple took 46 years to build—how was He going to rebuild it in just three days (2:20)? However, the Fourth Gospel records that many people believed in His name when they saw the signs that He did (2:23) and that after His resurrection, the disciples remembered this prediction and saw it as fulfilling the Scriptures (2:22).

While still in Jerusalem, Jesus encounters *Nicodemus* (2:24–3:21). **Nicodemus,** a ruler of the Jews, came to Jesus at night saying, "Rabbi, we know that You have come from God as a teacher, for no one could perform these signs You do unless God

---

Greek Highlight

Believe. Greek πιστεύω (**pisteuō**). The Greek word *pisteuo* means to *believe, trust, rely upon,* and its related noun is *pistis* (*faith*). In his Gospel, John never used the words *repent, repentance,* or *faith* to describe the way people are saved. Instead, he used *believe* since the term included all these ideas. John preferred the verb form to emphasize the act that is necessary for someone to be saved—total dependence on the work of another. John did indicate that believing can be superficial when it is merely intellectual without resulting in true salvation (John 2:23–24; 6:66; 12:42–43; see Jas 2:19). Jesus used a word-play when He said that people must do "the work of God" for salvation, for His point was that we must not try to work for it at all. We must simply *"believe in the One He has sent"* (John 6:29). Because this Gospel was written for the clear and simple purpose of persuading everyone who reads it to "believe Jesus is the Messiah, the Son of God, and by believing you may have life in His name" (John 20:31), it is no surprise that the Gospel of John is the most frequently distributed portion of the Bible to those curious about the gospel of Jesus Christ.

were with him" (3:2). Because Jesus "knew what was in man" (2:25), Jesus turns the conversation to Nicodemus's need for spiritual birth (3:3). Despite Nicodemus's position as a teacher of Israel, he cannot comprehend what Jesus is saying. John writes to illustrate Nicodemus's misunderstanding of Jesus and to present the reader with a well-developed overview of the message of salvation. Through this discourse John presents Jesus as the sole revealer of the message of the Father (3:13,34; cf. 1:18) and the only way to eternal life (3:16; cf. 1:3,12).

After this the focus briefly shifts back to *John the Baptist* (3:22–36). The **Baptist's disciples** become concerned when Jesus' disciples began baptizing more people than John the Baptist. Even so, the Baptist continued to baptize after Jesus was revealed, but John knew Jesus' salvation role would eclipse his (3:27–28). Therefore, the Baptist responded, "He must increase, but I must decrease" (3:30).

This is followed by Jesus' conversation with a *Samaritan woman* (4:1–42) by a historic well dug by the Old Testament patriarch Jacob. The fact that the conversation happens at all goes against the culture of the day because Jews did not associate with Samaritans (4:9). Jesus, however, was more concerned with the woman's spiritual

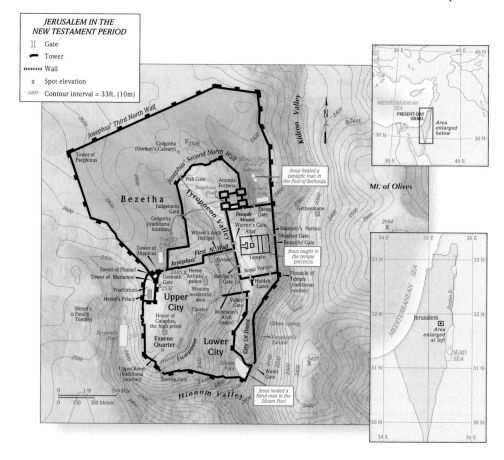

need than with her ethnicity. Jesus' knowledge of her bad marital situation causes her to recognize Him as a prophet (4:19). With this realization she asks Him if the proper place of worship was the mountain where the Jews worshipped or the mountain where the Samaritans worshipped (4:20). Jesus responds by explaining that soon worship would not depend on location but on whether one worshipped in spirit and truth (4:24). Jesus then revealed Himself as the Messiah she was anticipating (4:25–26).

After this the woman abandoned Jacob's well, leaving her water jar behind to tell others about the one who "told me everything I ever did" (4:39). **Many Samaritans believed** as a result of her testimony (4:39). Afterward, these people met Jesus personally and believed because of their firsthand experience with Jesus, declaring Him "the Savior of the world" (4:42).

When Jesus returned to Cana, He was approached by a *royal official* who begged Jesus to heal his son (4:46–54). Jesus' response was simply this: "Go . . . your son will live" (4:48–50). At that hour the son was healed (4:53). As a result of this sign, the royal official and his whole household believed (4:53). The Cana Cycle concludes as it began: with a **sign** that identifies Jesus as the fulfillment of **Jewish messianic expectations**.

The Festival Cycle (John 5:1–12:50)

While the Cana Cycle traces Jesus' ministry geographically from Cana to Cana, the Festival Cycle is arranged **thematically** around Jewish festivals. First we find Jesus at an *unnamed festival* (probably Passover) where He healed a man who had been lame for 38 years (chap. 5). Jesus commanded him, "Pick up your mat and walk!" (5:8). Because it was a Sabbath day, the Jewish leaders confronted the man and demanded to know why he was carrying his mat on a Sabbath (5:10). He explained that the One who healed him told him to carry it.

When the officials found out that Jesus healed the man, they began verbally attacking Him for breaking the Sabbath (5:16). Jesus explained, "My Father is still working, and I am working also" (5:17). The Jews redoubled their efforts to kill Him: "not only was He breaking the Sabbath, but He was even calling God His own Father, making Himself equal with God" (5:18). Ultimately, Jesus rebuked the Jewish leaders for their lack of faith (5:44), their rejection of His teachings and miracles (5:20), and their rejection of the message of John the Baptist (5:31–37). Jesus pinpointed their unbelief to their lack of belief in Moses' teachings. If they believed Moses, they would also believe Him, for Moses wrote of Him (5:46).

This second stage of the Festival Cycle took place during the Feast of Unleavened Bread (the *Passover*; chap. 6). Jesus fed 5,000 with only five loaves of bread and two small fishes. Leaving the multitude, the disciples attempted to cross the Sea of Galilee but encountered a storm. That night Jesus came walking to them on the water and calmed the storm. The following day Jesus rebuked them for their preoccupation with perishable bread and encouraged them to focus on the "spiritual food" (i.e., eternal life) which only He could provide. He tells them, "I am the bread of life" (6:35). Anyone who partakes of the "true bread from heaven" will have eternal life (6:48–58).

Jesus, the True Bread, therefore, supersedes the bread of the Passover. In response many of His disciples left Him (6:66).

Jesus makes two claims during the Feast of *Tabernacles* (chaps. 7–9): first, He is the "water of life" (7:37–39, author's translation); and, second, He is the "light of the world" (8:12). By making these claims at the Feast of Tabernacles, Jesus implies He is the Messiah. Because of His claims, the Jewish leaders attacked Him verbally (8:13). He offended some by telling them that they were slaves (8:33–36) and not true sons of Abraham (8:41). He even accused them of being sons of the devil (8:44). This section climaxes with the Jews picking up stones to stone Jesus because of His claim to be eternal (8:32,59).

In chap. 9, Jesus gave sight to a man born blind. This healing caused controversy among the Jewish leaders because He did it on a Sabbath. This sign illustrates Jesus as the Light of the world and reinforces the theme of spiritual "light and blindness" that was introduced in the prologue. Jesus explained that His mission was "to give sight to the blind and to show those who think they can see that they are blind" (9:39, author's translation). Jesus made clear that He was referring to spiritual blindness; the Pharisees were blind even though they claimed they could see (9:40–41).

Shepherd with flock of sheep.

The healing of the man born blind is followed by Jesus' Shepherd Discourse and His appearance at the Jewish Feast of *Dedication* (chap. 10). By picturing Himself as a shepherd, Jesus draws on a rich tradition of Old Testament texts about sheep and shepherds.[12] The religious leaders were thieves and robbers, whereas Jesus was the messianic Shepherd who knew the sheep by name, led them, and was willing to lay down His life for them (10:3,11). This flock contained not only Jewish sheep but Gentile sheep as well (10:16). All who enter this sheepfold must enter through Him; He is the door (10:7). They will know His voice and listen to Him (10:4). This chapter concludes with many of Jesus' hearers acknowledging that all John said about Him was true (10:41). The Jewish leaders, however, still did not believe, showing themselves not to be Jesus' sheep (10:25–26).[13]

The final and most climactic sign of the Festival Cycle is **Lazarus' resurrection** (chap. 11). This sign led the high priest to seek Jesus' death. He reasoned that "it is profitable for you that one man should die for the people, and the whole nation not perish" (11:50 LEB). Most likely, the high priest meant that it is better for Jesus to die than for Rome to destroy the whole nation because of their acceptance of Him. However, in truth the high priest's statement was prophetic; John viewed the high priest's decision to sacrifice Jesus' life as a prediction that Jesus would die as an atonement for sin (11:52).

Jesus as the Passover Lamb

John's references to the Passover in 11:55 may indicate that this statement is a part of a Passover Lamb motif introduced by the testimony of John the Baptist in chap. 1 (1:29). John is emphasizing that the lamb sacrificed in the Passover was actually a **prophecy** that looked ahead to the Messiah's death as a sacrifice for the people.

The Festival Cycle and the Book of Signs conclude with Jesus' *anointing*, His *triumphal entry* into Jerusalem, and the *coming of the Greeks* to see Jesus (12:1–50). Six days before Passover, Mary anointed Jesus' feet with an expensive **perfume** (12:1–7). This prompted Judas Iscariot, Jesus' betrayer, to criticize her for not selling it and giving the money to the poor (12:6). Jesus rebuked him saying, "Leave her alone, so that she may keep it for the day of my preparation for burial. For you have the poor with you always, but you do not always have me" (12:7–8 LEB). This interchange looked ahead to Jesus' death and for the second time in the Gospel reveals that Judas was the one who would betray Jesus (see John 6:7).

The following day at the **triumphal entry** (12:12–19), those who heard about Lazarus's resurrection gathered to welcome Jesus as the King of Israel by waving palm branches as He rode in on a donkey's colt. This fulfilled Zech 9:9: "Look, your king is coming to you . . . , on a donkey" (NLT). This great reception caused the Pharisees to lament, "You see? You've accomplished nothing. Look—the world has gone after Him!" (John 12:19).

The Book of Signs concludes by God-fearing **Greeks** coming to inquire about Jesus (12:20). Jesus interpreted their coming as a sign that His hour to be glorified has finally come (12:23). For this hour He would be lifted up on the cross and draw all to Himself (12:32). Despite the many signs He performed for them, they did not believe in Him. Nevertheless, many others did believe in Him even among the rulers; but because of the Pharisees, they kept their belief secret (12:42–43).

With this pronouncement in view, the Fourth Gospel concludes that unbelief should come as no surprise as it was anticipated in Isaiah (12:38–41; Isa 6:10; 53:1); and that Jesus came as the Light of the world (12:46); that belief in the Son is the only salvation (12:44,48); that eternal life comes through the Son (12:50); and that the Father speaks through the Son (12:44,49–50).

The Book of Glory (John 13:1–21:25)

Jesus' Farewell (John 13:1–17:26)

With the events of the Book of Signs completed, the next five chapters directly anticipate the approaching end of Christ's life and focus on His preparation of the disciples for the next stage in salvation history.

By the time of Jesus' **last supper**, Judas's heart was already set on betraying Jesus, and Jesus already knew that "the Father had given everything into His hands, that He had come from God, and that He was going back to God" (13:1–3). Jesus therefore got up from supper, laid aside His robe, and began washing the disciples' feet. After Jesus was finished washing His disciples' feet, He explained, "If I, your Lord and Teacher, have washed your feet, you also ought to wash one another's feet. For I have given

An olive grove at the church of St. Lazarus at Bethany. The church was built in close proximity to the traditional site of Lazarus's tomb.

you an example that you also should do just as I have done for you" (13:14–15). The foot-washing is, therefore, an action lesson that prepared Jesus' disciples for serving one another in such a way that their love and unity would show the world they were His disciples (13:35; 17:22).

After Jesus sent Judas out into the night, Jesus began to teach those who are "His own" (13:1). In this discourse (13:31–16:33) Jesus prepared His disciples for what was to come after He returned to the Father. He comforted them by promising to prepare a place for them and to bring them to Himself (14:2), to send the **Holy Spirit** to guide and teach them (14:26; 16:12–15), and to continue to abide with them even after His glorification.[14] Jesus promised to give them anything they asked in His name (14:13–15). He warned that tough times were ahead and that those who did not know the Father would drive them out of the synagogue and kill them (15:18–25; 16:2,20).

After His Farewell Discourse, Jesus prays His high priestly **prayer** for Himself, His disciples, and future believers (chap. 17). For Himself, Jesus prayed for the Father to glorify Him so that He may, in turn, glorify the Father (17:2). He also prayed that the Father would restore the glory He had before the world began (17:5). Jesus petitioned the Father to protect and unify the disciples as they were sent out in the world during the next stage of salvation history (17:11–18). Then Jesus prayed for future believers to have unity so they may be witnesses to the world (17:21–23). Jesus' prayer concluded by expressing His love for all who believe and His earnest desire for all future believers to be gathered to Him (17:24).

Olive trees in the traditional site of the garden of Gethsemane.

Jesus' Arrest and Trials (John 18:1–19:16)

Having finished His prayer, Jesus entered into the garden where He was met by Judas (His betrayer) and armed soldiers. Peter drew his sword and struck the servant of the high priest. Jesus rejected this intervention and went **willingly** to be judged by Annas the priest. Then Jesus was taken to Pilate the governor, who attempted to avoid being involved in Jesus' trials, but the Jews insisted that Roman law did not allow them to put anyone to death. Pilate, therefore, questioned Jesus concerning His claims to kingship and His origin (18:33–37). Jesus responded by acknowledging that He came into the world to testify of the truth and that His kingdom is not of this world (18:36–37). In the end Pilate attempted to have Jesus flogged and released, but the Jews insisted they would rather have a thief set free than Jesus and that, if Pilate thought otherwise, he was no friend of Caesar's (19:12). Ultimately Pilate conceded and allowed Jesus to be crucified, even though he found no grounds for charging Him (19:6,15–16).

Jesus' Crucifixion, Burial, and Resurrection (John 19:17–20:29)

Jesus was then crucified under a sign that read, "Jesus of Nazareth, King of the Jews." Through the course of His crucifixion, John recorded a series of **prophetic fulfillments**. First, the soldiers' *division of Jesus' clothes* is viewed as fulfilling Ps 22:18. Second, *Jesus asked for a drink*, thereby fulfilling Ps 22:15. After this, Jesus uttered the words "it is finished" and died. After Jesus' death, the Jews requested that those being crucified have their legs broken in order to expedite their death so they could be taken down before the Sabbath. However, because Jesus was already dead, they did *not*

The Garden Tomb is one site offered by tradition as the burial place of Jesus' body.

break His legs. Instead, they *pierced His side* with a spear, and at once blood and water came out. John viewed these aspects of Jesus' crucifixion as fulfilling two prophecies: "Not one of His bones will be broken," and "They will look at the One they pierced" (Exod 12:46; Num 9:12; Ps 34:20; Zech 12:10).

Jesus was buried in a **new tomb** by Nicodemus and Joseph of Arimathea (a secret disciple of Jesus, 19:38–42). However, when Mary Magdalene came to visit the tomb, it was **empty**. Peter and John, upon hearing the news, came and saw for themselves (20:3–10). Jesus then appeared to Mary Magdalene in the garden and His disciples on three separate occasions (20:11–19). During these appearances, Jesus comforted Mary, convinced Thomas of His resurrection, and reassured Peter that he was forgiven for denying Him.

Jesus showed Himself (*phaneroō*, full disclosure) to seven disciples who fished all night and caught nothing (21:3). Jesus provided them with an abundant catch, then had breakfast with them on the shore. Jesus asked Peter three times, "Do you love Me?" (21:15–17). Upon Peter's positive confession Jesus recommissioned him to service.

Epilogue (John 21:1–25)

John's Gospel concludes with a two-verse epilogue which verifies the authenticity of the Gospel account and observes that while Jesus did many other things, no one could possibly write them all down. If anyone did, even the whole world could not contain all of the books that would have to be written.

For Further Reading

Blomberg, Craig L. *The Historical Reliability of John's Gospel: Issues and Commentary*. Downers Grove, IL: IVP, 2002.

Carson, D. A. *The Gospel According to John*. Grand Rapids: Eerdmans, 1991.

Köstenberger, Andreas J. *Encountering John: The Gospel in Historical, Literary, and Theological Perspective*. Grand Rapids: Baker, 1999.

Morris, Leon. *The Gospel According to St. John*. NICNT. Grand Rapids: Eerdmans, 1971.

Towns, Elmer. *John: Believe and Live*. The Twenty-First Century Biblical Commentary. Chattanooga, TN: AMG, 2002.

Study Questions

1. How does John's Gospel emphasize the deity of Jesus?
2. How does this Gospel differ from the Synoptic Gospels?
3. How does John divide his story geographically and thematically?
4. Why does John place so much emphasis on believing the gospel?
5. How should this affect how you present the gospel?

ENDNOTES

1. John 13 presents the beloved disciple as present at the last supper. Matthew and Mark seem to indicate that only Jesus' 12 disciples were present at the last supper (Matt 26:20; Mark 14:17).

2. Cf. chaps. 13–16; 21:2.

3. John 15:15; the Twelve minus Judas.

4. Moreover, there would not be enough time for rumors to spread that he would live until Jesus comes (John 21).

5. Irenaeus, Clement of Alexandria, Tertullian, Theophilus of Antioch, Origen, and others ascribe the book to John.

6. John the Baptist appears 21 times in John's Gospel: 1:6,15,19,26,28,29,32,35,40; 3:23,24,25,26,27; 4:1; 5:33,35,36; 10:40,41.

7. For example, John assumes that his audience is already aware of the story of Jesus' anointing (chap. 12). Further, John seems to expect his audience to be familiar with the ceremonies of the Jewish festivals (chaps. 5–12).

8. Such as "Jews had no dealings with Samaritans" (4:9, author's translation), and that Mary was the one who washed Jesus' feet (11:12).

9. The Rylands Fragment evidences a first-century date for the Gospel.

10. However, it is unclear whether he saw Jesus as a Passover lamb as the apostle John did.

11. Ezekiel 2:1 and then about 90 times thereafter.

12. In the context of Jesus' rebuke of the Jewish religious leaders, Ezekiel 34 with its similar critique of the Jewish leaders and its promise of the perfect messianic shepherd's coming is probably the most foundational (see also Gen 48:15; 49:24; Pss 23:1; 28:9; 77:20; 78:52; 80:1; Isa 40:11; Jer 31:10; Ezek 34:1–11).

13. Jesus' Good Shepherd claims are fitting in the setting of the Feast of Dedication because the celebration focused on the deliverance of Israel through the Maccabean family. Jesus was the Messiah who, in the spirit of Judas Maccabeus, would shepherd His people to the promises of God at the Feast of Dedication.

14. Jesus said that He, not Israel, was the True Vine and they were the branches and that apart from abiding in Him they could do nothing (15:1–8; cf. Isaiah 5)

Chapter 9

ACTS
Taking the Message to the World

The Acts of the Apostles is the **second volume** of a two-part series. The Gospel of Luke was the first part. The writer Luke began telling the story of the life, ministry, death, and resurrection of Jesus Christ. He continued his story in Acts, telling how the message of Jesus was preached to the world after the ascension of Christ to heaven. The church began as a predominantly *Jewish* community in Jerusalem, and Luke tells how it became predominantly *Gentile*, reaching all the way to Rome. Luke emphasizes two gospel preachers, Peter and Paul, as the major characters in the dissemination of the gospel. Jesus is the main character in the Gospel of Luke, and the Holy Spirit is emphasized as the One continuing Jesus' ministry on earth in the book of Acts.

Key Facts	
Author:	Luke
Recipient:	Theophilus
Where Written:	Unknown
Date:	AD 60–62
Key Word:	Witness (Gk. *martus*)
Key Verse:	"But you will receive power when the Holy Spirit has come on you, and you will be My witnesses in Jerusalem, in all Judea and Samaria, and to the ends of the earth" (1:8).

AUTHOR

The authorship of the Gospel of Luke and the Acts of the Apostles intimately ties the books together. Both internal evidence and external testimony provide strong evidence that Luke wrote both books. Carson and Moo state, "Luke's authorship of these two books went virtually unchallenged until the onset of critical approaches to the New Testament at the end of the eighteenth century."[1] The reference to Theophilus as the addressee in the prologue of both Luke (1:1–4) and Acts (1:1–2) indicates that both books were dedicated to the same man and that Acts is picking up the story from the ending of Luke. The four "we" sections in Acts (16:10–17; 20:5–15; 21:1–18; 27:1–28:16) indicate that the author was **traveling with Paul** at those times. Paul specifically mentioned Luke as one of his companions in Col 4:14; Phlm 24, and 2 Tim 4:11. Luke was **a doctor** (Col 4:14). The book has an abundance of medical terminology and is written in excellent Greek style that would be expected of a physician (see the Gospel of Luke, Author). The book of Acts is an example of the careful research one would expect of a medical doctor (see Luke 1:1–4).

RECIPIENT

The primary recipient of both Luke and Acts was a man with the Greek name **Theophilus**: "lover of God" or "friend of God" (Luke 1:3; Acts 1:1). In Luke 1:3, he is addressed as the "most honorable Theophilus," indicating that he was a man of governmental rank (see Acts 24:3; 26:26 where the title is used for governors). Some have suggested that Theophilus might have been Luke's patron who paid the cost of the publication of the book(s).[2] Others have suggested that Luke might have been a slave freed by Theophilus. All of this, however, is speculation.

The fact that these books were circulated like the other Gospels indicates that Luke must have intended the books for more than just Theophilus, although he is the primary recipient. What made the book valuable to Theophilus would apply to others also.[3]

OCCASION AND DATE

Luke's prologue gives his purpose for writing to Theophilus: "so that you may **know the certainty** of the things about which you have been instructed" (Luke 1:4). Luke ended his Gospel with the crucified and risen Jesus commissioning His disciples as witnesses to take His message to the world. However, they are to wait first in Jerusalem until the promise of the Father comes, in the person of the Holy Spirit (Luke 24:49). Luke picked up the story in Acts, writing "all that Jesus began to do and teach until the day when He was taken up" (1:1–2).

If Luke used Mark as one of his sources for his Gospel, then the book must be dated no earlier than AD 70. It would seem strange for Luke not to mention an event so significant as the destruction of Jerusalem and the temple in the year 70. That puts the date of writing of the Gospel prior to AD 70. And since the Gospel was written before Acts, consider the following events in Acts. This book does not mention Paul's death (c. AD 68) or persecution of Christians under Nero (AD 64), indicating the date should be still earlier. Since the book ends prior to any decisive trial of Paul, it is likely that the book of Acts was composed around the year 62. This means the Gospel of Luke was **written around AD 60–62**.

GENRE AND STRUCTURE

Luke writes that he has "investigated everything from the very first" in the story of Jesus and that he has written "in an orderly sequence" so that Theophilus "may know the certainty of the things about which you have been instructed" (Luke 1:3–4). Darrell Bock describes Acts as **ancient historical writing** as well as biography.

> The problem here with classification is that the key character of Acts is God, not any of his servants. So if it is a biography, it is of a special kind, a "theography," if you will. This blurring of the genre lines points to the uniqueness of Acts and makes it hard to know if it should be classified as an ancient history (story of great deeds) or a special form of biography (story of God's directive, salvific work).[4]

Luke has given **several literary keys** which mark out the major sections of his book. In Acts 1:8, Jesus tells the disciples to be His witnesses to the world, going out in three concentric circles. First, they were to start in Jerusalem; second, they were to progress out to Judea and Samaria; and third, they were supposed to carry the gospel to the remotest part of the earth. This forms the outline of the book. Five additional summary statements are strategically placed as closing statements on the major sections. These alternate between saying that the word of God spread (6:7; 12:24; 19:20) and that the church grew (9:31; 16:5). The first two summaries close the first two geographical sections of the book; the last three conclude smaller subsections summarizing the missionary journeys from Syrian Antioch to Rome. Luke also recorded at least 23 speeches in Acts, making up about a third of the book.[5] These emphasize the **importance of personal testimony**, especially those which demonstrate the centrality of Christ and the sovereignty of God in the spread of the gospel.

Some have taken the book's purpose as an apologetic for the apostolic ministry of Paul. While this does not fit as the entire purpose, there are definite **parallels between Peter and Paul** in the book. Luke demonstrated that Paul, coming later from outside the circle of disciples, was indeed an apostle approved by God. His gospel message was divinely ordained; his mission to the Gentiles was conducted under God's approval and direction; and, like Peter, Paul was truly a man of God.

PETER AND PAUL COMPARED[6]			
Peter		*Paul*	
3:1–11	Healed a man lame from birth	14:8–18	Healed a man lame from birth
5:15–16	Peter's shadow healed people	19:11–12	Handkerchiefs and aprons from Paul healed people
5:17	Success caused Jewish jealousy	13:45	Success caused Jewish jealousy

Peter		Paul	
8:14–25	The Holy Spirit comes through Peter's laying on of hands	19:1–10	The Holy Spirit comes through Paul's laying on of hands
8:9–24	Dealt with Simon, a sorcerer	13:6–11	Dealt with Bar-Jesus, a sorcerer
9:36–41	Raised Dorcas to life	20:9–12	Raised Eutychus to life
12:1–19	Peter is imprisoned and miraculously released	16:16–34	Paul is imprisoned and miraculously released

Outline

I. The Church Comes into Existence in Jerusalem (Acts 1:1–6:7)
   A. The Church Was Founded in Jerusalem (Acts 1:1–2:47)
   B. The Church Expanded in Jerusalem (Acts 3:1–6:7)
II. The Church's Witness Spreads to Judea and Samaria (Acts 6:8–9:31)
   A. The Martyrdom of Stephen Precipitated a Scattering (Acts 6:8–8:3)
   B. Philip Went Out in Ministry (Acts 8:4–40)
   C. Saul Was Converted and Called into Ministry (Acts 9:1–31)
III. The Church's Witness Spreads to the Ends of the Earth (Acts 9:32–28:31)
   A. The Church Advanced to Syrian Antioch (Acts 9:32–12:24)
   B. The Church Advanced to Cyprus and into Asia Minor (Acts 12:25–16:5)
   C. The Church Advanced to the Western Shores of the Aegean Sea (Acts 16:6–19:20)
   D. The Church Advanced to Rome (Acts 19:21–28:31)

MESSAGE

The **birth and growth of the church** in Acts reveals God's plan to take the gospel message, as an extension of the Jewish messianic hope out of the Old Testament, from a completely Jewish setting in Jerusalem (Luke 1) to the heart of the Gentile world in Rome (Acts 28:16–31).

God's sovereignty plays an important part in the events of both volumes. Peter tells the Jews that what happened to Christ happened as part of the "predetermined plan and foreknowledge of God" (Acts 2:23 NASB). In Acts, God's sovereignty is seen in the way in which God used persecutions to take the gospel to the Gentile world.

The book of Acts also includes a defense of Christianity. While the Jews hated Paul and his message because of his inclusion of Gentiles, the Roman governmental authorities repeatedly declared the messenger of Christianity to be innocent of any crimes. In the end Paul was free to preach about the kingdom and teach "the things concerning the Lord Jesus Christ with full boldness and without hindrance" for two years in Rome (Acts 28:31).

I. The Church Comes into Existence in Jerusalem (Acts 1:1–6:7)

A. The Church Was Founded in Jerusalem (Acts 1:1–2:47)

Acts begins with the transfer of responsibility and authority to the **apostles**. Jesus commissioned them, ascended into heaven, and the Holy Spirit came down with power to begin saving lost Jews at first and eventually bringing Gentiles to salvation. Opposition quickly arose, both from within and outside the church. But the powerful moving of God's Spirit could not be stopped as the word of God spread and the number of disciples grew in Jerusalem.

Greek Highlight

Church. Greek ἐκκλησία (ekklēsia). The Greek noun *ekklesia* is a compound from the preposition *ek*, meaning out of, and the verb *kaleo*, meaning to call; thus *ekklesia* literally means called out ones. Despite the origin of the term *ekklesia*, its emphasis is not on a people called out but on a people gathered together, that is, an assembly or congregation. In secular Greek, *ekklesia* was commonly used for the assembled citizens of a city (see Acts 19:32,39–40). In the NT, *ekklesia* is found in the Gospels only three times, all in Matthew (16:18; 18:17), 23 times in Acts, and 62 times in all of Paul's letters combined. Jesus stated that He would build the *ekklesia* (Matt 16:18) and that the *ekklesia* must exercise discipline on members who sin (Matt 18:15–17). In the former passage Jesus used *ekklesia* in a corporate sense (all believers), and in the latter passage in the local sense (believers in a specific assembly). Today, 2,000 years later, the book of Acts provides the paramount description of the need for passionate and personal care for fellow believers, continual cultivation of spiritual growth among all members of the church, and the necessity for an unequivocal commitment to evangelism and discipleship in the church today.

Following the resurrection, **Jesus appeared for over 40 days**, giving convincing proofs of His resurrection and speaking about the kingdom of God. He told the disciples to wait in Jerusalem for the promise of the Father, the baptism with the Holy Spirit (1:3–5). The disciples had questions about the resumption of the kingdom program. Jesus instead emphasized the present responsibility to be His witnesses, from Jerusalem to the ends of the earth. Following the commissioning, **Jesus ascended to heaven** with a promise by angels that He would eventually return (1:6–11).

The apostles, some women and Jesus' brothers, a total group of about 120, returned to the **upper room** and devoted themselves to prayer. In order to be complete in their foundational group, the apostles chose Matthias as an apostolic replacement for Judas (1:15–26).

Ten days later on the **day of Pentecost**, with Jews gathered in Jerusalem from all over the known world, the Holy Spirit descended as the promised gift from the Father, just as Jesus had said He would (Luke 24:49; Acts 1:5).

The **coming of the Holy Spirit** upon the disciples was evidenced by the sound of a rushing wind and tongues like fire resting on each one as they spoke in the various languages the crowd understood (2:1–4). The diverse crowd of Jews in Jerusalem, "devout men from every nation under heaven" (2:5), heard them "speaking the magnificent acts of God" in their own languages (2:11). As some wondered what it meant, Peter gave the explanation in his first recorded sermon (2:14–40). Peter explained what they saw was what Joel predicted, "I will even pour out My Spirit . . . in those days" (2:18; cf. Joel 2:28–32). Peter argued that God had resurrected Jesus, a fact to which they were eyewitnesses (2:22). The Holy Spirit was demonstrating, through the disciples, that the Jesus whom they crucified was now "both Lord and Messiah!" (2:36).

Acts 2:4–11 gives a description of **tongues** as it was used by the apostles. Luke wrote that "they were all filled with the Holy Spirit and began to speak in different languages" (2:4). The word used here is *glōssa*, literally meaning "tongues." Those who heard the apostles speaking said they were hearing them in their "own native language" (2:8). The word here is *dialectos*, a word from which we get our word "dialect," meaning a variety of a language. God had given the apostles the ability to speak in languages they had not learned but that others could understand.

LUKE'S USE OF TONGUES IN ACTS[7]

Scripture	Situation	Purpose
1. Acts 2	Day of Pentecost (Jews)	To show the Jews that God was *beginning* a new body, i.e., the church
2. Acts 8	Samaritans	To show the Jews that Samaritans were added to *the church* on an equal basis
3. Acts 10	Gentiles (Cornelius's house)	To show the Jews that Gentiles were added to *the church* on an equal basis

Realizing they had killed the Messiah, the crowds "came under deep conviction" (literally, they were "pierced to the heart") and asked what they should do. Peter told them to repent (i.e., change their minds) about Jesus and come out from that "corrupt generation" that had killed Him (2:37–40). Such a turning would result in forgiveness of their sins. They were asked to be baptized in water in the name of Jesus. About **3,000** responded and were **baptized**. These formed a distinct community, the church under the apostle's instruction and in tight fellowship with one another. God added to their number daily (2:41–47). The church had begun and would continue to grow in power and numbers (2:47; 4:4; 5:14; 6:1,7; 9:31).

B. The Church Expanded in Jerusalem (Acts 3:1–6:7)

The Holy Spirit worked through Peter and John to heal a man lame from birth who was more than 40 years old (3:1–11; 4:22). The miracle happened just outside the temple, bringing a large crowd together as they realized that something supernatural had happened. Peter explained to the crowd that it was because of the risen Jesus working through them that the man was healed (3:12–26). Again Peter urged that they repent so that their sin of crucifying the Messiah might be forgiven. Such **repentance** would result in personal forgiveness, and if the nation that had crucified Jesus in ignorance repented, God would send Jesus, their appointed Messiah. This opportunity was available if only they were going to turn from their evil ways (3:22–26).[8]

The modern city of Jerusalem looking south through the Kidron Valley from Mount Scopus.

Immediately, there was **opposition by the Jewish leadership** (4:1–31). Peter and John were brought before the Jewish High Council to explain "by what power or in what name" (4:7) they had performed such a miracle. Peter again testified that Jesus, the One they crucified and whom God raised from the dead, was the only hope for the nation (4:12). The Jewish leaders saw the man who was healed, acknowledged the miracle, but continued to reject Jesus as their Messiah (4:13–22). Their main desire was to stop the witness of Peter and John. When Peter and John were released, they returned to the church and prayed for boldness and power to continue their witness (4:24–31).

Challenges also came from **within the church**. In an atmosphere of sacrificial and selfless giving, Luke wrote about Barnabas as a positive example (4:32–37). Barnabas sold land and gave the money to the apostles. Ananias and Sapphira wanted the same recognition Barnabas received. They sold some property but kept some money for themselves, an example of hypocrisy and greed (5:1–11). God responded in the death of Ananias and Sapphira in order to prevent this deadly sin from making further inroads into the church.

As **signs and wonders** took place (5:12–16), the church grew. Filled with jealousy, the Jewish leaders put the apostles in jail. When an angel released them and they returned to teaching in the temple, the Sanhedrin again questioned them. After being flogged, threatened, and released, they kept on preaching and teaching. Their claim was that they "must obey God rather than men" (5:17–40). In spite of the beating, the apostles rejoiced that they were considered worthy to suffer for Christ (5:41–42).

Also, more internal challenges crept in so that greed and selfishness grew within the church. The widows of the Hellenistic Jews were being overlooked in the daily servings of food (6:1–7). The church "addressed the problem" by selecting seven Hellenistic Jews who would do the work of serving to free the apostles for prayer and ministry of the Word. These were probably the first **deacons** and reflected a growing internal organization to meet the needs of the church.

At the end of the first major section of the book, Luke summarized that "the preaching about God flourished, [and] the number of the disciples in Jerusalem multiplied greatly" (6:7). Throughout the book of Acts, Luke traced the numerical growth of the church as an evidence of God's blessing.

II. The Church's Witness Spreads to Judea and Samaria (Acts 6:8–9:31)

In this second major section of his book, Luke introduced three men who were part of the movement of the church out of Jerusalem into the Gentile world: Stephen, Philip, and Saul (later Paul).

A. The Martyrdom of Stephen Precipitated a Scattering (Acts 6:8–8:3)

Luke shows how the **martyrdom of Stephen** precipitated a scattering of believers into Judea and Samaria (6:8–8:3). Stephen, one of "the Seven" (21:8), was "full of grace and power, . . . performing great wonders and signs among the people" (6:8). His preaching stirred the people until he was brought before the Sanhedrin. Following a lengthy speech, where he demonstrated that the present hostility to God's plan was not new in Israel (7:1–53), the Jewish leadership rose up in anger and stoned Stephen, making him the first martyr of the church. As they stoned Stephen, a man named Saul (Paul) was introduced as one approving of the execution (7:58).

B. Philip Went Out in Ministry (Acts 8:4–40)

Philip, another of "the Seven" was the first actively to take the gospel out of Jerusalem (8:4–40). Because of the persecution following Stephen's death, **Philip went to Samaria** where he performed miracles and cast out demons. Many became believers, including Simon, a magician or sorcerer. Previously, Simon had been a man who had astounded the people (8:9), receiving much attention because he claimed to be someone great, even accepting the title "the Great Power of God!" (8:4–15).

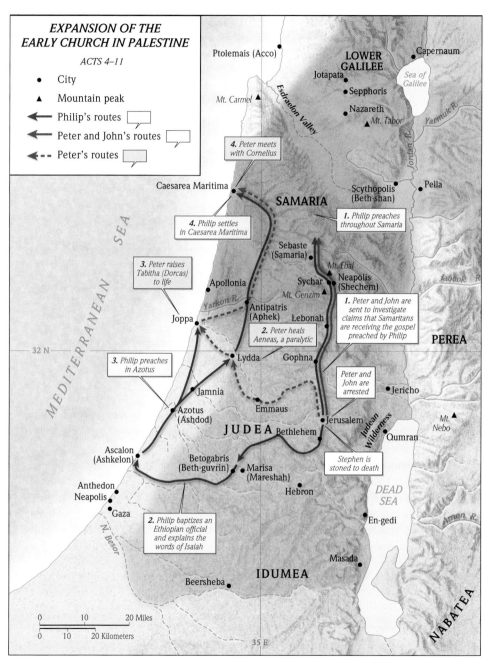

EXPANSION OF THE EARLY CHURCH IN PALESTINE

ACTS 4–11

- • City
- ▲ Mountain peak
- ← Philip's routes
- ← Peter and John's routes
- ◄-- Peter's routes

4. Peter meets with Cornelius

4. Philip settles in Caesarea Maritima

3. Peter raises Tabitha (Dorcas) to life

3. Philip preaches in Azotus

1. Philip preaches throughout Samaria

1. Peter and John are sent to investigate claims that Samaritans are receiving the gospel preached by Philip

2. Peter heals Aeneas, a paralytic

Peter and John are arrested

Stephen is stoned to death

2. Philip baptizes an Ethiopian official and explains the words of Isaiah

Ptolemais (Acco) • · Capernaum · LOWER GALILEE · Jotapata · Sepphoris · Nazareth · Mt. Tabor ▲ · Sea of Galilee · Mt. Carmel ▲ · Esdraelon Valley · Jordan R. · Yarmuk R. · Caesarea Maritima · SAMARIA · Scythopolis (Beth-shan) · Pella · Sebaste (Samaria) · Mt. Ebal · Neapolis (Shechem) · Sychar · Mt. Gerizim ▲ · Apollonia · Antipatris (Aphek) · Lebonah · Joppa · Yarkon R. · Lydda · Gophna · PEREA · Jabbok R. · Jamnia · Emmaus · Jericho · Azotus (Ashdod) · JUDEA · Bethlehem · Jerusalem · Qumran · Mt. Nebo · Judean Wilderness · Ascalon (Ashkelon) · Betogabris (Beth-guvrin) · Marisa (Mareshah) · Hebron · DEAD SEA · Anthedon Neapolis · Gaza · En-gedi · Arnon R. · N. Besor · Masada · IDUMEA · Beersheba · NABATEA · MEDITERRANEAN SEA · 32 N

0 10 20 Miles
0 10 20 Kilometers
35 E

In response to the Samaritans' conversion, Peter and John came down from Jerusalem, laid hands on the new believers, and imparted the Holy Spirit to them. The Jews and Samaritans were bitter rivals, and there was potential of forming a rival church. **Apostolic representatives** came from Jerusalem to Samaria, laid hands on the new believers, demonstrating continuity between the believers in Jerusalem and Samaria. When Simon saw that the Holy Spirit was given through the apostles, he offered to pay money for that ability. Peter spoke harshly to Simon, telling him of the need to repent of this wickedness (7:18–25).

Under divine leadership, Philip traveled south on the road to Gaza where he met an Ethiopian eunuch (8:26–39). After Philip explained Jesus to him from Isaiah 53, the eunuch responded with faith and was immediately baptized. The eunuch's return to Ethiopia is credited with spreading the gospel into Africa at that time.

C. Saul Was Converted and Called into Ministry (Acts 9:1–31)

A decisive event takes place when Saul is converted and called into ministry (9:1–30). Saul, a member of the Jewish Sanhedrin, was on the **road to Damascus** where he planned to arrest Jewish Christians. While traveling, Saul saw and talked with the risen Jesus, becoming blinded in the process. Later, in Damascus, a disciple named Ananias restored Saul's sight and baptized him. God told Ananias that

The city wall of biblical Damascus.

Saul was a chosen instrument who would bear the name of the Lord "to Gentiles, kings, and the Israelites" (9:10–19). Immediately, the converted Saul became a preacher who boldly proclaimed that Jesus was the Messiah. Due to opposition in Damascus, he fled to Jerusalem where further opposition led him to his own home in Tarsus (9:20–30).

In a **second summary statement** (9:31), Luke mentioned the growth of churches as they spread throughout all Judea, Galilee, and Samaria. They enjoyed peace, churches were built up, and many came to fear the Lord. Luke has now laid the groundwork for the future Gentile mission. The church has moved out to the transitional area of Samaria; and Paul, God's key instrument to the Gentiles, has been dramatically identified and converted.

III. The Church's Witness Spreads to the Ends of the Earth (Acts 9:32–28:31)

A. The Church Advanced to Syrian Antioch (Acts 9:32–12:24)

The next stage in the early church's mission sees the church advancing to **Syrian Antioch** (9:32–12:24). Up to this point the church had primarily been composed of Jews, and Peter was the leader of the church in Jerusalem. God intended His church to be inclusive of both Jews and Gentiles. In the first story Peter healed the paralyzed Aeneas (9:32–35) and raised Dorcas from the dead (9:36–43). The result of these miracles is that "many believed in the Lord" (9:42).

In the second story **Cornelius, a Gentile** military centurion living in Caesarea, was sovereignly prepared by an angel from God to receive the gospel (10:1–8). At the same time God gave Peter a vision of a sheet let down from heaven filled with animals and a message that Gentiles were no longer to be considered unclean. Rather, they were to be viewed as people needing the gospel on an equal level with the Jews (10:9–23). Peter acted on this information by preaching the message of Christ to Cornelius and his guests (10:23–48). As they came to believe the message through Peter's sermon, the Holy Spirit was poured out on these Gentiles in the same way the Jewish believers had experienced at Pentecost (10:47). The same Holy Spirit was given to **Jew and Gentile** alike as evidenced by the speaking in tongues and exalting God (10:46).

The next major account focused on a new center for the gospel ministry in Syrian Antioch (11:19–30). In the **dispersion of Christians** following the death of Stephen, some went to Antioch where they had success preaching the gospel to the Greeks. News of this response from Antioch prompted the Jerusalem church to send a representative, Barnabas, to evaluate the work. Barnabas is described as a "good man, full of the Holy Spirit and of faith" (11:24). Needing assistance, Barnabas brought Saul (Paul) from

Water was provided for Caesarea Maritima by an extensive system based on this Herodian aqueduct.

Tarsus to help. Antioch was the first place where the believers were called "Christians" (11:26).

While all this was happening, God demonstrated His sovereign approval of the church (12:1–23). The **separation** between Christianity and Judaism had grown larger. Herod Agrippa I sought to please the Jewish leaders by killing the apostle James (12:1–2) and putting Peter in prison (12:3–4). But Peter was miraculously released through the prayers of the church. While Peter went free, Herod died at the displeasure of God because of his arrogant assumption of a godlike position (12:20–23). The church was moving away from its Judaism foundation, and it had God's direction and approval to go to the Gentiles. Luke summarized that the Word continued to grow and be multiplied (12:24).

B. The Church Advanced to Cyprus and into Asia Minor (Acts 12:25–16:5)

Next, the church advanced to Cyprus and into Asia Minor (12:25–16:5). Barnabas and Saul returned from Jerusalem to Antioch, bringing John Mark with them. Through prayer and fasting, the Holy Spirit indicated to the church leaders that Barnabas and Saul were to be **sent out as missionaries** (12:25–13:3). Accompanied by John Mark, Barnabas and Saul traveled to Cyprus as their first destination.

With this Paul and his associates embark on their **first missionary journey** (13:4–14:27). While ministering on Cyprus, the Holy Spirit verified the appointment of Saul through a miracle he performed: a Jewish magician was struck blind, and a Gentile proconsul became a believer. In addition, Saul's name was changed to Paul; he was filled with the Holy Spirit and became the leader of the team (13:4–12). From Cyprus the team moved into Asia Minor (modern Turkey) to Pamphylia and then into the province of Galatia. At Perga, John Mark left and returned to Jerusalem (13:13; cf. 15:37–38). The two missionaries went north into Pisidian Antioch, Iconium, Lystra, and Derbe before backtracking and returning home.

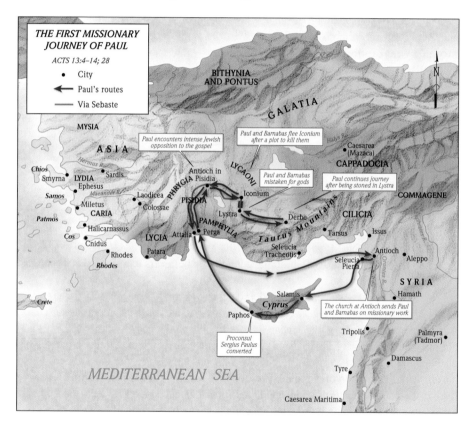

In Pisidian Antioch (13:14–52), Paul preached the gospel (13:16–41) in the synagogue, where some Gentiles were present: "When the Gentiles heard this, they rejoiced and glorified the message of the Lord, and all who had been appointed to eternal life believed. So the message of the Lord spread through the whole region" (13:48–49). The **response of the Gentiles** aroused the jealousy of the Jews, prompting Paul and Barnabas to tell them they would turn to the Gentiles (13:47). The Jews brought further persecution against Paul and Barnabas and drove them from the district. The missionaries simply shook the dust off their feet and went on to the next city. A pattern in Paul's ministry can be seen in this first experience. He would go to the Jews first, proclaiming Jesus as the fulfillment of the Old Testament Messiah. When the Jews rejected him, he turned to the Gentiles who readily responded in faith. This aroused the jealousy of the Jews who brought persecution on Paul and Barnabas.

In Lystra (14:8–20), Paul performed a **healing miracle**. The people, thinking the missionaries were gods, wanted to offer sacrifice to them. Shocked, Paul gave a second speech to point them to the Creator God who had spoken to them in nature. Soon Jews from Antioch and Iconium came and stirred up a mob, dragging Paul out of the city and stoning him. Some thought Paul had died; others said he was miraculously healed because he got up and returned to the city. After going on to Derbe and making many disciples there (14:21), the missionaries retraced their steps through the cities where they had been persecuted to strengthen the disciples and appoint elders in each city. They then returned to Syrian Antioch where they reported all that God had done in opening a door of faith to the Gentiles (14:27–28).

A serious argument arose when some came from Jerusalem to teach the need to circumcise new Gentile believers (15:1–35). The church of Antioch sent Paul and Barnabas to Jerusalem to settle the issue. **The Jerusalem Council** was held in AD 49 where it was determined that Gentiles do not have to follow the Mosaic law, which was a yoke even the Jews were never able to bear (15:10). The decision was that both Jews and Gentiles are saved by grace through faith alone (15:11). This was important information for the Gentiles who needed to know that they were "saved by grace through faith . . . not from works" (Eph 2:8–9). The most prominent leaders in Jerusalem sent a letter from the Jerusalem Council to the new churches stating the agreed-upon decision.

The Jerusalem Council: Who? When? What?

The Issue: Some men from Judea came to Antioch and argued, "Unless you are circumcised according to the custom prescribed by Moses, you cannot be saved!" (Acts 15:1). A delegation was sent to Jerusalem where some believers from among the Pharisees argued, regarding Gentiles who came to Christ, "It is necessary to circumcise them and to command them to keep the law of Moses!" (15:5).

The Solution: (1) Peter argued that God had already demonstrated that He had accepted Gentiles on the basis of faith alone (15:7–11). (2) Barnabas and Paul did not argue theologically but told stories of what they had seen God already do among the Gentiles (15:12). (3) James (Jesus' brother) demonstrated from Scripture that God would accept Gentiles as Gentiles (Amos 9:11–12). Therefore Gentiles should not be troubled with the law but be encouraged not to offend the Jews (15:13–21).

The Letter: A letter was issued declaring their official position (15:22–30) and circulated to the churches expressing apostolic authority.

THE SECOND MISSIONARY
JOURNEY OF PAUL

ACTS 15:36–18:22

- • City
- ▲ Mountain peak
- —— Via Egnatia
- ⤚ Pass
- ◄— Route of Paul and Silas

In due course the **second missionary journey** follows (15:36–18:22). Upon returning from Jerusalem, a decision was made to revisit the new believers from the first missionary journey (15:36–16:4). Paul and Barnabas had such a disagreement over taking John Mark along (see 13:13) that they split up their team and each went his separate ways. Barnabas took John Mark and returned to Cyprus. Paul chose **Silas** and took the northern route through Syria and Cilicia back to the churches of southern Galatia. In Lystra they added Timothy to the team. As the team ministered, the churches were strengthened in faith and daily increased in number (16:5).

C. The Church Advanced to the Western Shores of the Aegean Sea (Acts 16:6–19:20)

As the missionary team advanced westward, the Holy Spirit sovereignly guided their destination (16:1–12). Paul was prevented from preaching in certain places

(16:6–7), ending up in Troas where he received the "Macedonian call" (16:9–10) to take the gospel to Greece.

The first stop in Macedonia was **Philippi** (16:11–40) where God led Paul to find Lydia, the first convert in Europe. When demonic opposition came from a fortune-telling slave girl, Paul cast out the demon which resulted in Paul and Silas being put into prison (16:16–24). As they praised God through prayer and singing, God brought an earthquake which contributed to their release. In the process the jailer himself became a believer, along with his household. When the authorities realized that Paul and Silas were Roman citizens, they begged them to leave the city.

An overview of the Roman colony of Philippi. The great Roman road, the Via Egnatia, visible in the center of the photograph, brought Paul to Philippi from the nearby port of Neapolis.

Paul and his company went to **Thessalonica** where he preached only for three Sabbaths (17:1–9). While many believed, the Jews quickly became jealous, formed a mob, and dragged some of the believers before the city authorities, accusing them of preaching a king other than Caesar. Paul went to **Berea**, where the Jews were "more open-minded" and investigated the Scriptures to verify Paul's words (17:10–14). Not until the Jews from Thessalonica came was Paul driven away. Silas and Timothy remained in Macedonia while Paul went on to Athens.

In **Athens**, Paul was brought before the Epicurean and Stoic philosophers in the Areopagus (17:15–34). There, in another one of his sermons, Paul introduced them to the "unknown God," as noted on one of their altars on **Mars Hill**. Paul appealed to them to turn to the Lord before judgment came. The response there was small.

The rocky outcrop known as Mars Hill in Athens seen from the Acropolis.

Paul went to Corinth and worked as a tent maker to support himself. There Paul teamed up with Aquila and Priscilla in tent making until Silas and Timothy arrived with funds from Macedonia (18:1–5). The Jews in Corinth resisted Paul's message, so Paul took the church into the home of Titus Justus, "whose house was next door to the synagogue" (18:7). This was such a strategic decision that the Lord said to Paul in a night vision, "Don't be afraid, but keep on speaking and don't be silent" (18:9). After two and a half years, the Jews brought Paul before Gallio, the Roman proconsul, with charges that he persuaded men to worship contrary to the law. Gallio rejected the charge because Paul had done no crime or moral evil (18:14). Again Christianity was cleared by a Roman authority.

Leaving Corinth, Paul traveled to **Ephesus** (18:18–22), where he found an open door for ministry. However, having made a vow, he left for Jerusalem, promising, "I'll come back to you again, if God wills" (18:21).

After Paul left Ephesus, Apollos, an Alexandrian Jew, eloquent in the Scripture, arrived (18:24–28). **Apollos** had an understanding of salvation in the Old Testament up to the story of John the Baptist. So Priscilla and Aquila explained the truth of God to him more accurately. Apollos then went on to Corinth to minister.

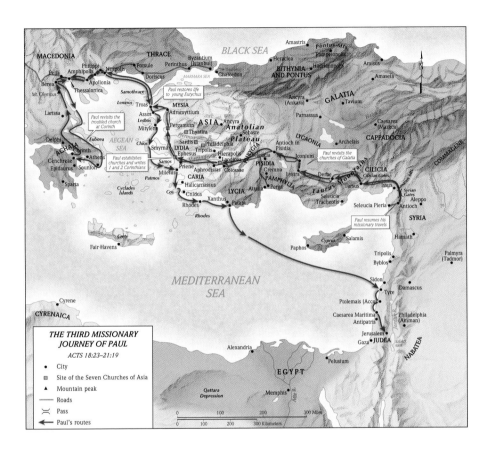

THE THIRD MISSIONARY
JOURNEY OF PAUL
ACTS 18:23–21:19

- City
- Site of the Seven Churches of Asia
- Mountain peak
- Roads
- Pass
- Paul's routes

Shortly after Paul arrived back in Antioch, he began his **third journey**, retracing the steps of his second journey, until he came again to **Ephesus** (19:1–19). Paul confronted 12 disciples of John the Baptist who did not know about Jesus. Paul taught them about Jesus, and the Holy Spirit came upon them. Paul continued to speak boldly in the synagogue for three months. Again Paul moved the church into a secular Gentile setting at the school of Tyrannus. Paul continued teaching there for two years so that all the Jews and Greeks in Asia heard the Word of the Lord (19:10).

Luke included a scenario in Ephesus to demonstrate Paul's God-given authority (19:11–19). Some Jewish exorcists attempted to cast out demons by Paul's formula, but **the demons attacked them** as imposters. Even demons knew that Paul was God's chosen instrument. This section ends with the summary, "The Lord's message flourished and prevailed" (19:20).

Ephesus, where Paul spent two and a half years in ministry. The view shows Curetes Street descending down to the Library of Celsus.

D. The Church Advanced to Rome (19:21–28:31)

Finally, as the culmination of the events recorded in the book of Acts, the church advanced all the way to Rome (19:21–28:31). Paul left Ephesus because the Gentile idol-makers caused a citywide riot due to loss of their revenue, obviously because of the influence of the Christian message (19:23–20:1).

Paul ministered to the churches through Macedonia and Greece (20:1–2) and backtracked again to Troas (20:3–6) where he raised a young man, **Eutychus**, from the dead who had fallen from a window and died (20:6–12). Paul traveled on to Miletus where he called the elders from Ephesus to meet with him (20:13–38). Following a tearful farewell, Paul traveled on to Tyre, to Caesarea, and finally to Jerusalem, even though he was repeatedly warned about dangers there (21:1–17).

In **Jerusalem**, Paul met with James and the elders and formed a plan to counter the criticism against Paul (21:18–26). However, the plan to follow Jewish customs failed, and Paul was seized by an angry mob who threatened to kill him. Paul was taken into custody by the Romans (21:27–22:29). Being allowed to speak to the crowd, Paul attempted to win them by relating his conversion experience. But the Jews refused to listen to Paul when he mentioned his commission to the Gentiles. When the Romans discovered that Paul was a Roman citizen, they treated him with respect.

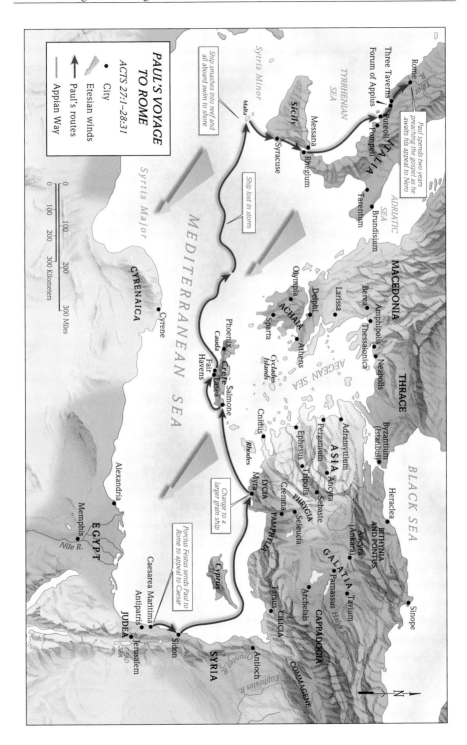

PAUL'S VOYAGE
TO ROME

ACTS 27:1–28:31

• City
Etesian winds
Paul's routes
Appian Way

Ship smashes into reef and all aboard swim to shore

Paul spends two years preaching the gospel as he awaits his appeal to Nero

Ship lost in storm

Change to a larger grain ship

Porcius Festus sends Paul to Rome to appeal to Caesar

0   100   200   300 Kilometers
0   100   200   300 Miles

TYRRHENIAN SEA
Syrtis Minor
Syrtis Major
MEDITERRANEAN SEA
ADRIATIC SEA
AEGEAN SEA
BLACK SEA

CYRENAICA
EGYPT
Nile R.
Memphis
Alexandria
Cyrene

Rome
Tiber R.
Three Taverns
Forum of Appius
Puteoli
Pompeii
ITALY
Messana
Sicily
Syracuse
Rhegium
Tarentum
Brundisium
Malta

MACEDONIA
Olympia
Delphi
Larissa
Berea
Amphipolis
Thessalonica
Neapolis
ACHAIA
Sparta
Athens
Cyclades Islands
Phoenix
Cauda
Crete
Fair Havens
Lasea
Salmone
Cnidus
Rhodes
Myra
LYCIA
THRACE
Byzantium (Istanbul)
Adramyttium
Pergamum
Ephesus
Tripolis
Crenna
Seleucia
PHRYGIA
PAMPHYLIA
ASIA
Ancyra
Sebaste
BITHYNIA AND PONTUS
Heraclea
Ancyra (Ankara)
Parnassus
Tavium
GALATIA
Archelais
Tarsus
CILICIA
CAPPADOCIA
COMMAGENE
Sinope
Halys R.
Cyprus
Caesarea Maritima
Antipatris
JUDEA
Jerusalem
Sidon
SYRIA
Antioch
Orontes R.
Euphrates R.
Dead Sea

N

Paul appeared in his own defense before the Sanhedrin, but a clash between rival groups was so violent the commander was afraid Paul would be torn apart (22:30–23:10). God, however, appeared to Paul that night with the reassurance that he would **appear in Rome for the cause of Christ** (23:11). God sovereignly disclosed a plot to murder Paul, so the Roman authorities protected Paul and delivered him safely to Felix, the governor, in Caesarea (23:12–35). A copy of the letter written by the Roman commander Lysias to governor Felix was included by Luke in the text, stating that the accusations against Paul centered on Jewish law and that he found nothing worthy of death or imprisonment (23:25–30).

Reconstruction of Caesarea Maritima where Paul was imprisoned for two years.

The reasons for holding Paul in prison for two years were pragmatic: the Roman commander did not show up (24:22–23); Felix, out of greed, was **hoping for a bribe** (24:26); and the Roman authorities were trying to gain the favor of the Jews (24:27; 25:9). During this time Paul repeated his defense three times, once before governor Felix (24:1–21), once before governor Festus (25:1–12), and once before both Festus and King Agrippa (25:13–26:32). Luke used these encounters to show a positive attitude by the authorities toward Paul and his message about Christ. Felix was frightened at Paul's preaching because it had to do with the judgment to come (24:25); Festus repeatedly stated that he found no charges to pass on to Caesar (25:18,20,25,27); and King Agrippa categorically stated that Paul was not worthy of either imprisonment or death and could have been released if he had not **appealed to Caesar** (26:31–32). Fearing for his life, under the threat of the Jews, Paul had used his option as a Roman citizen to appeal his case to the highest authority in Rome, that is, to Caesar (25:9–12). Because of that appeal, Festus was obligated to send Paul to Rome for trial.

During the trip to Rome, Paul directed the captain of the ship, the soldiers, the sailors, and all the prisoners through a storm at sea to safety on **Malta** (27:1–44). On Malta, Paul was unharmed in an encounter with a viper (28:1–6). In addition, Paul was able to perform miracles and heal people on the island. Arriving as a prisoner, Paul left Malta as an honored guest. In time Paul arrived in Rome, accompanied by brethren along the way (28:11–15).

The Island of Malta where Paul and the crew of the wrecked Roman freighter washed ashore.

In Rome, Paul was again treated with respect by the Romans, being allowed to stay with a soldier in his own rented quarters (28:16). The Jews there had heard nothing bad about Paul and so came to listen as he explained God's kingdom as centered in Jesus (28:23–24). As was typical of Paul's presentation, "Some were persuaded . . . , but others did not believe" (28:24).

In his concluding summary, Luke stated that **Paul stayed two full years** in his own rented quarters, preaching and teaching with all openness, unhindered in Rome itself (28:30–31). God's message and God's messenger were in Rome, the capital of the Gentile world, and he had complete freedom to preach about the kingdom of God and teach concerning the Lord Jesus Christ.

<u>CONCLUSION</u>

The gospel story began in the Jewish setting in Jerusalem where Jesus was shown to be their Messiah, but immediately the focus was to take the gospel to the world. The Great Commission, given by Jesus to His apostles, was carried to the Gentiles. When Paul ended up in Rome, he won palace guards to Christ, and through them the message of the gospel went out to the world (Phil 1:13; 4:22), just as Jesus had directed.

Study Questions

1. One of Luke's goals was to show the movement of the gospel from Jerusalem to Rome. How did God control circumstances so that His message was successfully communicated?
2. The book of Acts is about prayer and God's answers to them. Where and when did people pray, and what was the outcome?
3. Barnabas, whose real name was Joseph, was nicknamed "Son of Encouragement" (4:36). What are some of the ways in which God used him in the overall advancement of the gospel?
4. It was important for Luke to include evidences of believers praying in the book of Acts. What does this tell us about the importance of prayer in God's work?
5. In Acts 20:17–35 Paul passed the ministry from himself to the Ephesian elders in his farewell speech to them. What timeless principles of ministry can you find in that speech?

For Further Reading

Bock, Darrell L. *Acts*. BECNT. Grand Rapids: Baker, 2007.

Carson, D. A., and Douglas J. Moo. *An Introduction to the New Testament.* Rev. ed. Grand Rapids: Zondervan, 2005.

Ger, Steven. *Acts: Witness to the World.* Chattanooga: AMG Publishers, 2004.

Marshall, I. Howard. *The Acts of the Apostles.* TNTC. Grand Rapids: Eerdmans, 1980.

Pettegrew, Larry D. *The New Covenant Ministry of the Holy Spirit.* Grand Rapids: Kregel, 2001.

Polhill, John B. *Acts: An Exegetical and Theological Exposition of Holy Scripture.* NAC. Nashville: Broadman, 1992.

Toussaint, Stanley D. "Acts." *BKCNT.* Edited by John F. Walvoord and Roy B. Zuck. Wheaton: Victor, 1983.

ENDNOTES

1. D. A. Carson and Douglas J. Moo, *An Introduction to the New Testament,* rev. ed. (Grand Rapids: Zondervan, 2005), 291.

2. Ibid., 210.

3. Darrell L. Bock, *Luke 1:1–9:50,* BECNT (Grand Rapids: Baker, 1994), 15.

4. Darrell L. Bock, *Acts,* BECNT (Grand Rapids: Baker, 2007), 15.

5. For a list of the speeches, see Joseph A. Fitzmyer, *The Acts of the Apostles: A New Translation with Introduction and Commentary* (New Haven: The Anchor Yale Bible, 1998), 103–5. See also John B. Polhill, *Acts: An Exegetical and Theological Exposition of Holy Scripture,* NAC 26 (Nashville: Broadman, 1992), 43–47; Bock, *Acts,* 20–23; and Simon Kistemaker, "The Speeches in Acts," *Criswell Theological Review* 5/1 (1990): 31–41.

6. Modified from Stanley D. Toussaint, "Acts," in *BKCNT,* ed. John F. Walvoord and Roy B. Zuck (Wheaton: Victor, 1983), 349. For a more extensive comparison see Richard Belward Rackham, *The Acts of the Apostles* (London: Methuen, 1901; repr. Grand Rapids: Baker, 1964), xlviii.

7. Modified from Larry D. Pettegrew, *The New Covenant Ministry of the Holy Spirit* (Grand Rapids: Kregel, 2001), 152 (emphasis added).

8. For a full discussion of the post-resurrection offer of the kingdom, see Toussaint, 360–62.

Chapter 10

ROMANS
Righteousness by Faith

The apostle Paul's great epistle to the Romans has been called "the most profound work in existence" (Samuel Coleridge). Martin Luther called it the "purest gospel." The teaching of Romans is not only crucial for Christian theology, but the greatest revivals and reformations throughout the history of Christianity have resulted from an increased understanding and application of the teaching of this epistle. Mankind is faced with the question: How can a person be rightly related to the God who created the universe and will someday righteously judge all people? All are condemned by sin, with no hope of reconciliation with God on their own. Paul says the answer is the gospel of Jesus Christ, which reveals how one can be righteous before God by faith. What is more, the one who believes in Jesus will not continue in a life of sin but will daily be transformed into the character of Christ through the personal power of God's Holy Spirit.

The Roman Forum with columns of the temple of Saturn in the foreground.

Key Facts	
Author:	The apostle Paul
Recipients:	Believers at Rome
Where Written:	Corinth (Achaia, Greece)
Date:	Winter of AD 56–57
Key Word:	Gospel (Gk. *euangelion*)
Key Verses:	"For I am not ashamed of the gospel, because it is God's power for salvation to everyone who believes, first to the Jew, and also to the Greek. For in it God's righteousness is revealed from faith to faith, just as it is written: The righteous will live by faith" (1:16–17).

AUTHOR

The epistle to the Romans identifies its author as Paul, a slave of Christ Jesus (1:1). He twice refers to himself as an **apostle to the Gentiles** (11:13; 15:15–20). Paul's Hebrew name was Saul, and his Roman-Greek name was Paul. He probably had both names from childhood since he was born a Roman citizen (Acts 22:28) of Jewish parents (Acts 23:6; Phil 3:5). In his epistles he always refers to himself as Paul. Luke used the name Saul only in Acts 7–13, and Paul used it in describing his conversion experience (Acts 22:7,13; 26:14), since he was quoting Jesus in the Hebrew (or Aramaic) language.

Paul was probably born about 10 years after the birth of Jesus, in the city of Tarsus in Cilicia (modern southeastern Turkey; Acts 22:3). He is called a "young man" about AD 34 (Acts 7:58), and he called himself an aged man about AD 61 (Phlm 9).

Paul's father was apparently a merchant and a native of Israel. He was a **Roman citizen** (Acts 22:28) and a strict Pharisee (Acts 23:6). Paul had at least one sister and a nephew, who lived in Jerusalem (Acts 23:16). He probably never got married since he urged unmarried men and widows to "remain [single] as I am" (1 Cor 7:7–9; 9:5).

Paul learned the trade of tent making as a youth. He may have attended university in Tarsus, but he stated in Acts 22:3 that he was brought up in Jerusalem. He **studied under Gamaliel**, one of the most famous Jewish rabbis at Jerusalem (Acts 22:3).

Paul became a leader in the persecution of the Christian church soon after its birth (Acts 8:3; Phil 3:6; 1 Tim 1:13). There is no record that he saw or met Jesus before his conversion experience. **His conversion** to Christ came at the height of his opposition to the church while he was on his way to Damascus to arrest Christian Jews (Acts 9:1–18). Afterwards, Paul immediately became an enthusiastic witness for Christ.

Paul's principal **achievements** were twofold: (1) he wrote 13 books of the New Testament, which are a primary source of theological information; and (2) he was the principal leader in extending the church into Asia Minor and Greece, becoming known as the premier apostle to the Gentiles. Acts 13–28 focuses mainly on Paul's ministry.

Paul was a **unique Christian leader**, a fearless champion and exponent of Christianity, a genius of church planting and discipleship, and the most influential missionary, preacher, and teacher of the early church. Dedication and intensity were his primary attributes.

The book of Acts ends by describing Paul's first **imprisonment in Rome**. He was apparently released from this incarceration in about AD 62 and conducted a vigorous ministry in Crete, Asia (the province), Macedonia, and perhaps Spain. During Nero's persecution (c. AD 64–68), Paul was again arrested and put in a Roman prison. This time there was no hope of release (2 Tim 4:6). According to later church writers, he was beheaded (probably AD 66–67).

RECIPIENTS

The epistle was written to believers in Rome (1:7,15). At this time Rome was the largest and most important city of the world. Its population is estimated at one to four million. The emperor Nero began to rule in AD 54, but the Roman anti-Christian persecution had not yet begun. There was a large percentage of slaves and poor people. About a dozen Jewish synagogues were located throughout the city.

Paul did not start the church at Rome (1:13), and there is no definite record of how the church began. There are three principal suggestions:

1. Jews from Rome who were saved in Jerusalem on the day of Pentecost when the church began (Acts 2:10) returned to Rome and founded the church. A major support for this view is the fact the Roman emperor Claudius expelled all Jews from Rome in about AD 49 because of persistent riots that were occurring among the Jews due to arguments about Christ.[1] This indicates

Nero, Roman emperor from AD 54–68. Nero was emperor when Paul wrote his letter to the Romans.

that Christian Jews were evangelizing among Roman Jews within 16 years after the beginning of the church in Jerusalem. While there is no specific record that churches were established in Rome this early, the situation was certainly favorable.

2. The apostle **Peter** went to Rome in about AD 42 and founded the church. This is the Roman Catholic view. Peter would have been the first bishop of Rome and therefore the first pope. There are four principal objections to this view: (1) There is no

evidence that Peter was in Rome before AD 62 at the earliest. (2) In his prison epistles written from Rome (AD 61–62), Paul never mentions Peter. (3) Luke does not mention Peter in his record of Paul's arrival in Rome in Acts 27–28. (4) Paul states in Romans 15:20 that he didn't build "on someone else's foundation" (that is, he didn't try to establish churches where other apostles had already done so), yet he wanted to go to Rome to establish the brethren (1:11) and preach the gospel (1:15).

The Flavian Amphitheater in Rome, more popularly known as the Colosseum.

3. **Paul's converts** founded the church. Many of Paul's converts in Greece and Asia Minor later went to Rome. His greetings in Romans 16 reveal that Paul had many

personal acquaintances in the Roman church. Priscilla and Aquila were among those who had a church in their home in Rome (16:3–5). This view seems preferable.

The church in Rome probably consisted of at least five **household churches** rather than one large church. Five assemblies are apparently greeted in Rom 16:5,10–11,14–15. In addition, at the beginning of the epistle, Paul addresses the believers as "all who are in Rome" (1:7) rather than "the church at Rome."

The Roman church consisted of **both Gentiles and Jews**, but the majority was Gentiles. Paul emphasizes that he was an apostle to the Gentiles (Rom 1:5; 11:13; 15:16). In 9:3, he speaks of the Jews as "my" brothers, not "our" brothers. And in Romans 16 more than half the names of people greeted by Paul are Latin or Greek.

OCCASION AND DATE

The book of Romans was **written in Corinth**, in the province of Achaia. Paul said that he was leaving for Jerusalem soon (Rom 15:25). The last city Paul visited on his third missionary journey before beginning his return to Jerusalem was Corinth (cf. Acts 20:1–3). What is more, in Rom 16:1 Paul mentions Cenchrae as the home of Phoebe, who took the letter to Rome for Paul; Cenchrae was a seaport of Corinth, about four miles away (cf. Acts 18:18).

Paul's letter to the Romans was likely written during the **winter of AD 56–57** near the end of Paul's third missionary journey (c. AD 53–57). If the letter was written at Corinth, it must have been written during either Paul's second journey (c. AD 50–52) or his third. Priscilla and Aquila, whom he first met in Corinth during his second journey and who accompanied him to Ephesus thereafter, were back in Rome by the time Paul wrote Romans (16:3). And since Paul states that he is about to leave for Jerusalem (and then to Rome; Rom 15:25), this must have occurred during his third journey since Paul did not go to Jerusalem at the end of his second journey (Acts 18:22). Paul apparently spent the winter of **AD 56–57** in Corinth (cf. Acts 20:2–3), while preparing to take his monetary collection to the saints at Jerusalem (1 Cor 16:1–7). This would have been the best time to send the letter, in which he tells them that he hopes to visit them soon (Rom 1:10–15; 15:23–32).

While Paul was at Corinth near the end of his third journey, he contemplated his future ministry. He had to return to Jerusalem to deliver his collection of money from the churches of Asia Minor and Greece for distribution to needy saints. But after this he wanted to **extend his ministry** even farther west. This meant that he must go to Rome, Spain, and other areas of the western Mediterranean. Since there was already a flourishing church at Rome, Paul did not need to spend much time there. But he had always wanted to go to Rome (1:13; 15:22–24,28–29). He wanted to have some spiritual fruit there (1:13) and to share the benefits of his spiritual gifts with the believers (1:11). More than anything else, since no apostle had ever yet visited Rome, Paul felt that he needed to establish the Roman believers in their **faith and doctrine** (1:11).

To prepare them for his coming and to receive some financial support from them for his missionary journey to Spain (15:24,28), he wrote this epistle. In addition, Phoebe (16:1–2) was leaving for Rome, and so this was an appropriate time to send them a letter.

GENRE AND STRUCTURE

Epistles are the most common literary form in the New Testament. They are **occasional letters**; that is, they were designed to deal with specific situations. Their style was part everyday correspondence (like most personal letters today) and part literary production (with rhetorical strategies intended to advance theological and practical arguments). Paul's epistles typically begin with his name and some designation of his recipients, followed by a greeting, blessing, and thanksgiving to God for what he had recently heard about the recipients, then the body of the letter in which he presents both theological and practical concerns, followed often by a lengthy conclusion in which he summarizes his points and gives final greetings.

Paul's epistle to the Romans is Paul's most extensive theological writing. It stands first among the epistles because it is the longest and because it has always been considered **the most significant apostolic letter**. Many theological leaders, including Augustine, Luther, Melanchthon, and John Wesley, have claimed that Romans changed their lives and ministries more than any other part of the Bible.

The "occasional" emphasis in Romans focuses on **four issues**: (1) the *truth* about the gospel Paul has been preaching, especially in light of the negative response it has received from Jews (Romans 2; 4); (2) what *Jews* need to know about their place in God's program now that it has become clear that most of their fellow countrymen are rejecting God's Messiah (Romans 9–11); (3) the need for *Gentiles* to be humble about their inclusion in God's salvation program and about God's continued and future plans for Israel (because of the Abrahamic covenant); and (4) the *support* Paul is seeking from Roman believers for his expanded missionary program in the western Roman Empire (Romans 1; 15).

Outline

I. Introduction (Romans 1:1–17)
II. Doctrine (Romans 1:18–11:36)
    A. Condemnation: The Revelation of God's Wrath (Romans 1:18–3:20)
    B. Justification: The Imputation of God's Righteousness (Romans 3:21–5:21)
    C. Sanctification: The Impartation of God's Righteousness (Romans 6:1–8:39)
    D. Vindication: Israel's Rejection of God's Righteousness (Romans 9:1–11:36)
III. Duties (Romans 12:1–15:13)
    A. Toward the Brothers (Romans 12)
    B. Toward the Government (Romans 13)
    C. Toward the Weak and Strong (Romans 14:1–15:13)
IV. Conclusion (Romans 15:14–16:27)

MESSAGE

I. Introduction (Romans 1:1–17)

Paul introduces himself to the Romans as a **slave of Jesus Christ** and one who has been set apart to preach the gospel, focused on Christ Himself (1:1–6). Paul wants to visit them soon and lists some reasons he is longing to see them (1:11–15): he wants to share his spiritual gifts with them, establish them in their faith, be encouraged by them, and have some spiritual fruit among them.

Before moving into his doctrinal presentation, Paul states the theme of his letter in two ways: (1) the gospel is the power of God that leads to salvation (1:16); and (2) the righteousness of God by faith is revealed in the gospel (1:17). The first major portion of the body of Paul's letter to the Romans deals with **doctrine** (1:18–11:36), moving from condemnation (1:18–3:20) to salvation (3:21–8:39) to vindication (9:1–11:36). In the largest of these sections, Paul deals first with **justification** (3:21–5:21) and then with **sanctification** (6:1–8:39). After establishing the doctrinal foundation, Paul moves on to discuss the **duties** of Christians (12:1–15:13) and finally a conclusion.

II. Doctrine (Romans 1:18–11:36)

A. Condemnation: The Revelation of God's Wrath (Rom 1:18–3:20)

Paul begins the doctrinal portion of his epistle by describing the revelation of God's wrath on all mankind: everyone needs God's righteousness. He shows first that the **pagans** (unrighteous, idolatrous people) of the world are under God's wrath because they rejected the knowledge of God available in creation and turned to idolatry instead. God in turn gave them over to a life of immorality and depravity (1:18–32). Second, **moralists** (those who profess to have a personal moral code—both Gentiles and Jews) are under God's condemnation because, though they think they are righteous by their own standards, they don't match up to God's standards. Their deeds are evil and judgment awaits them (2:1–16). Third, **Jews** specifically are under condemnation because, though they have God's law and think they're righteous because of it, they are actually breaking it in many ways (2:17–3:8). Their hypocrisy even causes Gentiles to blaspheme and ridicule the God of the Bible. Possession of the law of Moses and circumcision are not sufficient for them to be counted as righteous before God. Finally, Paul shows that **the whole world** is under sin and therefore guilty before God. All are accountable, and no one can be justified by his works or the law (3:10–20).

Greek Highlight

Gospel, Good News. Greek εὐαγγέλιον (**euangelion**). The Christian *euangelion* (gospel) is the universal message of God's saving grace through faith in Christ, and the message of His kingdom over which Jesus reigns. Jesus preached the *good news* of God's coming kingdom (Matt 4:23) and substantiated His message by miracles (Matt 9:35). This *good news* of the kingdom's arrival will be preached to the world (Mark 13:10) and is worthy of sacrificial labor (Mark 8:35). Paul believed the *gospel* was an extension of OT promises (Rom 1:1–3; 16:25–26). Paul's gospel encompasses Jesus' entire life: His incarnation, sacrificial death, burial, resurrection, postresurrection appearances, and ascension (Rom 1:1–6; 1 Cor 15:1–8; Phil 2:9). It is the Spirit-empowered message (1 Thess 1:5) by which God calls all nations (Rom 1:5; 15:16–19) and reconciles people to Himself (2 Cor 5:18–21). Paul stressed that this glorious message of *gospel* that can bring about eternal life-change to all who believe should be boldly and unapologetically proclaimed by all believers to the entire world (Rom 1:16) knowing that all men will one day be judged by it (Rom 2:16; 2 Thess 1:8).

B. Justification: The Imputation of God's Righteousness (Romans 3:21–5:21)

The **answer** to mankind's dilemma is that God's righteousness is revealed to man through the gospel, bringing salvation by faith (3:21–8:39). Paul describes first the imputation of God's righteousness to man—justification (3:21–5:21)—and second the impartation of God's righteousness in and through man—sanctification (6:1–8:39).

Justification includes the imputation of God's righteousness by means of faith in Jesus Christ. This justification was provided by **Christ's substitutionary death** on the cross as a satisfaction for man's sin for all who come to Christ in faith (3:24–26). Justification by faith makes all equal before God and gives the law its rightful place of condemning sin (3:27–31).

Abraham illustrates the fact that justification is by faith alone (chap. 4). Paul quotes Gen 15:6: "Abraham believed God, and it was credited to him for righteousness" (4:3). When God offered Abraham an unconditional covenant with eternal promises, Abraham simply received it by faith, and God considered his faith as his being righteous before Him. Abraham was not justified by good works, by circumcision, or by the Mosaic law. He was **justified by faith**, as illustrated by his trust in God's promise that he would have a son in his old age (4:16–22). Everyone, says Paul, can be justified in the same way as Abraham: by faith alone in Christ alone (4:23–25).

Will such justification really last? In chap. 5, Paul shows why a believer can have **eternal confidence** of being justified before God. Justification brings total reconciliation with God. The believer now has peace with God (5:1) and a confident expectation (hope) for the future that is strengthened (not defeated) by afflictions. This is confirmed by the fact that God demonstrated His love for believers through Christ's death for them when they were still God's enemies (5:6–11). If Christ died for the ungodly, He will eternally save those who have been declared righteous in His sight.

Finally, Paul contrasts justification with condemnation (5:12–21). Christ's death provided justification which is **sufficient** to overcome all the effects of Adam's sin. When Adam sinned, he sinned as the head of the human race and therefore passed death on to all humanity (5:12). Christ, when He obeyed God as a sacrifice on the cross, died as the substitute for all. His righteousness has become the believer's position and destiny.

C. Sanctification: The Impartation of God's Righteousness (Romans 6:1–8:39)

This leads Paul into the second aspect of salvation: sanctification, the impartation of God's righteousness in and through the believer to conform him **progressively** to the character and image of Jesus Christ. The believer has been set free from the authority and rule of sin in his life (6:1–14). Since Christ was his substitute on the cross, the believer died with Christ and is identified with Him also in His resurrection. The believer should therefore consider himself dead to sin but now alive to God and God's righteousness. He should yield both himself and his body to God in order to live God's righteousness everyday (6:12–14).

Christians, in fact, are enslaved to God's righteousness. The believer is not free to sin now that he is under the grace of God (6:15). Obedience to a master makes one a slave of that master, and enslavement to a master determines one's ultimate destiny (6:16–23). The believer has been set free from slavery to sin and should now yield himself to his new master (God) to fulfill His righteousness. This brings **progressive holiness** (sanctification) in the present life. The believer's eternal life, however, is a gift from God (6:22–23) and can't be earned.

Paul moves next to the believer's relationship to the law of Moses. The believer has been **set free from the law** since he died to the law through the death of Christ (7:1–6). He has now been joined to Christ, and the expected fruit of such a union is holiness and obedience. The law does not produce sin (7:7–12). Paul wants to make sure his readers do not conclude that God freed believers from the law because the law is evil. Nor does the law cause death. Sin is the cause of death (7:13). The problem is that the sin principle indwells everyone, and the resulting struggle between what people know is right and what sin desires makes them unable to prevent wrong in their lives (7:15–20). The two laws or natures within them are constantly in conflict, and there is nothing inherently in them to enable them to win the battle (7:21–25).

There is a solution, however. The presence of the indwelling **Holy Spirit** has set believers free from the rule of sin and death. The Holy Spirit enables believers to fulfill God's righteous requirements (8:4). The flesh is unable to obey God, but believers are no longer simply in the flesh (8:5–11). They are in the Spirit, and God's Spirit lives within them (8:9).

Believers must now not live according to the flesh but through the Spirit put aside the sins they have been accustomed to committing (8:12–17). And they are to endure sufferings, both the internal struggle with sin and the external afflictions from the world (8:18–30). This can be done because of three facts: (1) the future glory that awaits believers is much greater than the present, brief sufferings (8:18–25); (2) the Holy Spirit helps believers in their weaknesses (8:26–27); and (3) the eternal purpose of God is working everything together for the good of believers, as it gradually conforms them to the character of Christ. In fact, being justified guarantees **final glorification** (8:28–30). Finally, believers are totally secure in Christ. Nothing will separate them from the love of God in Christ (8:31–39).

The ruins of Cenchrea with the waters of its bay seen in the background.

D. Vindication: Israel's Rejection of God's Righteousness (Romans 9:1– 11:36)

Now Paul returns to the **question of Israel** in order to vindicate God's righteousness in His dealings with the Jews. He shows that God's present rejection of Israel for their unbelief is not inconsistent with God's promises to them (9:6–13). God never promised that all the physical descendants of Abraham would be saved (shown first by God's choice of Isaac over Ishmael and then by God's choice of Jacob over Esau). Nor is God's rejection of Israel inconsistent with His justice (9:14–29). God can both extend mercy to those who accept it and harden those who don't. God is sovereign over His creation (9:19–21). He puts up with sinners (9:22) and prepares others for glory (9:23), now being demonstrated among Jews and Gentiles in the church (9:24–29).

Israel is guilty for **rejecting** God's righteousness by faith and trying instead to establish their own righteous (9:30–10:4). They ignored Old Testament teaching on the gospel of grace. It was always available through faith (10:5–10) to both Jews and Gentiles (10:11–13). The Jews simply need to acknowledge Jesus Christ as Lord and Savior (10:9–10), but most refuse to do this. The gospel was preached to Israel by the apostles God sent to them. They heard it (10:18) and understood it (10:19–20) but rejected it. They therefore stand under the condemnation of God (10:21).

But God is not finished with Israel. Israel's rejection by God is neither complete nor final. The rejection is not total (11:1–10) since God always has a **believing remnant** among His people, as seen in the case of Paul himself, Elijah and the 7,000 mentioned in the Old Testament, and many believing Jews in the present day. The rejection is also temporary since God is using the present hardness of Israel to pour out blessings on the Gentiles (11:11–15) and will one day restore the Jews as a nation in God's favor. Some Gentile believers mistakenly think that they as a race are now God's chosen people (11:17–24), but they do not have an unconditional covenant with God as Israel does. Israel's future restoration is certain, as one day all Israel will be saved (11:25–27) and God will have mercy on them as He has on the Gentiles now (11:28–32).

III. Duties (Romans 12:1–15:13)

The third major section of Romans describes the duties of those who are justified. These duties are toward the brothers (12:1–21), toward the government (13:1–14), and toward the weak and the strong (14:1–15:13). The foundation of all of **Christian conduct** is the consecration of the believer's life to God by presenting his body as an offering for God's service (12:1), and the transformation of the believer's life daily through the continual renewing of his mind and attitude (12:2).

A. Toward the Brothers (Romans 12)

Believers must live in humility and love toward the brothers and sisters in the assembly. They are to use their spiritual gifts in accordance with the ministry God has

Full moon rising over the Roman Colosseum, whose construction began in the early 70s by Vespasian. It was completed and opened in AD 80 by his son and successor, Titus.

assigned to them (12:6–8). They should **love others** sincerely and zealously and respond to evil treatment with blessing and humility, without taking vengeance (12:9–21).

B. Toward the Government (Romans 13)

Believers need to be in subjection to their government because its **authority ultimately comes from God**, and God has designed civil government to punish evil and reward good (13:1–7). The duty that a believer owes to others is to love them, since loving one's neighbor fulfills the requirements of the law toward others. The new age is at hand, and Christians must change their conduct to conform to the character of Christ (13:11–14).

C. Toward the Weak and Strong (Romans 14:1–15:13)

Paul ends his discussion of duties with four strong exhortations designed to promote **harmony in the church** between those who are weak in faith and those who are strong: (1) The weak and the strong must accept each other since both are accepted by God, both belong to God, and both will therefore be judged by God (14:1–12). (2) The strong believer should not cause the weak believer to stumble in his life but rather be concerned for him (14:13–18) and do what leads to peace and edification (14:19–21). (3) The strong believer needs to help the weak believer, just as Christ did not live to please Himself but took upon Himself the sins of the world (15:1–6). (4) Both the weak and the strong should accept each other, just as Christ has accepted both Jews and Gentiles in the Church for God's glory (15:7–13).

A street in Corinth from the first century AD with the Acrocorinth in the background.

IV. Conclusion (Romans 15:14–16:27)

Now Paul revisits his motivation for writing the letter. God has given him the ministry of **apostle to the Gentiles**, and he has preached the gospel to Gentiles all the way from Jerusalem to Illyricum (northwest of Greece). He now needs to go farther west, which will lead him to and past Rome. Everything Paul has accomplished among the Gentiles has been done by Christ Himself (15:18). Paul now wants the Romans to pray that he will at last be able to come to them in the blessing of God (15:22–33) after a brief detour to Jerusalem.

The final chapter is filled with **greetings** for those whom Paul knows by name in Rome. He mentions the one who is taking the letter to them—Phoebe (16:1–2). His greetings to various brethren in the church include his old friends Aquila and Priscilla. He also sends greetings from his companions in Corinth. The **final benediction** summarizes many of the topics Paul emphasized throughout the epistle (16:25–27).

CONCLUSION

The epistle to the Romans is Paul's theological and practical **magnum opus**. Having completed all his pioneer church-planting goals in the eastern Mediterranean region, he believed God wanted him to move westward beyond Rome (beginning at Spain). But he needed the support of the Roman church to do this. Many of the Romans, especially Jews, had received a distorted view of who Paul was and of the nature of the gospel he was preaching. Paul therefore threw "everything he had" into this letter in order to convince the believers at the center of the Roman Empire that they could trust him, his goals, and his preaching.

The **death and resurrection of Jesus Christ** were at the core of everything Paul preached. His message was this: God wanted Jews and Gentiles everywhere to be reconciled to Him. Because of their sin, the only way this could be done was to trust in Jesus Christ as Savior and Lord and receive His righteousness as a gift—through simple faith, just as Abraham had done centuries earlier (Gen 15:6). The rumor that many Jews had heard about Paul—that he taught Gentiles to disobey God's law and live in sin—was totally false. Paul taught that justified people entered a life of practical and progressive sanctification—growing in Christ by appropriating the Spirit's power to put away sins and love their brothers and enemies. God has not turned His back on

---

Erastus Inscription

Archeologists have discovered an inscription on part of a pavement (dating from c. AD 50) found near the theater in Corinth mentioning "Erastus" who was the aedile of the city of Corinth. An aedile was in charge of the financial matters of the city. Romans 16:23 says, "Erastus, the city treasurer . . . greet[s] you." This Erastus is probably the same person mentioned in this inscription, which can be translated, "Erastus, in return for his aedileship, laid (the pavement) at his own expense."

Israel or gone back on His covenant promises. All Israel will one day be saved after God completes his Gentile-focused plan and takes away Israel's blindness.

Meanwhile, Gentile believers need to recognize their status before God and not glory in themselves but in God and His grace. **Jesus came to save both Jews and Gentiles** and to receive all to Himself. Roman Christians should do no less.

Study Questions

1. How is righteousness related to faith?
2. What is justification, and what does Paul teach about it in Romans?
3. What are the fruits (results) of justification?
4. What did Paul mean by "grace" in Romans?
5. What is Paul's answer to the problem of sin in Romans 6–7?
6. In what way is the Holy Spirit important to living a Christian life?
7. What does Paul teach in Romans about the Jewish "remnant" and the future of Israel?

For Further Reading

Cranfield, C. E. B. *A Critical and Exegetical Commentary on the Romans.* 2 vols. Edinburgh: T&T Clark, 1975–79.

McClain, Alva. *Romans: The Gospel of God's Grace.* Winona Lake, IN: BMH Books, 1979.

Moo, Douglas J. *Romans.* NICNT. Grand Rapids: Eerdmans, 1996.

Morris, Leon. *The Epistle to the Romans.* Grand Rapids: Eerdmans, 1988.

Mounce, Robert. *Romans.* NAC. Nashville: B&H, 1995.

Murray, John. *The Epistle to the Romans.* Grand Rapids: Eerdmans, 1997.

Schreiner, Thomas. *Romans.* BECNT. Grand Rapids: Baker, 1998.

ENDNOTE

1. Acts 18:2; Suetonius, *Claudius*, 25.4; cf. Harry J. Leon, *The Jews of Ancient Rome*, updated ed. (Peabody, MA: Hendrickson, 1995), 23–27.

Chapter 11

1 CORINTHIANS
The Supremacy of Love

First Corinthians is a letter from a missionary pastor who came as a father (4:14–15) to address a local church about **local church problems.** He wrote with love and a spirit of gentleness, hoping the issues would be resolved so he did not need to come later with discipline (4:21). Some of the problems of the city of Corinth had become the problems in the church in Corinth. The church was exercising their spiritual gifts, but they were also immature and full of problems. Paul wrote to address those issues and answer questions the church had addressed to him.

Key Facts	
Author:	The apostle Paul and Sosthenes (1:1)
Recipient:	The church at Corinth (1:2)
Where Written:	Ephesus
Date:	AD 56
Key Word:	Love (Gk. *agapē*/*agapaō*)
Key Verse:	"Now these three remain: faith, hope, and love. But the greatest of these is love" (13:13).

AUTHOR

First Corinthians 1:1 identifies Paul as the author of this letter, a fact which is generally accepted (see also 1:12–17; 3:4–6,22; 16:21):

> Both 1 and 2 Corinthians are attributed to Paul in their salutations and show every historical and literary evidence of Pauline authorship. Indeed, the Pauline authorship of 1 Corinthians has **never been disputed** and the letter is already attested in the 90s by Clement of Rome (cf. 1 Clem. 37:5; 47:1–3;

49:5) and in the first decade of the second century by Ignatius (cf. Ignatius Eph. 16:1; 18:1; Rom. 5:1, etc.).[1]

What is more, the contents of this book coincide with what is known of Paul in his travels in Acts.

RECIPIENTS

The book is addressed "To God's church at Corinth, . . . with all those in every place who call on the name of Jesus Christ our Lord—both their Lord and ours" (1:2). Corinth was situated on the isthmus that joined the Ionian and Agean Seas. It was a maritime city that sat between the ports of Lechaion and Cenchreae in Greece. From the beginning of the letter, Paul was emphasizing the spiritual truth of one local "body of Christ" with application to all believers and/or all local churches (cf. 12:12–27).

The **city of Corinth**, a Roman colony, was the capital of the Roman province of Achaia. Situated on the Peloponnesian peninsula, the area was a center for commerce, bringing many travelers through the region. As a result, Corinth was known for its wealth and for being the center of the worship of Aphrodite, goddess of love and immorality, as well as other deities. From this city Paul wrote the first chapter of Romans containing the most graphic description of immorality in the New Testament. Some of that climate had infected the church there.

The columns of the temple of Apollo at Corinth.

OCCASION AND DATE

First Corinthians was written while Paul was in Ephesus near the end of his third missionary journey, putting the date at **AD 56** (16:5–9). Paul visited the city of Corinth for the first time on his second missionary journey (Acts 18:1–18). He planted a church, staying with them for a year and a half (Acts 18:11). On his third missionary journey, Paul's main stop was in Ephesus where he remained and ministered for about two and a half years (AD 53–56; cf. Acts 18:23–19:41). While in Ephesus, Paul heard some **negative news** about how the Corinthian church was handling an immoral situation. He wrote them a letter, which is now lost to us, but referred to in 1 Cor 5:9. A visit to Paul, from some of Chloe's household (1:11), followed this letter, reporting that the letter was misunderstood (5:10–11) and that there were quarrels among the people causing divisions in the church. In addition, several moral issues needed to be addressed. Around the same time Paul received a list of questions, possibly through the visit of Stephanas, Fortunatus, and Achaicus (16:17). In response, Paul wrote the letter known as 1 Corinthians.

GENRE AND STRUCTURE

First Corinthians is a **pastoral letter** to a local church from a father addressing his spiritually erring children (4:14–21). After the introduction (1:1–9), Paul immediately confronted the matter of divisions in the church at Corinth (1:10–4:21). The church needed to correct its spiritual unity before it could solve other issues. Second, Paul spoke to three moral issues in the church: incest (5:1–13); litigation between believers (6:1–11); and sexual immorality with prostitutes (6:12–20). Third, Paul gave **spiritual answers** to various questions passed on to him from the readers (7:1–16:12). Finally, he gave some closing exhortation, greetings, and a benediction (16:13–24).

Outline[2]

   I. Introduction (1 Corinthians 1:1–9)
  II. Reproof: "I Exhort You" (1 Corinthians 1:10–4:21)
 III. Correction: "You Have Become Arrogant" (1 Corinthians 5:1–6:20)
 IV. Instruction: "Don't Be Ignorant" (1 Corinthians 7:1–14:40)
  V. Teaching: "I Tell You a Mystery" (1 Corinthians 15:1–16:12)
 VI. Final Exhortations, Greetings, and a Benediction (1 Corinthians 16:13–24)

MESSAGE

The message of 1 Corinthians is that the problems of the local church are rooted in a sinful self-centeredness and can be effectively solved by spiritual men who have given themselves in sacrificial service to their Lord and so are walking in imitation of Christ. In addressing the problems, Paul told them to "imitate me, as I also imitate

Christ" (11:1; cf. 4:16). The letter demonstrates **a spiritual man's response** as correct doctrine is applied to life in the process of walking with God.

A look at the main issues brings a major theme to the forefront. While Paul addressed many subjects, the **central teaching** is the love chapter (chap. 13), and the **central example** is Christ in the illustration of the Lord's Supper (chap. 11). Through these issues the readers learn how to give up their own immediate goals and desires for a higher good that impacts the whole body of Christ.

I. Introduction (1 Corinthians 1:1–9)

Paul's introduction began on an encouraging note. After identifying himself as the author, and Sosthenes who was with him, Paul describes the church at Corinth in view of **God's sovereign call and sanctification** (1:1–3). Even though there were serious problems in this church, the readers belonged to God and were set apart in this evil city by His purposes for them. Paul also thanked God for His gracious giving of spiritual gifts to them. While there were problems in the exercise of those gifts, God had graciously been at work in them and would be to the end (1:4–9).

II. Reproof: "I Exhort You" (1 Corinthians 1:10–4:21)

Paul began the body of his letter with an issue that was at the root of their problems: the need for unity around the gospel message. Their problem was divisions centered on men (1:10–17). The focus of their problem was various groups siding with men they felt were the best representatives of their view of Christianity. This resulted in **divisions and quarrels** (1:10–17). Paul illustrated what he meant by naming the individuals and reminding them of the nature of his own ministry. His focus was not to build up a following but to preach the gospel and lift up the cross of Christ.

Paul corrected their worldly thinking which had caused these divisions (1:18–4:21). The **wisdom of God** was different from the wisdom of the world. God's wisdom triumphs over the wisdom of the world (1:18–2:5). The world looks at the message of the cross and sees foolishness, whereas it is really the power of God to save those who believe. In order to prevent boasting in human wisdom, God chooses to save and use those the world often rejects. As a result, glory appropriately goes to God. As an example, God took the human weakness of Paul's message, combined it with the power of the Spirit who taught him wisdom, and produced results now seen in the Corinthian church (2:6–13).

The unbeliever (*psychikos anthrōpos*) cannot accept the things of God, but the spiritual person (*pneumatikos*) has **the mind of Christ** (2:14–16). The Corinthians were operating as immature, baby Christians, still using the wisdom of the world, resulting in divisions among them. Paul was not able to speak to them as spiritual people (*pneumatikos*) but as to immature believers ("people of the flesh [*sarkinos*], as babies in Christ"). They were still fleshly (*sarkikos*), still controlled by the flesh and living like unbelievers, according to human wisdom (3:1–3).

Next, Paul explained how to view these various servants of God (3:5–4:5). Instead of being leaders of their sides, they were servants of God working among them (God's field, God's building; 3:9). Each of those servants was **accountable to God** for the type

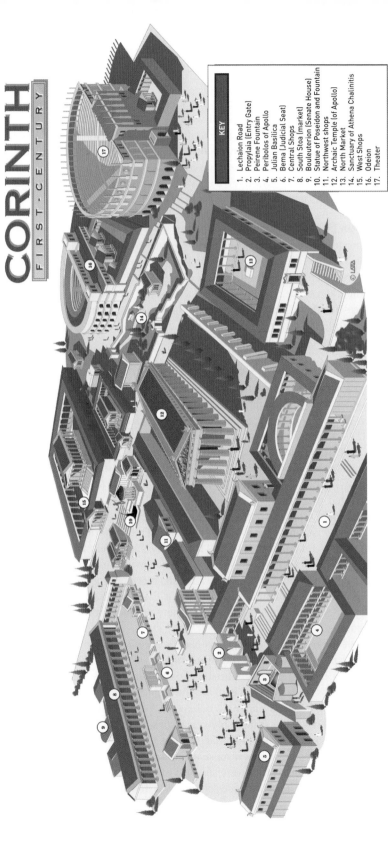

CORINTH
FIRST-CENTURY

Corinth First-Century Diagram.

of building produced from their service (3:10–17). If they built good things into God's building, they would be rewarded. If they built things that were of no lasting value and did not pass the test of fire, then they would lose their reward. The servants were not judged by the Corinthians; the servants stood accountable before God. Rather than boasting in certain men, the Corinthians should have viewed themselves as belonging to God who could raise up ministry from many sources. The various servants God had among them could only be evaluated correctly by the servants' faithfulness to God. Only God Himself can evaluate anyone correctly (4:1–5).

Also, Paul encouraged the readers to recognize their error and to **respond humbly** (4:6–21). They had taken a prideful position, whereas a servant must be humble in the world and before God. Speaking to them as their spiritual father, Paul's hope was that they would respond to this love and spirit of gentleness so that he might not have to come as a father with a disciplining rod (4:21).

III. Correction: "You Have Become Arrogant" (1 Corinthians 5:1–6:20)

Paul now wrote to address moral problems in the church. First, he responded to a report that had come to him regarding **immorality in the church**: a man was living with one of his father's wives, a sin the Gentiles did not even allow (5:1–13). The root problem was their arrogance. They were proud of their tolerance. Instead of dealing with the problem, they allowed it. Paul gave specific instructions. They were to put the man out of the protective assembly of the church, placing him in Satan's domain that could lead not only to the destruction of his flesh but also to the salvation of his soul. The principle and pattern for such a discipline came from Israel who made a clean break from leaven at Passover. The Corinthians were to make a **clean break with sin** as a result of accepting Christ, their Passover Lamb. God will appropriately judge those outside the church. The Corinthians were not to fellowship with a brother in the church who willfully sins without repenting.

Second, in the matter of **litigation between believers** (6:1–11), Paul was surprised that believers were taking Christian neighbors into civil courts for judgment. If saints will someday be responsible to judge both the world and angels, then believers are certainly competent to judge these small affairs also. They should choose a wise man from their own assembly and have him be a judge in the matter. In fact, it would be better not to sue a brother at all. Instead, they should be willing to take the wrong and be defrauded themselves rather than chance wronging and defrauding a brother. Finally, Paul told the Corinthians that to go before a pagan law court was inconsistent with their standing before God. Having once been a part of that unrighteous group who will not inherit the kingdom of God, they were now different because of their salvation. They needed to act accordingly.

The third problem area Paul addressed was **sexual immorality with prostitutes** (6:12–20). In Corinth, where prostitution was common, some felt it was not wrong to satisfy their physical lusts in this way. However, both the behavior and the perspective were wrong. Apparently some thought that since they were no longer under the law, all things were lawful. But they needed to see that not all things are beneficial for the believer. To give into sin is to become a slave of sin (6:12–14). Because our bodies belong to the Lord, and just as Jesus' body was raised again, so our physical bodies will be raised for a life beyond (1 Corinthians 15). Paul then gave **three arguments** against immorality (6:15–20). First, *a body which is a member of Christ* must never become a member of a harlot. Second, *immorality creates divisions* within the person. The person's body becomes one with the prostitute while the person's spirit is one with the Lord. In such a situation, the person is sinning against his own body. Third, the believer does not belong to himself and so is not free to do whatever he wants with his body. His body is a *temple of the Holy Spirit*, bought with a price. The responsibility is to glorify God with the body, not give it over to the fulfillment of its lusts. Self-serving and immediate gratification must give way to a rightful use of their bodies in service to their Lord.

The Lechaeum Road at Corinth. Lechaeum was one of two port facilities on either side of the Isthmus of Corinth that gave the city such strategic commercial importance.

IV. Instruction: "Don't Be Ignorant" (1 Corinthians 7:1–14:40)

In the third section of the letter, **Paul answered questions** posed to him by the Corinthians, as indicated by the repeated introductory phrase *"peri de."* This phrase is first found in 7:1 where Paul says, "Now in response to the matters you wrote about," followed later by other instances of *peri de*, introducing answers to further topics (7:25; 8:1; 12:1; 16:1,12).

To begin with, Paul answers questions regarding **marriage** (7:1–24). Questions came from some who wanted to take an extreme position. If sexual relations with a prostitute were bad, then perhaps all sexual relations were bad and should be avoided entirely. This affected those who were married and could encourage a change in that married state. First, sexual relations are not always evil, and *marriage is good*. Second, if a person struggles with temptation to immorality, then marriage is *God's provision* to handle that (7:1–7). Third, inside marriage, sexual relations are not only the norm but are expected, and *submission* of one's body to the mate is required. A married couple should *refrain* from sexual relations only by a mutual and temporary agreement. Fourth, while singleness may have its preferred benefits, God has gifted people to be in different situations, and marriage is a *legitimate* expression of one of those. Fifth, Paul recommended that those who are unmarried remain unmarried, but those who are not able to have self-control should marry and enter into those relations within the *proper context* (7:8–9).

Next, Paul answers questions about **divorce** and the solidarity of marriage (7:10–11). Husbands and wives should *not divorce*. Those who do should either *remain unmarried* or seek to *be reconciled* to their mate. When the marriage involves a believer and a *nonbeliever*, even then they should not seek to dissolve the marriage (7:10–16). God might use it to reach the unbeliever and the children. If the unbeliever decides to leave, however, then the believer should make a choice for peace. In such a case, they are not under obligation any longer to fulfill the duties of marriage. Finally, the basic principle is that people should remain in whatever condition they were in when they came to Christ (7:17–24). The goal is to pursue that which allows one to serve God best.

Next, Paul answered questions regarding **single people** (7:25–40). The second area of questions is related to the first, centering on whether single people should marry. Paul did not have a command here from the Lord but was only giving his opinion as one who had godly wisdom (7:25). This was wise advice, not moral command.

The principle is that the highest good results where one is able to give the most **undistracted devotion** to the work of the Lord. Instead of a self-serving mentality, in light of the present distress, it is best to remain in the single state (7:26–28). Those who are already married should remain that way. Paul's goal was not to downplay marriage as a legitimate option from God but instead to promote a situation where a believer's service to God was spared from trouble and distraction. Difficult circumstances can require believers to act as though they do not have certain privileges, like marriage; the unmarried state allows greater concern to be given to the things of the Lord (7:29–34).

Several **special cases** follow (7:36–40). First, a father has the freedom to give or withhold his virgin daughter in marriage (7:36–38). It is not sin for a father to give his virgin daughter in marriage, but, in keeping with Paul's previous advice, he does well if he decides not to give his daughter in marriage. While neither is sin, it is a matter of what is good and what is better. Second, the same applies to a woman who is now single because she has lost her husband (7:39–40). She is free to marry or to remain single, but the latter was preferable. The goal is to promote the condition in which the greatest service to the Lord might be rendered.

Paul next answered questions regarding certain aspects of **worship** (8:1–11:34). In this third area of questions, Paul addressed items related to worship: food offered to idols and the sharing in pagan festivals (8:1–11:1), the wearing of a head covering by women (11:2–16), and their approach to the Lord's Supper (11:17–34). Central to all of these topics is the theme of submission of self for a higher good of others.

In regard to **eating meat offered to idols** (8:1–13), Paul stressed that knowing your freedoms can have the impact of puffing up the one who claims freedom, but love has an impact on the one loved (8:1). Paul acknowledged that idols were not real gods; there is only one true God in heaven. Some who had come out of an idol-worshipping background may not have that understanding. So Paul pointed out that the strong can sin against the weak by indiscriminately using their freedom with the result of wounding the conscience of the weak. Ultimately one believer's freedom destroys the life of the weaker believer. Those who know truth must limit their freedom so as not to cause the weaker brother to stumble.

A **positive illustration** came from Paul's own life (9:1–27). As an apostle he had all the rights of apostleship including the right to be supported by those whom he served. Abstaining from those rights, Paul became a slave to any and all that he might win some for Christ. The ministry was the challenge; and, like an athlete, exercising self-control lest he be disqualified in the race and lose reward, he ran to win the prize.

A training track for foot racing at Olympia. Paul used running as an illustration of Christian endurance.

Greek Highlight

Resurrection. Greek ἀνάστασις (*anastasis*). The Greek noun *anastasis* is derived from the verb *anistemi*, meaning literally *to stand up* and then by extension *to rise up*. Both words could be used metaphorically. The word *anastasis* was common in the ancient Greek world; but it rarely referred to the resurrection of the dead, which is the dominant meaning of its occurrences in the NT. Two major events are described with the word *anastais* in the NT: the physical, bodily resurrection of Jesus in the past (Rom 1:4; 1 Cor 15:12–13), and the physical, bodily resurrection of believers in the future (John 5:29; 11:24–25; 1 Cor 15:42; Phil 3:11; Rev 20:5–6). The physical, bodily resurrection of Jesus Christ distinguishes the message of Christianity among all other belief systems. Thus, it is incumbent upon every person to accept the resurrection of Jesus Christ as fact in order to be truly "saved" (Rom 10:9).

Israel was a negative illustration (10:1–22). Israel had tremendous advantages and privilege but disqualified themselves by their indulgent, immoral, idolatrous behavior and so died in the wilderness. **Temptation** is common to all; but while those who are self-reliant and proud can quickly fall, those who depend on God's help and guidance will find their way to success. The application is made to the Corinthians. To participate in the pagan feasts was to share in the pagan's focus of the feast, and in attempting to share in the things of the Lord along with the things of demons, the believer provoked the Lord to jealousy.

Having argued for the need to curtail **Christian liberty** and having shown the danger of abusing liberty by indulgence, Paul came back to the matter of the impact of liberties on others (10:23–11:1). While all things are lawful, not all things are profitable or edifying. Believers may exercise their freedoms on their own, but when those freedoms might impact a weaker brother or an unbeliever, they need to be given up for the sake of the others. The goal in life is to do everything for the glory of God giving no offense to anyone—Jew, Gentile, or believer. In summary, Paul encouraged them to be imitators of himself, as he was an imitator of Christ.

The next issue was **head coverings** for women in worship (11:2–16). Commending the readers for remembering the things he taught, Paul gave further theological teaching behind the tradition. The divine order, as it was reflected in culture, was the first reason women should demonstrate submission by a head covering (11:3–6). Then he mentioned the order of creation (11:7–9), the observing angels (11:10–12), nature (11:13–15), and the fact that it was a recognized custom in the other churches (11:16). Paul commended them for something they were already doing. He spoke of it as something that "should" happen (11:10) and something that was "proper" for the women to do (11:13), but it was still a matter of **voluntary submission**. Paul's theme was that believers subordinate their freedoms and rights in order to lift another up. For the woman a head covering lifted up her husband as the head of their home and lifted up God as the Head of all.

In addressing the question of worship, Paul did not commend the Corinthians but rebuked them in their practice of observing the Lord's Supper (11:17–34). Their behavior was the exact opposite of the spirit of selflessness which he was trying to communicate. It was a glaring contrast to the act of our Lord in His sacrificial death that was memorialized in the Lord's Supper. Their current practice resulted in divisions instead of unity because of their self-serving behavior in the face of obvious needs in others. Instead of sacrificing for others, they were despising some church members and shaming those with needs. As a correction Paul rehearsed the pattern and **instruction for the Lord's Supper**, beginning with the night in which Jesus was betrayed (11:23–26). The elements of the Supper reflect Jesus' sacrificial death, and participation in the Supper proclaims that selfless act. Those who eat or drink in an unworthy manner are guilty of the sin of self-centered gratification, the sin which caused Judas to betray Jesus (11:27–34). Everyone should **examine his or her attitudes** before eating and drinking. Those who do not repent of such attitudes invite the Lord's discipline upon themselves. In keeping with the spirit of the sacrifice of our Lord, those who come together to celebrate the Lord's Supper should mutually submit to the needs of others.

Finally, Paul answered questions regarding key theological topics (12:1–15:58). The next section of the letter covered spiritual gifts (12:1–14:40) and the matter of resurrection (15:1–58). In the area of **spiritual gifts**, the emphasis again pointed away from self to a ministry to others. There may be many kinds of spiritual gifts, but they

Corinthian canal. Nero brought 6,000 Galilean slaves to work on the canal, but the project stopped at his death. The canal—four miles long and seventy-five feet wide—was completed between 1882 and 1893 and connects the Gulf of Corinth with the Aegean.

all come from the Holy Spirit as a common source, with a common purpose in serving the whole body. All believers have been baptized into the one body of Christ, the Church. Like the members of the human body, each person has his or her own role, and all are interdependent on the proper working of individual members. Paul moved the readers from a self-centered point of view to see themselves as part of a larger whole. Rather than being an end in themselves, they minister with others for a much larger goal. The fulfillment of individual roles by themselves will not lead to divisions within the body. Self-centeredness disrupts the smooth operation of the whole. The answer to that problem is Christlike love.

Almost as a parenthetical section, Paul moved from spiritual gifts to a focus on love which is something better (12:31b–13:13). Without love (*agapē*), spiritual gifts, as important as they are, have no value. In a brief, poetic section, Paul described love in action (13:4–7). In contrast to spiritual gifts, love is permanent. The need for gifts will pass away some day, but love will always be present. Pratt observes: "When Christ returns, there will be no need for prophecy, tongues, or the limited knowledge the church gains in this world. All these gifts only provide glimpses and foreshadows of the perfection that will come."[3] As in the movement from childhood to maturity, or moving from a reflection in a mirror to the real person, the Corinthians needed to move from what seemed important now to seeing the bigger picture: "As their church struggled in its worship, especially in the practice of prophecy and tongues, what was its highest priority? Paul's position was plain. The highest virtue for believers to pursue was to love one another."[4]

1 Corinthians 13:4–8

Love is patient;
love is kind;
Love does not envy;
is not boastful; is not conceited;
does not act improperly;
is not selfish; is not provoked;
does not keep a record of wrongs;
finds no joy in unrighteousness,
but rejoices in the truth;
bears all things, believes all things,
hopes all things, endures all things.
Love never ends.

Having pointed out the superiority of love, Paul now went back to the issue of **spiritual gifts** and demonstrated how his counsel applied (14:1–40). Taking the two gifts of tongues and prophecy as examples, Paul showed how the priority must be on ministry to others. Prophecy was to be preferred over tongues because of its value in communicating truth to edify others whereas tongues might end up with a limited audience. Orderliness was to prevail in order to provide the best atmosphere for others to hear and learn. The goal was to serve the greater body, not to emphasize individualism.

The Purpose for Tongues

The purpose of tongues, speaking in *other languages*, is given in 1 Cor 14:20–22. In 14:22, Paul said tongues were a sign for unbelievers; the gift of prophecy was for believers. In 14:21, Paul quoted from Isa 28:11, identifying the sign as given to "these people," a reference to the Jews, who were warned by Moses not to reject God's message (Deut 28:49). In his Pentecost speech in Acts 2:40, Peter responded to the question about the meaning of tongues (2:12), warning the assembled Jews to change their minds about Jesus and so "be saved from this corrupt generation!" God was going to bring judgment on the generation who had killed the Messiah. That judgment came from the Romans in AD 70 (see also Matt 23:34–39). Speaking in tongues was a warning to unbelieving Israel at Pentecost and an affirmation of the promise of Joel 2:28–29.

The Corinthian church was using tongues in the assembly of believers. Paul wrote to the Corinthians that, since tongues were for unbelievers, there was a better gift to use in the church, that of prophecy, or preaching in a known language (14:6–19). Of greater value than both of those gifts, however, was the exercise of Christlike love (13:1–2).

V. Teaching: "I Tell You a Mystery" (1 Corinthians 15:1–16:12)

The second theological topic was that of the **resurrection** (15:1–58). Some of the readers believed in Christ's resurrection but not in the resurrection of believers (cf. 15:12–13). To refute that idea, Paul presented the importance of **Christ's resurrection** in the understanding of the gospel message (15:1–11). Jesus died, was buried, and was raised on the third day; that is the gospel message. Numerous resurrection appearances, including one to Paul (cf. 1 Cor 15:8), testify that Jesus is alive.

But if some argue that there is no resurrection, then Christ was not raised either; and all the benefits of His resurrection are lost (15:12–34). However, since His resurrection is valid, based on eyewitness accounts, then **our resurrection** is a certainty as well. The fact that we will be raised should give motivation to endure suffering in ministry. Believers should separate from evil company that denies the resurrection and instead demonstrate a different lifestyle for those who do not know God (15:33–34).

With the fact of our resurrection established, Paul moved to the type of body we would have in the resurrection (15:35–49). Our body here in this life, which is from Adam and suited for this life, will be exchanged for a **new body**, suited for heaven, in the image of Christ. Whether we are raptured or die first, all believers will be changed from corruptible mortals to being clothed with incorruptible immortality. Then the final victory over death will be accomplished. The certainty of all this should motivate believers to selfless, steadfast, immovable service for their Lord (15:58).

Last, Paul answered final questions regarding the **collection** for the church in Jerusalem and the timing of a visit by Apollos (16:1–12). The fifth question was in regard to the collection Paul was taking up for the poor in the church in Jerusalem. Promoting selfless giving, Paul encouraged them to make the decision on a proportionate amount to give and then follow through so the offering would be ready when he came. Demonstrating his own selfless choices over his personal plans to come and spend time with them, Paul informed the Corinthians that there was an open door for service in Ephesus, and even if there were adversaries, he must stay and minister for the present.

The final question focused on the itinerary of Apollos who had been mentioned several times earlier in the letter (1:12; 3:4–6,22; 4:6). Paul's urging of Apollos to go to Corinth and Apollos's desire not to go at that time might be an indication to the Corinthians that neither of them had a desire to be treated as "party leaders" by the church. Each was involved in **ministry** to other believers, an example the Corinthians should follow themselves.

VI. Final Exhortations, Greetings, and a Benediction (1 Corinthians 16:13–24)

In the closing verses Paul encouraged the readers to a theological and spiritual **maturity** governed by love (16:13–14). He identified other servants of God to whom they needed to be in subjection, a direct counter to the partisan approach he had heard was present in them. After exchanging greetings, Paul gave one last instruction: "If anyone does not love the Lord, a curse be on him" (16:22). The encouragement here was toward devotion to the Lord, attached to a condemnation for those who live differently. It is followed with *"Maranatha!"* That is, "Lord, come!"

CONCLUSION

In this first letter to the Corinthians, Paul wrote to a church with **many problems and questions**. At the bottom of all the problems was a self-serving, indulgent attitude in contrast to the death of Christ as a self-giving sacrifice for the sin of others. Paul wrote to this group, addressing their errors, both in theology and in practice.

In the letter Paul led the readers away from personal gratification to a selfless love of others in the context of **service to God**. Their selfish attitudes had led them to focus on their immediate wants, whereas Paul led them to look at a bigger picture, beyond their own resurrection to the receiving of a glorified body in the image of their Lord. Living in light of this big picture and the final goal should influence any short-range goals of daily life.

Study Questions

1. Who are the four people Paul identified in 2:14–3:4, and what characteristics does Paul give for each?
2. What is the emphasis that Paul gave to the use of our bodies? How does that relate to the theme in the book of self-sacrificial service to others?
3. In 8:1–11:34, Paul addresses topics of Christian liberty and the exercise of our rights. How does this compare with our cultural view of exercising our rights and freedoms?
4. What guidelines did Paul suggest regarding the use of spiritual gifts?
5. How does the description of love that Paul gave in chap. 13 relate to the theme of the book and the need for self-sacrificing service to others?

For Further Reading

Barrett, C. K. *The First Epistle to the Corinthians.* New York: Harper & Row, 1968.

Blomberg, Craig. *1 Corinthians.* NIVAC. Grand Rapids: Zondervan, 1995.

Hawthorne, Gerald F., and Ralph P Martin, eds. *Dictionary of Paul and His Letters.* Downers Grove: IVP, 1993.

Lowery, David K. "1 Corinthians." *BKCNT.* Edited by John F. Walvoord and Roy B. Zuck. Wheaton: Victor, 1983.

Mitchell, Dan. *First Corinthians: Christianity in a Hostile Culture.* Chattanooga: AMG Publishers, 2004.

Pratt, Richard, Jr. *1 & 2 Corinthians.* HNTC 7. Nashville: B&H, 2000.

ENDNOTES

1. S. J. Hafemann, "Corinthians, Letters to the," in *Dictionary of Paul and His Letters,* ed. Gerald F. Hawthorne and Ralph P Martin (Downers Grove: IVP, 1993), 175. Paul also names Sosthenes as a coauthor. This may be the same Sosthenes mentioned in Acts 18:17.

2. Outline based on D. Mitchell, *First Corinthians: Christianity in a Hostile Culture* (Chattanooga: AMG Publishers, 2004), ix–x.

3. Richard Pratt Jr., *1 & 2 Corinthians,* HNTC 7 (Nashville: B&H, 2000), 234.

4. Ibid., 236.

Chapter 12

2 CORINTHIANS
Power in Weakness

This is the second letter in existence that Paul wrote to the Corinthian believers. This letter, 2 Corinthians, is **the most personal** of all Paul's letters as he reveals his own heart for this church and his ministry in general. This is a realistic letter about the ministry. It tells of the highs and lows, the joys and struggles, the privileges and sufferings of the minister. The frailty of the minister, however, is more than matched by the power of God.

Key Facts	
Author:	Paul and Timothy
Recipient:	The church at Corinth
Where Written:	Macedonia
Date:	AD 56
Key Words:	Ministry (Gk. *diakonia*) and glory (Gk. *doxa*)
Key Verse:	"Now we have this treasure in clay jars, so that this extraordinary power may be from God and not from us" (4:7).

AUTHOR

The salutation in 1:1 and a personal reference in 10:1 identify Paul as the author of this letter. Along with 1 Corinthians, the historical connections with Acts and the literary evidence easily fit Paul as the author. Since the second century, scholars have considered 2 Corinthians to be Pauline in authorship.[1] Most of the current scholarly debate regards the *unity* of the original composition (especially 6:14–7:1). Regardless, most still hold that Paul himself was the original author.[2]

RECIPIENTS

The book is addressed to "God's church at Corinth" (1:1; see 1 Cor 1:2). Paul adds here, "with all the saints who are throughout Achaia." Paul spent a year and a half in

Corinth during his first missionary journey (Acts 18:11) and another three months on his third journey (Acts 20:3). Luke's description of the third journey used the broader area descriptions of **Achaia** (Acts 18:21) and Greece (Acts 20:2), indicating Paul ministered outside the bounds of Corinth as well. Therefore, Paul intended this letter to be **circulated** throughout the area.[3]

OCCASION AND DATE

Paul wrote this letter about six months after he wrote 1 Corinthians while still on his third missionary journey somewhere in Macedonia. The date was in the **fall of AD 56.** After the visits and letters mentioned in the introduction to 1 Corinthians, Paul continued his contact with the church. The problems in the church were not resolved, so Paul made a second visit to Corinth from Ephesus, mentioned in 2 Cor 2:1–2 as a visit that caused them sorrow. Paul was challenged by some in the church when he arrived (2:5–8; 7:12).

When he returned to Ephesus, Paul wrote another letter, written with many tears "out of an extremely troubled and anguished heart" (2:4), and sent it with Titus to the Corinthian church. This third letter, like the first, is lost to us. At this point a disturbance in Ephesus occurred and Paul left for Troas (Acts 19:23–20:1). He was so anxious, however, over the response of the Corinthian church and the delayed return of Titus that even though he had an open door for ministry in Troas, he proceeded into Macedonia, hoping to find Titus (2:12–13). Somewhere in Macedonia, Paul met Titus who gave him the good news that the Corinthian church had responded favorably (7:5–7). With that news Paul wrote 2 Corinthians, his fourth letter to them. Shortly after that, Paul proceeded to visit them again for three months, his third visit (Acts 20:2–3; cf. 2 Cor 12:14; 13:1–2).

The Identity of Paul's Opponents

Paul's opponents in 1 and 2 Corinthians are different. In 1 Corinthians the people were divided against themselves and Paul. There is no mention of false teachers (1:10–17). Paul attempted to get the believers to work together on a common goal. In 2 Corinthians false teachers had come into the assembly denying Paul's apostleship. Thus Paul needed to **defend his apostleship** against them (11:4–5,12–13; 12:11).

GENRE AND STRUCTURE

Second Corinthians is **a pastoral letter** from Paul to the church in Corinth. It is the most personal letter of all Paul's letters. Following the introduction (1:1–11), Paul went immediately into a lengthy personal section giving an inside view of the ministry, centered on the anxiety he experienced when Titus did not come (1:12–7:16). He ended on a note of confidence when Paul met up with Titus. Paul encouraged the Corinthians to follow through on the collection they promised to take for the poor in

Jerusalem (8:1–9:15). The final section of the letter addressed those who still doubted his position as an apostle (10:1–13:10). Paul demonstrated that he was a true apostle and that God was working through him. He closed with instructions concerning preparation for his coming visit (13:11–14).

Outline

 I. Introduction (2 Corinthians 1:1–11)
 II. Personal Defense (2 Corinthians 1:12–7:16)
  A. Explanation of Paul's Previous Plans (1:12–2:13)
  B. Paul's Inside Perspective on the Gospel Ministry (2:14–6:10)
  C. Paul's Relationship with the Corinthians (6:11–7:16)
 III. Practical Needs (2 Corinthians 8:1–9:15)
 IV. Powerful Appeal (2 Corinthians 10:1–13:10)
 V. Conclusion (2 Corinthians 13:11–14)

MESSAGE

The message of 2 Corinthians is that the gospel ministry is carried out by the power of God through frail ministers. The key verse brings the theme to a climax as Paul related his own great inadequacy because of his physical limitations and **God's adequacy and power** through Paul's frailty. In a climatic statement Paul wrote, "But He said to me, 'My grace is sufficient for you, for power is perfected in weakness.'

The imposing rocky mass of the Acrocorinth.

Therefore, I will most gladly boast all the more about my weaknesses, so that Christ's power may reside in me" (12:9). This letter is an illustration of the power of God working in the life of Paul and the Corinthian church even though Paul was weak and frail yet powerful in the message of God.

I. Introduction (2 Corinthians 1:1–11)

Paul introduced himself as "an apostle of Christ Jesus by God's will" (1:1). He was indeed an apostle, but it was by the will of God, not by his own doing. As was his custom, Paul included a thanksgiving: he blessed God as "the God of all comfort" (1:3–11). In light of all the struggles he would talk about in this letter, he told the Corinthians that God is the one who **brings comfort out of affliction**. The reason God does so is that the comforted one might be a comfort to others in turn, the very thing Paul wanted to do in this letter. A specific incident in Paul's life brought him close to death. God had allowed this incident to motivate Paul to trust in God alone and not in himself (1:9). With this hope God rescued him, and Paul thanked the readers for being a part of this as they prayed for him. In this little scenario Paul admitted that he was weak and must trust God alone for the accomplishment of anything in ministry.

Greek Highlight

Counselor. Greek παράκλητος **(paraklētos)** The Greek word *parakletos* is derived from the verb *parakaleo* (lit. *to call alongside*; basically *to comfort, counsel, exhort*). It is also related to the noun *paraklesis* (comfort, exhortation). Both are much more common than *parakletos* but do not occur in John's writings, while *parakletos* occurs only in John's writings. In all four occurrences of *parakletos* in John's Gospel, Jesus used the term to refer to the Holy Spirit as our Counselor. The idea is that the Spirit comes alongside to aid us in the tasks Jesus gave us as His disciples. Thus, when translating its verbal form (*parakaleo*), the Holman Christian Study Bible does well in bringing out the full essence of the verb by using words like *encourage* (2 Cor 13:11), *comfort* (2 Cor 7:6–7,13), *plead* (2 Cor 12:8), or *urge* (2 Cor 9:5; 12:18). The believer should be encouraged that the One who serves as our Advocate (Jesus Christ in 1 John 2:1) and our *Counselor* (Holy Spirit in John 14:16) empowers us to offer the same impactful encouragement to other believers (2 Cor 7:6–7).

II. Personal Defense (2 Corinthians 1:12–7:16)

As he began the body of his letter, Paul allowed the readers to see **his vulnerability**. He told them why some of his plans changed, revealing his own anxiety over the delay of Titus with news from them (1:12–2:13). He interrupted this story with a lengthy aside, giving an inside perspective on the minister who is God's vessel (2:14–6:10). Finally, he returned to the story, letting them know what happened when Titus came with the news of their response (6:11–7:16).

The excavations of Corinth showing the shops in the agora.

A. Explanation of Paul's Previous Plans (1:12–2:13)

With regard to changes in Paul's plans, he wanted them to know that he had a proud confidence in his clear conscience. His conduct in the world and especially toward them had been in holiness and godly sincerity, not in the wisdom of the world. There was no validity to the charges that Paul was unpredictable and could not be trusted.

The first change grew out of his **original plan** to visit the Corinthians. He gave the detail of that plan and assured them that his intentions were sincere (1:17–22). The reason he did not come that way was so that he might not come to them in sorrow again. He wanted his next visit to be a joyful one. Instead, he wrote to them, sending Titus with the letter to show his love for them (1:23–2:4).

The second issue involved a **person** who had previously offended the church or Paul, or both (2:5–11). The church had punished the man. Now, since the man had repented, they should forgive him, comfort him, and reaffirm their love for him. Paul had forgiven the man, and so should they. The reason for the change was that they might not give an advantage to Satan who might use this as a weapon to defeat the church.

Finally, Paul explained how he ended up going from Ephesus to Troas and up into Macedonia (2:12–13). First, he had gone to Troas for **the sake of the gospel** and found an open door for ministry there. But he was so concerned for Titus and the news he heard from Corinth that he left Troas and went to Macedonia to try to find him. Paul described what it is like to be a minister for God, demonstrating his vulnerability and humanity.

B. Paul's Inside Perspective on the Gospel Ministry (2:14–6:10)

After mentioning the coming of Titus in 2:12–13, Paul wrote a **lengthy digression** about the ministry, picking up the story of Titus again in 7:5. In this digression Paul told what it was like to be the vessel God uses.

First, the **ministry is an opportunity** to display the glory of God (2:14–4:6). The word "glory" is a key word in this section, occurring 15 times. The glory of the ministry is compared to a glorious Roman triumphal procession where Christ is the conquering Ruler and His ministers are part of the procession (2:14–17). As they walk in the procession, the minister is an aroma of life to those who believe and an aroma of death to those who will not believe. Paul acknowledged that the minister is not competent in himself for such a powerful role. Unlike many others, the minister does not "market God's message for profit," but instead, he preaches it sincerely with accountability to God.

The Roman Triumphal Procession

Paul borrowed that picture of the Roman triumph and **applied** it to Christian workers led in triumph with Christ. The aroma of the knowledge of Christ is life to other believers, but it is the smell of death to those who reject Christ. Freeman and Chadwick note:

> A Roman military triumphal procession was one of the grandest spectacles of ancient times. It was granted to a conqueror only when certain conditions had been fully complied with. . . . When the day arrived the people crowded the streets and filled every place from which a good view of the procession could be obtained. . . . Fragrant odors from burning spices were profusely scattered through the temples and along the streets, filling the air with perfume. In the procession were the senate and chief citizens of the state, who by their presence honored the conqueror. . . . The general in whose honor the triumph was decreed rode in a chariot that was of peculiar form and drawn by four horses.[4]

Part of the glory of the ministry is reflected by those who receive it (3:1–3). Their **changed lives** demonstrate the impact of the gospel message as they become living letters of commendation, testimonies of God living in them.

Returning to the earlier statement about not being competent (2:16), Paul stated that the **competency** of the minister comes from God, making him competent as a servant of a new covenant (3:4–18). In a series of contrasts, Paul showed how the new covenant ministry has a far greater glory than the old covenant. The old was glorious but fading, like the face of Moses (Exod 34:29–35); the new is only increasing in glory as we are changed to become more and more like the Lord Himself.

Having such a glorious new covenant ministry means that the minister does not lose heart in the face of obstacles (4:1–6). Neither does he resort to deceptive tactics to sell the word of God. Those who do not accept the message are those who have been blinded by the god of this world. What is more, the minister does not preach himself, but he preaches **Jesus Christ as Lord**. In fact, the minister is simply one who has had the glorious light shine into his own heart.

Second, the minister accepts his weakness because of the opportunities it affords (4:7–5:10). The **weakness** of the minister is seen in contrast to the glory of the new covenant ministry. He is the vehicle for showing off the power of God (4:7–15). In a graphic word picture, Paul compared himself to a clay jar, out of which shines the "light of the knowledge of God's glory in the face of Jesus Christ" (4:6). The weakness of the instrument is intended to demonstrate a contrast to **the power and glory of God** and His message.

The struggles of the minister show off the life of Jesus in him (4:8–12). Also, the impact of the message gives hope in affliction (4:13–18). The minister believes the message he preaches and so is willing to endure whatever comes so that the message might spread to more people. He knows that the glory to come makes this present world's suffering appears to be only

Looking through a gate into the ancient city of Corinth.

a "momentary light affliction" (4:17). With a perspective on the **eternal**, not the temporal, Paul's preference is to be at home with the Lord rather than to be present in this body (5:1–10). The goal is to please Christ, whether here or there, because we know that believers will finally appear before the judgment seat of Christ.

Third, the minister endures hardship because of the message of the ministry (5:11–6:10). Paul wanted the Corinthians to understand his motivations of ministry in view of standing one day before the judgment seat (*bema*) of Christ (5:11–13). Knowing **the fear of God** moves the minister to persuade unsaved people to become Christians. On the one hand, it might sound like Paul was justifying himself, but he was only sharing this information about his ministry in order that they might answer his critics. He did not want his comments to be taken as the type of boasting that characterized his opponents. On the other hand, understanding the love of God, as demonstrated by the substitutionary death of Christ, produces a life that is no longer lived for self but for Christ (5:14–15). Those who are in Christ are new creatures; the old is gone. The God who has reconciled us to Himself has given us a ministry as **ambassadors of reconciliation**, motivating others into that same relationship (5:16–6:2). The minister, in response, endures many hardships in order not to discredit the ministry (6:3–10).

Throughout this lengthy digression Paul has pictured the **extremes of the ministry**. On the one hand, it is the glory of walking in the triumphal procession of Christ and of being an ambassador for Him. On the other hand are the frailty of the messenger and the difficulties of the ministry. The ministry is a struggle that makes incredible demands on the minister and takes him close to, if not into, death. Paul gave them this perspective so they could evaluate both him and the false teachers. The self-serving boasting of the false teachers did not fit this picture.

The bema or judgment seat at Corinth.

C. Paul's Relationship with the Corinthians (6:11–7:16)

Paul made application to the Corinthians. Now that Paul had spoken openly to the Corinthians, he invited them to be open with him (6:11–13). Such a relationship can only be maintained on **mutually shared grounds** (6:14–7:1). There is no common relationship between the things of God and the things of Satan. They cannot attempt to walk with Paul and also attempt to walk with these false teachers, whom he will later describe as servants of Satan (11:13–15). The relationship with another worker must be based on common separation from sin and holy living: "What does a believer have in common with an unbeliever?" (6:15). If they were going to be sharers with Paul in the ministry, they would need to separate themselves from these false teachers. Paul was confident they would do so.

Returning to the story about Titus, Paul explained that he had been at one of those low points in the ministry as he came into Macedonia. But God lifted him up by the coming of Titus and the news of the Corinthians' response, giving him joy and comfort (7:2–16). He rejoiced because their grieving according to the will of God produced a godly repentance. He also rejoiced because of a positive impact on Titus. Finally, Paul also rejoiced in his **renewed confidence** in them (7:16). With this matter now cleared, Paul turned to the mutual ministry in which they were both engaged: the offering for Jerusalem.

III. Practical Needs (2 Corinthians 8:1–9:15)

Paul spent the next two chapters emphasizing the practical needs of ministries to others. He especially focused on the **collection** for the church at Jerusalem. Paul urged the readers to follow through on their earlier commitment to give (8:1–15). Being in Macedonia, Paul told the Corinthians that the Macedonians were giving a contribution as well (8:1–5). In fact, they had gone beyond their ability to give, making it a **sacrificial gift**. Here were people ministering out of their weakness—an example of what he had just written about in this letter. In light of this, Paul urged the Corinthians to follow through on their previous commitments after the example of Christ's own giving of Himself (8:6–12). Sharing their abundance would bring equality as the needs of others were met (8:13–15).

Wanting to do "what is right, not only before the Lord but also before men" (8:21), Paul gave **detailed instructions** as to how the offering was to be taken (8:16–9:5). A delegation of three men was to handle the money as a precaution against any discredit in the administration of the gift (8:16–24). Moreover, the men had been sent on ahead to encourage the collection of the gift so that no one would be embarrassed by not being ready when Paul's delegation arrived. Paul was trying to avoid having the Macedonians, who were inspired by the desire of the Corinthians, disillusioned by failure of the Corinthians to follow through (9:1–5).

When the people in the ministry live out their commitments, the cheerful giver himself will be enriched in everything for his liberality, the needs of the saints will be met, and God will be praised (9:6–15).

Panorama from atop ancient Corinth. Roman walls are joined with walls from the period of the Crusades.

Paul's Thorn in the Flesh

A "thorn in the flesh" is an idiom for something painful (e.g., Num 33:55; Ezek 28:24). There are various interpretations for Paul's "thorn in the flesh." Many take this to be a physical ailment Paul experienced (see Gal 4:13–15). Others think it might have been continuing persecution from his enemies (see 2 Cor 12:10). Paul viewed whatever it was as a weakness, designed to keep him humble. He was content because it allowed the power of God to reside in him.

IV. Powerful Appeal (2 Corinthians 10:1–13:10)

Finally, Paul responded to those who criticized his apostleship. Turning to those who had attempted to discredit his ministry and apostleship, Paul emphasized his theme: the vessel is weak so that the power of God might be seen. First, he laid down a challenge to those who opposed him, challenging their perspective (10:1–18). They looked at the weak side of Paul, but he had divinely powerful weapons since he was acting on Christ's behalf (10:1–6). Paul warned them against **judging outward appearances** (10:7–12). He pointed out that his boasting centered on what God had chosen to do through him (10:13–18). He had not taken over another's territory, but his enemies were in the territory where Paul brought the gospel message.

Paul used the same technique of boasting the opponents had used (11:1–12:13). He joined his opponents in boasting, but he focused on his own weaknesses with a goal of showing how **the power of God** works through a weak vessel. The reason for Paul's boasting, even though it was foolishness, was because of his godly jealousy over them. He wanted to present them to Christ as a pure virgin, but he feared that Satan would deceive their minds and lead them astray from Christ, as evidenced that some were already following preachers with other messages. While unskilled in speech, his knowledge demonstrated he was still on the level of the most prominent apostles (11:1–6).

Paul used the financial arrangement of preachers who proclaimed the gospel to them. These men who were attacking Paul took financial support for their work; therefore they were not on the same basis with Paul since he ministered to the Corinthians at no charge. These men were **false apostles** who were operating under a disguise, just as Satan himself does (11:7–15).

Although boasting was foolishness, it was a technique they understood (11:16–21). Beginning with his own Jewish roots, Paul rehearsed a list of his sufferings, demonstrating his commitment as a servant of Christ (11:22–33). Paul could also boast in visions he saw, but since no one could verify them, he returned to his obvious weaknesses (12:1–6). To keep him from exalting himself, a **thorn in the flesh** was given to him to keep him humble. God refused to take the cause of his suffering away, and Paul was content with that because it allowed the power of God to reside in him (12:7–10). In conclusion, they should have been commending Paul as an apostle rather than challenging him. Paul had displayed signs, wonders, and miracles among them to demonstrate his apostleship (12:11–13).

Paul prepared them for his **planned third visit** (12:14–13:10). He assured them that he would not be a financial burden to them when he came. Like a parent, he would rather be spent for them than be a burden to them. Neither he nor Titus had taken advantage of them financially (12:14–18).

Paul also made clear that his real reason for writing was not to defend himself but to **build up his readers** by teaching them the biblical role of the ministry and the minister. He feared that he might find sin and a lack of repentance when he came (12:19–21). If so, there would be a need for discipline (13:1–4). Instead, Paul challenged the Corinthians to examine their behavior to see if they were living according to the faith (13:5–10).

V. Conclusion

In his brief conclusion (13:11–14), Paul exhorted his readers to respond maturely, giving the promise of God's love and peace. He exchanged greetings and closed with a benediction.

CONCLUSION

Paul built three main sections around his **theme of ministry** and the minister. First, affliction is shared by those who minister, so that they do not trust in themselves but in God. On the one hand, the ministry is like walking in a Roman triumphal procession. On the other hand, the minister is a fragile clay jar. He is willing to endure the afflictions that come because of the opportunities that ministry affords. The **fear of God** motivates the minister against discrediting the ministry. The **love of God** gives an opportunity to be an ambassador of the reconciliation for God with sinners.

Second, not wanting the Corinthians to discredit their ministry, Paul urged them to follow through on their previous commitment to give an offering. The results would impact both the giver and the recipient and bring praise to God.

Third, Paul displayed his own weaknesses in order that **the power of God** might be seen through him. Although Paul boasted in order to refute those who opposed him, he revealed his sufferings and weaknesses to demonstrate God's power through him to accomplish his ministry. Paul's hope was that the Corinthians might learn from this letter, reject the false apostles, and correct their error so that when he came he would see them living out the faith they professed.

Study Questions

1. Paul speaks of the inadequacy of the one who ministers. In what ways is the minister not competent for the ministry?
2. What is the glory of ministry that Paul explains in this letter?
3. What principles for financial stewardship can be drawn from chaps. 8–9?
4. Paul uses the root for the words "to boast" or "boasting" 13 times in chaps. 11–12. However, he writes that his boasting is in his weaknesses, not in his strengths. Make a list of the weaknesses Paul mentions in these two chapters. What can we learn about ministry from this list?
5. Satan is mentioned several times in this book (2:10–11; 10:4–5; 11:3,13–15; 12:7–9). What can we learn from these passages about Satan's tactics and our victory?

For Further Reading

Barrett, C. K. *The Second Epistle to the Corinthians*. New York: Harper & Row, 1973.

Garland, David E. *2 Corinthians*. NAC. Nashville: B&H, 1999.

Harris, Murray J. *The Second Epistle to the Corinthians*. NIGTC. Grand Rapids: Eerdmans, 2005.

Hughes, Philip E. *Paul's Second Epistle to the Corinthians*. NICNT. Grand Rapids: Eerdmans, 1975.

Lowery, David K. "2 Corinthians." *BKCNT*. Edited by John F. Walvoord and Roy B. Zuck. Wheaton: Victor, 1983.

Mitchell, Dan. *Second Corinthians: Grace Under Siege*. Chattanooga, AMG Publishers, 2008.

ENDNOTES

1. S. J. Hafemann, "Corinthians, Letters to the," in *Dictionary of Paul and His Letters*, ed. Gerald F. Hawthorne and Ralph P Martin (Downers Grove: IVP, 1993), 175.

2. See D. Mitchell, *Second Corinthians: Grace Under Seige* (Chattanooga, AMG Publishers, 2008).

3. See chap. 1, "How We Got the New Testament."

4. James M. Freeman and Harold J. Chadwick, *Manners and Customs of the Bible*, rev. ed. (North Brunswick, NJ: Bridge-Logos, 1998), 541–42.

Chapter 13

GALATIANS
By Grace through Faith

Paul writes with holy indignation over the news that the Galatians were being influenced by Judaizers who would have Gentile believers circumcised and live by the law. Because the Judaizers had attacked Paul's credentials as an apostle, he defends himself with proof of divine apostolic authority. Paul answers **the Judaizers** by stating Christian believers would be put in bondage and could never keep the law, just as no Jew had ever kept the law. He answers with sound doctrinal explanations and biblical illustrations and finally gives some practical exhortations for Christian living.

Key Facts	
Author:	The apostle Paul
Recipients:	Churches in the Roman province of Galatia
Where Written:	Unknown
Date:	About AD 49
Key Word:	Law (*nomos*)
Key Verse:	"We . . . know that no one is justified by the works of the law but by faith in Jesus Christ. And we have believed in Christ Jesus, so that we might be justified by faith in Christ and not by the works of the law, because by the works of the law no human being will be justified" (2:15–16).

AUTHOR

The apostle Paul can be called the "**apostle of Christian liberty**." He argued strenuously that Gentile believers were free from the law of Moses. During the first missionary journey, Paul and Barnabas, about AD 47–48, evangelized and planted churches in four cities in the southern territory of Galatia—Antioch, Iconium, Lystra, and Derbe. There they preached in Jewish synagogues, then reached out to Gentiles who lived in the region. Paul and Barnabas were driven out of Antioch and Iconium by angry Jews and subsequently rejected by city officials in Lystra. In spite of persecution, Paul and Barnabas organized churches and appointed elders in each church on their way back through these four cities (Acts 14:23).

RECIPIENTS

Galatians can be termed the "Magna Carta of Christian Liberty." It states unequivocally that salvation is by **grace alone**, through **faith alone**, in **Christ alone**, without works of any kind. People that Paul had evangelized in the Roman province of Galatia on his first missionary journey were in danger of turning from pure faith in Christ to a works-based system of salvation. They were accepting the Jewish rite of circumcision as necessary for salvation. Here Paul counters that heresy.

The central part of Asia Minor, or present-day Turkey, is an agricultural region. In the several centuries before Christ, this area was in turmoil with various tribes seeking control through military conquest. The Celts, or Gauls as they were also called, were among these tribal groups. In the west they settled in France, sometimes referred to as Gaul. They also settled in Ireland and Scotland where they were known as the Celts and spread the Gaelic dialect. In the early third century BC, a group of these Celtic Gauls helped the king of Bithynia defend his territory, then conquered the area around Ankara, the present capital of Turkey situated on a central plateau. When the Romans invaded the area, these **Gaelic peoples** had their own kingdom until their leader Amytyas died in battle in 25 BC, just six years after Caesar Augustus became Roman emperor.[1] Rome then managed the territory as an imperial province, adding some land to the southern part of the province. Rome called this province Galatia after the people who lived there. The land area is about the size of the state of Utah or Kansas, or about

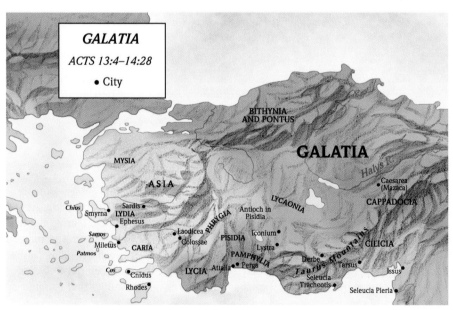

one-fourth of the land mass of the country of Turkey. Galatia was bordered by Pontus and Bithynia on the north, Cappadocia on the east, Cilicia and Pamphylia on the south, and Asia on the west. Galatia is mentioned six times in the New Testament.[2]

OCCASION AND DATE

Paul wrote Galatians **to counter the Judaizers**, a group of converted Jews who infiltrated the church and taught that one must keep the law of Moses in order to be saved. Paul wrote boldly and forcefully to argue for the freedom of the believer in Christ. In Paul's opinion Christian liberty hung in the balance not only for the Galatians but for all believers.

The question of when Galatians was written and to whom it was penned revolves around how the word "Galatians" was used in Gal 3:1. Does "Galatians" refer to the Gaulic tribesmen as an ethnic group, or is it a reference to those living in the Roman province called Galatia? The ethnic Gauls lived in the *northern* part of the Roman territory, but the cities Paul and Barnabas visited on their first missionary journey were located in the *southern* reaches of the province. Those who take the South Galatian view emphasize the fact that Barnabas is mentioned in the epistle to the Galatians, evidence that he had been there on the first missionary trip. But Barnabas did not accompany Paul on his second missionary journey. The second journey may have taken Paul and Silas into the northern part of the province according to Acts 16:6 which says, "They went through the region of Phrygia and Galatia."

If the South Galatian view is correct, the letter could have been written as early as **AD 49**, making it the first or earliest of Paul's epistles.[3] If the North Galatian view is correct, the letter must have been written after Paul and Silas toured that part of the province on their second missionary journey. The "Galatians" would be ethnic Gauls. Supporters of this view emphasize the Gauls' fickle character, which would have induced them to turn to Judaism after being converted to Christ. The date of writing would then be around **AD 55**.[4] However, neither view affects the basic meaning of the book.

In either case, Paul had heard of these believers' **departure from the pure gospel** he had preached to them. Since Paul could not soon return to this area, the situation was getting desperate. He wrote this brief letter of 148 verses with about 2,350 words. A letter this size might have required 9 to 16 separate pieces of papyrus written on one side each.[5]

GENRE AND STRUCTURE

The letter divides into **three major sections**: (1) a *personal* section (chaps. 1–2); (2) a *doctrinal* section (chaps. 3–4); and (3) a *practical* section (chaps. 5–6). The personal section contains units devoted to Paul's greeting and theme (1:1–9), his apostolic authority (1:10–17), his first visit to Jerusalem (1:18–24), his second visit to Jerusalem (2:1–10), and his rebuke of Peter at Antioch (2:11–21). The doctrinal section includes discussions of Paul's rebuke of the Galatians (3:1–14), the law and Abraham's covenant (3:15–22), the law and Christian faith (3:23–4:7), the folly of returning to the law

(4:8–20), and the allegory of Ishmael and Isaac (4:21–31). The concluding practical section discusses how to maintain Christian liberty (5:1–12), how to walk by the Spirit (5:13–26), how to serve others (6:1–10), and concluding remarks (6:11–18).

Outline

I. Personal Section (Galatians 1:1–2:21)
  A. Paul's Greeting and Theme (Galatians 1:1–9)
  B. Paul's Apostolic Authority (Galatians 1:10–17)
  C. Paul's First Visit to Jerusalem (Galatians 1:18–24)
  D. Paul's Second Visit to Jerusalem (Galatians 2:1–10)
  E. Paul's Rebuke of Peter at Antioch (Galatians 2:11–21)
II. Doctrinal Section (Galatians 3:1–4:31)
  A. Paul's Rebuke of the Galatians (Galatians 3:1–14)
  B. The Law and Abraham's Covenant (Galatians 3:15–22)
  C. The Law and Christian Faith (Galatians 3:23–4:7)
  D. The Folly of Returning to the Law (Galatians 4:8–20)
  E. The Allegory of Ishmael and Isaac (Galatians 4:21–31)
III. Practical Section (Galatians 5:1–6:18)
  A. Maintain Christian Liberty (Galatians 5:1–12)
  B. Walk by the Spirit (Galatians 5:13–26)
  C. Bear One Another's Burdens (Galatians 6:1–10)
  D. Concluding Remarks (Galatians 6:11–18)

MESSAGE

I. Personal Section (Galatians 1:1–2:21)

A. Paul's Greeting and Theme (Galatians 1:1–9)

In Paul's opening words (1:1–9), he refers to himself as an apostle of Christ and as such gives the basis for his authority to speak boldly for Christ. He addresses himself to "the churches of Galatia" (1:2), probably those he and Barnabas founded on their first missionary journey in Acts 13–14. Paul sends these believers grace and peace (1:3). **Grace** (Gk. *charis*) was a traditional Greek greeting but is heightened by the unmerited favor we have in Christ Jesus. **Peace** (Hb. *shalom*) was the traditional Hebrew greeting but is also enriched by the perfect peace we have with God through trusting Christ as our Savior. Paul omits any word of praise or thanks for these wayward saints. He even had praise for the Corinthians, despite their sin (1 Cor 1:4), but nothing good is said of the Galatians. Perhaps the sin of heresy is more serious than the sins of the flesh.

Greek Highlight

Grace. Greek χάρις (*charis*) The Greek noun *charis* refers to an unmerited favorable disposition toward someone or something. In the NT, *charis* is commonly used in relation to salvation, especially in Paul's writings. Paul used *charis* to explain that salvation comes from God's own choice to show favor in redeeming lost persons through faith in Christ (Rom 5:1; Eph 2:8–9; 2 Tim 1:9). However, God's *undeserved favor* is not toward those who have done nothing offensive; rather, God shows *grace* toward those who have sinned against Him and are actually His enemies (Rom 5:1–2,9–10; Eph 2:1–16; Col 1:21–22). Therefore, a better NT definition of *charis* would be *unmerited favor toward an enemy*—grace toward one who has forfeited any claim on God's favor because of sin and who deserves the opposite, God's judgment (Gal 1:6,15; 2:9,21; 5:4).

Instead, Paul accuses these Galatians of "so quickly turning away from Him" (Christ) to **"a different gospel"** (1:6). Paul uses two words meaning "another." One is *heteros*, another of a different kind; the other is *allos*, another of the same kind. Paul says the Galatians have turned to a completely different kind of gospel. Paul even warns that if he himself, or an angel from heaven, were to preach a different gospel, he would be under a curse (Gk. *anathema*, 1:8). Paul indicates that if anyone is currently preaching this false message, he is already under God's curse (1:9).

B. Paul's Apostolic Authority (Galatians 1:10–17)

Moving past the preliminaries, Paul first elaborates on his apostolic authority (1:10–17). Those causing trouble in Galatia were no doubt questioning Paul's apostolic authority, so Paul addressed that issue. **Paul's commission** came directly from Christ on the Damascus road, not from some human appointment (1:11–12). In fact, Paul notes, he was set apart and called by God from the time he was in his "mother's womb" (1:15). This is a way of saying that God's sovereign eternal plan was at work long before he personally met Christ while persecuting Christians. God's providence can be seen in our lives as well. When we glance back at our lives, we can see God's hand at work in mysterious ways to lead us to Himself. Paul's primary calling was to reach Gentiles with the gospel (1:16). But when God confronted Paul and changed his vocation, Paul had to sort it all out. From Damascus, Paul went into the desert territory of Arabia. There he realized that when he persecuted a believer he was persecuting Christ because all believers are part of Christ's spiritual body. Paul expresses this truth in Gal 2:19–20 as well as in Romans and 1 Corinthians.

C. Paul's First Visit to Jerusalem (Galatians 1:18–24)

Next Paul recounts his first visit to Jerusalem (1:18–24). The apostle traces his dealings with the other apostles of Christ to vindicate his apostleship. Three years after Paul's conversion, he went back to Jerusalem and met Peter for the first time (1:18).

They must have had a lot to discuss. Paul would find out more about the earthly ministry of Christ from Peter and be able to share with Peter what Christ had been teaching him by revelation and vision (2 Cor 12:1). Paul also met James, Jesus' earthly brother, who became a leader in the Jerusalem church. This brief visit lasted just 15 days. It was a **meeting of equals**. Paul then ministered in Syria and in Cilicia, returning to Tarsus in the Roman province of Cilicia where he was born. Paul was "personally unknown" to the churches in Judea, but they knew that he had become a believer and preached "the faith he once tried to destroy" (Gal 1:22–23). Paul remained in Tarsus until Barnabas came there to enlist him to teach new Christians at Antioch, the third largest city in the Roman Empire, just 300 miles north of Jerusalem (Acts 11:25–26).

Roman-age columns on the agora in Tarsus, the place of Paul's birth and early life.

D. Paul's Second Visit to Jerusalem (Galatians 2:1–10)

Paul writes, "Then after 14 years I went up again to Jerusalem with Barnabas" (2:1). If Paul was saved on the Damascus road in the year 32, then 14 years later would be about AD 46. This is sometimes called the "famine visit." Paul says they went to Jerusalem "according to a revelation" (2:2). This seems to be a reference to the prophecy of Agabus in Acts 11:28–30 who predicted a famine. The Antioch church then organized a relief mission led by Barnabas and Saul, as Paul was then called. A Gentile believer, Titus, was with Barnabas and Paul, and Paul makes the point that Titus was not "compelled to be circumcised" (2:3). The point of this is that the Galatian Judaizers were insisting that **Gentiles** had to **keep the Jewish law**, which included circumcision. But Paul includes Titus to demonstrate that the leaders of the Jerusalem church, including Peter, James the Lord's brother, and John stood for freedom from the law for Gentile converts. In this same meeting Paul was recognized as having a mission to Gentiles, just as Peter had a mission to Jews (2:7–8).

E. Paul's Rebuke of Peter at Antioch (Galatians 2:11–21)

Paul next relates an incident at which he rebuked Peter (2:11–21). Peter had come to the Syrian Antioch church and was mingling and eating with Gentile believers until some Jerusalem Jewish believers came there. Then Peter stayed aloof from the Gentile Christians (2:11–12). Even Barnabas was led astray with this **segregation**. But Paul says this was "hypocrisy" and was "deviating from the truth of the gospel" (2:13–14). The truth of the gospel is that belief in Christ is all that matters, not separating from

The tell of Lystra near Turkish valley Khatyn Serai.

supposedly unclean persons, practices, or foods. This led to Paul's key statement in Galatians, "We . . . know that no one is justified by the works of the law but by faith in Jesus Christ" (2:15–16). The grace of God is the all-important issue. Paul adds that "if righteousness comes through the law, then Christ died for nothing" (2:21). When Paul says, "I have been crucified with Christ," and "Christ lives in me" (2:19–20), he is expressing the truth of our **spiritual union with Christ**. By virtue of my union with Christ, when He died on the cross, I died with Him. My penalty has been paid in full. When He rose from the dead, I rose with Him and share His eternal life. This means every believer shares in all that Jesus Christ has done for us.

II. Doctrinal Section (Galatians 3:1–4:31)

A. Paul's Rebuke of the Galatians (Galatians 3:1–14)

"You foolish Galatians!" is how Paul begins chap. 3. Then he asks **six telling questions**. "Who has hypnotized you?" (3:1). "Did you receive the Spirit by the works of the law or by hearing with faith?" (3:2). "Are you so foolish?" (3:3). "After beginning with the Spirit, are you now going to be made complete by the flesh?" (3:3). "Did you suffer so much for nothing?" (3:4). "So then, does God supply you with the Spirit and work miracles among you by the works of the law or by hearing with faith?" (3:5). The answer to each of these rhetorical questions is that faith, and **faith alone**, has accomplished their salvation, not the works associated with the law of Moses.

Paul uses **Abraham as an example** of a person who was justified by faith. Abraham "believed God, and it was credited to him for righteousness" (3:6). Gentiles are saved in the same way. In fact, Abraham was a Gentile when God saved him. On the contrary, the law brings a curse with it. Paul then quotes Deut 27:26 from the curse uttered on Mount Ebal, "Everyone who does not continue doing everything written in the book of the law is cursed" (3:10). The law requires perfect obedience, and since no one is perfect, all are condemned by the law. Only faith in Christ's finished work can save anyone. Christ redeemed us by becoming a curse for us when He hung on the cross (3:13).

B. The Law and Abraham's Covenant (Galatians 3:15–22)

In the next section of his letter, Paul **contrasts law with promise**. God's promise to Abraham was in the form of a covenant (3:15–22). The Abrahamic covenant resulted in Christ's coming as the "seed" of Abraham (3:16). The law "came 430 years later" and cannot annul God's promises to Abraham (3:17). Does God grant Abraham an inheritance freely, or must some legal requirement first be met? If Abraham had to do something, as the law required, then God's promise is basically void (3:18).

This brings up the next question Paul asks: "Why then was the law given?" (3:19). This is a major issue. The law cannot give life (3:21), but it does have a purpose. It reveals our sinful character before God.

C. The Law and Christian Faith (Galatians 3:23–4:7)

After this Paul addresses the relationship between the law and Christian faith in greater detail (3:23–4:7). "Before this faith came, we were confined under the law, imprisoned" (3:23). The law locks us up, so to speak, but provides no remedy. Only faith in the blood of Christ can **atone for sin** and free us from the law's condemnation. "This faith" means faith in Christ. The law was also "our guardian" (Gk. *paidagogos*). Paul speaks as a Jew here when he says "our." The guardian was in charge of minor children from about the ages of 7 to 18. Children who become adults are "sons of God through faith in Christ Jesus" (3:26).

The **spiritual children of Abraham** have also been spiritually baptized into Christ (3:27–28). As such, all believers have the same spiritual standing in Christ. This does not mean that all distinctions are erased because God still has certain complementary functions for men and women in the home and in the church. The result, however, is that all believers are now considered sons, not slaves (4:1–3). Christ came at just the right time and redeemed us from the law. We are God's adopted children and call him "Father" (4:6).

D. The Folly of Returning to the Law (Galatians 4:8–20)

Paul proceeds to discuss the folly of returning to the law (4:8–20). In this passionate section, Paul **chides and pleads** with his recent converts. The fact that they were ceremonially observing "special days, months, seasons, and years" was an indication of the success the Judaizers were having among them (4:8–10). Paul urges them to remember what it was like when he first brought the message of Christ to them. They received Paul "as an angel of God, as Christ Jesus Himself" (4:14). Paul asks, "What happened?" (4:15). In fact, Paul notes, the Galatians would have done anything for him; they would have even "torn out" their eyes and given them to Paul (4:15). Paul now feels like a woman in childbirth, hoping these new believers will be formed properly in Christ (4:19–20). His appeal for them is personal. Will they turn back from their wayward path?

E. The Allegory of Ishmael and Isaac (Galatians 4:21–31)

The next section takes up the allegory of Ishmael and Isaac (4:21–31). Paul uses this **allegory** based on events in the life of Abraham **to illustrate** his message. Abraham had two sons, Ishmael and Isaac. Ishmael came from Hagar, his slave, and stands for a works-based solution to the problem of Sarah's barrenness (4:21–23). Isaac represents God's provision for His unconditional promise to Abraham (4:23). Hagar stands for Mount Sinai, or the law of Moses, and corresponds to the Jerusalem of Paul's day with its emphasis on keeping the law for salvation. Slavery to the law was the result. Sarah, the mother of Isaac, stands for freedom and Christian liberty (4:26–27). Paul even notes that the slave son, Ishmael, persecuted the freeborn Isaac (4:29). The conclusion to Abraham's dilemma was God's command to listen to Sarah who begged Abraham to "throw out the slave and her son" (4:30; see Gen 21:8–12). Paul's conclusion was that "we are not children of the slave but of the free" (4:31). Paul calls his readers "brothers," trusting they will respond positively and similarly cast out the Judaizers.

III. Practical Section (Galatians 5:1–6:18)

A. Maintain Christian Liberty (Galatians 5:1–12)

Paul next urges the Galatians to **stand firm** in Christ's liberty (5:1–12). This means not submitting to the Jewish rite of circumcision. Paul warns that to accept circumcision means one "is obligated to keep the entire law" (5:3). Paul says this would mean that "you have fallen from grace" (5:4). That should not be interpreted as losing one's salvation, as some modern-day skeptics claim. To "fall from grace" meant "trying to be justified by the law" (5:4). This attempt is useless because one is neglecting the grace method of salvation.

Paul also expresses in the next paragraph his positive hope for the Galatians he had evangelized. "You were running well," he notes (5:7). He adds, "I have confidence in the Lord you will not accept any other view" (5:10). But Paul also warns that "a little yeast leavens the whole lump of dough" (5:9). The answer would be to get rid of the leaven of law-keeping and return to living by grace.

B. Walk by the Spirit (Galatians 5:13–26)

Paul next issues several brief positive commands as part of his overall injunction for believers to "walk by the Spirit" (5:13–26). These practical **spiritual exhortations** are to "serve one another through love," to "love your neighbor as yourself," and to "walk by the Spirit" (5:13–16). When the Galatians follow these exhortations, Paul says, "You will not carry out the desire of the flesh." Here Paul uses a double negative (Gk. *ou mē*), for "absolutely not." Paul literally says that a person who truly walks in the Spirit, "will absolutely not" carry out the flesh's desires. How often do we walk that victoriously?

Paul then contrasts the works of the flesh with the fruit of the Spirit. The works of the flesh take effort while fruit bearing is the natural growth of real believers. The **fruit of the Spirit** is a ninefold result that includes "love, joy, peace, patience, kindness, goodness, faith, gentleness, self-control" (5:22–23). We should pray that these evidences of the Spirit's indwelling will be increasingly manifest in our lives.

C. Bear One Another's Burdens (Galatians 6:1–10)

In his final practical section Paul exhorts his readers to **serve others** (6:1–10). They are to "carry one another's burdens" (6:2) but at the same time to "carry his own load" (6:5). Both are true. We are also to restore a brother who has fallen into "any wrongdoing" (6:1), while we walk in the Spirit. This is a spiritual duty.

Paul then mentions **sowing and reaping** for his agricultural hearers. We reap what we sow and in proportion to what we sow: "The one who sows to his flesh will reap corruption from the flesh, but the one who sows to the Spirit will reap eternal life from the Spirit" (6:8). There are distinct times of sowing, growing, and stowing. Lastly, Paul challenges his readers to continue serving others. He urges the Galatians not to grow weary in doing good because, based on his sowing motif, "we will reap at the proper time if we don't give up" (6:9). We should "work for the good of all" but "especially for those who belong to the household of faith" (6:10). Paul hopes for a favorable response and outcome from his epistle to the Galatians. He seems hopeful that the Galatians will return to "grace living" and reject "legalistic Christianity."

D. Concluding Remarks (Galatians 6:11–18)

In his concluding remarks (6:11–18), Paul draws attention to the "large letters" he has written in his "own handwriting" (6:11). This may be an indication that he takes the quill in hand himself because of the urgency of the matter. Or, perhaps, Paul simply writes these last few lines by himself to **demonstrate the authenticity** of his letter.

He again speaks of those who want to "make a good impression in the flesh," which refers to the Judaizers' attempt to enslave the Galatians in the law through circumcision (6:12). Paul points out that even the "circumcised don't keep the law themselves" (6:13). They just want to brag about those they have entangled in their web of works. But Paul counters that, "as for me, I will never boast about anything except the cross of our Lord Jesus Christ" (6:14). What matters is not whether a person is circumcised. What does matter, Paul says, is "a new creation" in Christ (6:15). Later Paul will write about this **new creation**, "if anyone is in Christ, he is a new creation; old things have passed away, and look, new things have come" (2 Cor 5:17).

Lastly, Paul prays for a **blessing** on "all those who follow this standard" and for "mercy to the Israel of God" (6:16). The latter is not another name for the church but refers to Jewish believers rather than those unsaved Jews who are still "Israel of the flesh."

CONCLUSION

Paul's letter to the Galatians is still a trustworthy, up-to-date antidote for a works-based attempt to achieve heaven. Simple faith in Christ's death, burial, and resurrection as payment for our sin is the **only way** of salvation. Works of any kind cannot be added on and in fact may be an indication that one's faith is skewed and lodged on the wrong basis. Saving faith must be placed in Christ's finished work on the cross—nothing more and nothing less. Salvation is by **faith alone, in Christ alone, by grace alone**. This is God's plan, and it is so simple that a child can understand it. Yet the full nature of God's marvelous plan of salvation also goes far beyond our human comprehension.

Study Questions

1. What were Paul's personal motivations to write such a blunt letter?
2. What do we know about the main doctrinal problem Paul corrected in this letter?
3. When critics rejected Paul's apostleship, how did he prove his authority to correct the Galatians?
4. Why did Paul want his readers to reject the bondage that comes with obeying the law?
5. How did Paul describe freedom in Christ?

For Further Reading

Bruce, F. F. *The Epistle to the Galatians.* NIGTC. Grand Rapids: Eerdmans, 1982.

George, Timothy. *Galatians.* NAC 30. Nashville: B&H, 1994.

Hendriksen, William. *Exposition of Galatians, Ephesians, Philippians, Colossians, and Philemon.* NTC. Grand Rapids: Baker, 1968.

Kent, Homer A., Jr. *The Freedom of God's Sons: Studies in Galatians.* Grand Rapids: Baker, 1976.

Lightfoot, J. B. *The Epistle of St. Paul's to the Galatians.* Grand Rapids: Zondervan; reprint, 1965.

Schreiner, Thomas R. *Galatians.* ZECNT. Edited by Clinton E. Arnold. Grand Rapids: Zondervan, 2010.

ENDNOTES

1. See John Saul Howson, "Galatia," in *Smith's Dictionary of the Bible,* vol. 1, ed. H. B. Hackett (Grand Rapids: Baker, repr. 1971), 854–55; M. J. Mellink, "Galatia," in *The Interpreter's Dictionary of the Bible,* vol. 1, ed. G. A. Buttrick (New York: Abingdon, 1962), 336–38; and E. M. Blailock, "Galatia," in *The Zondervan Pictorial Encyclopedia of the Bible,* vol. 2, ed. M. C. Tenney (Grand Rapids: Zondervan, 1975), 624–26.

2. Acts 16:6; 18:23; 1 Cor 16:1; Gal 1:2; 2 Tim 4:10; and 1 Pet 1:1.

3. Supporters of the South Galatian view include William M. Ramsay, *A Historical Commentary on St. Paul's Epistle to the Galatians* (Grand Rapids: Baker; repr. 1965), 1–234; and such well-known commentators as F. F. Bruce, William Hendriksen, Homer A. Kent Jr., and Timothy George (see bibliography for latter four).

4. The North Galatian view is supported by J. B. Lightfoot, *The Epistle of St. Paul to the Galatians* (Grand Rapids: Zondervan; repr. 1966), 18–35, as well as by Theodor Zahn and James Moffatt.

5. Robert H. Gundry, *A Survey of the New Testament,* rev. ed. (Grand Rapids: Zondervan, 1981), 245.

Chapter 14

EPHESIANS
Wealth, Walk, and Warfare

Paul's letter to the Ephesians is a comprehensive presentation of the **universal church** or the body of Christ (1:22–23). This is said another way by Paul: believers are "in Christ" (1:1;10 times in Ephesians). Therefore, the believer has the heavenly privileges that Christ has (the theme of chaps. 1–3). The next section of Ephesians (4:1–6:9) exhorts believers to live (or walk) on this earth according to the riches they have in heaven. The final section (6:10–18) tells believers how to fight against evil powers they face on this earth.

Key Facts	
Author:	Paul
Recipient:	The Church at Ephesus
Where Written:	Rome
Date:	AD 61–62
Key Word:	Heavenlies (Gk. *epouranioi*)
Key Verse:	"For by grace you are saved through faith, and this is not from yourselves; it is God's gift—not from works, so that no one can boast. For we are His creation—created in Christ Jesus for good works, which God prepared ahead of time so that we should walk in them" (2:8–10).

AUTHOR

Conservative scholars contend that Paul is the author, based on both internal and external evidence. The internal evidence points to the salutation: "Paul, an apostle of Christ Jesus" (1:1), as well as familiar **Pauline vocabulary and theology**. There is also external evidence that Paul wrote Ephesians. The letter was frequently quoted as

EPHESUS
48 A.D. – 400 A.D.

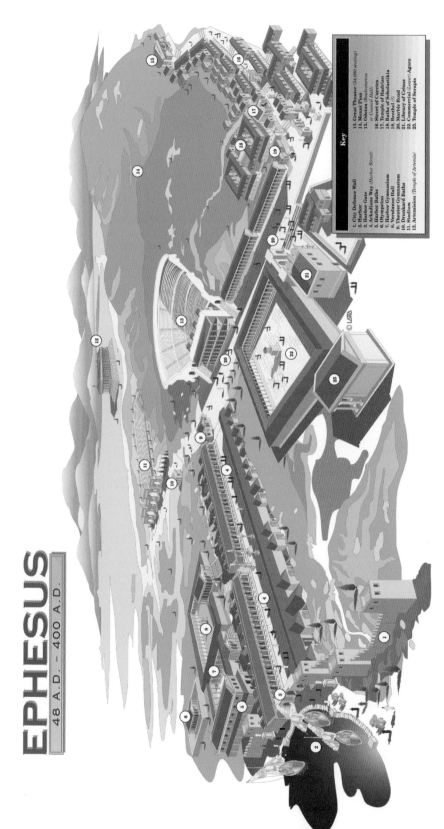

Key

1. City Defense Wall
2. Harbor
3. Harbor Gate
4. Arkadiane Way *(Harbor Street)*
5. Harbor Baths
6. Olympeion
7. Harbor Gymnasium
8. Theater Gymnasium
9. Drunkard Baths
10. Stadium
11. Artemision *(Temple of Artemis)*
12.
13. Great Theater *(24,000 seating)*
14. Mount Pion
15. Odeion *(Bouleuterion or Council Hall)*
16. Street of Curetes
17. Temple of Hadrian
18. Baths of Scholastikia
19. Brothel (?)
20. Marble Road
21. Library of Celsus
22. Commercial *(Lower)* Agora
23. Temple of Serapis

An artist's rendering of Ephesus.

written by Paul by many early church fathers in the second century, including Irenaeus, Clement of Alexandria, and Tertullian.

Those who deny that Paul wrote the book of Ephesians point to the **lack of personal references** found in most of Paul's other letters. However, there are several places where Paul speaks personally (6:24), and Paul says twice that he is the author (1:1; 3:1) and mentions three times that he is a prisoner (3:1; 4:1; 6:20). Some scholars believe the letter was written to be circulated among a number of churches in the region (cf. Revelation 2–3). If so, we would expect few specific personal references. Then again, Paul wrote, "Tychicus, our dearly loved brother and faithful servant in the Lord, will tell you all the news about me so that you may be informed. I am sending him to you for this very reason, to let you know how we are and to encourage your hearts" (6:21–22). Therefore personal references are not necessary, and any personal message by Paul would be delivered by Tychicus.

The Great Theater of ancient Ephesus as viewed from the Arcadian Way on the way to the harbor.

RECIPIENTS

The city of Ephesus was **the capital of Asia Minor** and the center of Roman authority in the area. It was connected to the sea by the Cayster River into its large man-made harbor. Today the artificial harbor is clogged with silt draining from the surrounding mountains. The city is built on a major road approximately two miles in length between two gently sloping mountains. The road through the city reached far into the interior of Asia Minor and was connected by highways to all the other chief cities of the province. Ephesus was easily accessible by both land and sea. Its location therefore contributed to its religious, commercial, and political importance. Because of this, Paul considered Ephesus as crucial for the evangelization of the area. He spent two years in Ephesus, and, as a result of his ministry, "all the inhabitants of the province of Asia, both Jews and Greeks, heard the message about the Lord" (Acts 19:10).

There are many myths about the religious idolatry of the city's past. However, it eventually became home to its native goddess, Diana (also called Artemis). Ephesus was famous for its **temple of Diana** (Acts 19:27) and its theater (Acts 19:29). The wealth of the temple gradually helped the city become the chief city of the province. Pilgrims from around the world came to worship and brought their wealth to sacrifice at the temple. In time the temple possessed most of the valuable land in and around the city and controlled fisheries and shops. Because people also stored their money for safe-keeping in the temple, it became the city's bank, and its priests became bankers of the ancient world.[1] Paul's ministry in Ephesus had become so effective that many turned away from idolatry—so much so that the artisans employed by the temple rioted in retaliation against Christianity (Acts 19:23–41).

OCCASION AND DATE

Because Paul speaks of himself as a "prisoner" (3:1; 4:1) and Acts ends with Paul in prison in Rome, this seems to be the obvious place from which this letter was written. Also, the phrase "I am an ambassador" (Eph 6:20) may suggest that Paul is in Rome, the city to which ambassadors from other nations were sent. If written during **Paul's Roman imprisonment**, the letter dates to approximately **AD 61–62**. In Rome, Paul was able to rent his own dwelling place, had a reasonable amount of liberty to preach and teach, and was able to write letters (Acts 28:30; Eph 6:19–20; Col 4:3–4). Perhaps he was motivated to write when news came about some problems in the Colossian church. Since the letters to the Ephesians and the Colossians are so similar and since the two cities were only about 100 miles apart, both letters may have been written and delivered about the same time.

GENRE AND STRUCTURE

The absence of personal greetings in this letter suggests to some scholars that perhaps, when Paul wrote, he intended for other churches in the province of Asia to read this letter along with the church at Ephesus. If so, Ephesians is a **circular letter**. Furthermore, some ancient manuscripts omit the phrase "at Ephesus" (1:1), and many scholars believe a space was left open so the names of other churches could be substituted when the messenger delivered them. However, it should be noted that we have no existing ancient manuscripts of the letter addressed to alternative locations—only Ephesus. In addition, the practice of leaving an open space for different recipient names to be inserted is not a known practice in the ancient world.[2]

There is great **similarity** between the style of Ephesians and Colossians, which leads many to conjecture that one of the letters is an imitation of the other. Many scholars who deny that Paul wrote Ephesians believe that a follower of Paul had a copy of Colossians and reworked it to produce Ephesians. However, as Clinton Arnold argues, "A much better explanation is to postulate the same author giving a fresh exposition of a similar theme (with different emphases) a short time later for a different audience."[3]

Outline

I. Doctrinal Section: The Position of the Christian (Ephesians 1:1–3:21)
   A. Spiritual Blessings in Christ
   B. The Body of Christ
   C. Being "in Christ"
II. Ethical Section: The Practice of the Christian (Ephesians 4:1–6:24)
   A. Church Unity
   B. Spiritual Warfare
   C. Knowing God

MESSAGE

A practical, and devotional commentary on this book is *Ephesians: The Wealth, Walk, and Warfare of the Christian* by Ruth Paxson,[4] who divides the book into three parts: (1) chaps. 1–3: The Wealth of the Christian; (2) 4–6:9: The Walk of the Christian; and (3) 6:10–23: The Warfare of the Christian. The letter to the Ephesians motivates the reader to triumph over in the challenges of this life and to experience the **abundant life** Christ offers. Paul says little about the local church or how it is organized; his emphasis is on the universal church, which is also called the body of Christ. This is in contrast to practical letters of Paul that deal with matters in local churches at Philippi, Corinth, and Thessalonica. The theme essentially highlights **three truths**: (1) the believer's exalted *position* in Christ; (2) the believer's *duty* to walk according to his position in Christ; and (3) that victory is *possible* because of the Word of God and the Holy Spirit.

I. Doctrinal Section: The Position of the Christian (Ephesians 1:1–3:21)

A. Spiritual Blessings in Christ

The first unit of the letter, 1:3–15, points to the unique position of believers "in Christ" where they are "blessed . . . with every spiritual blessing" (1:3). First is the work of the Father in choosing believers "before the foundation of the world" (1:4), where they were predestined to **adoption** as children of God. Paul concludes the section by saying, "According to His favor and will" (1:5).

The Library of Celsus at Ephesus. Though dating from a slightly later time than Paul, this beautiful building illustrates the wealth and culture of Roman Ephesus.

Second is the work of Jesus Christ as seen in **redemption** through His blood and forgiveness from sins. Then the believer can know the mystery of God's will, that in this new church age they have an inheritance as God's children. Paul ends this second section with the same conclusion, "so that we . . . might bring praise to His glory" (1:12).

Third, the Holy Spirit **seals** believers with His promise, and then the Holy Spirit becomes the down payment of their inheritance that guarantees their presence in the rapture (1:13–14). Again, Paul ends the third section saying, "to the praise of His glory" (1:14).

B. The Body of Christ

Paul's message in Ephesians pertains to the universal church, and this book represents his most mature theological and logical presentation on the subject. Contrast this with the letter to Philemon, which is poignant and personal; 2 Corinthians, which is somewhat disjointed and has little sequence of thought; and Galatians and 1 Corinthians, both of which were written with the white-hot heat of passion. Ephesians reflects **concentrated thought** that presumably took a long period of time to mature, rather than having been written hurriedly. Paul is a prisoner in Rome and therefore is somewhat limited as to where he can go and what he can do. For this reason he has time to think, reflect, and organize his thoughts with regard to the church, the body of Christ. Those who are "in Christ" are saved "by grace through faith," which is God's gift to believers (2:7–10).

Greek Highlight

Faith. Greek πίστις **(pistis)** *Pistis* carries a spectrum of meanings in the NT. It can refer to something completely *trustworthy*. Christ's resurrection is the *proof* (i.e. *trustworthy evidence*) that God will one day judge the world (Acts 17:31). *Pistis* may also refer to a *solemn promise* (1 Tim 5:12). It sometimes means the state of being *faithful or trustworthy*. God's *faithfulness* ensures He will fulfill His promises (Rom 3:3). *Pistis* may express belief with complete *trust*. The NT refers to the *faith* of OT characters (Rom 4:9,11–13,16; Heb 11:4–33,39) and of Christians (Heb 6:1; 10:39). In the Gospels faith is often expressed as reliance on the Lord's power over nature, illness, and spiritual powers (Matt 8:10; Mark 2:5; Luke 8:25). *Pistis* may refer to the doctrine of believers. Christians should contend for the faith (i.e., the body of apostolic doctrine) delivered to them (Jude 3,20). Ultimately the evidence that a person has placed true faith in Jesus Christ is if their practice/actions/words/deeds is in alignment to the truth they confess to obtain (Jas 2:14,17, etc.). Paul constructs the book of Ephesians with this in mind as he grounds his teaching on doctrine (chaps. 1–3) and then emphasizes obedient daily living (chaps. 4–6).

Paul uses the figure of **a temple** to describe the church (2:19–22). It is a **spiritual building** in which all the different elements (people groups) that make up a church are welded together into a collective unity. Notice that Paul says, "you also are being built together for God's dwelling in the Spirit" (2:22). The church is a society of people: "So then you are no longer foreigners and strangers, but fellow citizens with the saints, and members of God's household" (2:19). The church was built, yet it continues to grow. This speaks of the church located in a place, yet every time people are converted, they are added to the church. Once they are in a church, they can grow in Christ, which builds the strength of the church.

On the basis of this doctrinal statement regarding the church, Paul gives practical implications that believers should grow, should not sin, should be filled with the Spirit, and should love one another. Also, the earthly church should **reflect the heavenly church** because "we are members of one another" (4:25).

The second picture of the church is the bride of which Christ is the Bridegroom. Just as God compared Israel's relationship to Him to a **marriage** throughout the Old Testament (e.g., Hos 3:1), so the New Testament presents a union between Christ and the church. Both Christ and the church are bound by significant self-sacrifice on the part of both. The Christian must sacrifice himself for Christ, just as Christ made the ultimate sacrifice for him or her. The purpose of the bride or church is to be free from blemish and sin; it should be spotless.

The temple of Hadrian at Ephesus.

C. Being "in Christ"

One of the main subjects in Ephesians is being "in Christ." Paul portrays believers as having a special relationship with God because they are perfect in Christ "in the heavenlies." The concept of being "in Christ" is a description of being placed into Christ at salvation with an ongoing experience throughout one's Christian life. The believer enjoys an **intimate relationship** with Jesus Christ; just as a child is in the mother's womb before birth and is much a part of his mother, so the believer retains his individual personality while being "in Christ" and being intimately related to Him.

The concept of being "in Christ" grows out of the **promise** Jesus made in the upper room the night before He died when He said, "You are in Me, and I am in you" (John 14:20). When people receive Christ as Savior, Jesus enters their life ("I in you"). As a result of that initial experience of salvation, the believer is placed into the person or body of Christ who stands at the right hand of God the Father in glory. Being "in Christ" represents the believer's standing in glory.

Paul uses the phrase **"in Christ"** 170 times in his writings. It has been interpreted in various ways: (1) as a mystery religion that results in a *mystical relationship* that cannot be explained; (2) as a *sacramental orientation*: when believers receive the bread and cup, Christ enters their life symbolically; (3) as a republican view that in the act of justification the believer stands perfect in the righteousness of Jesus Christ; (4) as a *metaphorical* view, according to which the phrase means nothing more than an idiom or metaphor used to describe belonging to Jesus Christ; (5) as living in the *atmosphere* of Jesus Christ because the Greek preposition "in" is the dative; (6) as the *universal church* when the believer is placed into the body of Christ (the church in heaven), namely the church triumphant or victorious; (7) as being in the person or body of Jesus Christ who stands at the right hand of God the Father.

Whatever "in Christ" means, it does mean that the believer has a **new standing** in the heavenlies so that he has all the privileges of Christ in heaven. Hence, believers have all the benefits of Jesus Christ in heaven. This is why we pray in His name, and our requests are granted because we are "in Christ."[5] However one interprets the spiritual aspect of being "in Christ," Paul uses this term specifically of New testament church age believers (cf. 1 Thess 4:16).

II. Ethical Section: The Practice of the Christian (Ephesians 4:1–6:24)

A. Church Unity

Paul exhorted the people of Ephesus to be found "diligently keeping the unity of the Spirit with the peace that binds us" (4:3). Seven times in the next verses Paul describes the **unity** as "one body," "one Spirit," "one hope," "one Lord," "one faith,"

The Great Theater at Ephesus as viewed from the Harbor Road.

"one baptism," and "one God." He summarizes the **basis of unity** because there is "one God and Father of all, who is above all and through all and in all" (4:6). Remember that the Jews and Gentiles were initially having constant conflicts over circumcision (Acts 15) and legalism. A Jew would not enter a Gentile home; at the same time a Gentile was hardheaded toward the Jewish ceremonial law and its requirements of purity.

The answer to unity is the fact that we are "in Christ" and all of us are members of "the body of Christ." Both are not only **reconciled** to God the Father; both are reconciled to other believers so that "He might reconcile both to God in one body through the cross and put the hostility to death by it" (Eph 2:16). Notice that Paul never exhorts both factions to "make peace with one another." Instead, Paul exhorts them to be reconciled to Jesus Christ who is "our peace" (2:14). Therefore, the solution to unity was always Jesus Christ.

B. Spiritual Warfare

In all the cities where Paul ministered, perhaps the Ephesians had more evidence of Satanic activity and **demonic oppression** than any other place (Acts 19:11–20).

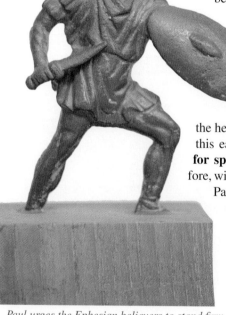

Therefore Paul warns "against the rulers, against the authorities, against the world powers of this darkness, against the spiritual forces of evil in the heavens" (Eph 6:12). Earlier Paul exhorted, "Don't give the Devil an opportunity" (4:27). Some scholars even believe Paul includes the evil world when he describes Christ as being set above "every ruler and authority, power and dominion" (1:21).

Spiritual warfare takes place both in the heavenlies and on earth. Remember, the key word in Ephesians is found in the phrase "in the heavenlies." Because the believer has victory in Christ in the heavenlies, he should and can have victory on this earth. So Paul exhorts believers to **prepare for spiritual battle** on this earth: "Stand, therefore, with truth like a belt around your waist" (6:14). Paul also exhorts you to take armor to your chest (6:14), sandal your feet with the gospel (6:15), wear the shield of faith (6:16), put on the helmet of salvation (6:17), and finally, use Scripture as "the sword of the Spirit" (6:17). The bottom line of spiritual warfare is Christ's authority over Satan and demons. When Christians are

Paul urges the Ephesian believers to stand firm (6:14).

equipped with their spiritual armor, they are equipped to stand firm and **win a victory** for Jesus Christ.

C. Knowing God

The book of Ephesians reveals Paul's desire that believers may know Christ more **intimately** by (1) having "a spirit of wisdom and revelation in the knowledge of Him" (1:17); (2) Paul prays "that the perception of your mind may be enlightened" (1:18); and (3) that they may understand "the immeasurable greatness of His power to us" (1:19). Because Paul had experienced this power in his own life, he wanted believers to experience the same victory. In his second prayer (3:14–21), Paul prays, "Now to Him who is able to do above and beyond all that we ask or think—according to the power that works in you" (3:20). Paul prays: (1) that the believers would "be strengthened with power . . . through His Spirit" (3:16); (2) that Christ "may dwell in your hearts through faith" (3:17); and (3) that the believers would be rooted and grounded in love to understand the length, width, and height of God's love (3:18). Paul's purpose is that Christ receives "glory in the church . . . to all generations, forever and ever" (3:21).

CONCLUSION

Some have called Ephesians a **trinitarian letter** because it reflects salvation obtained for believers by the Father, Son, and Holy Spirit. Yet everything is seen from the perspective of being "in Christ" in the heavenlies. Paul urges believers to subject all things to Christ's lordship, especially against a backdrop of spiritual warfare against pervasive evil where believers are constantly reminded of the riches and power they have in Christ. Believers are part of the body of Christ, and in Him they are "one" with others; specifically, Jews and Gentiles are one in Christ.

Study Questions

1. Make a list of various privileges the believer receives in Christ in the heavenlies.
2. Make another list of the various responsibilities mentioned in Ephesians that tell the believer how to walk.
3. What should a local church look like as we see the biblical ideal of the universal church?
4. What principles of spiritual warfare can be drawn from Ephesians that will give victory to the believer?

For Further Reading

Arnold, Clinton. "Ephesians." *Ephesians, Philippians, Colossians, Philemon.*
    Edited by Clifton Arnold. ZIBBC. Grand Rapids: Zondervan, 2002, 300–41.
Bruce, F. F. *The Epistles to the Colossians, to Philemon, and to the Ephesians.*
    NICNT. Grand Rapids: Eerdmans, 1984.
Hoehner, Harold W. *Ephesians: An Exegetical Commentary.* Grand Rapids:
    Baker, 2003.
Lincoln, A. T. *Ephesians.* WBC. Dallas: Word, 1990.
O'Brien, Peter. *Ephesians.* PNTC. Grand Rapids: Eerdmans, 1999.
Stott, John R. W. *The Message of Ephesians: God's New Society.* Downers
    Grove: IVP, 1979.

ENDNOTES

1. *The International Standard Bible Encyclopedia*, gen. ed. James Orr (Grand Rapids: Eerdmans, 1949), s.v. "Ephesus."

2. See Clinton A. Arnold, *Ephesians*, ZECNT (Grand Rapids: Zondervan, 2010), 26.

3. Ibid., 53.

4. Ruth Paxson, *Ephesians: The Wealth, Walk, and Warfare of the Christian* (Grand Rapids: Fleming H. Revell, 1939). A similar outline is found in Watchman Nee, *Sit, Walk, Stand* (Fort Washington, PA: Christian Literature Crusade, 1957).

5. Elmer Towns, *Understanding the Deeper Life* (Old Tappan, NJ: Fleming H. Revell, 1988), 122–29.

Chapter 15

PHILIPPIANS
The Mind of Christ

In this brief and intensely **practical letter** (approximately 94 sentences in English and approximately 60 sentences in Greek), the apostle Paul speaks to the vital necessity for all believers in Christ to live their Christian faith in a practical and relevant way in order to fulfill the plan of God for their lives. Paul reminds us that only when Christ Jesus is lived out in a believer's life will God the Father receive the fullest glory. Thus, Paul conveys his passion for all believers to have the mind of Christ as they function within the body of Christ. This letter does not attempt to establish church order, correct false doctrine within this church, or address issues of wrong living. Paul is simply rejoicing in everything that is happening to him because it is for the furtherance of the gospel. Prepare to hear from a fellow believer who, while confined in a Roman prison, encourages us never to cease exhibiting Christlike attitudes that produce true joy.

Key Facts	
Authors:	Paul and Timothy
Recipients:	The Church at Philippi
Where Written:	Rome
Date:	c. AD 60
Key Word:	To think, to mind, to have a certain attitude (Gk. *phroneō*)
Key Verse:	"Let this mind be in you which was also in Christ Jesus" (2:5 NKJV).

AUTHOR

The apostle Paul, a close friend of the people of Philippi and **founder of the Philippian church**, wrote this letter to them from his prison in Rome. Most scholars accept the genuineness of Paul's authorship. He stamps his imprint in the beginning, "Paul and Timothy, slaves of Christ Jesus: To all the saints in Christ Jesus who are in

Philippi" (1:1). Early external testimony also attributed the letter to Paul: Clement of Rome and Ignatius both quoted it.

RECIPIENTS

This 10-year-old church was established in Acts 16 after Paul obeyed a "vision" to leave Asia (Minor) and go to Europe to preach the gospel. Upon arriving in the **Gentile-populated city** of Philippi in Macedonia, Paul began immediately to preach the gospel to anyone who would listen. Eventually, the membership of the church was comprised of Lydia, a businesswoman and her household (Acts 16:14–15), a former demonic-possessed girl (Acts 16:16–18), a Philippian jailer and his household (Acts 16:25–34), and undoubtedly others. From these humble beginnings this church grew into a strong, healthy, mature, and God-honoring congregation.

Ruins of Philippi from atop the theater.

OCCASION AND DATE

This **intimate and personal letter** from Paul was written because the Philippians had heard that Paul was not doing well. Paul wrote this letter to encourage his friends in Philippi and to let them know he was rejoicing in the Lord. Perhaps Paul's friends at Philippi had believed his ministry was under lock-down conditions because he was in prison. Epaphroditus, whom they had sent to Paul, was near death after arriving in Rome. Paul drafted this letter and **sent it by Epaphroditus** to encourage them that God was still at work and that Epaphroditus was doing better and should be honored for his service for God to Paul (2:25–36). The letter was likely written around **AD 60** during Paul's Roman imprisonment.

Paul addresses many life issues with his friends in Philippi. As an extremely personal letter (second only to Philemon),[1] Paul always returns to the theme of making sure the recipients of this church retain a Spirit-controlled heart in order to respond to the circumstances of life with the mind (i.e., attitude) of Christ.

Summary of Correspondences between Paul and the Philippian Church

Communication 1: Acts 16 (Paul's first visit during his second missionary journey).

Communication 2: Acts 21 (During Paul's third missionary journey, Paul visits with them as he had to go through Philippi once again).

Communication 3: Correspondence during Paul's Imprisonment (Acts 21–28):

  A. The news gets to the Philippians that Paul was in prison.
  B. Epaphroditus is sent by the church to Paul (4:10,15).
  C. Paul receives news that Epaphroditus almost died (2:25).
  D. Paul learns that the Philippian church heard Epaphroditus was sick and that the church was worried about him (2:26).
  E. Epaphroditus delivers the book of Philippians back to the church at Philippi.[2]

GENRE AND STRUCTURE

In this **brief letter**, Paul emphasizes that believers can experience true joy by living out the mind of Christ within the body of Christ, adopting the attitude of remembrance (1:1–2), prayer (1:3–11), selflessness (1:12–20), confidence (1:21–30), unity, humility, selflessness (2:1–11), evangelism (2:12–18), servitude (2:19–30), gratitude (3:1–11), commitment (3:12–21), joy (4:1–9), and support (4:10–23).

Outline

  I. Greeting and Prayer (Philippians 1:1–11)
  II. Paul's Concern (Philippians 1:12–20)
  III. Paul's Personal Testimony, Part 1 (Philippians 1:21–30)
  IV. Christ's Example (Philippians 2:1–11)
  V. Believer's Witness (Philippians 2:12–18)
  VI. Co-laborers' Support (Philippians 2:19–30)
  VII. Paul's Personal Testimony, Part 2 (Philippians 3:1–11)
  VIII. Paul's Commitment (Philippians 3:12–21)
  IX. Final Exhortations (Philippians 4:1–9)
  X. Closing Words (Philippians 4:10–23)

MESSAGE

I. Greeting and Prayer (Philippians 1:1–11)

Paul expresses his deep, **heartfelt thanks** for the believers in Philippi and prays for them specifically; he "thanks . . . God for every remembrance of [them]" (v. 3), suggesting he prays for them every time he offers prayers (v. 4). Second, he fondly recalls their (financial) support in ministry (v. 5) and encourages them that God will continue to develop their already established faith (v. 6). Third, he tells them they hold a special place in his heart as partners in ministry (v. 7). Finally, he calls on God Himself to confirm to them that his feelings for them are indeed true (v. 8).

II. Paul's Concern (Philippians 1:12–20)

Paul knew it would be difficult for some believers in Philippi to believe God was still working mightily in his life even though he was in prison. Thus, Paul's hope was to offer **practical encouragements** to his friends at Philippi that they should not be tempted to doubt or allow their faith in God to be deflated—even in those seemingly dire circumstances. Paul actually reemphasizes this at the end of the letter in 4:6 when he kindly instructs his friends at Philippi to stop perpetually and habitually worrying.[3] In 1:12–20, Paul stresses that spiritual stability is needed in order to trust that God is at work even though the human eye cannot see the evidence of His working.

Paul's goal was to encourage the Philippian believers. He knew that if they could trust the sovereignty of God regarding his circumstances, they would be able to **serve God** more effectively where they were. Paul stresses that all of the hardships they had heard about—Paul's imprisonment; their messenger, Epaphroditus, coming close to death (2:25–30); their lack of physical resources to give further to Paul's needs (4:10); and so on—should be viewed through the eyes of faith in a God who is always in control. Paul observes, "What has happened to me has *actually* resulted in the advancement of the gospel" (1:12, emphasis added).

III. Paul's Personal Testimony, Part 1 (Philippians 1:21–30)

No matter what problems Paul faced, he concluded, "For me, living is Christ and dying is gain" (1:21). Paul experienced a **natural dilemma** that every person should feel about others within the body of Christ if they truly care for one another. If you care deeply about those to whom and with whom you minister, you will never be without the internal battle of asking, "Who will take care of them in my absence?" "At this point Paul seems to waver between alternatives, unable to reach a decision"[4] about his feelings regarding leaving this earth for heaven. Paul knew that in and of himself he did not have the authority or the foreknowledge to make the decision of the fate of his life. He is simply writing the expressions of his heart as he is experiencing them, confirming for us that such a display of emotions is both acceptable and expected from anyone who deeply cares for another.

And when a believer is persuaded that God is in control not only of his circumstances (1:12–18) but also of his life (1:21–26), one can feel free to "be real" in his relationship with his fellow man. Regardless of what happens in Paul's life, he desires for the Philippians to exhibit similar **confidence in Christ**. Paul emphasizes this point when he encourages them with these words, "Just one thing: live your life in a manner worthy of the gospel of Christ" (1:27).

IV. Christ's Example (Philippians 2:1–11)

Philippians 2:1–11 provides a profound example of how to live out **the mind of Christ**. Paul says believers should live in unity (v. 2), humility (v. 3), and selflessness (v. 4). He then gives Jesus Christ as the supreme example by which believers should live. He knew all believers would respect, revere, and desire to imitate Jesus Christ (v. 5). Paul rightly thought that if Jesus, the "head" of the body (Col 1:18), could live by these attitudes while He dwelt upon the earth (cf. John 13:15), then certainly the members of the body of Christ should live by them as well.

An inscription from the Roman period at ancient Philippi.

The incarnation proved not to have fractured the **unity** of the Godhead. Christ exemplified **humility** when He took upon Himself servant-oriented duties that led to His death. **Selflessness** is exhibited in the life of Jesus as He willingly offered His sinless life as a sacrificial payment for our sins upon a cross (v. 8b).

Greek Highlight

Think. Greek φρονέω **(phroneō)** Phroneo *(to think; to adopt the attitude)* is a key term in Paul's letter to the Philippians. Paul uses this word 23 times in all of his letters. Paul uses this word 10 out of the 23 times in this brief four-chapter letter to the believers in Philippi. In Philippians, Paul intentionally emphasizes that believers adopt a proper attitude toward life and ministry. He teaches that if believers adopt the attitude of Christ in their interactions with fellow believers and in their daily interactions with those unsympathetic to Christianity, they will experience the blessings that living out the mind of Christ produces—joy, peace, unity, protection, contentment, etc. The key usage of *phroneo* in the letter to the Philippians is Philippians 2:5 that states this emphasis clearly: "Make your own attitude that of Christ Jesus."

V. Believers' Witness (Philippians 2:12–18)

Evangelizing the world with the gospel message is required of all believers. It is both challenging and necessary to earn a hearing and the respect of an unbeliever so that he or she will willingly agree to listen to your message. Paul seemed to think that it was possible to fulfill both the Christian mandate and earn a hearing with unbelievers. How? By living a true and authentic life in accordance with who believers really are—children of God who conduct themselves as pure, holy saints with love for one another (2:12–15). Ultimately, Paul encourages believers that even though they will make every attempt to earn a hearing and the respect of the world, they never will be like the world because of a deep and spiritual difference (2:16).

The phrase "among whom you shine like stars in the world" (2:15) emphasizes the deep spiritual difference between a Christian and a lost person. "Stars" connotes that believers are not only to exhibit light in a dark world (Matt 5:14–16) but also are **spiritually different** within their core. Put another way, Matt 5:14–16 depicts the light we shed on others. Philippians 2:16 emphasizes that we are the "lightbulb" (a source of light) that is able to produce light as a result of the Holy Spirit's residence within each believer. Paul hoped the Philippians would exhibit a radiant testimony until their last moments on the earth (2:17–18).

Paul further demonstrates his passionate desire that the believers in Philippi remain **spiritually effective** and strong by encouraging them to "hold firmly the message of life" (2:16). "Hold firmly" (*epechō*, give heed, or stay the course) emphasizes a firm commitment to the faith necessary to remain as bright "stars" in this dark world. Paul's readers should have received his encouragement well because he exhibited this same level of spiritual commitment ("God consciousness") in his own life. The Philippians should have remembered hearing that Paul sang praises while suffering in the Philippian jail (Acts 16:25), along with hearing that he rehearsed praises to God while in confinement (Phil 1:12–18).

The agora (marketplace) in the ancient city of Philippi in Macedonia.

VI. Co-laborers' Support (Philippians 2:19–30)

Philippians 2:20 reminds us that we are known by the quality of our co-laborers. Interestingly, Paul's description of Timothy's **sincere character** is equally a commentary on his own sincere character: "For I have no one else like-minded who will genuinely care about your interests" (2:20). As Timothy genuinely cares for the people of Philippi, so does Paul because he is "like-minded."

Like-minded co-laborers are precious treasures to ministers. The church of Philippi was supported and served by these kinds of sincerely committed servants within the body of Christ. **Epaphroditus** was also a Christlike servant to Paul and to the people of Philippi. He experienced a close call with death during his time of serving Paul, yet he offered his life in the service of others (cf. the example of Jesus' selfless sacrifice for others). Even though he was physically unable to complete the intended human goals of traveling from Philippi and remaining with Paul during his confinement, Paul reminded the people of Philippi that anyone willing to lay down his life in the service of God was to be esteemed (cf. John 15:13).

VII. Paul's Personal Testimony, Part 2 (Philippians 3:1–11)

Paul uses his testimony to refuse the foundational tenants of false teachers who were propagating a works system of salvation. Paul suggests that his stellar **credentials** were superior to most false religious teachers (3:4–6). But he concluded that all his "good works" were insufficient to gain salvation (3:7–8a), and it was nauseating to him (3:8b) even to entertain that thought in light of Christ's work on the cross for salvation (2:6–11).

Paul rather leaned on the **righteousness of Christ** as payment for his sin (3:9). He wanted to commune with the Lord Jesus who provided salvation for him (3:10). Paul lived with the reality that as a result of his salvation he would someday see the Lord face-to-face (3:11). In sharing his testimony, Paul shows how a sincere testimony of Jesus Christ's life-changing power can both encourage the believer and serve as a powerful witness to an unbeliever.

Paul pursued Christ as passionately as a runner would pursue the goal and prize of **winning a race** (3:12–14). He reflected on how esteemed athletes would occasionally be summoned to be commended by a high official and how Paul himself longed to receive "God's heavenly call" (3:14,20–21).

A stone slab found at Philippi, inscribed in Latin.

VIII. Paul's Commitment (Philippians 3:12–21)

In Phil 3:12–21, Paul continues his encouragement to the people at Philippi with a vivid portrait of his commitment to unswervingly pursue an **intimate relationship** with Jesus Christ. To continue his plea for the people of Philippi to remain committed to Christ, he unfortunately had to address the reality that some "believers" had made a choice to defect from the faith and become "enemies of the cross of Christ" (3:18–19).

Just as Jesus had many "disciples" walk away from Him (John 6:66), Paul experienced his share of defectors from the faith (3:17–19); but he did not want the people of Philippi to be among their company.

IX. Final Exhortations (Philippians 4:1–9)

Paul publicly expresses his deep love and appreciation for all the people at Philippi: "My brothers, you are dearly loved and longed for—my joy and crown. In this manner stand firm in the Lord, dear friends" (4:1). Yet he corrected the disunity of some key influencers within the Philippian church (4:2). Paul expected a swift and **amicable resolution** so he did not belabor the situation longer than necessary.

True joy is not contingent upon circumstances but rather in knowing that an all-powerful and all-loving God is in control (1:12–20; 4:6–8). Paul proceeded to remind them in the next sentence that in all things, even after receiving a soft reproof from a friend, every believer can still experience joy (4:4). And when true **internal joy** is experienced, it can produce a level of "graciousness" (4:5) in our spirits that promotes further unity. When joy is fully experienced, it is the evidence of a level of trust and peace that can only be produced by God Himself.

Paul evidenced this level of **peace and joy** as he purposed in his heart to praise God even while he was in prison on his first trip to Philippi (Acts 16:25). Paul testified of God's sovereignty in his current confinement in Rome (Phil 1:12–16,18b), and thus offered himself as an example (4:9; see also 3:17; 1 Cor 11:1).

X. Closing Words (Philippians 4:10–23)

Paul experienced continued financial support from the people of Philippi (4:10,14–16) to the point that he could express sincere contentment that "I am able to do all things through Him who strengthens me" (4:13). Yet this victorious statement is found in the middle of his thoughts on how he had learned to be **content in all things** (4:11–13). Thus, Paul rehearses a strong truth that every believer should rest assured that the Lord Jesus Christ will empower them to be content in Christ in the midst of challenges and trials—confinement (1:12), slander (1:14–18), near death (1:21–26), suffering (1:28b–29), concerns for others (2:16,28), reteaching spiritual truths (3:1), eagerly awaiting heaven (3:20), correcting disunity (4:2–3), and lacking provisions (4:11–12). Paul proclaims that he is able to make it through life and be content in all things through Christ who strengthens him along the journey.

CONCLUSION

In this brief letter Paul provides practical answers to the frequently pondered question, "How can I truly bring glory to God?" Having the mind of Christ in the body of Christ is the way every believer can bring glory to God. Paul emphasized that we can experience true joy when we let the **mind of Christ** control our remembrance (1:1–2); prayer (1:3–11); selflessness (1:12–20); confidence (1:21–30); unity, humility, selflessness (2:1–11); evangelism (2:12–18); servitude (2:19–30); gratitude (3:1–11); commitment (3:12–21); joy (4:1–9); and support (4:10–23). A cursory reading of Philippians shows that Paul had "no sympathy with a cold and dead orthodoxy or formalism that knows nothing of struggle and growth."[5]

Paul ends this extremely practical letter with the ultimate purpose for why he strove to have the mind of Christ in the body of Christ and why he pleaded with other believers to do the same—*for the eternal* **glory of God** *the Father* (4:20; cf. 2:11). Paul knew that Christ—who sacrificed His own life on the cross, rose bodily from the grave, and who someday would greet Paul in heaven—was receiving all the glory for any and all of Paul's efforts. That was satisfaction enough for him and should be the goal for all who call themselves followers of Christ.

Study Questions

1. What was Paul's emotional and physical condition when he wrote to the Philippians?
2. According to Paul, how can we experience true joy?
3. In what ways does Paul liken the Christian life to a race?
4. In what ways did Paul express his love and appreciation for the Philippian Christians?
5. In what way does the "mind of Christ" reflect unity, humility, and selflessness?

For Further Reading

Bruce, F. F. *Philippians*. GNC. San Francisco: Harper & Row, 1983.

Gromacki, Robert. *Stand United in Joy: An Exposition of Philippians.* Woodlands, TX: Kress Christian Publications, 2003.

Melick, Richard R., Jr. *Philippians, Colossians, Philemon*. NAC 32. Nashville: B&H, 1991.

Silva, Moises. *Philippians*. 2nd ed. BECNT. Grand Rapids: Baker, 2005.

Thielman, Frank. *"Philippians."* In *Romans to Philemon*. Edited by Clifton E. Arnold. ZIBBC. Grand Rapids: Zondervan, 2002.

ENDNOTES

1. Richard Melick Jr., *Philippians, Colossians, Philemon*, NAC 32 (Nashville: B&H, 1991), 22.

2. Gleaned from Robert Gromacki, *Stand United in Joy: An Exposition of Philippians* (Woodlands, TX: Kress Christian Publications, 2003).

3. Harold J. Greenlee, *An Exegetical Summary of Philippians* (Dallas: SIL International, 2001), 224.

4. I-Jin Loh and Eugene A. Nida, *A Translator's Handbook on Paul's Letter to the Philippians* (Stuttgart: United Bible Society, 1977), 32.

5. A. T. Robertson, *Word Pictures in the New Testament*, vol. 4 (Nashville: Broadman, 1931), 446.

Chapter 16

COLOSSIANS
Preeminence of Christ

Epaphras came to Rome telling Paul of the problems in the church at Colossae. Some believers were insisting on observance of Jewish religious days, that is, strict diets, aestheticism of the body, mingled with "philosophy" and intercession to angels. Paul writes that Christ is their **only mediator** (1:15–26) and the gospel is fully revealed as the basis of Christian living (1:26–28; 3:1–3). Christ is the true wisdom (2:2–4), ascetic practices are wrong and useless (2:20–23), and the answer is found only "in Christ" (3:1–5).

Key Facts	
Author:	Paul
Recipient:	The church at Colossae
Where Written:	Rome
Date:	AD 62
Key Word:	Preeminence (Gk. *prōteuō*) (1:18 NKJV)
Key Verse:	Christ "also is the Head of [His] body, the church; seeing He is the Beginning, the Firstborn from among the dead, so that He alone in everything and in every respect might occupy the chief place [stand first and be preeminent]" (1:18 AMP).

AUTHOR

Many biblical scholars agree with the traditional view that Paul is the author of Colossians. **External evidence** supports Paul's authorship, such as the testimony of early church fathers like Irenaeus, Clement of Alexandria, and Tertullian. An abundance of **internal evidence** suggests Paul is the author as well (1:1,23; 4:18). The connection to Philemon, which is widely accepted as Pauline, also speaks to the genuineness of the letter. Note that Onesimus is commended in both letters (Col 4:9; Phlm

16). This would indicate that Onesimus was returning with Tychicus as they delivered the two letters (Col 4:7; Phlm 23).

Only recently have some critical scholars questioned Paul's authorship. They propose that some unnamed follower of Paul wrote the letter after his death using Paul's name to give the letter authority. They claim that the references to "wisdom," "knowledge," and "basic principles of the world" are terms used by Gnosticism, a heresy that did not invade the church until the end of the first century. However, precisely identifying the heresy has proved notoriously difficult for scholars. It is more likely that the heresy is some form of Jewish mysticism.[1]

Critics also claim that the "cosmic" or exalted manner of describing Jesus Christ in Colossians was not used until the second century. To support this view critics raise the same objection about John's Gospel and the Revelation. In order to counter false teaching, Paul focuses the reader on the **supremacy and preeminence** of Jesus Christ (1:15–20). Yet such "high" Christology is consistent with the exalted statements we read in the earlier undis-

A view of the tell of Colossae.

puted letters of Paul (Rom 10:6–13; 1 Cor 8:4–6; Phil 2:6–11).[2] Modern critics further deny Paul's authorship by pointing to words in Colossians not used elsewhere by Paul. But the uniqueness of the "Colossian heresy" suggests that Paul used appropriate words to deal with this particular pastoral situation.

RECIPIENTS

Colossae, Hierapolis, and Laodicea (4:13) form a triangle on the Lycus River in Phrygia (Asia Minor, today called Turkey) about 100 miles from Ephesus. As early as the fifth century, Colossae was recognized as a prosperous city, but at about the time of this letter, it was eclipsed by the other two cities and declined into a small town. Later the population moved to Chonai (modern Honaz), and today only a desolate, uninhabited mound marks its site.

Apparently, **Paul never visited Colossae** (2:1). The Colossians received the gospel through Epaphras (4:12–13), himself a Colossian. Perhaps when Paul was ministering in Ephesus and revival was spreading out from the city, the gospel touched Colossae: "And this [ministry in Ephesus] went on for two years, so that all the inhabitants of Asia, both Jews and Greeks, heard the message about the Lord" (Acts 19:10).

A **large Jewish population in** Colossae had a strong influence on the church. But the Jewish influence was not the same problem as that facing the Galatians and the issue at the Jerusalem conference: "Unless you are circumcised according to the custom prescribed by Moses, you cannot be saved!" (Acts 15:1). Since the "Colossian heresy" was a different issue, Paul needed to write a different letter to solve this unique problem: extreme self-denial, receiving authority from visionary experiences, intercession to angels, and the legalistic observance of religious traditions and holy days.

Laodicea, an important banking center in the Lycus Valley.

OCCASION AND DATE

Epaphras likely reported the details of this heresy to Paul in Rome (1:8). Epaphras was seeking advice from Paul and for some reason was detained in Rome as a prisoner (Phlm 23). Therefore, Paul decided to write to the Colossians and to get the letter into their hands as soon as possible. He sent the letter with Tychicus and Onesimus. Paul probably wrote Colossians in **late AD 62.**

Paul is a **prisoner in Rome** as he writes (Col 4:10; Phlm 1), living in his own rented house (Acts 28:16,30). Therefore, he has mental freedom to deal with the various issues brought to him. He has access to his companions and counselors on these issues (Col 4:10–15).

MESSAGE

I. Doctrinal Section: Christ's Preeminence and the Colossian Heresy (Colossians 1:1–2:23)

A. Paul's Prayer and Praise (Colossians 1:1–14)

Paul noted that the seed of the gospel was planted by Epaphras in Colossae and now was bearing fruit all over the world (1:6). This fruit was faith (1:4), hope (1:5), and love (1:8). Paul prays for the Colossians to have "knowledge of His [God's] will" (1:9). **Knowledge of God's will** counteracts knowledge of the Colossian heresy because it will help them "walk worthy" and please the Lord (1:10). Next Paul prays for the Colossians to be "strengthened with all power, according to His glorious might" (1:11). Victory in spiritual warfare is implied. We can be victorious just as Christ was victorious.

While the sister book, Ephesians, emphasizes the members in the body of Christ, that is, "members of one another" (Eph 4:25), Colossians puts emphasis on Christ as **the head of the body**. Here Paul cites an early Christian hymn. While the name "Jesus" or the office of Christ is not referenced in this hymn, the expanded translation below uses the title "Christ" in places of pronouns referring to Him. This amplification helps the worshipper focus on Christ's greatness:

> He [Christ] is the image of the invisible God, the firstborn over all creation. For everything was created by Him [Christ], in heaven and on earth, the visible and the invisible, whether thrones or dominions or rulers or authorities—all things have been created through Him [Christ] and for Him [Christ]. He [Christ] is before all things and by Him [Christ] all things hold together. He [Christ] is also the head of the body, the church; He [Christ] is the beginning, the firstborn from the dead, so that He [Christ] might come to have first place in everything. For God was pleased to have all His fullness dwell in Him [Christ], and through Him [Christ] to reconcile everything

to Himself by making peace through the blood of His [Christ's] cross—
whether things on earth or things in heaven. (Col 1:15–20)

The first part of this **hymn** praises Christ for His work as Creator God, and the
second part deals with His role as Redeemer God. Christ has made the Father know-
able to all believers, available and approachable at all times (1:15–17).

B. Christ's Exaltation (Colossians 1:15–23)

Ministers have quoted hymns in their sermons throughout the church age, perhaps because Paul did it in this letter or sermon. While we do not have an external
copy of this hymn, most believe the early church used it to worship Christ. The first
verse exalts Christ for His **preeminence** in creating all things (1:15–17) and asserts
Christ's equality with the Father (1:15,19) and declares that Christ created thrones,
dominions, rulers, and authorities (1:16). This is most likely a description of heavenly
powers, both angelic and demonic, which become the foundation for dealing with the
"Colossian heresy" later in the letter.

Greek Highlight

Firstborn. Greek πρωτότοκος **(prōtotokos).** *Prototokos (firstborn),* derived
from *protos* (first in time or rank) and *-tikto* (give birth to), appears eight times
in the NT. All six occurrences in the singular refer to Jesus, and it is possible
that *prototokos* was a title for the incarnate Christ (Heb 1:6). With the exceptions of Luke 2:7 and Heb 11:28, where *prototokos* clearly refers to firstborn
children, the remainder of the references emphasizes rank and/or promi-
nence that one enjoys. Aside from these two verses, the force of *-tikto* is lost
in the NT. The term thus takes on the sense of "preeminence in rank or time."
Jesus' preeminent status over His creation is seen in Col 1:15. As Creator
"He is before all things" in supremacy (Col 1:17a) and is "the firstborn from
the dead" (Col 1:18; Rev 1:5): the first to be resurrected and the One having
authority over the resurrection of the dead. Additionally, Jesus' postresurrection transfiguration is a preview of the glorious transfiguration of the saints in
the future (Rom 8:29). All believers in Jesus Christ will benefit from devoting
many days of prayerful mediation over the letter to the Colossians in order to
reinforce their faith in Jesus Christ as it contains some of the most profound
teachings on the deity of Christ (esp. 1:15–23; 2:9).

The second verse exalts Christ for His **redemption** (1:18–20). Jesus is praised as
the "firstborn from the dead," that is, the resurrection (1:18), so that "all His [God's]
fullness dwells in Him" (1:19). What is fullness? The term denotes the salvation of
many, "to reconcile everything to Himself" (1:20). Paul concludes again with the cosmic or heavenly emphasis, "whether things on earth or things in heaven" (1:20).

C. Wisdom (Colossians 1:24–2:3)

Paul explains that true **biblical wisdom** was found in Old Testament truth but was now "fully known" (1:25). He explains, "the mystery hidden for ages and generations but now revealed to His saints" (1:26). And what is that mystery? It is "Christ in you, the hope of glory" (1:27). The indwelling Christ is half of the truth predicted by Jesus the night before He died: "You are in Me, and I am in you" (John 14:20). The other half is our position in Christ (Col 1:27).

The essence of God's mystery or wisdom is Jesus Christ. Paul summarized, "that they may have all the riches of assured understanding, and have the knowledge of God's mystery—Christ" (2:2). When they have Christ, they have "all the treasures of wisdom and knowledge" (2:3).

D. The Colossian Heresy (Colossians 2:4–23)

The heresy of the Colossians was grounded in *gnōsis*, that is, unknowable wisdom and mystery. (Technically, the cult of Gnosticism did not develop into a full threat to the church for half a century though its seeds were manifesting themselves early.) Epaphras came to Rome telling Paul of the problem(s) in the church. Paul seems to sum up this heresy in the phrase, "philosophy and empty deceit based on human tradition, based on the elemental forces of the world" (2:8). This "philosophy" was not what is taught in today's colleges, that is, a historical survey of the way individual philosophies have thought and the assumptions of their views. No, Paul seems to use the word "philosophy" to sum up the particular way the Colossians thought.

First, their problem seems to be that of **emphasizing Jewish rites** of circumcision (2:11), kosher food (2:16), Sabbath keeping (2:16),

Marble bust of Claudius from the island of Malta, dating from the first century.

and laws of purification (2:14). Paul answers the circumcision issue reminding the Colossians that they have spiritual baptism, "Having been buried with Him in baptism . . . raised with Him" (2:12). No other initiatory rite is needed. Paul answers the food issues reminding them, "These are a shadow of what was to come" (2:17). Paul said

Christ fulfilled the law. With that, Sabbath keeping is no longer necessary because Christ fulfilled the law, taking "it out of the way by nailing it to the cross" (2:14).

Second, the heresy seemed to involve the **worship of angels**. This was probably not Jewish inspired, but it could be (1) venerating angels to the point of worshipping them; (2) using angelic intercessors for their prayers; or (3) entering the heavenly or cosmic world where both angelic and demonic spirits operate so that they want to influence their normal world by heavenly beings. Paul answers this problem with a biblical explanation of the heavenlies: "Set your minds on what is above" (3:2). Since Christ has been raised and lives in heaven, "For ye are dead, and your life is hid with Christ in God" (3:3 KJV).

Third, Paul deals with **asceticism**, which practiced self-denial for spiritual results. Paul asks, "Why do you live as if you still belonged to the world? Why do you submit to regulations: 'Don't handle, don't taste, don't touch'?" (2:20–22). What were the Colossians doing "promoting ascetic practices, humility, and severe treatment of the body" (2:23)? Paul answers, telling them, "They are not of any value in curbing self-indulgence" (2:23).

II. Ethical Section: Identification with Christ and Personal Remarks (Colossians 3:1–4:18)

A. Living in Two Worlds (Colossians 3:1–4:6)

New Testament believers live in two realms. They live on this earthly realm, and they live in the heavenly realm above, in keeping with the term Paul used in Ephesians, "in the heavenlies." Paul reminded them of this **earthly life**, "As you have received Christ Jesus the Lord, walk in Him" (Col 2:6). That earthly walk was to "put to death what belongs to your worldly nature: sexual immorality, impurity, lust, evil desire, and greed" (3:5). That list includes other sinful acts (3:5–9). The Colossians

Exterior view of the archways in the top tier of one of the great theaters at ancient Laodicea. Laodicea was 10 miles west of Colossae.

were to set their minds on what is above, not on what is on the earth (3:2). Paul also focused on their **heavenly standing**, "You have been raised with the Messiah, seek what is above, where the Messiah is, seated at the right hand of God. Set your minds on what is above" (3:1–2). Paul reminds them, "You have died, and your life is hidden with the Messiah in God" (3:3).

Paul again presents the **struggles within believers** between the old man and the new man (3:9). Victory comes from "being renewed in knowledge according to the image of your Creator" (3:10).

Paul then turns from negative issues to **positive admonitions** for Christian living (3:12–4:6): "Put on heartfelt compassion, kindness, humility, gentleness, and patience, accepting one another and forgiving one another if anyone has a complaint against another. Just as the Lord has forgiven you, so you must also forgive" (3:12–13). "Put on" (3:12) is an aorist imperative, implying a sense of urgency. Paul is saying that it is important to put on the following characteristics. First, they are to remember they are "chosen ones" (3:12), so they should act accordingly. Second, they must accept other believers (the basis is that all are one in the body of Christ because they died together and were raised together (3:11). Third, they must forgive as they have been forgiven (3:14). Fourth, they are admonished to let the peace of Christ control their hearts (3:15); and fifth, they must let the words of Christ dwell and rule them (3:15). The sixth exhortation involved actions, namely, "Do everything in the name of the Lord Jesus" (3:17). The phrase "in the name" suggests that **believers are ambassadors** for Christ and therefore must live Christ-centered lives. All their words, actions, and attitudes should honor Him.

Paul adds a section of **practical observations** addressed to wives, husbands, children, fathers, slaves, and masters (3:18–4:1). Their relationships should reflect their enthusiasm for serving the Lord, not humans.

Paul ends this practical section with an emphasis on **prayer**. They are to give constant attention to prayer with an alert attitude, that is, keep awake or be spiritually watching. Paul applies this truth so "that God may open a door to us for the message" (4:3): not the prison door, but opportunities to minister what answers the "Colossian heresy," that is, "the mystery of the Messiah" (4:3), which is the true answer to the Colossian heresy.

B. Conclusion (Colossians 4:7–18)

Paul writes to the Colossians on behalf of **Timothy** after he receives a report from Epaphras about some heretical matter that apparently he could not handle. He sends this letter by **Tychicus** and **Onesimus** because Epaphras is detained (perhaps in prison). Paul praises **Epaphras** who has ministered in the church and rejoices at the good news he heard about the church.

CONCLUSION

Paul prays that the Colossians may have clearer knowledge and spiritual discernment (1:3–12). He uses an early hymn for lofty praise of Christ, that is, that Christ is the invisible representation of the invisible God. Christ is the Creator, **the Head of the church**, and has redeemed all things to Himself. Paul lays the foundation to answer their doctrinal problems by reminding them that the mystery is "Christ in you, the hope of glory" (1:27).

Paul wants them to **walk in Christ** as they have received Him. Christ triumphed over evil, fulfilled the law, and nailed it to the cross. Therefore, there is no reason to observe the Jewish law. He also deals with the issues of worshipping angels and asceticism.

The Colossians must set their minds on things above (3:1–3), which means control the actions of their earthly life by the riches they have been given in heaven. Their new union with Christ demands putting away all kinds of sin and putting on holiness in this life.

Paul gives practical directions to husbands, wives, children, slaves, and masters. Finally, he prays for them and asks that he might have future liberty to preach the gospel. He requests that they allow the Laodiceans to read their letter, and they must read the letter to them. (Some scholars believe this is a reference to the letter to the Ephesians.)

Study Questions

1. In what ways are Ephesians and Colossians similar?
2. What is the theme of Paul's hymn that praises Christ (1:15–20)?
3. What was the nature of false teaching at Colossae?
4. Explain the spiritual death, burial, and resurrection of the believer with Christ.
5. How should the heavenly standing of a believer influence his earthly state?
6. What is the wisdom of Christ that counteracted the Colossian heresy?

For Further Reading

Bruce, F. F. *The Epistles to the Colossians, to Philemon, and to the Ephesians.* NICNT. Grand Rapids: Eerdmans, 1984.

Garland, David E. *Colossians and Philemon.* NIVAC. Grand Rapids: Zondervan, 1998.

Harris, Murray J. *Colossians and Philemon.* Exegetical Guide to the Greek New Testament. Nashville: B&H Academic, 2010.

Moo, Douglas J. *The Letters to the Colossians and to Philemon.* PNTC. Grand Rapids: Eerdmans, 2008.

Wright, N. T. *The Epistles of Paul to the Colossians and to Philemon.* TNTC. Grand Rapids: Eerdmans, 1986.

ENDNOTES

1. See the discussion of the "Colossian heresy" in Andreas J. Köstenberger, L. Scott Kellum, and Charles L. Quarles, *The Cradle, the Cross, and the Crown* (Nashville: B&H Academic, 2009), 605–9.

2. See ibid., 602.

Chapter 17

1 THESSALONIANS
The Return of Christ

The Christians at Thessalonica experienced a **miraculous transformation** of their lives when they turned from idolatry to Christ. Paul spent only a short time with them, but by the time the apostle wrote to them a few months later, they had come together as a dynamic Christian fellowship. This epistle is one of Paul's most personal letters—an intimate, affectionate, heart-to-heart talk with a young church. With tact and humility, the apostle reminds them of the sincerity of his founding visit with them, defends himself against false rumors that enemies of Christianity had been spreading, and comforts them about concerns they have related to the death of loved ones and Christ's imminent return.

Key Facts	
Author:	The apostle Paul
Recipients:	The church at Thessalonica (Macedonia)
Where Written:	Corinth (Achaia, Greece)
Date:	AD 51
Key Word:	Sanctification (Gk. *hagiasmos*)
Key Verses:	"For they themselves report what kind of reception we had from you: how you turned to God from idols to serve the living and true God and to wait for His Son from heaven, whom He raised from the dead—Jesus, who rescues us from the coming wrath" (1:9–10).

AUTHOR

Paul identifies himself as the author of 1 Thessalonians twice in the epistle (1:1; 2:18), giving internal evidence of his authorship. Paul notes that Silas (Silvanus) and Timothy are with him (1:1). Both had accompanied him during the evangelization of Thessalonica and were well known to the readers.

211

External evidence also testifies to Paul's authorship. Köstenberger, Kellum, and Quarles write,

> The early church unanimously accepted the letter as both Pauline and canonical. Irenaeus quoted 1 Thess. 5:23 and identified that quotation as the words of the "apostle" in his "first epistle to the Thessalonians" (*Against Heresies*, 6.5.1). Clement of Alexandria (c. 150–215; *Paedagogus*, 5) and Tertullian (c. 160–225; *Against Marcion*, 5.15) also acknowledged that the letter was Paul's own composition.[1]

RECIPIENTS

The city of **Thessalonica** was named by Cassander, one of Alexander the Great's generals, after his wife, Alexander's half-sister, about 315 BC. It became the capital of **Macedonia** in 148 BC, and a free city in 42 BC, upon which it was able to choose its own government officials (cf. Acts 17:6). It was a seaport on the Egnatian Way, the principal Roman road east and west between Rome and Asia Minor. It had a harbor in the Thermaic Gulf at the northwest corner of the Aegean Sea. During Paul's time it was the chief seaport of Macedonia. The population of Thessalonica in Paul's day was

The triumphal Arch of the Emperor Galerius built over the Egnatian Way in Thessalonica.

about 200,000, mostly Greeks. It was an important trade center and a prosperous city. Idolatry was the common religious practice of the people. There was a Jewish synagogue in the city, and the Jewish population was fairly large and influential (cf. Acts 17:5–6). There was also a large Roman segment in the city, with a strong devotion to emperor worship (cf. Acts 17:7).

The church at **Thessalonica** was founded by Paul during his second missionary journey (c. AD 50–52). After receiving a vision and call to go to **Macedonia** while he was at Troas in Asia Minor (Acts 16:9), he went to Philippi (with Timothy, Silas, and Luke) and planted a church there during a probable two-month stay under intense persecution (Acts 16:12–40). Then (with Timothy and Silas) he followed the Egnatian Way west 100 miles to Thessalonica. Acts 17:1–10 describes his ministry there, probably during the winter of AD 50–51. He preached Jesus Christ as God's Messiah (who suffered and rose from the dead) for three Sabbaths in the Jewish synagogue. Acts 17:2 says he "reasoned with them from the Scriptures." The results were that some Jews believed, many God-fearing Gentiles believed, and many prominent women of the city believed, but unbelieving Jews stirred up a riot against Paul. By the time of the writing of 1 Thessalonians, the believers were organized as a church (1 Thess 1:1) with leaders (5:12). The congregation was composed of pagan Gentile converts (1:9), Jewish converts (Acts 17:4), and working-class people (1 Thess 4:11). It was thriving but persecuted (3:3).

OCCASION AND DATE

After quickly evangelizing Thessalonica, Paul, Silas, and Timothy went west 50 miles to Berea (Acts 17:11–15). There Paul preached in the Jewish synagogue for about seven weeks, with a good response. However, he was driven out by jealous Jews from Thessalonica. Paul then went to Athens, where he had a poor response from the intellectuals of the city. Shortly after Silas and Timothy joined Paul at Athens (1 Thess 3:1), Paul sent them back to Macedonia to check on and encourage the new churches at Thessalonica and Philippi (3:1–5).

Paul then went on to Corinth, probably arriving in the spring of AD 51. He had a successful 18-month ministry at Corinth (c. AD March 51 to September 52). Silas and Timothy returned to Paul at Corinth from Macedonia about May of **AD 51**. They brought a good report about the churches there but also mentioned some problems that needed to be solved (cf. 1 Thess. 3:6–7; Acts 18:5). Paul then wrote his first epistle to the Thessalonians in spring or early summer of AD 51 (cf. Acts 18:1,11). He told them in the letter that he had already twice been hindered from returning to see them and therefore had sent Timothy in his place (1 Thess 2:17–18). The mention of Timothy's arrival from Thessalonica in 1 Thess 3:6 corresponds closely with the description in Acts 18:5.

Acts 18:12 states that **Gallio** was proconsul of Achaia during the time Paul was in Corinth. An ancient inscription discovered in Delphi has enabled scholars to date Gallio's service in Corinth to the time period beginning in July of AD 51. Paul wrote to the Thessalonians in AD 51 during his second missionary journey (c. AD 50–52), possibly during the spring of the year. This makes 1 Thessalonians **one of Paul's earli-est epistles** (only Galatians may be earlier).

Overlooking Berea in Macedonia. This is the city to which Paul escaped from Thessalonica after the Jewish leaders sought to harm him.

GENRE AND STRUCTURE

First Thessalonians is one of Paul's most intimate and personal epistles. It is simple and basic in structure and content. Paul's approach is gentle and loving. He writes with an air of expectancy concerning the return of Christ. The letter has no Old Testament quotations. Paul presents his ideas as revealed by the Lord Himself. Paul is concerned to answer some of the questions currently troubling the believers at Thessalonica (cf. 4:9; 5:1).

Four major purposes for the writing of 1 Thessalonians may be seen in the letter: (1) to commend the Thessalonian believers for their faith; (2) to exhort them to continue in sanctification (holy living); (3) to answer false charges that had been leveled against Paul by some at Thessalonica, such as that he preached for money, that he was a selfish flatterer, insincere, or fickle and afraid of persecution; (4) to clarify their understanding of the rapture in relation to those believers who had already died.

The epistle divides easily into **two major sections**. The first is personal and historical, containing a commendation of the readers (for their fruitfulness, their reception of the gospel, and their current proclamation of the gospel, 1:1–10); a recounting of Paul's conduct at Thessalonica during his second missionary journey (his motives, his affection, and his integrity, 2:1–12); and a statement of Paul's concern for the believers (their suffering and persecution, his desire to see them and know how they're doing, 2:13–3:13). In chap. 4, Paul says, "Finally then, brothers" (4:1), and begins the second major section—practical and informative. This section contains exhortations for the believers to be sanctified in their lives (4:1–12), explanations concerning the resurrection and the rapture and how they relate to both dead and living saints (4:13–18), an extended description of the coming Day of the Lord (5:1–11), and some exhortations about the conduct of the church (5:12–22).

Outline

I. Salutation and Paul's Personal and Historical Situation
    (1 Thessalonians 1:1–3:13)
II. Paul's Practical and Informative Remarks (1 Thessalonians 4:1–5:22)
III. Conclusion (1 Thessalonians 5:23–28)

MESSAGE

I. Salutation and Paul's Personal and Historical Situation (1 Thessalonians 1:1–3:13)

"We always thank God . . . our visit." (1:2; 2:1)

Since some of the Thessalonian believers were beginning to suspect Paul of being insincere toward them, he begins his epistle by establishing again his **past relationship** to them. He thanks God for their faith, hope, and love (cf. 1 Cor 13:13) and commends them for their fruitfulness (obedience to God), their reception of the gospel, and their proclamation of the gospel to others (1:2–10). The theme of the epistle is given in 1:9–10: they turned to God (past) and now wait for Christ to return from heaven (present), who will deliver believers from the wrath to come (future).

Three time periods are described here. First, when Paul visited them with the gospel, in the *past*, they "turned to God from idols" (1:9); they responded to Christ by faith and were born again. Second, they were now, in the *present*, serving "the living and true God" (1:9) (rather than the idols and false gods they formerly worshipped). Third, one day in the *future*, Jesus would come from heaven and rescue them "from the coming wrath" (1:10). What "coming wrath" is this? Since Christ's appearance "from heaven" is described in 4:15–17 as the rapture, this "coming wrath" must be God's wrath during the *future* tribulation (the Day of the Lord; 5:3,9). Jesus is the One who "rescues" believers from a wrath which itself is still "coming." Paul seems to have preached this message to the infant church while he was still in Thessalonica. It serves as a summary of Paul's prophetic teaching, which he expands in 4:13–5:11.

THE RAPTURE AND THE SECOND COMING CONTRASTED	
Rapture	*Second Coming*
Believers are judged and rewarded (1 Corinthians 3).	Unbelievers and Israel are judged (Matthew 25).
Christ comes to claim His bride, the church (1 Thessalonians 4).	Christ comes with the bride (Revelation 19).
Christ comes in/to the air (1 Thessalonians 4).	Christ returns to Earth (Matthew 25; Revelation 19).
The focus is comfort (1 Thessalonians 4).	The focus is judgment (Revelation 19).
The church is emphasized (1 Thessalonians 4).	Israel and the world are emphasized (Revelation 12–19).
The rapture is imminent (John 14; 1 Thessalonians 1).	Many signs are predicted (Matthew 24; Revelation 6–18).
The tribulation begins (Revelation 1–6).	The messianic kingdom is established (Revelation 20).

Paul next describes his **past conduct** among the Thessalonians (2:1–12). When he first ministered among them, he was not deceitful or insincere. In fact, he would have given them his own life; such was his affection for them (2:1–8). Furthermore, he worked hard to make his own living so that they would not have to support him. He was blameless and treated them like his own children. This was the way in which they had received his teaching: as the Word of God. They had even suffered for that Word (2:9–16).

Lastly, Paul shows his **concern** for the Thessalonians (2:17–3:13). It was not insincerity that had taken Paul away from them. He wants to see them, to encourage them, and to know how they are now. While he was at Athens, Paul became so concerned about their welfare that he sent Timothy to see how they were doing. Paul's desire and prayer for them is that they might become mature and steadfast in their faith and love.

II. Paul's Practical and Informative Remarks (1 Thessalonians 4:1–5:22)
"Walk and please God . . . encourage one another." (4:1; 5:11)

The will of God for the Thessalonian believers is that they might be **progressively sanctified** and have a strong hope for the future. They should abstain from immorality of every sort (4:1–8). They should live a life of love toward others—both believers and outsiders.

Concerning their fellow believers who have died, they should remember that at **the rapture** they will all be resurrected and translated (glorified) together, to be with Christ forever (4:13–18). The fact that both dead and living believers (those "in Christ") will be "caught up" (Gk. *harpazō*) together points to the promise of a future event.

Because of the promise of the rapture, believers will not suffer the **wrath** of the Day of the Lord (5:1–11). In the meantime they may suffer the wrath of men and Satan. Therefore, in these last days it is necessary to be watchful so that they will not be found in the same stupor in which unbelievers are living. As they wait and watch, they should edify one another, respect their elders and leaders, and remain blameless toward God and the world (5:12–22).

Greek Highlight

Caught Up. Greek ἁρπάζω **(harpazō).** Harpazo (catch up, snatch up) is often invested with the idea of force. In this sense *harpazo* refers to an arrest (Acts 23:10) and to the near forceful capture of Jesus by a crowd (John 6:15). The term is not limited to the physical realm. The evil one *snatches away* the message of the kingdom sown upon men's hearts (Matt 13:19), Jude exhorts believers to *snatch* some men from the fire (Jude 23), and no one is able forcefully to *carry off* the sheep belonging to the Good Shepherd (John 10:11,28–29). Elsewhere, the term is used of supernatural phenomena and does not carry the concept of force. Paul received glorious revelation after being *caught up* into paradise (2 Cor 12:2,4). The Holy Spirit *carries* Philip away and transports him to Azotus (Acts 8:39). Believers will one day be *caught up* to meet their returning Lord (1 Thess 4:17). Paul encourages all believers to be comforted by this reality (1 Thess 4:18) knowing that no force is able to prevent or suspend God from gathering His children—as He Himself will come to gather His children home (1 Thess 4:16).

III. Conclusion (1 Thessalonians 5:23–28)

Paul closes by praying for their complete **sanctification** with the assurance that God will bring it to pass. He requests prayer for himself, greets the brethren, and blesses them.

CONCLUSION

The Christians at Thessalonica were a joy and an inspiration to Paul and became devoted followers of Christ. In reading this epistle, we get a clear glimpse of how dear Paul was to his new, struggling churches and the importance he assigned to his apostolic gift and his continuing relationship to the churches he had founded. It also shows how quickly false teachers were able to spread false rumors and errant teachings among the believers and how frustrating this was to Paul.

Study Questions

1. What does this epistle teach about the strategy of evangelism for a local church?
2. At the end of each chapter, Paul discusses the return of Christ. What can be learned about what our attitude should be as we expect His return?
3. What does this epistle teach about sanctification of a believer?
4. What are the main things that will happen on the "Day of the Lord"?

For Further Reading

Fee, Gordon D. *The First and Second Letters to the Thessalonians*. NICNT. Grand Rapids: Eerdmans, 2009.

Green, Gene L. *The Letters to the Thessalonians*. PNTC. Grand Rapids: Eerdmans, 2002.

Hiebert, D. Edmond. *The Thessalonian Epistles*. Chicago: Moody, 1992.

Stallard, Mike. *First & Second Thessalonians: Looking for Christ's Return*. Chattanooga: AMG Publishers, 2009.

Thomas, Robert L. *"1 and 2 Thessalonians."* In *EBC*. Grand Rapids: Zondervan, 1996.

Walvoord, John F., and Mark Hitchcock. *1 & 2 Thessalonians Commentary*. Chicago: Moody, 2012.

ENDNOTE

1. Andreas J. Köstenberger, L. Scott Kellum, and Charles L. Quarles, *The Cradle, the Cross, and the Crown* (Nashville: B&H Academic, 2009), 433.

Chapter 18

2 THESSALONIANS
The Day of the Lord

Paul's second epistle to the Thessalonians emphasizes a different aspect of future events from the first epistle. Whereas 1 Thessalonians teaches the imminence (any-moment possibility) of the Lord's return to "catch up" believers to Himself in the rapture, 2 Thessalonians emphasizes the **coming judgment** on the enemies of Christ and focuses on Satan, the Antichrist, and the world. The eschatological passage in 2 Thessalonians 2 describes the great tribulation and the destiny of Satan's false messiah. The epistle focuses on the "revelation" of Christ (1:7) and the Day of the Lord rather than on the rapture and the "day of Christ" (Phil 1:10).

Key Facts	
Author:	The apostle Paul
Recipients:	The church at Thessalonica (Macedonia)
Where Written:	Corinth (Achaia, Greece)
Date:	AD 51
Key Word:	Lawlessness (Gk. *anomia*)
Key Verse:	"Therefore, brothers, stand firm and hold to the traditions you were taught, either by our message or by our letter" (2:15).

AUTHOR

Paul identifies himself twice in 2 Thessalonians as the author of the epistle (1:1; 3:17). As in 1 Thessalonians, he again notes that Silas and Timothy are with him (1:1). No early church writer questioned the authenticity of Paul's authorship. The style, vocabulary, and teaching of 2 Thessalonians demonstrate that the epistle is Pauline. However, some critics claim that 1 and 2 Thessalonians are so similar that it is correct to assume someone other than Paul is trying to imitate him in 2 Thessalonians.

However, it is likely that the similar words, tone, and attitudes demonstrate that the same author, Paul, wrote both, one letter shortly after the other to the same church.

RECIPIENTS

This epistle is addressed to "the church of the Thessalonians" (1 Thess 1:1; 2 Thess 1:1).

Paul started this church during his second missionary journey (c. AD 50–52) after he left Philippi (about 100 miles to the east). Acts 17:1–10 describes his ministry in **Thessalonica** (AD 50–51). Paul taught the gospel of Christ, "reasoning with them" from the Old Testament Scriptures for three weeks in the Jewish synagogue.

He focused on **three truths**: (1) the promised Messiah had to suffer and die (probably based on passages such as Isaiah 53); (2) the Messiah had to rise from the dead (also predicted in Isaiah 53); and (3) Jesus of Nazareth was this predicted Messiah. As a result, some Jews believed the gospel, as well as many Greeks (especially those who had already believed in the God of the Old Testament). Acts 17:4 notes that quite a few leading (prominent) women of the city also believed. However, unbelieving (zealous) Jews stirred up a riot against Paul (Acts 17:5). For further information about Thessalonica, see 1 Thessalonians.

The ancient agora in Thessaloniki.

OCCASION AND DATE

Paul likely wrote both epistles to the Thessalonians **from Corinth** during his 18-month stay there. According to Acts, Paul, Silas, and Timothy were present together in Corinth (Acts 18:5). The one who delivered 1 Thessalonians to the church apparently brought back a further report from Thessalonica. Some of the news was good; the brethren were continuing to grow and remained faithful in spite of persecution. But other news was bad. The persecution was intensifying. There were false reports (pretending to be from Paul himself) that **the rapture** had already happened and believers had missed it and that **the Day of the Lord** (the predicted tribulation) had already come. Some believers were apparently quitting their work and occupations in order to wait for Christ's return from heaven.

In view of these reports, Paul quickly wrote his second epistle to the church at Thessalonica. It contained both (1) commendation and (2) doctrinal and practical correction. It dealt with new questions that had been raised among the Thessalonian believers. Paul's answers extend his teaching and exhortations to higher levels. Second Thessalonians apparently followed the first epistle by no more than a few months. The probable date for the writing of the second epistle is therefore the summer or fall of **AD 51**.

GENRE AND STRUCTURE

Second Thessalonians is a brief but **intense letter** expressing Paul's concerns for the suffering of the Thessalonian believers and for their apparent confusion about the future. Three major purposes may be discerned: (1) exhortation—to exhort and motivate the Thessalonians to persevere in suffering (chap. 1); (2) doctrine—to clarify the events and order of the Day of the Lord and the tribulation (chap. 2); (3) practice—to correct those who were refusing to work (chap. 3).

COMPARISON OF 1 AND 2 THESSALONIANS	
1 Thessalonians	*2 Thessalonians*
Teaches the imminent return of Christ	Corrects misunderstandings about Christ's return
Focuses on the church	Focuses on Satan, the Antichrist, and other enemies of Christ
Teaches the *parousia* (coming, presence) of Christ	Teaches the revelation (apocalypse) of Christ
Focuses on the day of Christ	Focuses on the Day of the Lord
Emphasizes comfort of believers	Emphasis on judgment of those who oppose
Thanks God for their faith, love, and hope	Thanks God for their faith and love

Outline

MESSAGE

I. Salutation (2 Thessalonians 1:1–2)

Since someone had falsely told the Thessalonians that the Day of the Lord had already arrived, Paul writes to instruct them concerning the **last days** and to show them how to live while waiting for the Lord to return. He includes Silvanus (Silas) and Timothy in his salutation since Silas had helped him in his initial evangelistic visit to Thessalonica (Acts 17) and Timothy had served throughout Macedonia (Acts 16–18).

II. Introduction: Commendation (2 Thessalonians 1:3–12)

Paul begins on a positive note, commending the believers for their **endurance and faith** under severe persecution and thanking God for their faith and love (1:3–4; not hope because they had apparently lost it because of unsettling rumors). In speaking

The seafront promenade of Thessaloniki, Greece, on a clear spring day.

of the coming judgment of God on the world, Paul assures the believers that God will take vengeance on their persecutors and will be glorified over them at the end of the age (1:5–12).

III. Warning: Do Not Be Upset (2 Thessalonians 2:1–12)

In his first epistle, Paul had foretold the sudden and imminent rapture of the church (1 Thess 4:16–17). He had then warned them about the coming of the **Day of the Lord** (5:1–10), which would surprise the unbelieving world "like a thief in the night" (1 Thess 5:2). The Thessalonians had clearly understood that this was associated with tribulation and suffering. But then they had been deceived by someone who brought them a letter presumably with Paul's (forged) signature stating that the Day of the Lord had already arrived (2 Thess 2:1–2). They believed the false report, apparently because of the persecution they were undergoing. But that raised a major theological problem. If the Day of the Lord had in fact arrived, what should they now believe about the rapture of the church? Had it already occurred and they missed it? Were they left behind? Or was Paul's teaching wrong?

Greek Highlight

Coming, Presence. Greek παρουσία (parousia). *Parousia* means *presence* or *coming*. In the sense of *presence*, it refers to the physical proximity. Paul speaks of the obedience of the Philippian church during both his *presence* and his *absence* (Phil 2:12) and of the *presence* of his fellow laborers (1 Cor 7:6–7). Elsewhere, *parousia* refers to the *coming* or *arrival* of men or events. Paul mentions the *coming* of Titus (2 Cor 7:6–7), and he hopes to *come* again to the Philippians (Phil 1:26). *Parousia* occurs most often in relation to the *coming* of the Lord Jesus as human history moves to closure. His *coming* will be preceded by the *coming* of "the lawless one," the Antichrist (2 Thess 2:8–9). The glorious *coming* of Jesus will be accompanied by the destruction of all His enemies, a resurrection of the dead in Christ, and a gathering of the saints still living (1 Cor 15:23–25; 1 Thess 4:15–16; 2 Thess 2:1). The study of the *parousia* of the Lord has often been a topic reserved for the most erudite scholars. It must be remembered, however, that Paul taught this glorious doctrine unapologetically to a young burgeoning church comprised of many new believers. All believers should consider its depth of meaning as an opportunity to experience teaching about the love, power, and promises of God in a profound way.

Paul's second epistle makes clear that the persecutions suffered by the church should not be confused with **judgments** God will pour out on the world of unbelievers in the Day of the Lord. He begins the second chapter stating that he wants to clarify some things regarding "the coming of our Lord Jesus Christ and our being gathered to Him" (the rapture; 2:1). The Day of the Lord will not begin until "the man of lawlessness" (the Antichrist) has been revealed (2:3). He will be known by his blasphemous character (2:4–5), by the removal of the restrainer (2:6–7), and by the power of Satan that backs him up (2:8–10). He will be destroyed by God (2:8). He will deceive many (2:9–11), and everyone who falls into his deception will be judged by God (2:12).

NAMES OF THE ANTICHRIST	
The little horn	Daniel 7:8; 8:9
The coming prince	Daniel 9:26
The king who will do whatever he wants	Daniel 11:36
The man of lawlessness	2 Thessalonians 2:3
The son of destruction	2 Thessalonians 2:3
The lawless one	2 Thessalonians 2:8
The Antichrist	1 John 2:18
The beast out of the sea	Revelation 13:1; 17:8

Besides the revelation (unveiling) of the man of lawlessness, something else **has to occur before** the Day of the Lord can begin: the "apostasy" (Greek *apostasia*, 2:3). This has been interpreted in numerous ways but probably refers either to the rapture (translated as "departure") or a rebellion (defection) against God by falsely professing believers or the unbelieving world at large. If it refers to the rapture, Paul uses the word to refer to back to "our being gathered to Him [Christ]" in v. 1. If it has an "apostasy" or "rebellion" in view, perhaps Paul is thinking of the warnings he will later give in 1 Timothy 4 ("in later times some will depart from the faith," 4:1) and 2 Timothy 3 ("difficult times will come in the last days," 3:1), though the terms used there are different. A problem with this latter view is that no such "apostasy" or "falling away" appears in this context in 2 Thessalonians and would not seem likely to be understood this way by the original readers in AD 51. Thus, Paul teaches that the rapture will precede the removal of the "restrainer," the revealing of the Antichrist, the time of tribulation, and the final Day of the Lord.[1]

IV. Appeal: "Stand Firm" (2 Thessalonians 2:13–3:5)

The Thessalonian believers have been **chosen and called** to sanctification and salvation. They should continue to stand firm and to be established in good works (2:13–17). This should include prayer for the spread of the gospel through Paul and others. He also asks them to pray that he will be "delivered" from evil men as he preaches the word. Paul is confident they will continue to obey and will remain steadfast (3:1–5).

V. Command: "Imitate Us" (2 Thessalonians 3:6–15)

Finally, Paul commands the Thessalonians not to be idle or lazy. They must **separate themselves** from brethren who live unruly or disobedient lives (3:6). They should follow Paul's example and teaching, working for their own food and persisting in doing good (3:7–13). People who do not work become meddlers and busybodies. Did these people quit working because they were waiting for the rapture? Paul does not command them to stop meddling but to get to work. Working will take care of the meddling. The people of the church should have no fellowship with such people who refuse to work. However, these kinds of disobedient people should still be admonished as brothers, not treated as enemies (3:14–15).

The highway near Thessalonica (modern Salonica) going toward Athens.

VI. Benediction (2 Thessalonians 3:16–18)

Paul closes with a short benediction, in which he emphasizes the **God of peace** who can give them peace at all times and in every way (3:16). He also underscores the fact that he is writing his final greeting with his own hand, as he does in every epistle (3:17). The Thessalonians need to take notice of this and be sure they verify any future reports or communications they may receive claiming to be from Paul. Finally, as Paul does in almost all his epistles, he ends with a blessing and salute to the grace of Christ.

CONCLUSION

Second Thessalonians is an example of how concerned the apostle Paul was about his infant churches, especially when they were influenced by false teachers. The doctrine of the rapture should have been a **joyous and expectant** doctrine but became a cause of alarm and confusion. The believer looks forward to being "caught up" and "gathered" to the Lord. We may suffer persecution in the meantime, but we do not fear Christ's return. In the meantime we are to remain faithful in serving the Lord. The churches of Macedonia ultimately continued to be a blessing to Paul, as seen in his later references to their love and generosity (Rom 15:26; 2 Cor 8:1–5).

Study Questions

1. Why do you think the Thessalonians thought their persecutions might indicate that they were already in the Day of the Lord?
2. What is your view of the rapture, and how does it fit with the details of 1 and 2 Thessalonians?
3. List all of the words you can find that refer to God's judgment and state who is being judged or punished in each case.
4. In 2:6, Paul uses a *neuter* expression to refer to "what currently restrains" the man of lawlessness, but in 2:7 he uses a *masculine* expression ("the one now restraining"). What do you think this may indicate concerning the identity of the restrainer?
5. In what way is the promise of Christ's return a comfort to believers?

For Further Reading

Couch, Mal. *The Hope of Christ's Return: A Premillennial Commentary on 1, 2 Thessalonians*. Chattanooga: AMG, 2002.

Green, Gene L. *The Letters to the Thessalonians*. PNTC. Grand Rapids: Eerdmans, 2002.

Stallard, Mike. *1 & 2 Thessalonians: Living for Christ's Return*. Chattanooga: AMG, 2009.

Thomas, Robert L. "1 and 2 Thessalonians." In *EBC*. Grand Rapids: Zondervan, 1996.

Walvoord, John F., and Mark Hitchcock. *1 & 2 Thessalonians Commentary*. Chicago: Moody, 2012.

ENDNOTE

1. See details in Tim LaHaye, Thomas Ice, and Ed Hindson, *Popular Handbook on the Rapture* (Eugene, OR: Harvest House, 2012).

Chapter 19

1 TIMOTHY
Pastoral Principles

Paul's letters to Timothy and Titus are collectively known as the **Pastoral** Epistles. They express Paul's love for the church and his advice to pastors. Paul wrote 1 Timothy to encourage Timothy to live the gospel and fight to defend it (1:18–19). The apostle then gave instructions about public prayer (2:1–7) and about the role of women (2:8–15) and men (3:1–16) in the church. He predicted and warned against false (demonic) doctrine in the church (4:1–5) and that the gospel and truth were the defense against error (4:6–16). Paul instructed Timothy in the care of widows (5:1–16) and recognition of elder leaders (5:17–25). Finally, Paul exhorted young Timothy to stand against false doctrine and false living, that is, "Fight the good fight for the faith" (6:12).

Key Facts	
Author:	The apostle Paul
Recipient:	Timothy
Where Written:	Macedonia
Date:	AD 64
Key Words:	Fight (Gk. *agōnizomai*) or warfare (Gk. *strateia*)
Key Verse:	"Fight the good fight for the faith" (6:12).

AUTHOR

Paul wrote this letter (1:1) in keeping with **internal evidence** revealing him to be the author. Not only does the opening verse attribute the letter to "Paul, an apostle of Christ Jesus" (1 Tim 1:1), but it is hard to imagine how someone other than Paul could have penned the letter, attributed it to Paul, and fabricated an entire set of circumstances surrounding the writing of the letter (e.g., 1 Tim 1:3–7,18–20), all without deceptive intent, as part of an allegedly accepted ancient practice. It seems much more plausible to take the ascription of authorship to Paul at face value, especially since there is little evidence for the existence of pseudonymous letters in the first century AD.

There is also **external evidence** from early church fathers such as Ignatius, Polycarp, Irenaeus, Tertullian, and Clement of Alexandria who all say Paul is the author. However, about a hundred years ago modern scholars suggested the letter was written in the second century by an unknown author but attributed to Paul. These critics give three reasons: (1) the letter reflects advanced church internal organization of the second century unknown to the primitive church of Paul's day; (2) the letter contains words and style allegedly different from Paul's other letters; and (3) the letter deals with Gnostic heresies that did not appear in the church until after AD 100 when Paul had passed off the scene.

However, the **controversy** is a modern one; no one from the first century until modern times ever doubted Paul's authorship. To answer the critics: (1) Since Paul is the chief architect of church order and organization, we would expect him to deviate from synagogue order and give the embryonic order for authority for worship in the emerging church (he suggests elders and bishops are the same office). (2) The differences in vocabulary and style are demanded because Paul is dealing with different content (personal encouragements and corrections); he is writing to a coworker and not an entire church. (3) The Gnostic problem, while in full bloom after the first century, began its inroads during Paul's lifetime.

The critics also claim there is no room in the book of Acts (chap. 28) for the events of 1 Timothy, 2 Timothy and Titus to take place. This problem is **completely solved** when we recognize that Luke does not end his historical story of the early church but simply stops the story because he had to stop somewhere (and possibly because these are all the events that had happened when Luke wrote). The abrupt ending of Acts suggests the work of the church goes on while Luke's story stopped in Rome. Paul's life probably did not end in Acts 28. He was most likely released from prison, probably because there were no accusers against him (Acts 28:21). Paul enjoyed two or three years of continued ministry, visiting Colossae (Phlm 22), Philippi (Phil 2:24), and the Island of Crete where he left Titus to "set right what was left undone and, as I directed you, to appoint elders in every town" (Titus 1:5). Paul also placed Timothy over the church at Ephesus (1 Tim 1:3). He probably did this at a distance. Most feel Paul never visited Ephesus again after his tearful departure (Acts 20:25; 2 Tim 1:4). Paul probably left Trophimus sick at Miletus (2 Tim 4:20), then went to Macedonia by way of Troas (2 Tim 4:13). Paul may have written 1 Timothy there in the **summer of AD 64**.

Curetes Street in ancient Ephesus with the Library of Celsus in the background.

RECIPIENT

Timothy was probably converted to Christianity as a youth when Paul visited his home in Lystra on the first missionary journey with Barnabas (Acts 16:1–3), so Paul writes "to Timothy, my true son in the faith" (1 Tim 1:2). However, **Timothy** was reared by his godly mother Eunice and influenced by Lois, his godly grandmother (2 Tim 1:5). Apparently, he memorized large sections of the Old Testament (2 Tim 3:15), having been instructed by these women. Many believe Paul and Barnabas stayed in Timothy's home on that first visit, and when Paul was stoned (Acts 14:19; some thought Paul was dead), Timothy was an eyewitness to the stoning, if not the event. At least the young lad saw the results. When Paul challenged Timothy to "share in suffering for the gospel" (2 Tim 1:8), Paul may have been reminding him of his sufferings at Lystra.

On his second trip to Lystra, Paul chose Timothy to go with him and assist in ministry. On that trip Paul removed any obstacle Timothy might have had to ministry by having the young man **circumcised** (Acts 16:3). Apparently Timothy's father, a Greek (Acts 16:1,3), had an agreement with Eunice that she could teach Timothy the Hebrew faith, but he could not be circumcised until his manhood when he could make the choice. This might be the occasion where Timothy was ordained to the gospel ministry.

As Paul writes, he recharges Timothy with the same "charge" he received at his ordination: "I am giving you this instruction in keeping with the prophecies previously made about you" (1 Tim 1:18). It happened when **the church laid hands** on Timothy as they recognized his spiritual gifts for ministry (2 Tim 1:6).

Timothy worked alongside Paul or was sent on occasions on behalf of Paul to minister. It is evident from the two letters addressed to Timothy that Paul had great love for "**my true son in the faith**" (1 Tim 1:2). It is evident from the phrase Paul used to describe their closeness: "For I have no one else like-minded who will genuinely care about your interests" (Phil 2:20), which literally means "equal soul." Timothy was a son, brother, fellow worker, companion, and like-minded with Paul.

Timothy was Paul's **personal appointee** to lead the church at Ephesus and represented Paul in that city. Maybe Timothy felt he was too young to seize leadership, or perhaps it was Timothy's timid or reluctant nature. Or perhaps he had not yet broken his tie to being a "second man" to Paul and had not yet become the strong leader he could become. But Paul motivated him, "Let no one despise your youth" (1 Tim 4:12). Paul constantly exhorts Timothy to be firm, bold, and decisive. Paul challenges him, "Fight the good fight for the faith" (1 Tim 6:12).

OCCASION AND DATE

Paul writes this letter **after his first imprisonment** in Rome (Acts 28; see introductions to Ephesians, Philippians, Colossians, and Philemon). Paul was probably released in the fall of AD 62 and then began revisiting the churches in the spring of AD 63. At that time Paul writes to Timothy who is ministering in Ephesus, perhaps one of the reasons Paul did not go to Ephesus after his release; he did not want to "overshadow" the image of Timothy's leadership. Paul was probably in Macedonia (1:3) when he wrote. It is possible that he may have gone on into Greece. Jews with Gnostic tendencies who wanted to be known as "teachers of the law" (1:7) were spreading their heresy. Paul told Timothy, "Instruct certain people not to teach other doctrine or to pay attention to myths and endless genealogies" (1:3–4).

Paul **bolsters Timothy's faith** to face these doctrinal problems and teach the sound doctrine: "Pay close attention to your life and your teaching; persevere in these things, for by doing this you will save both yourself and your hearers" (4:16). Paul warns against these teachers, "If anyone teaches other doctrine and does not agree with the sound teaching of our Lord Jesus Christ and with the teaching that promotes godliness" (6:3). Against these opponents Timothy is to "fight the good fight for the faith" (6:12) and to "guard what has been entrusted to you" (6:20).

GENRE AND STRUCTURE

Paul's first letter to Timothy is the earliest of the Pastoral Epistles and opens with an introduction (1:1–3), followed by instructions on how to fight heresy and defend the truth (1:4–20). This is followed by instructions on public prayer (2:1–8), the role of women in the church (2:9–15), standards for church leaders (3:1–16), how to contend against false doctrine (4:1–16), and the ministry of church leaders and the place of widows in the church (5:1–25). The letter closes with a charge to church leadership (6:1–19) and a conclusion (6:20–21).

The re-erected marble façade of the Library of Celsus at ancient Ephesus.

Outline
I. Introduction (1 Timothy 1:1–3)
II. Church Instructions (1 Timothy 1:4–3:16)
A. Defend the Faith (1 Timothy 1:4–20)
B. Public Prayers (1 Timothy 2:1–8)
C. Role of Women (1 Timothy 2:9–15)
D. Church Leaders (1 Timothy 3:1–16; 4:6–5:2,17–25)
III. Personal Instructions (1 Timothy 4:1–5:25)
A. Preach the Truth (1 Timothy 4:1–5)
B. Minister to the Needy (1 Timothy 5:3–16)
C. Charge to Leaders (1 Timothy 6:3–19)
IV. Conclusion (1 Timothy 6:20–21)

MESSAGE

Defend the Faith (1 Timothy 1:4–20)

Paul is concerned about false teaching that was slipping into the church. Just as right teaching will lead to godliness and right living, so **false teaching** will lead to perversion and to the destruction of believers. The key role of the pastor is to provide proper biblical teaching: "This charge I commit to you, son Timothy . . . having faith and a good conscience" (1 Tim 1:18–19 NKJV).

False teachers in the church (1:20) were disturbing the congregation (1:3). Those who turned away from the faith were guilty of "paying attention to deceitful spirits and the teachings of demons" (4:1). While the New King James Version calls this "doctrines of demons," this does not mean demons are the subject matter of false teaching, but rather **demons** are the **source** behind false doctrine that was infiltrating the church. Those who believe and practice the heresy taught by these false teachers were pulling their listeners away from godly living and Christian service. They had "wandered away from the faith" (6:10). Therefore, Timothy is told first to "have nothing to do with irrelevant and silly myths" (4:7). Second, Timothy is exhorted to expose errors, teach doctrine, and drive away those who believe and teach error (1:19–20). "If you point these things out [error and doctrine of demons] to the brothers, you will be a good servant of Christ Jesus" (4:6).

Third, Timothy is to **separate from false teachers** who are being judged (or have been judged) by God (1:19–20). Fourth, being a pastor/elder is hard work so Paul told Timothy to teach the truth with authority (4:11–13,16). Paul's strong admissions are balanced with practical advice for all pastors.

Public Prayers (1 Timothy 2:1–8)

The early pastors were men of prayer (Acts 6:4). Here Paul directs men (*aner*, males) to pray. This does not mean men only should pray in church services; it directed prayer "in every place" (2:8). And it includes all kinds of prayer: (1) intercession (*deēsis*, petition for need), (2) prayers (*proseuchē*, personal devotion to God), (3) intercession (*enteuxis*, confidence the answer will come), (4) giving thanks (*eucharistia*, offer gratitude).

Paul directs that prayer be made "for kings and all those who are in authority" (2:2), so that believers may live a "tranquil" (outer life) and "quiet life" (inner life). Paul even wants prayer for the Roman government that arrested and eventually will execute him. The basis of answered prayer is the "one mediator between God and humanity" (2:5).

Paul declared there is **only one mediator** for salvation—not many or one among many—it is the man Christ Jesus. Because Jesus came in the flesh, He "gave Himself—a ransom for all" (2:6). Paul wants all saved because Jesus died for all. But this is not universalism; each must come to "the knowledge of the truth" (2:4).

Role of Women (1 Timothy 2:9–15)

Paul is not sexist or chauvinistic in describing the role of women but believes men and women are equal before God (Gal 3:28). He wants women to please God and others by their inner character, not by outer clothing, hair, or ornaments (2:9–10). He recognizes **unique male and female roles** and that Adam was created first and Eve taken *from* his side as a helper (Gen 2:20) to rule creation *by* his side (Gen 2:21–22). Eve's choice brought sin into the world, but "she will be saved through childbearing" (1 Tim 2:15). This does not mean a woman goes to heaven because she gives birth to a child but is a reference to Eve's having children that would eventually lead to the Christ child who would offer salvation to all (Gen 3:15).

Church Leaders (1 Timothy 3:1–16; 4:6–5:2; 5:17–25)

Paul describes the **qualifications of a bishop** (another word for a pastor is "elder"; 5:17). He does not give a job description but rather explains their inner character, knowing that it will guide how they perform their function. The same is true of his description of *deacons* (Gk. *diakonos*). His purpose was this: "I have written so that you will know how people ought to act in God's household, which is the church of the living God" (3:15). Paul made clear that **belief and behavior** cannot be separated. He

The Great Theater of Ephesus with the Arcadian Way in the background leading to the ancient harbor.

does not want church leaders to live like the false teachers exhibiting conceit, slander, and greed (6:3–5). Paul's standards for bishops and deacons were the same instructions given to Timothy to "pursue righteousness, godliness, faith, love, endurance, and gentleness" (6:11).

Paul tells Timothy that elders/bishops should be paid (5:17–18). They should be protected from rumors and slanders: "Don't accept an accusation against an elder unless it is supported by two or three witnesses" (5:19). In 5:20, they are to "police themselves," so to speak, so they can lead the church with **humility and dignity**. His admonition is this: "Don't be too quick to appoint anyone" (5:22), but a man must be tested first; "if they prove blameless, then they can serve" (3:10). Paul's words in 5:24–25 are reminiscent of the adage, "Time will tell what's in a man."

Greek Highlight

Deacon, Servant. Greek διάκονος (**diakonos**). *Diakonos* frequently refers to a *servant* who attends to others' needs. Those responsible for serving a meal (John 2:5,9) and the attendants of a king are *servants* (Matt 22:13). The person desiring a position of greatness must become a *servant* (Mark 10:43). One can also serve a spiritual power. False apostles are called *servants* of Satan (2 Cor 11:15), and Paul is a *servant* of the gospel (Eph 3:17). Elsewhere, *diakonos* retains the idea of service, while adopting the more technical sense of a church leadership position (i.e., deacon), Paul may use this technical sense when he calls Phoebe a *servant* of the church in Cenchreae (Rom 16:1). In 1 Tim 3:8–13, Paul delineates the qualifications for holding the diaconate. Lastly, *diakonos* may refer to a *promoter*. Paul rhetorically asks if Christ is one who promotes sin (Gal 2:17). In I Timothy, Paul writes a younger minister reminding him that in addition to having the organizational leadership structure in order, the leadership ought to remember that their role is to lead as servants, serving God as they serve people in their leadership roles.

Preach the Truth (1 Timothy 4:1–5)

In chap. 1, Paul begins dealing with the false teaching of Judaizers. Now he turns his attention to the early problem of Gnosticism. There are "deceitful spirits" (v. 1) which are the subtle influences of demons, that is, **doctrines motivated by demons** to get people to "depart from the faith" (v. 1). The "later times" could be preceding the rapture at the end of the church age, or it could be subtle temptations that attack a church in its natural growth pattern to maturity. Later in the book of Revelation, Jesus commends this church at Ephesus for resisting false teaching: "You [the church at Ephesus] have tested those who call themselves apostles and are not, and you have found them to be liars" (Rev 2:2). Paul identified **two acts of heresy**: forbidding marriage and abstinence from food. Paul's answer is that God created both of these, and believers are to receive them with thanksgiving (4:3).

Minister to the Needy (1 Timothy 5:3–16)

Paul explains that the church should care for those who are "genuinely **widows**" (5:3). He gives the criteria for "the real widow" (5:5) and stipulates that each: (1) is a Christian, that is, trusts God (5:5); (2) has no family to care for her (5:4–5,8); (3) gives herself to Christian matters (5:5,10); (4) is at least 60 years old (5:9); and (5) doesn't give herself to pleasure (5:6).

Charge to Leaders (1 Timothy 6:3–19)

Paul begins with the conditional clause, "If anyone teaches other doctrine" (6:3), which involves teaching heresy, he gives a negative description of such a one (6:4–5). Then Paul describes (1) the life of a **godly teacher** (6:6–10); next, (2) the goals of such a teacher (6:11–16); and finally, (3) the duties of a teacher (6:17–19).

CONCLUSION

Paul writes to Timothy, the son of an unnamed Gentile father and a Jewish mother, Eunice, and grandmother, Lois. These women were responsible for Timothy's biblical training. He probably enjoyed Old Testament salvation but was converted to Christianity on Paul's first trip to Lystra (Acts 14:6–22). Timothy is described as a disciple when Paul visited Lystra again (Acts 16:1). Paul's refers to Timothy as his own son in the faith (1:2).

First Timothy is the earliest of the three pastoral letters and was written around AD 64 after Paul was released from his Roman imprisonment. This letter contains the **earliest instructions** for church leaders and orderly arrangement of the local church. These instructions were simple, embryonic explanations and, according to Dean Alford, "are altogether of an ethical, not of a hierarchical kind."[1] The simple nature of the early church is vastly different from the wide and exhaustive infrastructure of the modern church.

Paul addresses the problem of heretical *Judaizers* and early evidences of *Gnosticism*. Some in the church had turned aside from biblical Christianity altogether, while others were denying essential truths. Some had "depart[ed] from the faith" (4:1), thus Paul's warning: "Perhaps God will grant them repentance leading them to the knowledge of the truth" (2 Tim 2:25).

Timothy does not appear to be a bold leader but **seems to be timid** and somewhat retiring. Paul constantly charges him to take leadership, teach correct doctrine, and "holding faith, and a good conscience" (1 Tim 1:19 KJV). Paul ends, "Timothy, guard what has been entrusted to you, avoiding irreverent, empty speech and contradictions from the 'knowledge' that falsely bears that name" (6:20). According to tradition, Timothy died a martyr's death around the turn of the century.

Study Questions

1. What in Timothy's background influenced him to have the meek retiring personality that appears in this letter?
2. What was the nature of false teaching in Ephesus that was threatening the church?
3. What kind of leaders did Paul want in churches?
4. Describe the simple infrastructure that Paul suggested for churches.
5. What can we learn about prayer from this letter?

For Further Reading

Guthrie, Donald. *The Pastoral Epistles.* TNTC. Grand Rapids: Eerdmans, 1990.

Hughes, R. Kent, and Bryan Chapell. *1 and 2 Timothy and Titus.* Wheaton: Crossway, 2000.

Kent, Homer. *The Pastoral Epistles.* Chicago: Moody Press, 1986.

Köstenberger, Andreas J. "Church Government." In *Encyclopedia of Christian Civilization.* Vol. 1: *A–D,* ed. G. T. Kurian. Oxford: Blackwell, 2011.

Köstenberger, Andreas J., and Thomas R. Schreiner, eds. *Women in the Church: An Analysis and Application of 1 Timothy 2:9–15.* 2nd ed. Grand Rapids: Baker, 2005.

Lea, Thomas D., and H. P. Griffin Jr. *1, 2 Timothy, Titus.* NAC. Nashville: B&H, 1992.

ENDNOTE

1. Dean Alford, as quoted in introductory notes in E. W. Bullinger, *The Companion Bible* (Grand Rapids: Kregel, 1999), 1799.

Chapter 20

2 TIMOTHY
Final Words

This tender letter was written by Paul to Timothy his "dearly loved son" (1:2) **just before Paul's martyrdom**. It contains the final words Paul wrote that were inspired and preserved in the canon. Apparently Timothy was leading the church in Ephesus, so Paul wrote, "I long to see you so that I may be filled with joy" (1:4). After this letter no further mention is made of Timothy (with the possible exception of Heb 13:23), and tradition claims Timothy was martyred about the end of the century.

The **dominant theme** is the church's departure from the truth (1:15; 2:18; 3:8; 4:4). Paul recounts, "all those in Asia have turned away from me" (1:15); "at my first defense, no one stood by me, but everyone deserted me" (4:16); and "Demas has deserted me" (4:10). Therefore, Paul's theme is be "strong in the grace that is in Christ Jesus" (2:1); "preach the word" (4:2 KJV); and "what you have heard from me in the presence of many witnesses, commit to faithful men who will be able to teach others also" (2:2).

Paul is not concerned with providing instructions regarding church organization, leadership, and ministry (as in 1 Timothy), but he warns, "difficult times will come in the last days" (3:1). Paul's major concern with regard to Timothy is rather this: "continue in what you have learned and firmly believed" (3:14). In a moving **final appeal**, the aged apostle urges Timothy, "I solemnly charge you before God and Christ Jesus, who is going to judge the living and the dead, and because of His appearing and His kingdom: Proclaim the message" (4:1–2).

In this letter Paul traces the faith of Timothy to his grandmother, Lois, and his mother, Eunice (1:5). Timothy is reminded that he was taught the Scripture as a child (3:15). He is also reminded of the occasion when Paul placed his hands on Timothy's head in ordination (1:6); therefore, Paul exhorts Timothy, "share in suffering" (2:3) and "continue in what you have learned and firmly believed" (3:14).

Key Facts	
Author:	The apostle Paul
Recipient:	Timothy at Ephesus
Where Written:	In prison in Rome
Date:	AD 66, just before Paul's execution
Key Word:	Be strong (Gk. *endunamō*)
Key Verse:	"Continue in what you have learned and firmly believed" (3:14).

AUTHOR

There is strong **internal evidence** that Paul wrote 2 Timothy. Paul claims to be the author (1:1). Everything about this letter is Pauline: sentence structure, vocabulary, and thought development. At the outset Paul refers to "the promise of life in Christ Jesus" (1:1), which is his comfort as he faces death. The style and tone reflect the attitude of a Christian leader who expects to be executed soon. A number of early church fathers claim Paul was the author, giving **external evidence** to Paul's authorship. However, some modern scholars argue that 2 Timothy was not written by Paul but by an anonymous follower after Paul's death. They claim the language is different, especially from the other prison letters. However, the doctrine in this letter is consistent with 1 Timothy and the rest of Paul's letters. Also, the letter is different because it reveals an intimacy that would reflect Paul's need and concern when facing death.[1]

Paul is a **prisoner** (1:8,16), and the apostle talks of his confinement: "I suffer, to the point of being bound like a criminal" (2:9). However, Paul's confinement is much more severe at this time than his first Roman imprisonment. Paul apparently had been tried in court during this second imprisonment and was awaiting execution: "The time for my departure is close" (4:6). When Paul was in prison in Rome the first time, he had no accusers (28:21–22) so he was released. In his first imprisonment Paul had "his own rented house" (Acts 28:30); that is, he was under house arrest. During his first prison confinement, he had access to his friends and received visitors (Acts 28:17–31; Col 4:10–14; Phil 1:13–14). But Paul was released and visited the churches, including the island of Crete where he left Titus to straighten out church ministry (Titus 1:5). As he traveled, Paul was apparently arrested in Troas (2 Tim 4:13) where he left behind his coat and books. But this second time in prison, Paul is isolated from friends (2 Tim 4:11). Apparently only Luke could visit Paul in prison, and that may have been for medical treatment.

Paul strikes a victorious chord even though **facing death**: "For I am already being poured out as a drink offering, and the time for my departure is close" (4:6).

Tradition suggests that Paul died in Nero's persecution after the great fire in Rome (July 19, 64). That persecution continued until Nero's death in AD 68. Paul died during the height of this persecution about AD 66.

Interior of the Mamertine Prison in Rome. The stairs descend to a lower level called the Tullianum. According to tradition, this is the site where Paul may have been imprisoned in the weeks preceding his death. From here Paul would have written 2 Timothy.

RECIPIENT

As Paul is facing many hardships and persecution in prison, he remembers his **faithful coworker** Timothy who had not given up (1:3–5). Timothy persevered in contrast to those who had left the ministry. "All those in Asia" had "turned away," including Hymenaeus and Philetus (1:15). Demas was previously commended as a "coworker" (Phlm 1:24) but deserted Paul because "he loved this present world" (4:10). Paul doesn't mention whether Crescens and Titus had valid reasons for leaving, but one went to Galatia and the other to Dalmatia (4:10).

Paul knew Timothy's faith was true because he remembered, "your sincere faith that first lived in your grandmother Lois, then in your mother Eunice, and that I am convinced is in you also" (1:5). Paul knows Timothy first learned the Scriptures as a child (3:15). When Paul adds, "All Scripture is inspired by God" (3:16), he referred to the Old Testament as a whole and to every part of the whole. Timothy had learned, or memorized, large portions of Scripture.

A bust of the emperor Nero.

But Paul wants Timothy to "stir up the **gift of God**" (1:6 NKJV). The word *anazopureo* is the picture of hot coals without a flame, but when they are stirred up, or breath is blown upon them; they burst once more into flames. The word "spirit" (1:7) in the next verse is the breath to "keep ablaze the gift of God" (1:6). Paul exhorts Timothy, "Don't be ashamed" (1:8), "be strong" (2:1), "share in suffering" (2:3), "continue in what you have learned" (3:14), "persist . . . whether convenient or not" (4:2), and "endure hardship" (4:5).

Paul's strongest command is "Preach the word!" (4:2 NKJV). The idea of **preaching** is to **announce boldly** as a herald (*kerusso*, to proclaim). Because of this objective Paul tells Timothy, "Study to shew thyself approved unto God" (2:15 KJV). The Greek word *spoudazo* is a workman giving diligence or exerting oneself to do his best, that is, exhibit excellence. Paul wants Timothy to be "approved to God" (2:15); this is done by "correctly teaching the word of truth" (2:15). Paul exhorts Timothy, "Hold on to the pattern of sound teaching" (1:13); "guard, through the Holy Spirit . . . that good thing entrusted to you" (1:14); "commit to faithful men who will be able to teach others" (2:2).

OCCASION AND DATE

Paul is in prison and knows he will be **executed soon**. He wants to see Timothy one last time. He asks, "Make every effort to come to me soon" (4:9). Then it appears

Paul begs, "Make every effort to come before winter" (4:21). It is not so much that Paul needs encouragement, but the aged apostle wants to encourage Timothy to carry on the ministry after he is gone. Paul does not need encouragement, he testified, because "the Lord . . . will bring me safely into His heavenly kingdom" (4:18). This certainly will motivate Timothy to continue in the ministry.

Paul asks for his coat and papers: "When you come, bring the cloak I left in Troas with Carpus, as well as the scrolls, especially the parchments" (4:13). These seem to be incidental to Paul's relationship to Timothy. Paul is **encouraging** Timothy, like a coach challenges a discouraged team, to strive with all your might until the end of the game. This letter must have been a terrific blow to Timothy. Whether Timothy arrived before Paul was executed is not known. But Paul looked death confidently in the face and was ready to meet the Lord. He left churches all over the Roman Empire and believers everywhere. But Paul also had some friends who stood with him. The greatest thing Paul had was his own **integrity**. He could say, "I have fought the good fight, I have finished the race, I have kept the faith" (4:7). He knew there was a "crown of righteousness" reserved for him in glory (4:8). Paul ends, "Grace be with you!" (4:22). The pronoun "you" is plural, suggesting the letter is not to Timothy alone but also to those with him, perhaps even to us who read it centuries later.

This letter is written shortly before Paul's death. It appears Paul was released from his first Roman imprisonment (AD 63) and that he traveled first to churches he planted in Greece and then Asia Minor. This would have taken him approximately one year. He visited Crete with Titus and left him there to establish the churches. Since no sailing took place in the winter months in the Mediterranean, Paul was most likely arrested in Troas as he traveled overland around two years after his release (AD 65). His second imprisonment took place in the fall and winter of AD 65–66. Therefore it seems that Paul wrote 2 Timothy in **AD 66**.

Outline

   I. Perseverance (2 Timothy 1:1–18)
  II. Propagation (2 Timothy 2:1–26)
 III. Perilous Times (2 Timothy 3:1–9)
 IV. Perfect Word (2 Timothy 3:10–17)
  V. Precious Ministry (2 Timothy 4:1–22)

MESSAGE

I. Perseverance (2 Timothy 1:1–18)

Paul had been personally abandoned by many, and others had abandoned Christianity. In the face of rejection and disappointment, Paul remembers Timothy, his faithful coworker: "I constantly remember you" (1:3). Paul uses the majority of this letter to urge Timothy to *persevere*. Paul does not give in to Timothy's timid spirit but exhorts him to "stir up the gift of God" (1:6 NKJV). "God has not given us a spirit of fearfulness" (1:7). Therefore Paul the apostle urges Timothy, the disciple, "Don't be ashamed of the testimony about our Lord" (1:8). The basis of perseverance is God who "has saved us and called us with a holy calling" (1:9). For this reason Paul could testify, "I am not ashamed, because I know the One I have believed in and am persuaded that He is able to guard what has been entrusted to me until that day" (1:12).

Greek Highlight

Apostle. Greek ἀπόστολος (*apostolos*). The Greek noun *apostolos* comes from the common verb *apostello* and literally means "one sent forth with a message." The original 12 disciples were chosen and named apostles by Jesus (Matt 10:2; Mark 3:14; Luke 6:13); they were trained by Him (see Acts 1:15–26) and were invested with His authority to lead the church to accomplish the task He gave it (Matt 28:18–20). Apostles had to be eyewitnesses of Jesus' resurrection (Acts 1:22; 1 Cor 9:1; 15:8–9). Together with prophets, *apostles* were foundational for the early church (Eph 2:20), particularly in being responsible for giving divine revelation to God's people (Eph 3:5). Only 15 people are clearly referred to as apostles in the NT: the original 12, Matthias (Acts 1:26), Paul, and Barnabas (Acts 14:14). The noun did not attain the significance of being sent with authority until its adoption by Jesus and the NT writers and serves as a vivid reminder of both how Christianity engaged relevant social terms to convey spiritual truths in an understandable way.

II. Propagation (2 Timothy 2:1–26)

Paul wanted Timothy to see the **future generations** of ministry duplication. The first generation was Paul who preached the gospel. The second generation was Timothy who received the gospel from Paul. The third generation was the ones to whom Timothy preached, that is, "commit to faithful men" (2:2). This third delegation produces men of faith. The fourth generation is the "others" who were taught by faithful men in the third generation, "teach others also" (2:2). The key to Christianity is **passing our faith on** to others. Paul calls Timothy a "son" (2:1 NKJV), suggesting four generations: father (Paul), son (Timothy), grandsons (faithful men), and great-grandsons (others).

Paul gives other **illustrations** of faithfulness in ministry: a *soldier* (2:3–5); an *athlete* (2:5); a *farmer* (2:6–13); a *craftsman* (2:14–19); a *serving dish* (2:20–22); and a *servant* (2:23–26).

III. Perilous Times (2 Timothy 3:1–9)

The King James Version describes the conditions as "perilous times" (from *chalepos*, which means "hard or difficult times"). These conditions apply primarily to **the end times**, although they can also apply to all ages throughout the church age. Foreseeing these trends, Paul says, people will be "lovers of self" (3:2) and "lovers of money" (3:2) Then Paul describes them as "boastful, proud, blasphemers" (3:2). Some will even express rebellion against their own parents (3:2). Paul foresees a time of unrestrained self-centeredness that will characterize the "last days" (3:1).

Paul adds "ungrateful, unholy, unloving, irreconcilable, slanders" (3:2–3). Paul sees the pervasive influences of sin on individuals so that people are "without self-control" (3:3). Paul continues, "brutal, without love for what is good, traitors, reckless, conceited" (3:3–4). Paul must have spoken of modern America when he added, "lovers of pleasure rather than lovers of God" (3:4). Paul predicts a great **outward show** of formal but spiritually empty religion. Paul described this phenomenon as follows: "holding to the form of religion, but denying its power." So Paul exhorts Timothy to "avoid these people!" (3:5).

IV. Perfect Word (2 Timothy 3:10–17)

Paul reminds Timothy he had "fully known" (3:10 KJV) his doctrines (*parakolou theou*, translated in Luke 1:3 [NKJV], "perfect understanding"). Before following someone, check out their lives, their beliefs, and what they accomplished with their ministry. Paul invited Timothy to do that. Then Paul reminded Timothy of the various places where he had suffered persecution, mentioning Lystra, Timothy's hometown. Perhaps Paul wanted Timothy to remember that he was stoned there (some think Paul died and was resuscitated, 2 Cor 12:1–10). Paul was telling Timothy to be willing to die for the truth, just as he was.

The essence of faith is "the sacred Scriptures" (3:15; *gramma*, the word meaning "writings"). The inspired Scriptures are the basis of salvation but must be affirmed by faith. Then Paul told Timothy why the Scriptures are important: "All Scripture is inspired" (3:16; *pasa graphē* [singular], suggesting the whole is inspired as well as the parts). Inspiration is *theopneustos*, which means literally "God breathed." Since God is perfect and all-knowing, when He breathed inspiration on the Scriptures, they were perfect. Also, since God breathed His life or Spirit into the Scriptures, those who read and believe will receive the life of God. When the Scriptures are applied for doctrine, reproof, correction, and instruction in righteousness, the man of God will be "complete, equipped for every good work" (3:17).

V. Precious Ministry (2 Timothy 4:1–22)

Paul tells Timothy, "I solemnly charge you" (4:1, *diamarturomai*, which is more than directions or even a command; it carries a **moral obligation** that Timothy must pledge to fulfill). And what is that imperative? It is this: "Preach the word!" (4:2 NKJV), a formal presentation of God's Word with authority. Paul then told Timothy, "rebuke, correct, and encourage" (4:2). It is not Timothy's opinion that he is to preach; it is what God commands so do not be afraid. Paul returned to the theme of the end times because "they will not tolerate sound doctrine" (4:3). Paul told Timothy to "endure hardship" (4:5). He also exhorted him, "Do the work of an evangelist" (4:5). No pastor can simply pray and preach; they must be soul-winners if they expect the congregation to win souls.

Paul knew his ministry was almost over, yet he was satisfied that he had given and done everything he could. So he describes his **coming execution** as follows: "I am already being poured out as a drink offering" (4:6), a picture of a worshipper bringing an offering to God for no other purpose than to worship God. It was not a guilt offering or atonement of sin. Just as a worshipper freely gives to God, expecting nothing in return, Paul offers his coming death as worship to God.

A great leader said, "I am immortal until the will of God for me is accomplished."[2] So Paul has "finished his race"; he testified, "I have kept the faith" (4:7). Now the "crown of righteousness" (4:8) awaits Paul, similar to a laurel wreath being placed on the head of winners at an athletic contest. He has played the game by God's rules and is the winner. The **crown of righteousness** that all believers receive will be cast at Jesus' feet (Rev 4:10–11) in worship of Him.

These verses read like a thundering crescendo that brings a symphony to its proper climax. The music is over, the message has come to a proper conclusion, and the expectation engendered by the music itself is properly satisfied. Paul could say with Jesus, "It is finished!" (John 19:30).

Ancient bridge over the Tiber River in Rome. According to reliable tradition, Paul was executed on the banks of the Tiber during the reign on Nero.

CONCLUSION

This is the **third letter** by Paul known as the "Pastoral Epistles" (or books). They were written in the following order: 1 Timothy, Titus, and 2 Timothy. When Paul wrote 2 Timothy, he was **again in prison** in Rome, having been arrested for preaching the gospel (2:9). A number of people have deserted Paul. These people could have made a statement for Christ, but when Paul needed them the most, they deserted him. Some in Asia Minor had deserted Paul (4:16). Alexander, a metal worker, may even have testified against Paul. Yet Paul testified that the Lord Himself had stood with him and he was given a temporary reprieve (4:17). Onesiphorus had come to Rome and searched for Paul until he found him (1:16–18). Luke is with Paul; perhaps he was allowed to visit Paul as a physician. Paul had sent Tychicus, his personal mail carrier, who carried this letter to Timothy. Also, perhaps Tychicus was to take over duties in Ephesus when Timothy came to Rome to see Paul. Some feel Paul wrote this second letter because he was afraid Timothy would not get to Rome before he was executed. Therefore, this letter would tell Timothy what Paul wanted to tell him face-to-face.

This letter is **more personal** than 1 Timothy. Winter was coming; Paul wanted his coat and books. The letter was written in the face of growing persecution and hardships. Paul does not promise blue skies over the rainbows but rather suffering and difficulties. Yet in the face of all these problems, "There is reserved for me in the future the crown of righteousness, which the Lord, the righteous Judge, will give me on that day, and not only to me, but to all those who have loved His appearing" (4:8).

Statue of St. Paul Outside the Walls basilica where Paul was buried.

Study Questions

1. What was Paul's condition when he wrote 2 Timothy?
2. What were the main differences between Paul's first and second imprisonments?
3. What Christians were standing with Paul and who deserted him? What were their motivations?
4. What is Paul's main exhortation to Timothy in this letter?

For Further Reading

Earle, Ralph. *1, 2 Timothy*. EBC. Grand Rapids: Zondervan, 1978.
Guthrie, Donald. *The Pastoral Epistles*. TNTC. Grand Rapids: Eerdmans, 1990.
Hughes, R. Kent, and Bryan Chapell. *1 and 2 Timothy and Titus*. Wheaton: Crossway, 2000.
Kent, Homer. *Pastoral Epistles*. Chicago: Moody Press, 1986.
Lea, Thomas D., and H. P. Griffin Jr. *1, 2 Timothy, Titus*. NAC. Nashville: B&H, 1992.

ENDNOTES

1. Andreas J. Köstenberger, L. Scott Kellum, and Charles L. Quarles, *The Cradle, the Cross, and the Crown: An Introduction to the New Testament* (Nashville: B&H Academic, 2009), 638–42.

2. David Livingstone, as quoted by Kenneth Boa, "Discerning the Will of God," accessed December 1, 2011, http://bible.org/article/discerning-will-god.

Chapter 21

TITUS
Good Works

Paul's short epistle to Titus is a practical book focused primarily on **church ministry** and secondarily on **Christian discipleship**. Though it contains a classic description of the grace of God in salvation (2:11–14; 3:4–7), there are six references to "good works" on the part of the believer (1:16; 2:7,14; 3:1,8,14). Paul shows that good works come after saving faith (2:14; 3:8) and are a visible sign of salvation (1:16). "Sound doctrine" (healthy teaching) must be adorned with good behavior and holy living (2:10). Titus is one of the Pastoral Epistles and is most like 1 Timothy in its content.

Key Facts	
Author:	The apostle Paul
Recipient:	Titus (and believers in churches at Crete)
Where Written:	Macedonia (Philippi or Thessalonica)
Date:	About AD 63
Key Words:	Good works (Gk. *kala erga*)
Key Verses:	"For the grace of God has appeared, with salvation for all people, instructing us to . . . wait for the blessed hope and appearing of the glory of our great God and Savior, Jesus Christ . . . a people . . . , eager to do good works" (2:11–14).

AUTHOR

The author of the epistle to Titus was **the apostle Paul** (1:1), though this is disputed by most critical scholars. See 1 Timothy for the evidence and arguments for Paul's authorship of the Pastoral Epistles. Titus was apparently quoted by Clement of Rome in his Epistle to the Corinthians (AD 95).[1] It was also cited in the Epistle of Barnabas and the Epistle to Diognetus (second century).

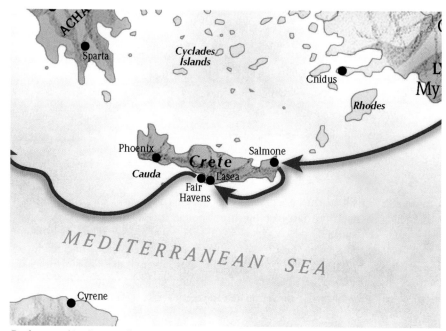

Paul stopped in Crete on his voyage to Rome. Many scholars believe Paul was released from house arrest in Rome. Between this time and the time of his second imprisonment in Rome, he and Titus preached the gospel on Crete.

RECIPIENT

Paul addresses the epistle to "Titus, my true son in our common faith" (1:4). Both of Titus's parents were Greek (cf. Gal 2:3). He is not mentioned by name in the book of Acts. He was probably converted through the ministry of Paul (Titus 1:4). **Titus** went with Paul and Barnabas to Jerusalem for the Jerusalem Council about AD 49 (Gal 2:1) and was an example of one who was saved by faith in Christ apart from circumcision and was not compelled to be circumcised at Jerusalem (Gal 2:3).

Titus was **Paul's representative** to the church at Corinth during the third journey (2 Corinthians 7–8). He had a genuine spiritual concern for the believers at Corinth (2 Cor 8:16–17). Titus later joined Paul in Macedonia to report on conditions in the Corinthian church and delivered Paul's second epistle to the Corinthians. He was also given some responsibility to help gather the financial collection for the poor saints in Jerusalem (2 Cor 8:16–23).

Nothing further is known of Titus until after Paul's first Roman imprisonment. He was Paul's representative to the **Cretan churches** after Paul founded those churches and moved on (Titus 1:4–5). Later Paul urged Titus to join him at Nicopolis for the winter (3:12). He was with Paul in Rome for part of his last imprisonment. Paul mentioned to Timothy that Titus had gone to Dalmatia (2 Tim 4:10), which was a Roman province with part of Illyricum northwest of Greece.

Tradition says that Titus in his later years was the overseer of the Christian work on Crete and that he died there. In character Titus was consecrated, bold, zealous, wise, and practical. He apparently replaced Timothy as Paul's representative to Corinth because he was bold and courageous enough to withstand the opposition and stubbornness at Corinth. Like Timothy, Titus, who was wholly Gentile, was a young and **gifted coworker** of Paul for many years, but unlike Timothy, Titus had a strong personality.

OCCASION AND DATE

The epistle to Titus was probably written about the same time as 1 Timothy (c. AD 63) and in the same location (Macedonia). It was composed after Paul's release from prison in Rome, likely in **AD 62**, but before Paul's arrest later by Nero (c. AD 64–67). It was probably written soon after 1 Timothy.

Titus was in Crete when he received this epistle from Paul (1:5). **Crete** is a mountainous **island** in the Mediterranean Sea southeast of Greece, measuring about 160 miles long by 35 miles wide. It had many large coastal towns, which were probably the focus of Paul's witness. The island had been the site of a great civilization in the past. The inhabitants depended on the sea for their living through both fishing and shipping. There were Jewish Cretans in Jerusalem for the Feast of Pentecost when the Christian church began (Acts 2:11), but there is no record of converts returning to Crete or the existence of a church on Crete before Paul's ministry there.

Agios Pavlos is a small village on the southern coast of Crete. Paul left his protégé Titus on Crete to "set right what was left undone" and to appoint elders in every town.

The Cretan people had a **negative reputation** in the Mediterranean world. Paul quotes the Cretan poet Epimenides as saying that Cretans were "always liars, evil beasts, lazy gluttons" (1:12). Many classical writers had written of the untruthfulness of the Cretans. The Greek verb *kretizein*, meaning "to act as a Cretan," became synonymous with the idea of "playing the liar." The writer Leonides called the Cretans "brigands, piratical, unjust."

Sometime following Paul's release from prison in Rome, Paul visited and evangelized a number of towns on the island of Crete (c. AD 62–63). Titus apparently accompanied him, and Timothy may have been there as well. Perhaps Paul was drawn to Crete because of having spent some brief time harboring there during his **voyage to Rome** as a prisoner (Acts 27:7–9). When Paul traveled on, he left Titus at Crete to take care of things in the churches that remained to be done (Titus 1:5), and perhaps at this time Paul went on to Ephesus with Timothy. After Paul went to Macedonia (1 Tim 1:3), he wrote 1 Timothy to Timothy at Ephesus and then wrote this epistle to Titus at Crete. He asked Titus to meet him at Nicopolis (on the west coast of Greece) the following winter and sent the letter with Zenas and Apollos (Titus 3:13).

The letter gives evidence that disorder and false teaching were threatening the churches on Crete (1:10–11) as well as inconsistent living by church members and the need for instruction concerning church organization. Even worse, they were allowing false teachers to wreak doctrinal havoc among the churches. The problems in Crete were partly caused by **moral laxity and careless behavior** among the Christians. The young women were flirtatious, the old women were gossips, and the men were ethically and theologically careless. Paul emphasizes that they did not receive salvation by works (3:5–6), but six times he feels the need to urge them to do good works.

GENRE AND STRUCTURE

Titus displays the epistolary genre typical of the apostle Paul. Of major significance is the letter's **similarity to 1 Timothy**. Except for the salutation (1:1–4) and the closing (3:12–15), only two doctrinal passages (2:11–14 and 3:4–7) have no resemblance to 1 Timothy.

There are **differences** as well, however. Timothy was working with an older established church (Ephesus, founded at least 10 years earlier), while Titus was left to take care of what had not yet been done or to arrange orderly practices in the churches—appoint elders, institute sound biblical teaching, and teach believers good Christian ethics. First Timothy is full of second-person-singular imperatives directed to Timothy regarding his personal ministry (such as "fight the good fight" and "guard the deposit"), but Titus has few such imperatives (2:1,15).

Paul wrote in order to (1) *encourage and strengthen* Titus in his mission on Crete; (2) *reinforce* Titus's authority among the churches on Crete; (3) *instruct* Titus and the churches in church organization; (4) *preach* on Christian behavior and good works; and (5) *ask* Titus to meet him in Nicopolis that winter and to help Zenas and Apollos on their journey.

Outline

MESSAGE

I. Introduction (Titus 1:1–4)

Paul introduces himself as "a slave of God, and an apostle of Jesus Christ"—that is, his objective in life day by day is to do whatever God and the Lord Jesus want him to accomplish. Jesus called him to be an apostle, and he emphasizes this to Titus in order to reinforce his authority as Paul's representative to the newly founded churches on Crete.

Paul says **his mission** is to build faith, to impart knowledge of the truth, and to proclaim eternal life (1:1–3). Titus is his true (genuine) child in the faith (1:4). Probably Paul was instrumental in Titus's conversion to Christ, perhaps at Antioch in Syria.

II. The Task of Titus (Titus 1:5–16)

The body of the letter outlines the task Paul left Titus to accomplish on Crete. He is to set in order the things that are still undone. First, he needs to **appoint elders** in every city (1:5–9). Elders are local church leaders who have the responsibility in each church to guide believers like a shepherd leads his flock. The elders are described in 1 Timothy 3 as "overseers," emphasizing their leadership authority. These elders should be spiritually mature and in subjection to sound teaching. They must be above reproach or publicly blameless (1:6–9), particularly in their family life, self-control, goodness, and faithfulness to the Word of God.

Titus must also **reprove the rebellious** people who are influencing the churches (1:10–16). They practice deceit and need stern reproof (1:10–13). Their deeds are worthless (1:14–16). The Cretans were by nature unruly and ungodly, especially since they were being influenced by Judaizers who continually opposed Paul's gospel of grace.

III. Sound Teaching (Titus 2:1–15)

Positively, Titus must **exhort with sound doctrine** (teaching that edifies). Good Christian behavior that fits sound doctrine must be commanded (2:1). The old men should be sober (serious and self-disciplined); the old women should be holy in their behavior; the young women should be sober, loving, chaste, and in subjection; and the

Elders

The position of elder was restricted to men who met the qualifications set forth in Titus and 1 Timothy. The term "overseer" (Greek *episkopos*, sometimes translated as "bishop") refers to the same individual as "elder" (Greek *presbuteros*, literally "old man"). This is shown by two sets of passages:

- Titus 1:5: "Appoint elders in every town."
- Titus 1:7: "For an overseer, as God's administrator, must be blameless."

The "for" at the beginning of 1:7 indicates a connection back to 1:5, showing that the overseer is an elder. Paul listed the qualifications of overseers because they were the individuals he wanted Titus to appoint (elders, v. 5).

- Acts 20:17: "[Paul] sent to Ephesus and called for the elders of the church."
- Acts 20:28: "The Holy Spirit has appointed you as overseers, to shepherd the church of God."

At the end of his third missionary journey, Paul called the "elders of the church" of Ephesus together for a meeting. In verse 28 he addressed them as "overseers."

The same correlation between "elder" and "overseer" can be seen in 1 Pet 5:1–2. The term "overseer" refers to the leadership position with its authority. The term "elder" refers to the leader's maturity or inward character. Each church appears to have had multiple elders (see Acts 14:23; 15:4; 20:17,28; Phil 1:1; 1 Tim 5:17; Titus 1:5). The authority of each elder was confined to one local church (Phil 1:1; Jas 5:14; Titus 1:5; 1 Pet 5:1–2). The function of an elder/overseer was to rule the church (1 Tim 3:4–5; 5:17). They were the "spiritual fathers" of the Christian "household," the shepherds of the local flock (Acts 20:28; 1 Pet 2:25; 5:2,4). In the early church, elders were appointed by apostles or their representatives (Acts 14:23; 1 Tim 5:17–24; Titus 1:5). Following the initial appointment, each church recognized future elders by noting their qualifications (1 Tim 3:1–7).

young men should be sober (serious minded). Titus must be an example to all of them, sound in life and teaching (2:7–8). Slaves should be obedient and respectful (2:9–10).

The reason for living a godly lifestyle is God's grace (2:11–14), which teaches all believers that they should live soberly and righteously because of the **"blessed hope" of Christ's return** and the believer's redemption and purification. Paul here speaks clearly and candidly of the deity of Jesus Christ as "our great God and Savior" (2:13).[2] Titus should therefore exhort and reprove with authority (2:15).

IV. Good Works (Titus 3:1–11)

Believers must be subject to **governmental authority**, as people who are "ready for every good work" (3:1). Having been saved "not by works of righteousness that we had done, but according to His mercy" (3:5), they were justified by God's grace (3:7) and should live a life of good works toward all men.

Titus should **speak confidently** of these things (3:8–11). Good works are useful for all, and Titus must avoid and reject contentious men. Anyone in the churches who continues to be divisive after two warnings should be treated as a sinner and be rejected (presumably kept out of church gatherings and not be allowed to teach believers).

V. Closing (Titus 3:12–15)

Paul closes the epistle by **asking Titus to meet him** at Nicopolis for the winter, as soon as either Artemas or Tychicus, two of Paul's other coworkers, could arrive to take Titus's place on Crete. Nicopolis ("city of victory") was a town in Epirus on the west coast of Greece, built by Caesar Augustus in 30 BC to honor his victory over Mark Antony at the battle of Actium in 31 BC. Paul could have reached Nicopolis by traveling west from Philippi on the Egnatian Way (a Roman road) to the Adriatic Sea, then south. He possibly planned to use the town as a base from which to evangelize Epirus (the western area of Greece).

Palace of Minos on Crete.

The teacher Apollos and a lawyer named Zenas brought the epistle to Titus. Paul then asked Titus and the Cretan churches to help them financially so they could continue their journey without difficulty ("lacking nothing"). This is Paul's **final exhortation** for the believers: Devote yourselves to helping urgent needs so as not to be unfruitful in sharing what you have.

CONCLUSION

Titus and Paul had been coworkers for many years, and Paul had come to trust Titus to solve some really tough problems (see 2 Corinthians 7–8). Now, following Paul's release from imprisonment in Rome, they had made a joint spiritual investment in the founding and growth of churches on the Greek-speaking island of Crete. The converts in these churches were not all devoting themselves to growing in Christ, and Titus's job was to direct them to that important task.

Study Questions

1. What topics do 1 Timothy and Titus have in common?
2. How are atonement, redemption, and sanctification related to one another?
3. How does the emphasis on good works in Titus relate to the similar emphasis in the epistle of James?
4. In what ways can a Christian "adorn" the doctrine of God in the way Paul means it in Titus?
5. How could you find out more about the history of Christianity in Crete?

For Further Reading

Getz, Gene A. *The Measure of a Christian: Studies in Titus.* Ventura, CA: Regal Books, 1983.

Knight, George. *The Pastoral Epistles.* NIGTC. Grand Rapids: Eerdmans, 1992.

Köstenberger, Andreas J. "1–2 Timothy, Titus." In *EBC.* Edited by Tremper Longman III and David E. Garland. Grand Rapids: Zondervan, 2005.

Lea, Thomas, and Hayne Griffin. *1, 2 Timothy, Titus.* NAC. Nashville: B&H, 1992.

Towner, Philip H. *The Letters to Timothy and Titus.* NICNT. Grand Rapids: Eerdmans, 2006.

ENDNOTES

1. *1 Clement* 2.7; 33.1.
2. See Daniel B. Wallace, *Greek Grammar Beyond the Basics: An Exegetical Syntax of the New Testament* (Grand Rapids: Zondervan, 1996), 276.

Chapter 22

PHILEMON
Social Dynamics of the Gospel

Onesimus was Philemon's **runaway slave** who met Paul in Rome. There Onesimus came to faith in Christ through contact with the apostle Paul. Philemon had the right to put Onesimus to death, but Paul interceded for him in this short epistle, which emphasizes the social dynamics of the gospel.

Key Facts	
Author:	The apostle Paul
Recipient:	Philemon, his wife (and the church looking over his shoulder)
Where Written:	Rome where Paul was under house arrest
Date:	AD 60–62
Key Word:	Brother (Gk. *adelphos*)
Key Verse:	"And if he [Onesimus] has wronged you in any way, or owes you anything, charge that to my account" (18).

AUTHOR

Paul is in Roman custody awaiting trial by the emperor, Nero. After his third missionary journey, Paul was in the Jewish temple area in Jerusalem when a riot broke out because some Jews thought Paul had brought Gentiles into the temple area. He was rescued by Roman authorities but later falsely accused by the Jews (Acts 24:5–6). An assassination attempt was even planned on Paul's life by a band of extremist Jews (Acts 23:20–21). When it looked like he would not be given a fair trial in Israel, Paul invoked his right as a Roman citizen to **appeal his case to Caesar** (Acts 25:10–11). Roman authorities transported Paul to Rome for trial, but he was accompanied by Luke and Aristarchus (Acts 27:1–2). Paul awaited trial for two years and was allowed to live "in his own rented house" and to receive visitors (Acts 28:30). The date is around **AD 60–62**, and Paul pens four epistles during this stay in Rome—Ephesians, Philippians, Colossians, and Philemon.

RECIPIENT

Philemon was a **wealthy slave owner** who lived in Colossae, along the Lycus River valley about 100 miles east of Ephesus. Colossae was an influential city on the major trade route to the east. Philemon came to faith in Christ as a result of Paul's three-year stay in Ephesus on his third missionary journey. Paul was instrumental in his salvation (v. 19). The church in Colossae actually met in this rich man's home.

The Lycus River Valley as seen from Colossae. At the time this letter was written, the church at Colossae met in the home of Philemon.

OCCASION AND DATE

The epistle to Philemon is Paul's appeal to Philemon, a wealthy believer in Colossae, to receive back his runaway slave, Onesimus, who came to Christ through Paul's ministry in Rome. The key theological idea of this epistle is that of **imputation**, placing something on another's account. Just as Christ took our sins upon Himself, so Paul asks Philemon to place the guilt, or debt, of Onesimus upon Paul. Paul expresses this in v. 18.

The first century AD in the Roman Empire forms the backdrop for this epistle. **Slavery** was a major institution in that era. Out of a population of approximately 200 million in the Roman Empire, there could have been as many as 60 million slaves. Many slave owners had a dozen or more slaves, and some owned hundreds. Slaves were not of any particular nationality or race. Many were skilled and well trained. A family might own a doctor, a teacher, chaperones, cooks, house servants, nurses, and other caregivers. Some slaves helped manufacture items for sale, transported goods, or worked in agriculture. Some were skilled writers or copyists. Some individuals became slaves to pay off debts. Most slaves were considered the property of their owners. They could be bought and sold and used for any purpose. Slaves could be beaten for wrongdoing and even crucified for running away. But slaves were also an investment, costing the equivalent of one to two years' income of an average worker.[1] The Old Testament laws regarding slavery were much in contrast with the Roman practice. Slaves were treated like household members (Lev 25:53) and could become partakers of the Abrahamic covenant (Gen 17:27). During the sabbatical year they were to be freed (Exod 21:2). If a slave was harmed, he was to be set free (Exod 21:26–27); and if someone killed a slave, severe punishment could result (Exod 21:20). Runaway slaves were not to be hunted down or returned to their masters (Deut 23:15–16).

In this epistle Paul masterfully sought to bring **Christian compassion** into the Roman slavery system where it concerned Christians. Paul urged Onesimus to return to Philemon and urged Philemon to receive Onesimus as a brother in Christ. Paul may have had Onesimus in mind when he addressed slaves and slave owners in Eph 6:5–8 and in Col 3:22–25, both of which were written about the same time as the epistle to Philemon.

Eleven persons, including Paul, are mentioned in this little letter. Six of them—Timothy, Epaphras, Mark, Aristarchus, Demas, and Luke—are with Paul in Rome. Timothy is mentioned in the initial verse with Paul as a sender. Epaphras (v. 23) is a fellow prisoner with Paul and sends his greetings. Mark, Aristarchus, Demas, and Luke are called Paul's coworkers and also send greetings (v. 24). Apphia is greeted warmly by Paul and is probably Philemon's wife (v. 2). Archippus has some responsibilities in the local congregation and may be the son of Apphia and Philemon (v. 2). Colossians 4:7–9 informs us that Paul sent Tychicus to accompany Onesimus back to Philemon. This leaves the three prominent persons about whom this epistle revolves—Paul (the author; see above), Philemon (the recipient; see above), and Onesimus.

Onesimus was a slave of Philemon. However, he took the opportunity to escape and made his way Rome. He apparently paid for his escapades with money or other valuables stolen from Philemon. However, in God's providence Onesimus met **Paul** in Rome, and Paul led him to a saving knowledge of Jesus Christ. Now as a Christian, Onesimus is urged by Paul to return to **Philemon** and make things right. Paul writes this short epistle to smooth the way for Onesimus's reception by Philemon. The Greek word *doulos* means slave, one who is the servant of another. The New Testament uses this common word 126 times, and Paul uses *doulos* twice to refer to Onesimus in v. 16. Roman slaves had no rights, and Philemon could have put his runaway slave to death.

GENRE AND STRUCTURE

Paul's epistolary prologue takes up the opening unit (vv. 1–3). The first main section of the body of the letter includes Paul's prayer and praise for Philemon (vv. 4–7). The second major unit contains Paul's plea for profitable Onesimus (vv. 8–21). The letter concludes with Paul's personal prospects (v. 22) and a postscript (vv. 23–25).[2]

Outline

I. Prologue (Philemon 1–3)
II. Praise for Philemon (Philemon 4–7)
III. Plea for Onesimus (Philemon 8–21)
IV. Postscript (Philemon 22– 25)

MESSAGE

I. Prologue (Philemon 1–3)

In his prologue, or opening remarks, Paul identifies himself as the writer. Paul does not call himself an apostle here as he does in seven other epistles but rather refers to himself as **a prisoner** for Christ's sake. This is more personal and also quite touching. Outwardly, Paul is Nero's prisoner, but inwardly he is a prisoner of Christ. Timothy was with Paul in Ephesus and is probably known to Philemon, so he joins Paul in strengthening the appeal to Philemon. Apphia, Philemon's wife, would have had the day-to-day responsibility for the slaves so she was perhaps as much a party to the decision to receive back Onesimus as was her husband. Archippus, their son, is mentioned as a fellow soldier. This evokes images of being fit, well trained, effective, brave, and a hard worker. The letter is also addressed "to the church that meets in your home" (v. 2). The church would be looking over Philemon's shoulder, so to speak, as he read the epistle from Paul. They could bring appropriate pressure should Philemon lean otherwise than Paul appeals.

Paul sends the believers **grace and peace** as he does in six other epistles. We have peace by being in the spiritual state of a proper relationship with God. God's grace, His unmerited favor shown to us in Christ, is what brings this about, and all is hallowed by the name of our Lord Jesus Christ.

II. Praise for Philemon (Philemon 4–7)

Next Paul offers thanksgiving as he does in every epistle except Galatians. When Paul says he prays for "you," hearing of "your love and faith," he uses the singular and is speaking of Philemon. Paul says that Philemon's love goes out to all the saints, and that must also include Onesimus since he is now a believer.

Philemon's **partnership**, or sharing (Gk. *koinonia*) in the faith, will be effective because of his full understanding of God's goodness. The word "effective" is used in the New Testament only here and in two other places.[3] The more we comprehend of God's grace, the more eager we are to share it, as was true of Philemon.

Paul also mentions that Philemon has been a source of refreshment for the saints. Since he has been refreshed by Christ, he can now refresh others. The implication is that his maturity in Christ will find expression in Philemon's treatment of Onesimus.

III. Plea for Onesimus (Philemon 8–21)

Paul begins v. 8 with the phrase "For this reason." This is the application of vv. 4–7. Paul is an apostle of our Lord Jesus Christ. He could boldly command Philemon to **receive Onesimus back** in a kindly and godly manner but instead "appeals" to him. The intimate union of Paul and Philemon in Christ makes such a frank appeal possible. In v. 9, Paul makes three appeals. First, he appeals to Philemon "on the basis of love." It could be a reference to Christian love in general, to the love that Paul and Philemon have for each other, or just Philemon's love for Onesimus. Second, Paul refers to himself "as an elderly man." Paul's failing powers have been worn down in the Lord's service. Third, Paul says that he is "a prisoner of Christ Jesus." The weakness of his age, aggravated by the helplessness of his bonds, should evoke some sympathy from Philemon.

In vv. 10–11, Paul **tenderly appeals** for Onesimus as his "son" in the faith. He actually calls him his own child. Paul only uses this word (Gk. *teknon*) to refer to two other individuals, both of whom he led to Christ.[4] Paul "fathered" Onesimus while "in chains" in Rome. This spiritual relationship Paul has with Onesimus is deep and tender. Notice that the name "Onesimus" comes last in the sentence that begins in v. 9. It is the perfect touch of heart rhetoric.

Figure of a slave seeking refuge at an altar. Onesimus, Philemon's slave, found refuge and freedom in Christ through the ministry of Paul.

In v. 12, Paul says he is **sending Onesimus back** to Philemon. Onesimus had been a personal attendant of Paul, waiting on and serving some of Paul's needs while in chains (v. 13). To have kept Onesimus would have been to reap a benefit from Philemon, willing or not. Philemon's good had always been given willingly (v. 14). What unselfishness on the part of Paul to send Onesimus back, and what courage of conscience and faith on the part of Onesimus as he stands before Philemon while the latter reads the epistle. By law Philemon could treat Onesimus as he pleased—whether to allow him to live or put him to death.

In vv. 15–16, Paul introduces a new reason for Onesimus's return. "Perhaps," Paul says, in **God's providence** Onesimus the runaway, was sent away, as it were by God, to become a believer. Now Philemon can receive him back as if he had been loaned to the Lord. Onesimus returns not as a slave but "as a dearly loved brother" (v. 16). This concept is the antithesis to the principle of slavery and even the ultimate existence of slavery. Both master and slave are "in the Lord." Therefore, Paul assumes Onesimus's debt, even as Christ assumed ours.[5] "Charge that to my account" is Paul's way of appealing for forgiveness and restitution. Thus, this letter is a model for Christian social responsibility.

Paul himself (Gk. *ego*) takes up the pen at this point and formally mentions his own name as in a **legal document**. "I will repay it" (v. 19) is emphatic in the original letter. But Philemon is asked to consider that he actually owes Paul his own life. He is obligated to Paul spiritually, but Paul does not dwell on this fact.

Paul calls Philemon "brother" and asks that he might have joy and be refreshed by Philemon, even as Philemon has refreshed others (v. 20). Paul also expresses his **confidence** in Philemon's "obedience" (v. 21) to his request. This is a little more direct than his other tactful appeals, but it is the obedience as to a father and a benefactor. Paul also trusts that Philemon "will do even more than I say" (v. 21). What would that be? Certainly welcomed and forgiven but freed? If Onesimus were released, it would show the effect that true brotherhood in Christ has on slavery.

IV. Postscript (Philemon 22–25)

Having concluded his formal appeal for Onesimus, Paul tells Philemon that he believes he will be released soon through the prayers of Philemon and others.[6] He asks Philemon to "prepare a guest room for me" (v. 22). How can Philemon pray for Paul's release and then refuse to release Onesimus? The mention of Paul's coming to Colossae might also spur Philemon on with his decision about Onesimus.

In his final postscript, Paul mentions some of those who are with him. Epaphras is called a "fellow prisoner in Christ" and sends greetings to Philemon and the church at Colossae (v. 23). Mark, Aristarchus, Demas, and Luke are called "co-workers" (24). But in Col 4:10 Aristarchus is also termed a "fellow prisoner," simply in view of his constant association with Paul at that moment. He is with Paul so much that he is virtually under the same house arrest, though not in chains.

Mark was the nephew of Barnabas. He accompanied Paul and Barnabas on their first missionary journey but then "left them and went back to Jerusalem" (Acts 13:13) not even halfway through the mission. Paul later refused to allow Mark to accompany them on a proposed second journey. Instead, Mark went with Barnabas. Paul then selected Silas as his second missionary partner. However, Mark's failure was not final. He recovered and became a close disciple of Peter. Peter even calls him "Mark, my son" (1 Pet 5:13). Mark also penned the Gospel of Mark. Paul wrote his final epistle from the Mamertine Prison in Rome and told Timothy, "Bring Mark with you, for he is useful to me in the ministry" (2 Tim 4:11). Mark's restitution, like that of Onesimus is a model of Christian forgiveness. **Demas** is also mentioned as a "co-worker" in v. 24 and sent his greetings with Paul in Col 4:14. Unfortunately, Demas later defected from Paul and apparently from Christ. Paul's final words about Demas are found in 2 Timothy 4. Paul says, "Demas has deserted me, because he loved this present world" (v. 10). **Luke**, of course, was the writer of the Gospel that bears his name and also of the book of Acts. He joined Paul's missionary company at Troas on Paul's second journey (Acts 16:10).

Paul concludes all 13 of his epistles with a **one-sentence benediction** like the one in v. 25: "The grace of the Lord Jesus Christ be with your spirit." God gives us grace for our daily walk with Him. He infuses His grace into our inner spirit. We can be aware of His unmerited favor at all times. Paul uses "your" in the plural as he ends this epistle. The grace of Christ extends to the spirit of all of the believers who are there with Philemon.

CONCLUSION

Philemon is **Paul's shortest epistle**, but it is packed with practical and spiritual truth. Martin Luther said, "We are all the Lord's Onesimi," using the Latin plural of Onesimus. Just as Onesimus owed a great debt he could not pay, so do we. Christ came to Earth to pay a debt He did not owe because we owed a debt we could not pay.

Study Questions

1. Under what circumstances did Paul pen the letter to Philemon?
2. What was the nature of the relationship between Philemon and Onesimus at the time Paul wrote to Philemon, and how did Paul envision this relationship changing?
3. Where did Philemon live, and how did he become a believer in Christ?
4. How does Paul's intercession for Onesimus picture what Christ has done for believers?
5. What was slavery like in the Roman Empire at the time of Paul?

For Further Reading

Barth, Markus, and Helmut Blanke. *The Letter to Philemon: A New Translation with Notes and Commentary.* Grand Rapids: Eerdmans, 2000.

Bruce, F. F. *The Epistle to the Colossians, Philemon, and the Ephesians.* NICNT. Grand Rapids: Eerdmans, 1984.

Lucas, R. C. *The Message of Colossians and Philemon.* Leicester, UK: IVP, 1980.

Müller, Jac J. *The Epistles of Paul to the Philippians and to Philemon.* Grand Rapids: Eerdmans, 1955.

Ray, Charles. *Timothy, Titus, and Philemon: Goals to Godliness.* Chattanooga: AMG Publishers, 2007.

ENDNOTES

1. See Markus Barth and Helmut Blanke, *The Letter to Philemon: A New Translation with Notes and Commentary* (Grand Rapids: Eerdmans, 2000), 1–102, which deals extensively with slavery at the time of Paul.

2. James A. Borland, "The Epistle to Philemon," in *King James Bible Commentary* (Nashville: Thomas Nelson, 1999), 1666–69.

3. First Corinthians 16:9 and Heb 4:12. The latter refers to God's Word as a two-edged sword. In the Greek papyri, the word is used of a mill in working order and of a finely plowed field.

4. These two are Timothy and Titus. See 1 Tim 1:2 and Titus 1:4.

5. See Heb 4:15 and 7:25.

6. When Paul says "your" prayers, he uses the plural. Philemon and the other believers at Colossae have been praying for Paul's release.

Chapter 23

HEBREWS
Jesus Our Great High Priest

During difficult times of hardship and persecution, Christians are often told to "trust Jesus and have faith." But often during these times, trusting and having faith seem most difficult to hold on to. Doubt and despair tug at our souls, dragging us away from faith and telling us no one understands our despair. We may even start to wonder if we could lose our faith altogether. Hebrews, unlike any other book of the New Testament, calls us back to endure in our faith and to hold fast to Jesus' message. It reminds us that Jesus Himself was no stranger to suffering: As God's Son, He was greater than the prophets and the angels, yet He entered humanity to suffer in our place. Through His endurance He became our Great High Priest. As the author of Hebrews unfolds these truths, it becomes clear that we are not alone in our sufferings; we are surrounded by a crowd of faithful witnesses, and we too must continue in faith, focusing on Jesus, our Great High Priest, as we run the race toward God's everlasting kingdom.

Key Facts	
Author:	Unknown
Recipients:	Unknown
Where Written:	Unknown
Date:	Before AD 70
Key Word:	Better (Gk. *kreittōn*)
Key Verses:	"Therefore since we have a great high priest who has passed through the heavens—Jesus the Son of God—let us hold fast to the confession. For we do not have a high priest who is unable to sympathize with our weaknesses, but One who has been tested in every way as we are, yet without sin. Therefore let us approach the throne of grace with boldness, so that we may receive mercy and find grace to help us at the proper time" (4:14–16).

AUTHOR

The letter to the Hebrews is anonymous. Unlike the other epistles, it is unsigned. Many have held **Paul** as the author of Hebrews. There are several points of contact between the content of this book and the content of Paul's other letters:

1. Jesus' preexistence and creatorship (Heb 1:1–4; Col 1:15–17)
2. The giving of gifts by the Holy Spirit (Heb 2:4; 1 Cor 12:11)
3. The humiliation of Christ (Heb 2:14–17; Phil 2:5–8)
4. The new covenant (Heb 8:6; 2 Cor 3:4–11)

However, even the early church was not in total agreement about who wrote it. Though the Eastern church held that Paul was the author early on, the majority of the Western church did not hold to Pauline authorship until the late fourth and early fifth centuries. Pauline authorship was then accepted in the West until it was challenged again during the Reformation. Some **obstacles** to Pauline authorship are as follows:

1. Hebrews is anonymous, whereas Paul's 13 other letters begin by naming him as the sender.
2. Hebrews contains no greeting or prayer for the people as Paul's letters traditionally do.
3. Hebrews does not use the phrase "Christ Jesus," as Paul's letters often do.
4. Stylistically, the Greek of Hebrews seems more polished than that of Paul.
5. The vocabulary and argumentation are different from Paul's letters.
6. The author of Hebrews states that salvation was "first spoken by the Lord and was confirmed to us by those who heard Him" (2:3). This seems inconsistent with Paul's claims elsewhere that he did not receive the gospel from any man but through a vision of Jesus Christ (Gal 1:12).

In light of the challenges to Pauline authorship, it is better to admit that the **identity** of the author of Hebrews is **uncertain**. A few things are more certain: (1) assuming that the Timothy mentioned in 13:23 was the same that traveled with Paul on his second and third missionary journeys, the author was someone who knew Timothy and lived in the first century AD; (2) the author had a

An artist's presentation of the garments of the high priest.

thorough knowledge of the Old Testament; and (3) he was an eloquent speaker and/ or writer. Regardless of the author's identity, the early church had reason for associating it with Paul or one of his close associates and for accepting it into the canon. While some questions are unanswered, the church in practice has agreed with the early church's decision to accept it into Scripture. Christians view Hebrews as an important witness to Jesus' identity and ministry as the Son of God and our Great High Priest.

RECIPIENTS

Just as we are unsure of the identity of the author of Hebrews, we are equally unsure of where the people who received it lived. We may have a clue in 13:24 where it states that "[t]hose who are from Italy greet you." However, this statement can be interpreted in two ways: (1) "Those from Italy" could refer to people who were from Italy but were living in a foreign land sending their greetings home (similar to the situation with Paul's friends Aquila and Priscilla); this would mean that the letter was written to Italy. (2) The phrase could refer to believers in Italy sending their greetings to an unspecified city, thus the letter was sent from Italy. Therefore, without any explicit mention of the book's audience, we can only speak in general terms about the characteristics of the audience rather than their geographic location. The content and argumentation of the letter seem to indicate that the recipients were **Jewish believers** familiar with the Old Testament and tempted to go back to Judaism by observing Old Testament feast days and temple practices, including animal sacrifices.

OCCASION AND DATE

Internal evidence implies that Jewish Christians were considering returning to the sacrificial system of old covenant Judaism.[1] These are urged to hold firm to their confession (3:16,14; 4:14; 10:23) and argue that now that Jesus is the Great High Priest of a new covenant there is no going back to the old covenant sacrificial system of Judaism. A date of **pre-AD 70** seems likely. The sacrificial ritual is consistently described in the present tense (7:8; 9:6–7,9,13; 13:10). This may indicate that the temple is still in use and that the book should be dated sometime before the temple's destruction in AD 70. What is more, since the author of Hebrews is showing that Jesus made the greatest and final sacrifice when He offered Himself, it is hard to believe he would not have explicitly pointed out the relationship between Jesus' ultimate sacrifice and the destruction of the temple.

GENRE AND STRUCTURE

Some view Hebrews as an **epistle**; however, while the book has an epistolary conclusion, it does not begin with an epistolary greeting or blessing. Others, noting the book contains oral features, have described Hebrews as a **sermon** or even as a series of sermons. Without knowing for certain if this book is a single letter, a single sermon, or a series of sermons, the book's structure is difficult to identify and outline. For this reason there is no universally agreed outline for the book of Hebrews.

Outline

I. Theological Declaration: Superiority of Christ (Hebrews 1–6)
   A. Jesus the Son Is Superior to Angels (1–2)
   B. Jesus the Son Is Superior to Moses (3:1–6)
   C. Having a Great High Priest: Hold Fast and Draw Near (Heb 4:14–16)
   D. The Son as the Great High Priest (Heb 5:1–7:10)
II. Biblical Explanation: Priesthood of Christ (Hebrews 7–10)
   A. Priesthood in the order of Melchizedek (Hebrews 7)
   B. Priest of the New Covenant (Hebrews 8)
   C. Priestly Sacrifice of Christ (Hebrews 9–10)
   D. Transition: Since We Have a Great High Priest, Draw Near, Hold Fast, and Consider (Heb 10:19–25)
III. Practical Application: Living by Faith (Hebrews 11–13)
   A. Examples of Faith (Hebrews 11)
   B. Lifestyle of Faith (Hebrews 12–13)

MESSAGE

I. Theological Declaration: Superiority of Christ (Hebrews 1–6)

A. Jesus the Son Is Superior to Angels (1–2)

The author of Hebrews sees himself as living at a significant time in history because while "long ago" God spoke through the prophets, during his time He has spoken through His Son, Jesus (1:1; 2:9). As God's Son, **Jesus is superior** to the prophets and even the angels. As God's Son, He is the radiance of God's glory and the exact representation of His nature.

Though the Son's coming did not occur until "these last days," the Son has been at work in the world long before this time. In fact, He is credited as the **Creator of the world** (1:2–3) who laid the foundation of the Earth and made the heavens with His hands (1:10). In addition, He is credited as the One who sustains the world by the power of His word. Despite the sustaining of the world by the Son, its inhabitants sinned and were in need of purification. The Son, therefore, came into the world to bring it back to its original state by making purification for the sin of the people. Since God's children (mankind) were flesh and blood, the Son, too, became like them so that He could become a merciful and faithful high priest in order to give a sacrifice for their sin (2:14–18).

After this was completed, Jesus returned to His position of authority in heaven. While this position was in many respects a return, He was now not only the Creator and Sustainer of the world but also its **Redeemer** and **High Priest**. Therefore, while He was for a little while made lower than the angels, He has now been crowned with glory and honor and all created things are now under His authority (2:6–8). He is now the Heir of all things and has a more excellent name than even the angels (who would now worship Him). This position of honor will remain His even after the heavens and the Earth, which He made, become worn out like old garments. And as old garments they will be changed, but He will remain the same.

Warning 1: Do Not Neglect Such Great Salvation (2:1–4)

Because this Son, Jesus, is greater than the prophets and the angels, there is a **greater responsibility** for those who hear the message to accept it and a **greater judgment** for those who do not. Looking back to Old Testament law, the author of Hebrews reasons that "if the message spoken through angels was legally binding and every transgression and disobedience received a just punishment, how will we escape if we neglect such a great salvation?"

B. Jesus the Son Is Superior to Moses (3:1–6)

In chapter 2, the author called Jesus "a merciful and faithful high priest" who made "propitiation for the sins of the people" (v. 17). This theme is developed greatly throughout the remainder of the book. But presently the author continues to emphasize the unique importance of Jesus' sonship by comparing him to **Moses**. Moses is the prophet who wrote the first five books of the Old Testament, liberated the people from slavery in Egypt through miraculous means, and led the people to the Promised Land. The Jews of Jesus' day were even expecting a prophet like Moses to come (Deut 18:15–19). With these things in mind, Moses could be viewed as the premier prophet in all of God's salvation history, until the coming of the Son. From this comparison the author concludes that while Moses was a faithful servant of God, Jesus' position as a faithful Son is worthy of more glory than Moses' position as a servant.

Warning 2: Don't Harden Your Heart but Enter God's Rest (3:7–4:13)

Having compared Jesus to Moses, the author now compares the people that followed Moses with those who are following Jesus. He explains that those who followed Moses in the wilderness had **unbelieving hearts** and sinned against God. Consequently, though they had heard God's message, they were not able to enter because their hearing was not united with belief (3:19). We too have heard this message, and this rest is still available for those of us who believe and continue to the end (4:2). He therefore gives the second warning of the book, "Today if you hear His voice, do not harden your hearts" (4:7) and resolves, "let us then make every effort to enter that rest, so that no one will fall into the same pattern of disobedience" (4:11).

C. Having a Great High Priest: Hold Fast and Draw Near (Heb 4:14–16)

In the final three verses of chap. 4, the warning in 3:7–4:16 is buffered with a **message of hope**: We should stand firm in our confession because we have something that those following Moses did not have, that is, Jesus the Son of God as our great High Priest. He sympathizes with our weaknesses and gives us confidence to approach the throne of God to receive mercy and grace in our time of need. These three verses serve as a transition to the next chapter and instills a curiosity in his audience for what he is about to say concerning Jesus' distinctive priesthood.

South end of the Wilderness of Paran where the Israelites wandered.

D. The Son as the Great High Priest (Heb 5:1–7:10)

Chapter 5 begins by comparing **Jesus' priesthood** with that of Aaron's. There are some similarities: (1) in both priesthoods, God chose men to be the high priest; (2) both offered gifts and sacrifices for the sins of men; (3) both in their humanity dealt gently with us and were sympathetic to our weaknesses. However, key differences set Jesus' priesthood apart from Aaron's: (1) though Jesus was in all ways tempted as we are, He did not sin; (2) as a sinless priest, Jesus did not have to offer sacrifices for Himself as Aaron did; (3) Jesus was not of the Levitical priesthood descended from the Levites but is God's Son, and a priest forever "in the order of Melchizedek"; (4) Jesus was perfect and became to all those who obey Him the source of eternal salvation.

Warning 3: Don't Fall Away from the Faith (5:11–6:20)

Having just made the comparison between the priesthood of Aaron and that of Melchizedek, the author of Hebrews expresses concern for his audience. They have become "dull of hearing." Though by this time they should be ready for in-depth teaching, they are still spiritual infants. He therefore rebukes them for their lack of maturity and the danger of falling away from the faith. But he buffers this warning with **the assurance** that, despite the fact that he is talking with them in this way, he is convinced of better things for them: God is not unjust. He will not forget their deeds and love. If they are patient like Abraham; they, too, will inherit God's promises. God cannot lie, and they too will enter into the holy place that Jesus, their High Priest, has entered before them.

II. Biblical Explanation: Priesthood of Christ (Hebrews 7–10)

A. Priesthood in the Order of Melchizedek (Hebrews 7)

After the third warning, the author picks up where he left off in 5:10, continuing his discussion on the importance of **Melchizedek**. He looks to Genesis 14, the passage where Abraham pays Melchizedek a tithe and notes that (1) Melchizedek was a priest of God; (2) his name means "king of righteousness"; (3) his title "king of Salem" means "king of peace." So it can be said that he is both a priest and a king of peace and righteousness. Beyond this, however, the biblical narrative is silent concerning Melchizedek's identity and origin. No genealogy is given, and his parents are not named. There is no word as to his birth or his death. This silence shrouds in mystery the identity of Melchizedek as a priest and king. Literarily speaking, he mysteriously enters the narrative and then exits. This mystery deepens when one considers what relationship this "priest of God" has with the priests and kings of Israel under the law of Moses.

The author of Hebrews begins to answer this question by explaining that Abraham's tithe to Melchizedek shows that Abraham and all of his priestly descendants are inferior to Melchizedek. He does this in two steps. First, he explains that the one who pays the tithe is inferior to the one who receives it. Since Abraham paid the tithe to Melchizedek, he acknowledged that he was inferior to Melchizedek who received it. Second, the author reasons that Abraham's tithe to Melchizedek shows the Levites to be inferior as well. Levi (from whom the Levitical priests are descended) was still in Abraham's loins when he paid the tithe; therefore his children were participating in this gift along with him. For the modern reader this second step in the author's line of reasoning is somewhat foreign. His main point, however, is clear enough: the Melchizedekian priesthood is greater than Abraham and the Levitical priesthood which descended from him.

The temple veil is a curtain that separated the most holy place from the holy place. Only the high priest was allowed to pass through the veil and then only on the Day of Atonement.

B. Priest of the New Covenant (Hebrews 8)

A question likely to be looming in the mind of the reader is, "How can Melchizedek's priesthood replace the Levitical priesthood when the Levitical priesthood is sanctioned by the law of Moses?" The author of Hebrews argues that Moses' law appointed priests who were weak and needed to offer sacrifices for their own sins before offering sacrifices for the people (7:27). Because these priests were mortal, a whole succession of priests was needed. There was, therefore, a need for a priest based not on the old law but on something **more permanent**. The author finds this permanence in Jesus' priesthood because it is not based on the old law but on God's promise, which came after the law. This promise, is referred to is Ps 110:4, which states that the messianic King would be "forever, . . . a priest like Melchizedek." Since this priesthood is based on this promise rather than on the law, Jesus is not disqualified by being born of the kingly line of Judah rather than the priestly line of Levi. On the contrary, He is a priest of a different sort, a holy, innocent, undefiled priest whose office is permanent and **heavenly**. As such, He has offered himself as a once-for-all sacrifice and is "able to save those who come to God through Him, since He always lives to intercede

---

Greek Highlight

Covenant. Greek διαθήκη *(diathēkē)*. A *covenant* (*diatheke*) is a legal arrangement between two parties (Gal 3:15) or a document transferring property from the deceased to an heir (Heb 9:16). The Greek OT influenced the use of *diatheke* in the NT, where the *covenant* was an agreement by which God's people related to Him. The NT frequently mentions three OT *covenants*: (1) the Abrahamic *covenant* (Gen 12:1–3; 15:1–21; 17:1–27), (2) the Mosaic *covenant* (Exod 20:1–24:8), and (3) the new *covenant* (Jer 31:31–34); and it often focuses on the relationship between the Mosaic and new *covenants* (e.g., 2 Cor 3:6, 14). Over half of the occurrences of *diatheke* occur in Hebrews, where Jesus is portrayed as mediator of the new *covenant*, a *covenant* superior to the Mosaic *covenant* (Heb 7:22; 8:6,8–10; 9:15). As the Mosaic *covenant* was inaugurated with blood, so the new *covenant* was inaugurated with Jesus' blood (Heb 10:18–28; 13:20; cf. Matt 26:28; 1 Cor 11:25).

---

for them" (7:25–27). Jesus should therefore be seen as "the guarantee of a better covenant" than that of Moses and the Levitical priests (7:22–24).

C. Priestly Sacrifice of Christ (Hebrews 9–10)

In chap. 8, the author of Hebrews develops what it means for Jesus to be the mediator of this **better covenant**. He quotes Jeremiah 31 at length to give scriptural proof for his claim that a new covenant has come which supersedes the old. From this passage he concludes that "by saying, a new covenant, He has declared that the first is old. And what is old and aging is about to disappear" (8:13).

With this in view, the author turns his attention to presenting Jesus as "a minister of the sanctuary and the true tabernacle" (8:2). He begins by painting a picture for his readers of the earthy sanctuary of the first covenant. He reminds them that the earthly tabernacle was made up of two rooms. The first was called the holy place and was opened to the priests every day. The second room was called the holy of holies and was only open to the high priest once a year whenever he sacrificed on the Day of Atonement (9:1–7; 10:3). This limited access to God and continual need for sacrifice reveals the old system's limitations. It could not fully restore the worshipper's relationship with God, and the blood of animals could not take away sins (9:8–10; 10:4). The old system was insufficient and needed to be replaced.

With these deficiencies in view, Jesus' priestly duties were not performed in an earthly sanctuary, a mere copy of the heavenly, but in the **heavenly sanctuary** itself (9:24). When Jesus did so, He did not offer the blood of animals continually, but with His own blood once for all (9:12). Because Jesus offered this greater sacrifice in a greater sanctuary, He has removed sin and attained eternal redemption for all of God's people and has enacted the **new covenant** predicted by Jeremiah (9:11–13; 10:16–17). By doing so, He has brought forgiveness; and where there is forgiveness, there is no longer any need for an offering for sin (10:18).

D. Transition: Since We Have a Great High Priest, Draw Near, Hold Fast, and Consider (Heb 10:19–25)

In light of what Jesus has done, the author encourages his audience to: (1) have **confidence** to enter into the holy place through Jesus' blood; (2) draw near with a sincere heart in full assurance of faith with a clean conscience and pure bodies; (3) hold fast to their confession without wavering; (4) not forsake assembling together with other believers; and (5) encourage one another as they see the day of salvation drawing near (10:19–25).

Warning 4: Do Not Shrink Back in Your Confession (10:26–39)

Now that Jesus has replaced the sacrificial system, there is no other sacrifice for those who reject Him. The author therefore warns his readers to **persevere** in their confession; those who shrink back are (1) trampling on the Son of God; (2) profaning the blood of the covenant; and (3) insulting the Spirit of grace. Such people will suffer God's punishment. Therefore, the author encourages his readers to look back to earlier hardships and to continue to endure in doing God's will. In this way they can receive God's promises rather than His judgment.

III. Practical Application: Living by Faith (Hebrews 11–13)

A. Examples of Faith (Hebrews 11)

In chap. 10, the author of Hebrews encourages his audience to find support and encouragement by assembling together with other believers. Once again he turns his attention to the fellowship of a **common faith**. He explains that "faith is the reality of what is hoped for, the proof of what is not seen" and that through faith our ancestors were approved (11:1). He mentions Abel, Enoch, Noah, Abraham, and Sarah and then explains that all of these "died in faith without having received the promises, but they saw them from a distance, greeted them, and confessed that they were foreigners and temporary residents on the earth" (11:13). These people sought after a heavenly country which was **better** than their own, and God prepared a heavenly city for them. His list continues with accounts of the faith of Isaac, Jacob, Joseph, Moses, and Rahab. He laments that he does not have time to talk about Gideon, Barak, Sampson, Jephthah, David, and Samuel, and the prophets who "who by faith conquered kingdoms, administered justice, obtained promises, shut the mouths of lions, quenched the raging of fire, escaped the edge of the sword, gained strength after being weak, became mighty in battle, and put foreign armies to flight" (11:33–34). He notes that these did not receive what was promised during their lifetime because "God had provided something better for us, so that they would not be made perfect without us" (11:40). These examples show that Christians are not alone in their trials but are united in the faith and hopes of all who have come before them. Beyond this, Christians see the promises of God from long ages past becoming a reality within their own lifetime.

B. Lifestyle of Faith (Hebrews 12–13)

Fix Your Eyes on Jesus and Endure Discipline (Heb 12:1–17). In light of these examples of faith, the author of Hebrews encourages his readers to fix their eyes on Jesus with the same intensity that a runner fixes his gaze on his goal. And like a runner they must continue with **endurance** and rid themselves of any sin that could trip them up in the race of life. Jesus Himself modeled this; by fixing His eyes on the joy ahead, He endured the cross, despised the shame, and sat down at the right hand of the throne of God (12:1–3). By looking to Jesus, the readers could see that their sufferings were small compared to His. They had not yet suffered to the point of shedding blood as He did.

If Jesus, God's Son, endured this kind of suffering, it follows that Christians might suffer in a similar way. God disciplines those He loves (12:5–6). The author, therefore, encourages his audience that their endurance is a form of **God's discipline** which reveals that they are God's beloved sons. While this discipline will seem unpleasant for them at the time, it is for their betterment and will yield the fruit of peace and righteousness afterwards (12:11).

Mount Sinai Versus Mount Zion (Heb 12:18–24). In this section the author emphasizes the blessings of their stage of salvation history by turning his attention to a comparison between two holy mountains. The first is **Mount Sinai** where Moses received the law. He reminds his readers that when God made Himself known on this mountain, it was touched with blazing fire, darkness, gloom and a whirlwind, and the sounds of trumpets. God's words filled the air in such a frightening way that those who heard begged that no further words be spoken to them. The people could not even touch the mountain, or they would be put to death. Moses himself said, "I am terrified and trembling" (12:21). Rather, they had come to **Mount Zion** and the city of the living God (the heavenly Jerusalem). Here the mood is one of celebration and of fellowship. Here there are myriads of angels gathered, along with the assembly of the firstborn whose names have been written in heaven—that is, God who is the judge of all, the spirits of righteous people made perfect, and Jesus (the Mediator of the new covenant).

Warning 5: Do Not Reject the Words of God (12:25–29)

For the fifth time in the book, the author pauses to warn his audience. This time, the **warning** is, "Make sure that you do not reject the One who speaks. For if they did not escape when they rejected Him who warned them on earth, even less will we if we turn away from Him who warns us from heaven" (12:25). God is going to shake the world and remove everything that can be shaken. However, the kingdom we receive is a kingdom that shall not be shaken; the readers should therefore offer their service to God with reverence and awe because God is a consuming fire (12:26–29).

Practical Exhortations and Benediction (13:1–25). The end of the book is comprised of a long list of practical exhortations encouraging readers to be hospitable, moral, prayerful, continually praising God, holding to the truth, and so forth. The letter concludes with a short benediction which: (1) wishes the readers that God will equip them with all that is good to do His will; (2) urges them to receive His word of exhortation; (3) informs them that Timothy was released and may come with him to visit soon; and (4) greets all the leaders and saints.

CONCLUSION

Hebrews, perhaps more than any other book of the New Testament, calls us to **endure in our faith** and to hold fast to Jesus' message. It reminds us that many people of faith have endured hardship and endured even when God's promises seemed lifetimes away. It reminds us that Jesus Himself was no stranger to suffering; as God's Son, He was greater than the prophets and the angels yet entered humanity to suffer in unthinkable ways. In all of this, He did not sin. Through His endurance Jesus has set an example for us in righteousness and became a greater **high priest** than the world has ever known. We are not alone in our sufferings; we are surrounded by a crowd of faithful witnesses; and we, too, must continue in faith, focusing on Jesus our Great High Priest as we run the race toward God's everlasting kingdom.

Study Questions

1. Hebrews has a major emphasis on endurance for salvation. How does this fit with other New Testament texts which seem to indicate that salvation is eternally secure?
2. If Jesus is the High Priest and no other sacrifices are needed, what implications does this have for the concept of the priesthood of the believer?
3. Why is this book so helpful for Jewish Christians?
4. If Jesus is our High Priest whose sacrifice of Himself is sufficient to pay for our sins, do we need anything else to save us?
5. Have you trusted the sacrifice of Christ for your salvation?

For Further Reading

Bruce, F. F. *The Epistle to the Hebrews.* NICNT. Grand Rapids: Eerdmans, 1990.

Ellingworth, Paul. *The Epistle to the Hebrews: A Commentary on the Greek Text.* NIGTC. Grand Rapids: Eerdmans, 1993.

Ger, Steven. *Hebrews: Christ Is Greater.* Chattanooga: AMG, 2009.

Guthrie, George H., and Janet Nygren. *Hebrews: Running the Race Before Us.* Grand Rapids: Zondervan, 2009.

Hughes, Philip E. *A Commentary on the Epistle to the Hebrews.* Grand Rapids: Eerdmans, 1997.

Johnson, Luke Timothy. *Hebrews: A Commentary.* Louisville: Westminster John Knox, 2006.

ENDNOTE

1. While this book has practical application for Gentiles, the fact that circumcision is not mentioned is evidence that the book was more concerned with a Jewish return to Judaism than a Gentile conversion into Judaism.

Chapter 24

JAMES
Faith That Works

James may have been the first New Testament letter written. It ties the Old and New Testament together. He writes to the "the 12 tribes in the Dispersion," and obviously he means Christian Jews living outside the Holy Land. James was the half brother of Jesus Christ and was converted when Jesus appeared to him in His resurrected body (1 Cor 15:7). Apparently, he never left Judea and was one of the pillars in the church at Jerusalem (Gal 2:9). James reflects the **Hebrew mind**: he is conscientious, austere, and legal. Tradition tells of his martyrdom in AD 62. James writes to Christians who are still attending the synagogue (2:2). He writes with short, pithy sentences that encapsulate a truth, a style found in the wisdom books of the Old Testament.

Key Facts	
Author:	James, son of Mary and Joseph, half brother of Jesus
Recipients:	To the 12 tribes in the Dispersion
Where Written:	Unknown
Date:	AD 40–42
Key Word:	Trials (Gk. *peirasmos*)
Key Verse:	"A man who endures trials is blessed, because when he passes the test he will receive the crown of life that God has promised to those who love Him" (1:12).

AUTHOR

Most Bible scholars agree that James, **the half brother** of the Lord (Gal 1:19), wrote this epistle. However, two other persons by the name of James are mentioned in the New Testament who might have written this epistle. First is an apostle, James the son of Zebedee (Matt 4:21), who probably did not write the epistle. This James was martyred by Herod (Acts 12:2) and would not have been available to write this letter.

The next James was an apostle (Matthew 10), called James, the Less (Mark 15:40). He was probably the son of Alphaeus (Matt 10:3) and possibly the son of Mary (Matt 27:56; Mark 15:40). However, little is known of him, so most scholars think he was not responsible for the strong convictions of this epistle.

James, the half brother of Jesus, was strong enough to preside over the disagreement at the **Jerusalem Council** (Acts 15), and because of his influence that came out of that Council, he seems to be the most likely author of this epistle.

James was first mentioned in Matt 13:55, when the children of Mary, the mother of Jesus, were mentioned: "James, Joseph, Simon, and Judas [or Jude]." The word "James" is English from the Hebrew "Jacob." At this place Matthew uses the normal word for "brother," but some have tried to interpret the expression otherwise. The Greek Orthodox Church holds that the four "brethren" of Jesus are considered "half brothers," the son of Joseph by a former marriage. But there is no evidence to support this view. The Roman Catholic Church regards them as cousins—sons of a sister of the virgin Mary. However, Matthew uses the Greek word *adelphos* for "brother," and so does Paul in Gal 1:19, suggesting that James was the firstborn to Joseph and Mary after the virginal conception of Jesus.

A model of Jerusalem in the first century AD showing the Roman fortress Antonia with its four massive towers just north of the Temple Mount. To the left of the fortress is the Pool of Bethesda where Jesus performed one of His miracles.

James and the other half brothers of Jesus **did not recognize** His messiahship, nor did they believe in Him (John 7:5). Paul explains that the resurrected Jesus appeared to James (1 Cor 15:7), and this experience apparently led to James's faith in Jesus as the Messiah. As one of the leaders of the early church, it is natural to assume that James was converted to Jesus Christ after the crucifixion and resurrection and quickly became the leader of the Christian community in Jerusalem by common consent of the early Christian believers.

The **early church fathers** give evidences of the epistle of James. Origen (c. AD 200) quoted the epistle of James but declared he was uncertain which James wrote it. Indirect references (phrases taken from the epistle of James) were found prior to the time of Origen. These go back to Clement of Rome who wrote at the end of the first century. However, these quotes are general biblical truths that could be paraphrased from James or other sources.

Gentile Christians were not as concerned about the law as were Jewish Christians, that is, the controversy of faith versus the law. As the church became more Gentile focused and less Jewish focused, less attention was given to the book of James. However, the book of James provides a **balanced picture** of good works as evidence of true faith. James had no use for people who only had a religious profession or who did not live according to the Word of God (1:23). He also had a deep distrust for rich people (1:10; 5:1–3), while he exercised sympathy for the poor (2:5). James did not call himself an apostle, nor did he elevate himself even to being worthy to be called "brother," but he introduces himself, "James, a **slave** of God and of the Lord Jesus Christ" (1:1).

RECIPIENTS

The epistle is addressed to "the 12 tribes in the Dispersion" (1:1). Thus, it appears that James was writing to fellow **Jewish Christians** residing across the Roman Empire. Many of them may have visited Jerusalem for the various feasts and would have sought instruction and direction from a leader of the primary church of Christianity: the Jerusalem church. They would have wanted to know what it meant to be a Christian in their daily lives as messianic believers.

OCCASION AND DATE

While some scholars believe James wrote this book toward the end of his life (c. AD 62), other scholars believe he wrote the book at an earlier date, that is, approximately **AD 40**, which is probably more accurate. Therefore, James's letter could be one of the earliest (if not the earliest) books of the New Testament.

First, James calls the leaders of the church "teachers" and "elders" (3:1; 5:14) rather than using later terms such as "bishops" and "elders." While these later terms may have been used in Gentile churches outside Jerusalem, James would have used the **earlier terms** and identified church leaders by their spiritual gifts and accumulated wisdom from an advanced age.

Second, James identified Christians still meeting in **synagogues** (2:2), which seemed to be an early practice until Paul went to Corinth where the church began meeting next door to the synagogue and the Lord Jesus seemed to confirm their leaving the synagogue (Acts 18:9–11). Again, remember, James is writing to Jewish Christians whose tendency would probably be to remain in the synagogue as long as possible.

Third, many **later truths** found elsewhere in New Testament letters are not mentioned in the epistle of James. No mention is made of the great truth of justification by faith, being "in Christ," the church age, and the truth found in the book of Hebrews that the death of Jesus Christ once and for all ended the sacrificial practice in the temple.

Fourth, James does not mention the controversy over **circumcision** of new Gentile converts that erupted in Acts 15, which took place after the epistle was written. Note what is said of this later controversy: "Some men came down from Judea and began to teach the brothers: 'Unless you are circumcised according to the custom prescribed by Moses, you cannot be saved!'" (Acts 15:1). Since James did not mention this controversy at all, it is often assumed that he wrote early, perhaps within 10 years of the death of Christ. Because there were not many Gentiles in the early church, there was little need to deal with this issue. This situation also seems to reflect the early date for the book.

This book by James is **not the only letter** that James had a part in writing. After the Jerusalem Council, Luke records: "They wrote this letter to be delivered by them: From the apostles and the elders, your brothers, To the brothers among the Gentiles in Antioch, Syria, and Cilicia: Greetings" (Acts 15:23). This letter explained the position of the early church: "Then, being sent off, they went down to Antioch, and after gathering the assembly, they delivered the letter. When they read it, they rejoiced because of its encouragement" (Acts 15:30–31). While James is not specifically mentioned, he undoubtedly wrote or gave his approval to the writing of this letter since he was the leading spokesman at the Jerusalem Council (Acts 15:13).

GENRE AND STRUCTURE

Since James was a half brother of the Lord Jesus, one would expect a number of quotations from Jesus in his epistle. These are found in "free reference" inasmuch as James does not cite the Gospels directly but quotes things Jesus would have said. For example, compare the following: Jas 1:2 with Matt 5:11; Jas 2:5 with Matt 5:3; Jas 3:12 with Matt 7:16–20; Jas 4:10 with Matt 18:4; Jas 5:1 with Luke 6:24; and Jas 5:12 with Matt 5:34–37.

James has some striking **aphorisms** in his epistle (a concise statement of a principle that also defines its meaning):

- "An indecisive man is unstable in all his ways" (1:8).
- "Man's anger does not accomplish God's righteousness" (1:20).
- "Don't you know that friendship with the world is hostility toward God?" (4:4).
- "Resist the Devil, and he will flee from you" (4:7).
- "The urgent request of a righteous person is very powerful" (5:16).

James was also descriptive in his language, using **word pictures** or similes:

- "For the doubter is like the surging sea, driven and tossed by the wind" (1:6).
- "Now when we put bits into the mouths of horses to make them obey us, we also guide the whole animal" (3:3).
- "And consider ships: Though very large and driven by fierce winds, they are guided by a very small rudder wherever the will of the pilot directs" (3:4).
- "You don't even know what tomorrow will bring—what your life will be! For you are like smoke that appears for a little while, then vanishes" (4:14).

Outline

I. Faith Tested (James 1)
II. Faith Authenticated (James 2)
III. Faith Demonstrated (James 3–5)

MESSAGE

Trials (James 1:1–4,12)

Wherever Jewish people went, they were often shunned, neglected, or persecuted. When a Jew took on the faith of Jesus Christ, there was additional reason to face persecution. So James begins by describing their faith as tried by fire: "Consider it a great joy, my brothers, whenever you experience various trials, knowing that the testing of your faith produces endurance" (1:2–3). Therefore, one of the principles of living an effective Christian life in a sinful world is knowing how to respond to all types of trials and testing.

James tells believers six things about **trials**. First, they are *inevitable*. When he says "whenever," he is instructing them to expect afflictions and trials just as Jesus instructed His disciples that they would be persecuted and even martyred (John 15:18–25).

Second, trials are part of the Christian *experience*. Christianity is not just an intellectual religion, nor is it merely a physical or racial religion. Christianity is an experience that involves the total personality: intellect, emotion, and the will or power of choice that involves self-perception and self-direction. New believers come to know Jesus Christ who saves them. Second, they experience love when they are accepted in Jesus Christ. And third, they make a decision to follow Jesus Christ. So just as they experienced the joys of Christianity, they also will experience trials.

Third, James predicts that there will be "various" trials, which means *many kinds* or sources of trials. These would include financial, business, cultural, and family trials.

The fourth area of testing involved their faith. The original language reads "your tested faith." The core of their relationship with Jesus Christ will be tested. For those who give their faith up easily when tested, this shows that they did not originally have real saving faith.

The fifth element demonstrates the *results* of testing. Why is this so? Because James wrote, "Knowing that the testing of your faith produces endurance" (1:3). In other words, when you are tested, this will help you grow spiritually. Testing will make the Christian mature, complete, and lacking nothing.

Sixth, James wants the believer to "consider it a great joy" (1:2–4), which means looking beyond a trial to see what good can come out of it.

Wisdom (James 1:5–8; 3:13–18)

James is probably referring to the wisdom books of Proverbs, Ecclesiastes, and Song of Songs when he uses the term "wisdom." His definition of wisdom could be characterized in everyday terms as "habitually living according to the principles of God." He tells leaders to give themselves to the Word of God in order to find out how to make good **practical decisions** and how to direct their lives according to the plan of God.

James teaches that God is waiting to give wisdom to anyone who asks for it: "Now if any of you lacks wisdom, he should **ask God**, who gives to all generously and without criticizing, and it will be given to him" (1:5). The phrase "without criticizing" means that God will not find fault with those who acknowledge their need of wisdom, nor does God "slap the hand" of those who ask for it. The person who seeks wisdom must not be "double minded" or "unstable" (1:8 KJV). Does James have someone in mind when he speaks about the "double minded"? It is those who second-guess God's plan and God's Word (1:22–25). The true believer should draw near to God in obedience, love, and service (4:8), then express wisdom in humility (3:13), yieldedness (4:7), seriousness (4:9), and correct speech (1:19).

What does James say about the wisdom that comes from God? "But the wisdom from above is first pure, then peace-loving, gentle, compliant, full of mercy and good fruits, without favoritism and hypocrisy. And the fruit of righteousness is sown in peace by those who make peace" (3:17–18).

Greek Highlight

Wisdom. Greek σοφία **(sophia).** The Greek word *sophia* means wisdom, intelligence, or knowledge which refers to skill in living more than to the attainment of facts. In the Old Testament, *wisdom* is viewed as coming from the Lord. Solomon stated that "the fear of the LORD is the beginning of knowledge" (Prov 1:7). Paul understood *sophia* in light of the Old Testament. He viewed worldly wisdom and God's wisdom as direct opposites (cf. 1 Cor 2:1–9; Col 2:23). The Greco-Roman world depended on human intellect to gain wisdom, whereas New Testament writers, like James (1:5), viewed such wisdom as a gift given by God to help believers navigate the challenges of life.

Poverty and Riches (James 1:9–11; 4:13–17; 5:1–6)

James writes much about the poor. He is repeating God's **concern for the poor** from the Old Testament (Pss 18:27; 112:9; 113:7; Isa 11:4). He wants those who follow Jesus Christ to help meet the practical needs of the poor (1:27; 2:8). The poor should not be segregated in the Christian community and most definitely not given the lower seat in the assembly (2:1–8).

James says, "The brother of humble circumstances should boast in his exaltation; but the one who is rich should boast in his humiliation because he will pass away like a flower of the field" (1:9–10). **Humility** is the underlying virtue in James's letter. The lowly should accept the exaltation (promotion) with humility, and the rich should accept humiliation (demotion) with the same kind of humility. Thus, James emphasizes that if the rich oppress the poor (5:1–6), they will face the imminent judgment of God's wrath.

Doing the Word (James 1:22–25)

One of the most **practical principles** of James' wisdom involves being a "doer" and not just a "hearer" of the Word of God (1:22–25). He adds that those who only hear the Word of God "deceive" themselves (1:22). That man is "looking at his own face in a mirror" whereas the King James Version calls it the "natural face" (1:23). The original Greek uses the word *genesis* (only here, in 3:6, and Matt 1:1), which literally means "looking into the face of his birth." When this person walks away from this mirror, he has seen what he really looks like, yet he still has a much higher opinion of himself than he should. While not stated in this reference, it is implied throughout James that this person is haughty and has a high opinion of himself. However, James wants us to look ourselves in the mirror and not forget "what kind of man" we are (1:24). That one "is not a forgetful hearer but one who does good works," so that person "will be blessed" (1:25). Therefore, James believes the credible Christian is the one who lives by the principles of the Word of God, that is, proves to be a doer of the Word.

Bronze mirror.

Faith and Works (James 2:10–26)

James is probably best known because of his teaching on faith and works. Some have felt James's view of works is in **contrast** to Paul's teaching on faith. Paul declares, "We have been declared righteous by faith" (Rom 5:1), whereas James seems to say the opposite: "You see that a man is justified by works and not by faith alone" (Jas 2:24). Others view James as a **complement** to Paul's teaching. Paul urges his readers to do good works but only as a natural outcome of Christianity or the fruit of their faith (Romans 12; Gal 5:18,22–23; Eph 2:10; Titus 2:7). In the same manner James constantly tells a person to live by good works that grow out of a life of faith: "Show me your faith without works, and I will show you faith from my works" (Jas 2:18).

Martin Luther had such a deep reaction against the improper teaching of salvation by works that he fully embraced the doctrine of justification by faith found in the apostle Paul. Martin Luther called the epistle of James an "epistle of straw." Luther even doubted if James should be in the canon. However, its inclusion in the canon came early and is well attested.

James writes to many Jewish believers who are apparently confused about their new role as Christians. While they lived in the past under the law as Jews, now they are saved by faith (2:14–26). James deals with those who feel they can live by faith, but they don't have to "work out" their practical obedience to Scripture. Perhaps they believed they could live as they wanted. But James uses **negative motivation**: "You believe that God is one; you do well. The demons also believe—and they shudder" (2:19). Another negative illustration is aimed at the rich (a recurring theme in James): "'Go in peace, keep warm, and eat well,' but you don't give them what the body needs, what good is it?" (2:16). James says that faith is "dead by itself" (2:17). He concludes, "Show me your faith without works, and I will show you faith from my works" (2:18).

James uses two **Old Testament illustrations** to show the works of people who have been saved by faith. First, *Abraham* offered his son Isaac to God. James makes the statement, "You see that faith was active together with his [Abraham's] works, and by works, faith was perfected" (2:22). Then James uses the illustration of *Rahab* the prostitute when he said, "Wasn't Rahab the prostitute also justified by works when she received the messengers and sent them out by a different route?" (2:25). He concludes, "For just as the body without the spirit is dead, so also faith without works is dead" (2:26).

The Tongue (James 3:1–18)

James believes that the **tongue** could probably do more damage than all temptations to the child of God. He begins by indicating that even though we should keep the law, "we all stumble in many ways" (3:2). The chief source of stumbling is our tongue, or the words we speak.

James gives **three pictures** to describe the tongue. First, it is like a *small bit* put into the mouth of a horse to make the animal obey (3:3). Second, the tongue is like a *small rudder* of a large ship; even though driven by fierce winds, the ship is controlled by a small rudder. Third, the tongue is like a *small fire* that ignites a large forest fire (3:6). Because the tongue pollutes the whole body (3:6), James says it creates a fire of hell, that is, *Gehenna*. This seems to be a reference to the fires of destruction associated with the judgment of God. Authentic Christians will obey the wisdom of biblical principles by controlling what they say, hence controlling their actions.

A small spark can ignite a forest fire.

Healing (James 5:13–18)

James introduces the section on **praying for the sick** by pointing to the consequences of sin, *"so that you won't fall under judgment"* (5:12). James deals with the suffering, sickness and healing. He asks the question, "Is anyone among you suffering? He should pray" (5:13). Then he goes on to comment, "The prayer of faith will save the sick person, and the Lord will restore him to health" (5:15).

Before praying for someone who needs healing, examine whether sin has made them sick. Notice **the promise of healing** is attached to the condition of confessing sin and getting forgiveness: "If he has committed sins, he will be forgiven. Therefore, confess your sins to one another and pray for one another, so that you may be healed" (5:15–16). So sick people must deal with their sins for healing as well as church leaders.

The **elders of the church** must be involved in praying for healing. James tells us to "call for the elders" (5:14). Why elders and not a traveling evangelist or some other person? Because elders have spiritual oversight of the flock of God, and they probably know of any sin or rebellion in the life of the sick person that may have led to his or her illness. Because elders have the command to "shepherd God's flock among you" (1 Pet 5:2), they must exercise "watch care" and pray for those in their flock. Therefore, based on their spiritual relationship of the sick person, they can provide healing for the soul before they provide prayer for the body.

When praying for healing, ask God to give the sick person **spiritual and physical** life. Remember, the Bible teaches, "Every generous act and every perfect gift is from above" (Jas 1:17). Therefore, it is God who gives good health and healing.

Finally, the **key** to healing is not your faith, nor is it the severity of the disease. Healing comes from God. When you exercise the "prayer of faith," remember it is faith in the *source* of healing—God Himself. Since God can do all things, God can heal anyone. But since God does not do everything that is asked of Him but only does His will, let's pray in the will of God. Let's pray "not My will, but Yours, be done" (Luke 22:42).

CONCLUSION

James writes to believers who are suffering **trials and temptations** because of their faith in Jesus Christ. He uses the style of the wisdom literature of the Old Testament, that is, a number of pointed truths written in a solitary sentence that are clustered together to make a point. He tells his readers to expect trials and enjoins them to demonstrate their faith by their works. James is hard on the rich, especially when they exploit the poor. He puts great value on God's wisdom and emphasizes a proper relationship between faith and works.

Study Questions

1. How should a believer react when facing trials?
2. What is the genre (style) of James's writing?
3. In what ways do Paul and James agree about faith and works? How do they seem to disagree?
4. What is the basic contribution of the book of James to the rest of Scripture?
5. How does James's personality influence the book?

For Further Reading

Davids, Peter H. *The Epistle of James: A Commentary on the Greek Text.* NIGTC. Grand Rapids: Eerdmans, 1982.
Martin, Ralph P. *James.* WBC. Waco, TX: Word, 1988.
Maynard-Reid, P. V. *Poverty and Wealth in James.* Maryknoll, NY: Orbis, 1987.
Moo, Douglas J. *The Letter of James.* PNTC. Grand Rapids: Eerdmans, 2000.

Chapter 25

1 PETER
Holy Living

The apostle Peter is one of the most interesting men of the New Testament. But though he is the most prominent apostle in the Gospels, he wrote only two New Testament books. By the time he wrote his first epistle, things were getting dangerous for Christians in Asia Minor. Peter called them "**pilgrims**" of the "Dispersion" (scattering), referring to their position in the world as aliens and strangers. Perhaps they had been scattered by persecution (Acts 8:1). Or the term "pilgrim" may be a spiritual metaphor relating them to the Christian task of living in a pagan world. In any case, about AD 64, the year Nero began his violent outrage against believers in Rome, Peter wrote to exhort Christians to persevere through increasing sufferings with a confident expectation of Christ's return.

Key Facts	
Author:	The apostle Peter
Recipients:	Believers in the provinces of Pontus, Galatia, Cappadocia, Asia, and Bithynia (northern Asia Minor)
Where Written:	Probably from Rome
Date:	About AD 64
Key Words:	Hope (Gk. *elpis*), suffering (Gk. *pathema*)
Key Verses:	"Dear friends, don't be surprised when the fiery ordeal comes among you to test you as if something unusual were happening to you. Instead, rejoice as you share in the sufferings of the Messiah, so that you may also rejoice with great joy at the revelation of His glory" (4:12–13).

AUTHOR

The stated author of 1 Peter is the **apostle Peter** (1:1), and he claims to be a "witness to the sufferings of the Messiah" (5:1). He states that he wrote the letter with the help of Silas (Silvanus, 5:12), who appears to be the Silas of Acts 15:22 and 1 Thess 1:1. The author calls Mark "my son" (5:13). Since Peter was known to be close to Mark (see Acts 12:12), and Mark was reported to be the disciple and interpreter of Peter in Rome, this statement points to Petrine authorship. The author writes with a tone of authority; this would be expected from an apostle, especially the leading apostle. The letter was universally accepted in the early church as being authored by Peter.

Some scholars have objected to the idea that Peter wrote the epistle. For example, some say that Peter could not write the excellent style of Greek that is found in 1 Peter. However, Peter probably was at least bilingual, since both Aramaic and Greek were spoken in Galilee. Furthermore, Peter had the assistance of **Silvanus** (1 Pet 5:12), who was a Roman citizen like Paul (Acts 16:37–38) and knew Greek well (see Acts 15:22–23,27).

It is also alleged that the epistle reflects the persecution by the Roman emperor Trajan (AD 98–117) rather than that of Nero (AD 64–68). Peter was obviously dead by the time of Trajan (having been executed by Nero). However, nothing in 1 Peter requires a later persecution. Apprehension arose among Christians throughout the empire when **Nero** began his murder of Christians. Peter may have warned the Christians of Asia Minor what was coming. The reference to "fiery ordeal" (4:12) may allude to both the burning of Rome (July 64) and the burning of Christians as human torches by Nero.

Peter's birth name in Hebrew was **Symeon** (Acts 15:14), which was usually spelled in Greek as Simon (Matt 4:18). His father was named Jonah (in Hebrew; John in Greek; Matt 16:17), and he had at least one brother, Andrew. By the time he met Jesus, Peter was married (Matt 8:14). His early home was at Bethsaida (John 1:44), northeast of the Sea of Galilee. He was not trained in rabbinical or scribal studies (Acts 4:13). His adult occupation was fishing (Matt 4:18), including a partnership with James and John (Luke 5:10). During this time Peter's home was at Capernaum, on the northwest shore of the Sea of Galilee (Mark 1:29).

Peter first met Jesus through his brother Andrew, who was a disciple of John the Baptist (John 1:35–40). On that occasion Jesus gave Simon a **new name**: *Kepha* (Aramaic "stone" or "rock"), translated throughout the New Testament as Peter (Greek *petros*, "stone"). Later, while Peter and his brother were fishing (Luke 5), Jesus called Peter to become his disciple, and the following year he appointed Peter as one of his 12 apostles (Luke 6). Peter's name heads every list of the apostles in the New Testament. He became their spokesman and one of Jesus' **inner circle** of three disciples (Peter, James, and John). Following Christ's resurrection, Peter was commissioned to "feed Christ's sheep," that is, to lead the other apostles and believers (John 21:15–19).

Fishing boats on the Nile River in Egypt.

After the coming of the Holy Spirit at Pentecost (Acts 2), Peter entered the most fruitful period of his life (Acts 1–12)—preaching in Jerusalem, Judea, and Samaria; working miracles; and bringing the gospel to Gentiles at Caesarea (Acts 10). His apostleship was principally to the *Jews* (Gal 2:7–9), but it is possible that he evangelized *Gentiles* in Asia Minor (1 Pet 1:1). He apparently went to Rome at some time between AD 62 and 65, and wrote his two epistles during the next few years. According to later church writers, Peter died during Nero's persecution (before AD 68) by being **crucified upside down**. The New Testament describes Peter as a man of energy, enthusiasm, boldness, faith, leadership, and devotion to Christ. His favorite names for himself were Peter (1 Pet 1:1) and Simeon (2 Pet 1:1). In the Gospels, he is known mainly as Simon Peter.

RECIPIENTS

The epistle is addressed to people in **five Roman provinces** in Asia Minor: Pontus, Galatia, Cappadocia, Asia, and Bithynia (1:1). The book of Acts indicates that Paul worked mainly in the southern half of Asia Minor (Acts 16:6–7), so Peter may be writing to those who lived generally to the north of Paul's area of ministry.

The recipients are called "pilgrims" (NKJV) or "temporary residents" of the "**Dispersion**" (1 Pet 1:1 NKJV) and "sojourners" (2:11 NKJV). These terms refer to their position in the world as aliens and strangers, who were scattered throughout northern Asia Minor. They may have been recent converts to Christ (cf. 2:2; 3:21). Some of the readers were slaves (2:18).

There are three views as to the **race or nationality** of the recipients: (1) *Jewish Christians*, because of references to the Diaspora (1:1) and the fact that Peter was primarily an apostle to the Jews; (2) *Gentile Christians*, because the readers apparently had a pagan lifestyle before their conversion (1:14,18; 2:10; 4:3–4); and (3) *mixed churches* of both Jewish and Gentile Christians, because every known church in Asia Minor at this time was mixed.

OCCASION AND DATE

The probable date of writing of 1 Peter is between AD 62 and 67. Tradition affirms that Peter died during the persecution of Nero (AD 64–68). Nero died in AD 68. In 2 Peter, Peter states that he is approaching death (1:14–15), whereas in 1 Peter he gives no hint of his death. Therefore 1 Peter was probably written around AD 64 and no later than AD 67. Peter apparently was not yet in Rome when Paul wrote Romans (AD 56/57) or when Paul arrived in Rome (AD 60). If 1 Peter was written in Rome, then probably the epistle was written after AD 62, when Paul was released from his first imprisonment. And if 1 Peter was written to warn believers in Asia Minor concerning the threat of Neronian persecution, the date of writing would be AD 64 or thereafter. It seems, therefore, that the probable date is most likely **AD 64**.

Four locations have been suggested as the place where 1 Peter was written.

The first is **Babylon in Mesopotamia**. The major

Nevsehir is the capital of the region of Cappadocia where some of the recipients of Peter's first letter lived.

support for this view is 1 Pet 5:13, where Peter sends his readers greetings from "Babylon." A large Jewish synagogue/community existed in Babylon that would have been an attractive audience to draw Peter to that city. However, there is no evidence that Peter was ever in Babylon or that a church was there in the first century. Early tradition puts the activities of Peter in the West, not in the East.

The second possibility is **Babylon in Egypt** (old Cairo). There was a village in Egypt named Babylon (mentioned by Strabo about AD 18), but there is no evidence that Peter was there. The village was small (a military station), and the Egyptian church never claimed this identification.

The third suggestion is **Antioch in Syria.** Galatians says Peter went to Antioch (Gal 2:11). The believers were first called Christians in Antioch (Acts 11:26), and 1 Peter is the only New Testament epistle to use the term "Christian" (1 Pet 4:16). Antioch was also the place to which Christians were "scattered" (cf. Acts 11:19). This is an idea Peter uses throughout the letter. However, no ancient tradition claims this view.

The fourth is **Rome**. Peter died in Rome in about AD 65–68 during the persecution of Nero, according to such early writers as Clement of Rome, Gaius, Tertullian, and Porphyrius. Tradition places Peter's last residence and preaching in Rome (cf. Eusebius). The term "Babylon" used in Rev 14:8; 17:5,18 may also refer to Rome. The term would symbolically indicate a complex of arrogant idolatry combined with the power of empire (like the historical Babylon), which had become known for its persecution of the saints of God. This could easily apply to Rome. The historic Babylon was the location for Jewish exiles in 586 BC and 1 Peter calls Christians exiles (*Diaspora*), pilgrims, strangers, and sojourners (1:1,17; 2:11). Perhaps the literal name "Rome" was not used in the letter for the sake of security in order to avoid bringing persecution on the Roman church.

The Christians of Asia Minor were experiencing **trials of their**

The interior of the Colosseum at Rome showing the area beneath the arena. Although the Colosseum wasn't completed until over a decade after Peter's death, it became one of the places of "the fiery ordeal" of which Peter warned.

faith (1 Pet 1:6–7), including (1) slander by their fellow citizens (2:12); and (2) possibly state-organized persecution, particularly by Nero and his provincial officials (4:12). Paul may have been recently executed (c. AD 64–66), and Peter may have felt it necessary to step in with a letter of encouragement and exhortation to the churches of Asia Minor.

GENRE AND STRUCTURE

First Peter is a **general epistle** or "catholic" epistle, intended for a larger group than most of the New Testament epistles that were addressed to local churches or individuals. However, this letter was not sent to the entire universal church. Nor is it simply a "letter"; it was intended to be widely distributed as a message of hope and exhortation. The Old Testament is cited a number of times (1:16,24; 2:6–10,22; 3:10–12,14; 4:18; 5:5). Some have suggested that the epistle may be a commentary on Psalm 34, a psalm of faith and righteous conduct in spite of suffering. Also, this letter contains parallels with Romans, Ephesians, Hebrews, James, the speeches of Peter in Acts, and the teachings of Jesus.

Outline

I. Character of the Believer's Salvation (1 Peter 1:1–12)
II. Challenge of the Believer (1 Peter 1:13–2:10)
III. Conduct of the Believer (1 Peter 2:11–5:11)
IV. Conclusion (1 Peter 5:12–14)

MESSAGE

Peter addresses his readers as "pilgrims of the Dispersion" (1:1 NKJV)—scattered aliens—who live in (northern) Asia Minor. His readers were chosen by God, foreknown by God, sanctified by the Spirit, sprinkled with the blood of Christ, and forgiven of all sins (1:2).

I. Character of the Believer's Salvation (1 Peter 1:1–12)

In the future, believers will receive an **inheritance from God**, described as a living hope (1:3), an imperishable inheritance (1:4), and a salvation that is certain to be revealed in the last time (1:5). For the present, believers should rejoice in spite of trials and in spite of the absence of Christ. The purpose of trials is to refine believers' faith (1:6–9).

II. Challenge of the Believer (1 Peter 1:13–2:10)

Peter gives believers a **fourfold challenge**. First, believers should *be holy* in the light of the approaching return of Christ, in the light of the holy character of God, and in the light of salvation by an exalted Savior (1:13–21). Second, believers should *love one another* with fervent love, based on their purification through faith in Christ and their rebirth by the Word of God (1:22–25). Third, believers should *grow*, laying aside their previous life of sin (2:1–3). Fourth, believers should *live as priests*, recognizing their position as living stones in the spiritual household and temple of God (2:4–5). Christ is the chief cornerstone of salvation, and believers form a royal priesthood, the chosen people of God (2:6–10).

III. Conduct of the Believer (1 Peter 2:11–5:11)

Peter explains and illustrates the expected **conduct of believers**. He begins with a summary: (1) abstain from fleshly desires; and (2) live with honorable conduct so outsiders may be converted (2:11–12). After this Peter elaborates on the essence of believers' conduct by noting that they must live out their Christian lives in submission, suffering, and service.

First, believers are to live in **submission to civil government** (2:13–17), to their masters (2:18–25), to their husbands (3:1–7), and to the brethren (3:8–12). They should submit to civil authorities, in order to do the will of God and silence unbelievers (2:13–16). Believers who are slaves should submit to their masters because God rewards those who endure unjust suffering (2:18–20). Christ is an example of unjust suffering. Though He committed no sin, He accomplished the believer's substitution and reconciliation through suffering (2:21–25).

Believing **wives** should submit to their husbands so their husbands will come to faith in Christ (3:1–2). A woman's true beauty is in her character and conduct (3:3–4). Believing husbands have an obligation to understand and honor their wives. Finally, believers should be submissive to one another, living together in unity and

Shepherd and his sheep.

love. The Old Testament promises a long and good life to those who live righteously and seek peace (3:8–12).

Second, in light of persecution, believers face the possibility of **suffering for righteousness**. They must respond with consecration to God and readiness to testify of their faith (3:14–15). The result of such a response will be a good conscience on the part of the believer and the shame of those who slander and abuse (3:16). Christ is an example of the importance of suffering unjustly and the result of enduring such suffering. After Christ suffered and died, He was raised from the dead and announced His victory to the enemies of God. The ark of Noah illustrates what happens to those who are saved, which is a picture of Christian baptism, and submitting to baptism is an act of a good conscience toward God (3:18–22).

Believers now live for God; therefore, they must **turn from sin** (4:1–2). They must pray, love one another fervently, be hospitable, and use the gifts and abilities that God has given them in ministry (4:7–11). They should expect suffering to come and respond with joy. They will suffer for the name of Christ and because they are Christians; however, their suffering should never be because of sin (4:12–15). They should maintain their good conduct while they suffer, since God is always faithful to them (4:17–19).

Third, believers must live out their Christian lives in *service* to others. Peter exhorts Christians as a fellow elder and as one who has witnessed Christ's sufferings and a future partaker of Christ's glory (5:1). The elders should take Peter's exhortation seriously and carry out their duties willingly and humbly, in shepherding God's flock of believers knowing they will receive a crown of glory when Christ returns (5:2–4). Believers should trust God for all their anxieties because God is concerned for them (5:7). The devil is always searching for some way to attack and defeat them; therefore believers need to resist the devil firmly.

IV. Conclusion (1 Peter 5:12–14)

Peter identifies Silvanus as the writer of the letter, and himself as the author (5:12). The epistle is Peter's **exhortation and testimony**. He closes with greetings from the church in "Babylon" (presumably Rome) and from Mark (5:13–14).

CONCLUSION

The major purpose of 1 Peter is practical **exhortation** (5:12). Peter exhorts the believers to: (1) live in accordance with the hope they have received through Christ and (2) endure suffering triumphantly and joyfully in light of the coming eternal glory promised to the followers of Christ. The theme is living with hope in the midst of suffering. Some subthemes include: (1) holiness in the midst of paganism, (2) Christ as an example of suffering and endurance, and (3) how to bear suffering triumphantly.

Study Questions

1. How does Peter's apostolic authority make itself known in this epistle?
2. Make a list of all the commands (imperatives) in the epistle. Group them by topic and write a paragraph summarizing what Peter wants his readers to do.
3. How does Peter connect the concepts of rejoicing and suffering to the doctrines of Christian hope and salvation?
4. Why do you think Peter calls himself an "elder" in 1 Pet 5:1, and how does Peter use this concept in his exhortations in that chapter?
5. How can Christians today use Peter's statements in 1 Pet 5:8–10 in their lives?

For Further Reading

Davids, Peter H. *The First Epistle of Peter*. NICNT. Grand Rapids: Eerdmans, 1990.

Grudem, Wayne. *1 Peter*. TNTC. Grand Rapids: Eerdmans, 1988.

Hiebert, D. Edmond. *First Peter: An Expositional Commentary*. Chicago: Moody, 1984.

Jobes, Karen H. *1 Peter*. BECNT. Grand Rapids: Baker, 2005.

Schreiner, Thomas R. *1, 2 Peter, Jude*. NAC. Nashville: B&H, 2003.

Chapter 26

2 PETER
Growing in Grace

Second Peter contains the **final exhortations and warnings** of the aging apostle. He says that he wants to leave behind some things through which he can continue to exhort or "motivate" his readers (1:13)—to stir up their minds and ears by reminding them of his previous teachings. It is also one of several New Testament epistles that describe in great detail a rising tide of false teachers (chap. 2) and warn true believers to oppose them and shun their false doctrine.

Key Facts	
Author:	The apostle Peter
Recipients:	Believers in Asia Minor and elsewhere
Where Written:	Probably from Rome
Date:	About AD 65–67
Key Words:	Grow (Gk. *auxanō*), knowledge (Gk. *gnosis*)
Key Verses:	"I consider it right, as long as I am in this bodily tent, to wake you up with a reminder, knowing that I will soon lay aside my tent, as our Lord Jesus Christ has also shown me. And I will also make every effort that you may be able to recall these things at any time after my departure" (1:13–15).

AUTHOR

Simon Peter is identified as the author of this epistle (1:1). One of the most important Christian writers of the third century, Origen, attributed the epistle to Peter (c. 250). It was also accepted as Peter's work by Cyril of Jerusalem (386), Athanasius (370), Augustine (430), and Jerome (420). The epistle was probably used in the first century by Clement of Rome in his letter to Corinth (95), by several apocryphal books in the second century (including Pseudo-Barnabas), and by Irenaeus (c. 200). Significantly, when Eusebius divided Christian writings into "genuine," "disputed," and "spurious," he did not place Peter among the "spurious writings" (c. 320). Many critical scholars reject this and believe that the letter is pseudepigraphal (written by someone else).

The strongest **internal evidence** for the Petrine authorship of 2 Peter is that the name Simon (Simeon) Peter appears in the text at 1:1, and he identifies himself as an apostle of Jesus Christ. There are also a number of personal allusions in 1:12–18. For example, Peter mentions his approaching death (1:14; cf. John 21:18). His use of the word "exodus" (departure) for death in 1:15 appears to allude to the story of the transfiguration of Jesus (cf. Luke 9:31). In fact, the author claims to have been an eyewitness of the transfiguration (1:16–18). There is also a possible allusion to Peter as the source of the Gospel of Mark (see authorship of Mark) when Peter writes, "And I will also make every effort that you may be able to recall these things at any time after my departure" (1:15).

In addition, the author refers to an **earlier epistle** which had been written by him to the same readers (3:1); this epistle was likely 1 Peter. The writer even claims to know Paul (3:15–16), as Peter would certainly have done.

Lastly, there are many **similarities in vocabulary** between 2 Peter and Peter's speeches in the book of Acts, as well as with 1 Peter: (1) "obtained" (2 Pet 1:1; Acts 1:17); (2) "godliness" (2 Pet 1:3–7; 3:11; Acts 3:12); (3) "lawless" (2 Pet 2:8; Acts 2:23); (4) "putting off" (1 Pet 3:21; 2 Pet 1:14); (5) "cease from sin" (1 Pet 4:1; 2 Pet 2:14); (6) "eyewitness" (1 Pet 2:12; 3:2; 2 Pet 1:16); (7) "supply" (1 Pet 4:11; 2 Pet 1:5,11); (8) "love of the brethren" (1 Pet 1:22; 2 Pet 1:7); (9) "manner of life" (1 Pet 1:15,18; 2:12; 3:1–2,16; 2 Pet 2:7; 3:11); and (10) "without blemish or spot" (1 Pet 1:19; 2 Pet 3:14).

Many critical scholars, however, despite this evidence, reject the Petrine author-ship of 2 Peter and believe the letter is pseudepigraphical, offering **several objections**

Roman aqueduct at Caesarea where Peter first baptized Gentiles.

to support their claim. Critics argue that the second epistle of Peter is not quoted or directly referred to positively until the time of Origen (c. 250). Didymus called it "spurious" (fourth century AD). Eusebius placed it among the disputed books (c. 320), along with James, Jude, and 2 and 3 John. He admitted that no long line of tradition for 2 Peter could be traced up to the fourth century. However, it may be that the letter was not circulated widely because of persecution or because it was kept by an isolated group of churches. The epistle is still better attested historically than many of the secular writings of the period (Herodotus, Thucydides, etc.).

Internally, critics claim there are **differences** between 1 Peter and 2 Peter in style, thought, and vocabulary. First Peter has 369 words that are not used in 2 Peter. Second Peter has 230 words that are not used in 1 Peter. They claim the two epistles have only 100 words in common. First Peter is warm and intimate, whereas 2 Peter seems detached and theological. First Peter stresses the suffering, death, resurrection, and ascension of Christ, whereas 2 Peter mentions only the transfiguration and prophecies concerning Christ.

Moreover, 2 Peter refers to a collection of Paul's letters and to Paul as "our beloved brother" (3:15–16 NKJV). Some critics maintain that Peter would not have commended his rival Paul. And many think that collections of apostolic writings were not made as early as the lifetime of Peter (however, they have no proof for this claim). Critics also claim 2 Peter is dependent on the epistle of Jude and assume the apostle Peter would not have borrowed material from Jude, who was not an apostle.

The following may be said in **answer to these objections**: (1) Peter apparently used different secretaries for the two epistles (a common practice); this would account for the differences in style and vocabulary. (2) Paul's letters were probably collected early by such men as Luke, Silas, Timothy, and Paul himself (cf. Col 4:16). (3) Peter and Paul were not rivals (cf. the parallels between 1 Peter and Romans and Ephesians). (4) It is not certain that 2 Peter is dependent on Jude. Jude could have used 2 Peter as a source.

The only **alternative** to Peter's authorship of the epistle is that it is a deliberate forgery (someone else wrote it and put Peter's name on it). However, the early church was strongly opposed to the passing off of pseudepigraphical books as genuine.[1] Second Peter is universally recognized as having a much higher quality than any pseudepigraphical book. Furthermore, it is unlikely that the whole church could have been totally deceived about the actual author of an epistle claiming to have been written by the chief of the apostles.

RECIPIENTS

The original readers of 2 Peter were **probably the same** as for the first epistle— Christians mainly in northern Asia Minor. According to 2 Pet 3:1, Peter had written a previous letter to his readers; that letter would most likely be 1 Peter. There are some problems with this view. Second Peter does not refer directly to any of the content of 1 Peter. Furthermore, when Peter refers to a letter written by Paul (3:15), the reference appears to be to Rom 2:4. This implies either that the readers of 2 Peter were in Rome or that the epistle of Paul to the Romans had already been sent out to the churches of Asia Minor as a circular letter, since Peter implies that his readers already knew what

Paul had written. In actuality, 2 Peter may have gone out to a wider audience than 1 Peter, since no addressee is given. But it is clear that he expects them to have already read his previous letter.

OCCASION AND DATE

Apostasy and false teachers were already infiltrating Christian churches. Believers needed to be aware of these false teachers and how to combat their teachings. They also needed reassurance concerning the fulfillment of the prophecies of Christ's return, since many false teachers were mocking these promises. Since Peter was expecting death soon, he wanted to leave some exhortations and instructions for the churches about these matters.

Peter probably wrote this epistle during the years **AD 65–67**. He makes clear that he expects to die soon (1:14), and these threats may have arisen because of Nero's persecution (AD 64–68). Since 2 Peter was written after 1 Peter (dated AD 64–67), the earliest possible date seems to be AD 65. The latest possible date for the writing of 2 Peter is AD 68. Nero died in the year 68; since Peter died at the hands of Nero, he must have written the epistle during or before AD 68, most likely in Rome. Tradition is clear that **Peter died in Rome** (for example, Papias, in the second century), so Peter's final epistle was most likely written there also.

GENRE AND STRUCTURE

Peter's first epistle emphasizes the sufferings and redemption of Christ and the resultant suffering of Christians. His second epistle focuses instead on the glory of Christ and the certainty that should come from the apostolic teaching about him. The first epistle contains much about opposition from the **outside** (persecution). The second warns about the growing apostasy **within** (false teaching).

There is also an emphasis in this epistle on **prophecy**—true and false. One of the classic biblical passages on the **inspiration** of Scripture comes at the end of chap. 1: "First of all, you should know this: no prophecy of Scripture comes from one's own interpretation, because no prophecy ever came by the will of man; instead, men spoke from God as they were moved by the Holy Spirit," (1:20–21). This is followed immediately by a lengthy warning in chap. 2 that "there will be false teachers among you," bringing in "destructive heresies." These coming false prophets and teachers are described in gruesome detail, after which Peter returns to the truths of God's true prophecy (3:2–13)—that which is trustworthy and designed for salvation (3:9).

Outline

I. Exhortation: Growth and Fruitfulness (2 Peter 1:1–15)
II. Prophecy: True and False (2 Peter 1:16–3:13)
III. Exhortation: Growth and Holiness (2 Peter 3:14–18)

MESSAGE

I. Exhortation: Growth and Fruitfulness (2 Peter 1:1–15)

Peter introduces himself as an apostle and servant of Jesus Christ and notes that he is writing to people who hold the same faith and doctrine as do he and the other apostles.

The basis for Christian growth is the divine power of God, which through the knowledge of God and God's promises enables believers to share in the divine nature. Peter describes the process of growth (1:5–7) as beginning with faith, and including such other Christian virtues as goodness, knowledge, self-control, perseverance, godliness, brotherly affection, and love. Growth is vitally important for spiritual vitality, for **assurance of salvation**, and for a reward in the kingdom of God (1:8–11). Peter believes his readers have a need for reminders, to arouse their memory of what he has already taught. Since Peter knows that he will die soon, he is putting into writing the things he wants them to remember (1:12–15).

II. Prophecy: True and False (2 Peter 1:16–3:13)

Peter shows that the return of Christ is guaranteed, first through the eyewitnesses of the Lord Jesus Christ and second through the Scriptures (1:16–21). The testimony of the apostles concerning **the return of Christ** and the majesty of Christ confirms the prophecies of His return. More particularly, the reality of the transfiguration of Christ and the testimony of God the Father from heaven (see Mark 9:7) guarantees the certainty of Christ's return (1:17–18). Second, the Scriptures themselves show the certainty of prophecy, since they are not from man but from God (1:19–21).

Peter then issues a **warning** against false prophets and false teachers. Just as there were false prophets among the people in the Old Testament, there would also be false teachers in the Church, professing Christ but denying the truth. Their methods are deceptive: they will teach heresies and deny Christ Himself, using sensuality and exploitation to bring others under their influence (2:1–3). But their judgment is certain. The certainty of the judgment of false teachers is illustrated by the punishment of angels, the people of the ancient world in the worldwide flood, and the people of Sodom and Gomorrah. God will deliver the godly, but He will judge the unrighteous (2:3–10).

The **false teachers** are self-willed, ignorant, licentious, and greedy. They are following the example of Balaam in the Old Testament. Their teaching is worthless and unproductive. Their method is to entice others with empty words and an appeal to the flesh. They attempt to draw Christians themselves away from their pure commitment to Christ, particularly those who are new in the faith. The result for those who are thus enticed and entrapped is spiritual slavery. These have returned to corruption, which for them is a worse state than their previous unbelief (2:10–22).

Concerning true prophecy, however, Peter reaffirms the **promise of the coming of Christ**. Scoffers will arise, who will argue that since Christ has not yet returned, He never will (3:1–4). They willfully ignore both the past judgments of God and His future judgment of the world (3:5–7). God's attitude toward the promise of Christ's return is totally different. The reason for the apparent delay of Christ's return is the

First-century AD ruins outside the synagogue at Capernaum with Peter's memorial in the background. The memorial is built on what may have been Peter's house.

different time perspective of God and His patience with mankind so that all might be saved (3:8–9). The judgment of the world is nevertheless certain. It will arrive suddenly and bring total destruction on the present world. Believers must pursue holiness and have an attitude of expectancy—both of judgment and of blessing (3:10–13).

III. Exhortation: Growth and Holiness (2 Peter 3:14–18)

Believers need to become holy and be diligent to **pursue sanctification**. Believers also need to recognize that the patience of God in delaying the return of Christ is to give the world more time to be saved. This has been further substantiated by the revelation that God has given to the apostle Paul—whose epistles have equal authority with the rest of the Scriptures (3:14–16).

In addition, believers need to **guard against error**, being careful not to fall away from their steadfastness in the Christian faith. And finally, believers need to grow in their experience of the grace and knowledge of Jesus Christ (3:18). This is the best safeguard against apostasy and false teaching.

CONCLUSION

Peter appeared to have two major purposes in writing this epistle: (1) to **exhort the believers** to growth, confidence, and steadfast faith; and (2) to **expose false teachers** and instruct believers in how to deal with them. Many pastors and teachers since Peter's day have testified that the great apostle succeeded magnificently in this endeavor. Christians can trust the eyewitness testimony of Peter and the other apostles (1:16–19), as well as the divinely inspired words of Scripture that were written as selected men were moved and inspired by the Holy Spirit (1:20–21).

In spite of the attempts by destructive false teachers to move believers away from this confidence (2:1–19), God will have the last word. After giving humanity every possible opportunity to avail themselves of the gracious redemption accomplished through Christ, God will ultimately dissolve this Earth and begin the final stage in his eternal plan with a "**new earth**" and "**new heavens**," where "righteousness will dwell" (3:10–13). Meanwhile, as Peter says, what sort of people should we be "in holy conduct and godliness" (3:11)?

Study Questions

1. What do you think Peter means by "share in the divine nature" (1:4)?
2. How can believers "confirm" their calling and election (1:10)?
3. Are there any anti-Christian "scoffers" (3:4–5) in our day? Are they saying anything similar to Peter's quotation of those of his day?
4. In what way does Peter's statement in 3:8–9 explain why the fact that Christ has not yet returned should not be called a "delay"?
5. Why does Peter bring up the illustration of the Genesis flood in 3:5–6? What is his point as it relates to the immediate context?

For Further Reading

Davids, Peter H. *The Letters of 2 Peter and Jude*. PNTC. Grand Rapids: Eerdmans, 2006.

Green, Gene L. *Jude and 2 Peter*. BECNT. Grand Rapids: Baker, 2008.

Green, Michael. *2 Peter and Jude*. TNTC. Grand Rapids: Eerdmans, 1987.

Hiebert, D. Edmond. *Second Peter and Jude: An Expositional Commentary*. Greenville, SC: BJU Press, 1989.

Mounce, Robert H. *Born Anew to a Living Hope: A Commentary on 1 and 2 Peter*. Grand Rapids: Eerdmans, 1982.

Schreiner, Thomas R. *1, 2 Peter, Jude*. NAC. Nashville: B&H, 2003.

ENDNOTE

1. For more information on the issue of pseudepigraphy in the New Testament, see D. A. Carson, "Pseudonymity and Pseudepigraphy," in *Dictionary of New Testament Background*, ed. Craig Evans and Stanley Porter (Downers Grove: IVP, 2000), 857–64; Terry Wilder, *Pseudonymity, the New Testament, and Deception* (Lanham, MD: University Press of America, 2004).

Chapter 27

1 JOHN
Blessed Assurance

John's Gospel presented "signs" in order to bring people to the belief that Jesus was the Messiah (20:30–31). Those who believed were given the right to become children of God. These children were brought into **fellowship with God** the Father through Jesus the Son. However, not all who professed faith in Christ were truly walking with God. Their lives did not reflect the changed life that results from experiencing fellowship with God. They walked in darkness rather than light and refused to acknowledge any sin in their lives. Some taught false doctrines about Jesus, and some abandoned the faith, leaving the church altogether. John writes this epistle to assure believers of their position as children of God and to call illegitimate children and their teachings into question.

Key Facts	
Author:	John
Recipients:	Believers
Where Written:	Unknown
Date:	AD 85–95
Key Word:	know (Gk. *oida* and *ginōskō*)
Key Verse:	"I have written these things to you who believe in the name of the Son of God, so that you may know that you have eternal life" (5:13).

AUTHOR

This epistle begins without any introductory greeting or without identifying the author by name. Internal evidence shows that the writer is an eyewitness (1:1–4) and writes his audience as one in a position of authority (1:6; 2:15,24,28; 3:14; 4:1; 5:21). The author uses simple Greek sentences and incorporates themes which contrast opposites such as light and darkness, life and death, love and hate, and truth and lies. People are said to fit into one or the other of each of these opposites. All of this internal

302

evidence is consistent with **Johannine authorship**. Likewise, external evidence supports this conclusion.[1] For more about John, the son of Zebedee, see the introduction to John's Gospel.

RECIPIENTS

The epistle's lack of formal epistolary introduction limits the scope of how much can be known about the epistle's original audience. The author did not greet a specific church or group because he wanted the letter to be circulated among as many churches as possible. Certainly, the epistle is intended for believers (1 John 2:12–14,19; 3:1; 5:13), and its message is one that has application to all churches.

An ancient baptistery in Ephesus, the city in which John ministered late in the first century.

OCCASION AND DATE

Internal evidence indicates that some members of their body were abandoning their confession of faith and leaving the church. Some were even teaching that Jesus did not have a physical body. John, therefore, writes this epistle in order to (1) teach his readers discernment about who is and who is not in proper relationship with God; (2) affirm his readers in their faith; and (3) warn them concerning the teachings of the false teachers. John concludes that those who leave their church fellowship have made clear that they were not in true fellowship with God in the first place. Those who have fellowship with God will walk in light rather than darkness, love one another, believe in the name of Jesus, affirm that Jesus came in the flesh, and follow God's commandments.

No specific information in 1 John assists in pinpointing an exact date when it was written. However, church tradition suggests that John was in the later years of his life and living in Ephesus when he wrote this letter. Many scholars conclude that the epistles were written soon after he completed his Gospel. In addition, these letters do not seem to indicate that the persecution under Domitian (c. AD 95) had yet begun. Therefore an acceptable date range for all three epistles is between AD 85 and 95.

Outline

   I. Introduction (1 John 1:1–4)
  II. Walking in the Light (1 John 1:5–2:29)
 III. Fellowship in Love (1 John 3:1–5:13)
 IV. Conclusion (1 John 5:14–21)

MESSAGE

In this letter, just as in the Gospel, John affirms that a person's assurance of eternal life is not something to be experienced only after death, but it begins and is experienced in the believer at the moment of salvation. All true believers, therefore, are not only looking ahead in faith toward something future but can already know certain things. Therefore, much of 1 John focuses on reaffirming what the readers already know. Therefore, John uses the words *oida* and *ginōskō* (both meaning "to know") 77 times in 32 verses, many of which are reaffirming what his audience already knows, including: (1) the truth (2:2); (2) that they have a relationship with God (2:3–5,13–14); (3) that He hears and grants their prayer requests (5:15); (4) that Jesus was righteous, did not sin, came to take away sin, and that when He appears we will be like Him (2:29; 3:2); (5) that sin is not characteristic of someone in fellowship with God (3:15; 5:18); and (6) the final hour is at hand (2:18).

I. Introduction (1 John 1:1–4)

As one of Jesus' disciples, John was among the first to hear Jesus' message and to receive eternal life (cf. John 1:35–39). He begins by reminding his readers that he was an eyewitness to the historical Jesus and was among those who experienced fellowship with the resurrected Jesus during His postresurrected ministry. Now John continues fellowship with Jesus and God the Father. While he is writing with the authority of an apostle, he is also writing as a fellow believer, extending his hand of fellowship to all who believe. His hope is that this letter will bring his readers into the fellowship he is experiencing and that through this letter their joy may be complete.

II. Walking in the Light (1 John 1:5–2:29)

In the first major section of the letter, John writes about believers enjoying fellowship with God and walking in the light (1:5–2:2). After establishing his credibility in the prologue, John summarizes the message that he has heard as "God is light, and there is absolutely no darkness in Him" (1:5). With this message in view, he reasons that anyone in their assembly who claims to have fellowship with God but continues to walk in darkness (sin) is deceiving himself and others. However, those who walk in the light (righteousness) of Jesus are forgiven, cleansed from their sins, and experience true fellowship (1:6–10). John's hope is that his letter will serve to help his reader avoid sin, but he is careful to remind his readers that salvation cannot be equated with sinless perfection. If anyone denies their need of forgiveness, they are making God out to be a liar and remain in darkness. However, if anyone does sin, they have not lost their salvation. Rather, Jesus remains their Advocate with the Father. His bodily sacrifice is sufficient to pay, not only for their sins but for the entire world's sins (2:2). However, they must accept Jesus as their Advocate.

After this, John moves on to speak about believers' assurance of salvation and their keeping of Jesus' commandments (2:3–15). Those who keeps Jesus' commandments can have assurance of salvation when they are in proper relationship with Him, and God's love is perfected in them (2:3,5). When they obey His commandment to love one another, they walk as Jesus walked (2:6). They do not love the world or the things of the world (2:15).

Greek Highlight

Fellowship. Greek κοινωνία (**koinōnia**). *Koinonia* most often carries the sense of communion or fellowship, referring to an association involving close mutual relations. This idea of mutual involvement is seen in extrabiblical usage, where *koinonia* can refer to marriage (3 Macc 4:6). Because of a common Spirit, Christians have fellowship with God and one another (1 John 1:3,6–7). This kind of intimate fellowship was displayed among the sharing community of the early church (Acts 2:42). *Koinonia* may also refer to the way in which this fellowship is portrayed, namely, through sharing, generosity, or participatory-feeling. Paul speaks of the Corinthian church's generosity in sharing a financial gift (2 Cor 9:13). By extension *koinonia* may refer to the financial contribution itself (Rom 15:26). It may also express participation or common fellowship in a task or cause. All believers have a common participation in the faith (Phlm 6) and in Christ's body and blood (1 Cor 10:16). Near the end of the first century, *koinonia* was a vital quality to have among the believers as they began to face organized threats upon the maturing church. Thus, *koinonia* is a requisite characteristic for believers today in order to maintain a healthy church in the twenty-first century.

However, those who profess to know Jesus yet do not keep His commandments are liars, and the truth is not in them (2:4). From this it can be concluded that the way people treat others is a window into their soul. Those who love one another are walking in the light and have the sure footing the light provides. Those who hate others are walking in darkness and do not know where they are going because they remain blinded by the darkness (2:9,11).

John's first admonition is that believers do not love the world (2:12–17). Having emphasized the need for love, John admonishes them that (1) their sins have been forgiven, (2) they know Jesus and the Father, (3) God abides in them, and (4) they have overcome the wicked one (2:12–14). However, they live in a world full of sin and temptation. John therefore admonishes them not to love the sinful world or the things of the world (2:15–16). Rather than getting entangled with the lusts of the world, their focus should be on God's will. He explains that the world is passing away but that the one who does the will of God will remain forever (2:17).

John makes clear that the "Antichrist is coming" in the future (2:18). But in the meantime many antichrists are already here (2:18–23). Unfortunately, John's readers knew this truth all too well (2:20–21); some from their own church were antichrists. Apparently, some individuals in their fellowship were denying that Jesus was the Christ, thereby proving to be antichrists and liars (2:19,22–23). John reminds them that Jesus claimed that the one who denies the Son cannot know the Father, but the one who confesses the Son has the Father as well (2:22; cf. John 5:32–38; 8:18). John comforts his readers by explaining that those individuals who left their church fellowship were never really a part of it in the first place (2:19).

John's second admonition is that his readers abide in the truth (2:24–28). In light of these antichrist-like false teachers, John reminds his readers that they have already been equipped to resist the lies of the world. If they allow the gospel to abide in them, they will abide in the Son and in the Father and have live life eternal (2:24–25). Jesus the Son has anointed them with the Holy Spirit who will guide them away from false teachers and lead them into truth (2:26–27). If they abide in Jesus, when He returns, they will have confidence and not be ashamed. He therefore admonishes them to abide in the truth.

III. Fellowship in Love (1 John 3:1–5:13)

Earlier in chap. 2, John focused on the importance of loving one another and not loving the things of this world. Now he returns to this theme by focusing on God's love for them. God displays His love by calling them His children (3:1). This title is just the beginning; God has not fully revealed what they will become, but they will become like Jesus because they will see Him as He is (3:2).

In the meantime, all who look forward to the second coming of Jesus purify themselves just as He is pure (3:3). In fact, John goes as far as saying that "everyone who remains in Him does not sin; everyone who sins has not seen Him or known Him" and "everyone who has been born of God does not sin, because His seed remains in him; he is not able to sin, because he has been born of God" (3:6,9). Jesus came to destroy the works of the Devil, and therefore those who are of Jesus should have no association with sin, which is the work of the Devil (3:8–9). In other words, sin is something foreign to the child of God and something that opposes the reason Jesus came into the world. Jesus came to live in believers and lead them away from sin. These statements need to be balanced with John's previous statement, "I am writing you these things so that you may not sin. But if anyone does sin, we have an advocate with the Father—Jesus Christ the Righteous One" (2:1). With this broader context in view, John's statements should not be taken to mean that any single instance of sin disqualifies someone as a true child of God. However, John's statements in chap. 3 make clear that sin is something that should rarely appear in the lives of children of God.

John's third admonition is for believers not to be surprised by hate (3:10–15). John illustrates his description of the children of God by citing the Old Testament account of Cain and Abel. The interplay between Cain and Abel represents what it means to be a child of God and a child of the Devil. Abel in his righteousness offered an offering that was acceptable to God, but Cain in his unrighteousness did not. As a result, Cain hated his brother because of his righteousness and

Second-century Roman baths in the upper agora at Ephesus.

murdered him. John, therefore, admonishes his readers, "Do not be surprised, brothers, if the world hates you" (3:13). The children of the Devil will hate the righteous; and he who hates is a murderer and does not have eternal life (3:15; cf. John 5:18). The children of God, on the other hand, love one another. Therefore, those who love one another know that they have passed from death to life (3:14).

What is the source of this love, which so defines a child of God (3:16–23)? It is Jesus' own self-sacrifice. We, therefore, should love one another even to the point of laying down our own lives for one another (3:16). This means the things that we own should be available to others in need. If we see our brother in need but close our hearts to him, the love of God does not abide in us. Our love should not simply be of words but of action (3:17–18). Displaying this kind of love will give us assurance that we are of the truth and give us confidence before God. With this confidence we know that we shall receive whatever we ask in prayer (3:19–22) and that we obey God's commandments to believe in His Son and to love one another (3:23).

John's fourth admonition is that believers must test the spirits (3:24–4:6). In light of John's comments, it becomes clear that one's belief in Jesus and one's love for others are evidence that one is abiding in Jesus. But what is the evidence that this relationship is reciprocal and Jesus is abiding in us? John explains that the answer lies in the Spirit that God has given to His children (3:24). But he cautions them not to believe every spirit but to test the spirits to see whether they are of God (4:1). If a spirit does not confess that Jesus Christ has come in bodily form, then that spirit was not sent from God but is the spirit of the Antichrist (4:2–3).[2]

Despite John's admonition for believers to test the spirits, he is confident that the Spirit within them has already conquered the spirit of the evil one. He explains, "You are from God, little children, and you have conquered them, because the One who is in you is greater than the one who is in the world" (4:4). What is more, they will be able to discern the spirit of truth from the spirit of error by remembering one simple truth—"We are from God. Anyone who knows God listens to us; anyone who is not from God does not listen to us" (4:6).

After this admonition John returns again to his discussion of love (4:7–21). In this section, perhaps more than any other, John drives his point home concerning why love is so characteristic of those who have fellowship with God. He explains that love is the nature of God. Therefore, everyone who loves is born of God and knows God; the one who does not love as he ought does not know God (4:7–8). Jesus' self-sacrifice for our sins has made this love possible and is the model we should follow. Therefore, true love is not that we love God but that He first loved us and sent His Son (4:9–10).

John then reviews what he has told them up to this point concerning love and abiding with an unseen God (4:12–21):

- God is love and he who abides in love abides in God and God in them (4:8,16).
- We love because He first loved us and sent His Son (4:10,19).
- Love for one another is evidence of abiding with God and that His love is perfected in us (1:9,11; 3:14; 4:12).
- God's Spirit is evidence that God abides in us (3:24; 4:13).
- Whoever confesses that Jesus is the Son of God abides in Him (2:22; 4:15).
- Whoever claims to love God must love their brother also (2:9–10; 3:17–18; 4:21).

In the midst of this review, John explains that this love they are now experiencing should put any fears to rest that they have concerning the day of judgment. Perfect love casts out fear; he who fears has not yet been made perfect in love (4:18). But he warns them that in the meantime their relationship with God will be evidenced through their relationships with one another—if they cannot love their brother whom they can see, how can they love God whom they cannot see (4:17–21)?

John now turns his focus to the certainty of God's witness (5:1–13) and the importance of the life and teachings of Jesus. Belief in Jesus is essential for becoming a child of God. Everyone who loves God will also love Jesus (5:1). This love is displayed through obeying God's commandments. And these commandments are not burdensome because those born of God have victory over the world through their faith and their belief that Jesus is the Son of God (5:4–5).

God's Spirit bears witness to Jesus' life and death.[3] This witness is greater than the witness of men because it is from God about His own Son. This witness lives in believers, but those who do not believe God are making Him out to be a liar. This is the testimony the Spirit brings, "God has given us eternal life, and this life is in His Son. The one who has the Son has life. The one who doesn't have the Son of God does not have life" (5:11–12). This testimony should give us assurance that those who believe in the name of the Son of God have eternal life (5:13). In sum, while the witness of men can be fallible, God's witness cannot be fallible. All believers have this testimony inside them in the form of God's Spirit. This testimony should give believers everywhere assurance that their belief in the name of the Son of God has given them eternal life.

IV. Conclusion (1 John 5:14–21)

In closing, John reminds his readers that eternal life is not the only certain thing in life. First, they can be certain that when they ask anything according to God's will, He hears their prayers. Therefore, if anyone sees a brother sinning, they should pray for him, and God will give him life.[4] Second, they can be certain that whoever is born of God will avoid sin and is not touched by Satan (5:18). Third, they know they are of God, but the whole world is under the power of Satan (5:19). Fourth, the Son of God has come and has given understanding so that they can know the true God and His Son Jesus Christ and have eternal life through Him (5:20). Then, almost as an afterthought, he concludes with, "Little children, guard yourselves from idols" (5:21).

CONCLUSION

John's first epistle is addressed to a church where some had abandoned their confession of faith and left the church while others were teaching that Jesus did not have a physical body. In response John wrote his letter in order to: (1) equip his readers to discern who was and who was not in proper relationship with God, (2) affirm his readers in their faith, and (3) warn them concerning the teachings of false teachers.

John maintained that those who left the fellowship of believers showed by their departure that they were not in true fellowship with God in the first place. Those who have fellowship with God will walk in light rather than darkness, love one another, believe in the name of Jesus, affirm that Jesus came in the flesh, and follow God's commandments. Believers must test the spirits and stay away from that which is false.

Study Questions

1. What people/groups today can be said to be antichrists (2:18)?
2. What did John mean when he said that the water and blood testify concerning Christ (5:6)?
3. What reasons in chap. 5 give assurance to believers that they have eternal life?
4. What sin leads to death?
5. What can we know about the nature of God (1:5; 4:8)?

For Further Reading

Akin, Daniel L. *1, 2, 3 John*. NAC. Nashville: B&H, 2001.
Brown, Raymond E. *The Epistles of John*. AB 30. New York: Doubleday, 1982.
Johnson, Thomas. *1, 2 and 3 John*. NIBC. Peabody, MA: Hendrickson, 1993.
Kruse, Colin G. *The Letters of John*. Grand Rapids: Eerdmans, 2000.
Ryrie, Charles. "Epistles of John." In *Wycliffe Bible Commentary*. Chicago: Moody Press, 1992.
Stott, John R. W. *The Letters of John*. TNTC. Grand Rapids: Eerdmans, 1988.

ENDNOTES

1. Church fathers such as Irenaeus (c. 140–203), Clement of Alexandria (c. 155–215), Tertullian (c. 150–222), and Origen (c. 185–253) present John as the author.

2. These false spirits do not seem to be denying the existence of Christ but that Jesus actually had a physical body. Theologically speaking, this denial undermines the gospel itself; if Jesus didn't have a physical body, then His sacrifice would not be sufficient to atone for the sins of mankind. Beyond this, it undermines many statements in the Gospels that give evidence that Christ had such a body (Luke 24:39,43; John 19:28,34; 20:20,27).

3. John also states that the water and the blood bear witness to Him (5:6). There is no universal agreement concerning how water and blood bear witness to Jesus. Possibilities include: (1) Jesus' own baptism and crucifixion; (2) Jesus' baptizing ministry (baptizing others in the Spirit) and crucifixion; (3) natural birth and crucifixion; (4) Jesus' body was made up of the elements of water and blood—proponents of this view cite ancient Jewish sources that held that the human body is composed of two elements: water and blood; (5) the sacraments of baptism and the Eucharist. See Colin G. Kruse, *The Letters of John* (Grand Rapids: Eerdmans, 2000), 174–78.

4. That is, if it is not a sin leading unto death. For a detailed discussion on the sin that leads to death, see Raymond E. Brown, *The Epistles of John*, AB (New York: Doubleday, 1982), 612–19.

Chapter 28

2 JOHN
Avoid False Teachers

J esus taught that the greatest commandment was loving God and loving our neighbor as ourselves. In his farewell discourse, Jesus taught that His disciples would be known by their love for one another (John 15:12). However, as John emphasized in his first letter, fellowship with God is not only a matter of love but also of **sound doctrine**. Followers of Jesus must be careful not to sacrifice truth in the name of love. In this second letter John warns his readers to have nothing to do with false teachers; to show hospitality to them would be to share in their wickedness.

Key Facts	
Author:	John "the Elder"
Recipients:	The "elect lady and her children"
Where Written:	Unknown
Occasion/Date:	AD 85–95
Key Word:	Remain (Gk. *menō*)
Key Verse:	"Anyone who does not remain in Christ's teaching but goes beyond it, does not have God. The one who remains in that teaching, this one has both the Father and the Son" (vv. 9–10).

AUTHOR

While 1 John is anonymous, 2 and 3 John attribute authorship to someone who calls himself "the Elder." While scholarship has not come to a consensus concerning who this elder is, similarities between the first letters attributed to John indicate that both were written by the **same person**. These similarities are as follows: The historical situations between 1 and 2 John are similar. The first epistle speaks of people who "went out" and "who [deny] the Father and the Son" (1 John 2:19–23). Similarly, the second letter speaks of deceivers who "have gone out into the world" and "do not confess the coming of Jesus Christ in the flesh" (2 John 7). Both books call these false teachers "antichrists" (1 John 2:18); both stress the importance of the love command and that it was received "from the beginning" (1 John 3:11,23; 4:7; 2 John 4,6); and both rejoice in seeing their children walking in the truth of the gospel.[1]

Others have proposed that the elder is not the apostle John but another person named John who had a position in the early church. This view finds support in a citation of Papias by Eusebius.[2] However, the consistency of literary style, vocabulary, and topics evidence that the writer of the Gospel of John also wrote the three letters of John.

RECIPIENTS

The recipient is identified in the opening verse as the "elect lady and her children." There is debate as to whether this should be taken: (1) literally, meaning a Christian woman and her children; or (2) figuratively, as a title representing a local church. To date, no other manuscript has been discovered that uses these expressions with the title "elect lady" for a church. Nevertheless, this does not rule out the possibility that this was a figurative title for a church. Three reasons for a **figurative meaning** are as follows: (1) The New Testament refers to the church as "the bride of Christ," and the Old Testament uses the imagery of a "wife" to describe Israel. (2) The church in Rome is described as "she who is in Babylon" (1 Pet 5:13 NKJV). This furthers evidences feminine personifications of the church. (3) The occurrence of both "the elect lady and their children" and "children of your elect sister" in the same letter makes a literal meaning less likely. The "children" obviously are the members of the church. With these reasons in view, a figurative/symbolic usage seems more likely. Either way, the recipients of this letter are followers of Jesus whom John wants to encourage and protect.

OCCASION AND DATE

The occasion and date are similar to 1 John (**AD 85–95**; see notes on 1 John). In 2 John, the apostle focuses on making sure churches do not extend hospitality to false teachers and thereby unknowingly support their itinerate ministry. He instructs them not to allow false teachers into their homes or even recommend them to others and for them to go on their way (vv. 10–11).

GENRE AND STRUCTURE

Second John is a typical first-century letter consisting of an introduction (vv. 1–3), a body (vv. 4–11), and a conclusion (vv. 12–13). It is personal and pastoral yet poignant and powerful.

Outline

I. Introduction: Grace, Mercy, and Peace (2 John 1–3)
II. Body: Truth and Deception (2 John 4–11)
III. Conclusion: I Hope to Be with You (2 John 12–13)

of the epistle of Jude was the last of these—the brother of James and **half brother of Jesus**—since the author of Jude introduces himself as "Jude, a slave of Jesus Christ, and a brother of James" (Jude 1). He seems to talk about the apostles as though he were not one of them (cf. Jude 1,17–18). His self-identification as the **brother of James** indicates that he expected his readers to be familiar with the name and reputation of his brother, the well-known leader of the early church at Jerusalem (cf. Acts 12–21) and author of the epistle of James.

Some scholars believe the author of Jude was the apostle who asked Jesus on the night before he died, "Judas (not Iscariot) said to Him, 'Lord, how is it You're going to reveal Yourself to us and not to the world?'" (John 14:22). This apostle had a father or a brother named James (Luke 6:16; Acts 1:13) who was not the half brother of Jesus. Hence, he identified himself at the introduction of this letter as "the brother of James." Although this identification is possible, it was not accepted by the earliest Christian authors. The name "Jude" is actually "Judas" (Greek *Ioudas*; Hebrew *Judah*). Jude was therefore a **namesake** of the tribe of Judah of which he was a member. Perhaps he was converted to Christ, along with James, after the resurrection of Jesus (cf. John 7:5; Acts 1:14; 1 Cor 9:5). In his epistle he calls himself a "slave" of Jesus Christ (v. 1). In one of his epistles, Paul suggests that Jude was married and was often accompanied by his wife on his travels (1 Cor 9:5).

The epistle of Jude is listed in the Muratorian Fragment (c. AD 170) and is cited in *The Martyrdom of Polycarp* (second century AD). Several early church fathers disputed the authenticity of the book, particularly because of its brevity and its quotation of **nonbiblical sources** (Jude 9,14–15), and some questioned it because Jude was not an apostle. However, the church fathers Athenagoras and Clement of Alexandria (second century) accepted the epistle as canonical and ascribed it to Jude. Later Didymus, Athanasius, Augustine, Jerome, and others recognized its authenticity (fourth century).

RECIPIENTS

The recipients are stated by Jude to be "called," "loved by God," and "kept by Jesus Christ" (v. 1). He calls them "dear friends" (v. 3) and makes several personal references to his knowledge of them (cf. vv. 5,12,17,20). It is probable, therefore, that the recipients of this epistle were **believers** in **various churches** among whom Jude had some ministry and whom he now wanted to warn concerning the presence and deceit of various false teachers who had "come in by stealth" among them (v. 4). Either Israel (Palestine) or Asia Minor would be good possibilities for their location.

OCCASION AND DATE

Jude states that he had originally planned to write an epistle concerning the doctrine of salvation (v. 3), but he now felt it more urgent to warn them concerning the presence of false teachers and to exhort them to **contend for purity of doctrine**. The false teachers, who had come into the churches unnoticed (v. 4), were apparently libertine Gnostics. They were antinomian (from *anti-nomos*, against law), rejecting

Christian moral instruction (v. 4). They were unspiritual (*psuchikoi*), not possessing the Spirit of God (v. 19). They were in bondage to the world (v. 8). They rejected Jesus and denied the truth concerning Him (v. 4). They blasphemed angels (vv. 8,10), and were known for their complaints and cynicism (v. 16). They thought salvation was gained through esoteric (secret) teaching, not through the atonement of Christ. In general, they denied God's revelation in Christ.

If **2 Peter** was written first, perhaps Jude, as he studied Peter's epistle, realized the mockers and false teachers had already arrived and were busily infiltrating the churches. He therefore wrote his epistle to warn believers concerning the growing apostasy and to exhort them to be faithful to apostolic doctrine and to fight for it.

Jude was probably written between **AD 60 and 80**. A crucial factor concerns the relationship of Jude to 2 Peter. There are many similarities between Jude and 2 Peter, particularly between Jude 4–19 and the second chapter of 2 Peter.

SIMILARITIES	Jude	2 Peter
False prophets introduce heresies	4	2:1
Sinful angels	6	2:4
Sodom and Gomorrah's judgment	7	2:6
Despise authority	8	2:10
Blaspheme glorious beings	8	2:10
More abusive than angels	9	2:11
Like unreasoning animals	10	2:12
Greedy like Balaam	11	2:15
Utter arrogant, bombastic words	16	2:18

Four principal views relating to these similarities are possible: (1) Both epistles were written *independently* of each other. This is possible but improbable because of the many similarities and apparent borrowing (the similarities are even in the same order in each epistle). (2) Both epistles used a *common source*. But there is no objective evidence of such a source. (3) *Peter borrowed from Jude*. This view is widely held, especially among biblical critics. However, it is not the most likely explanation, for the reasons listed below under the last view. Jude, who was not one of the 12 apostles, would have been much more likely to have used Peter's epistle than *vice versa*. (4) *Jude borrowed from 2 Peter*. This view is most likely, since Peter mentions the coming of the false teachers as still somewhat future (2 Pet 2:1), whereas Jude states that they are already present (Jude 4). In addition, Jude's reference to the apostolic warning concerning mockers and scoffers (Jude 17–18) appears to refer to the warning of Peter in 2 Pet 3:2–4 and perhaps to that of Paul (cf. Acts 20:28–30; 2 Tim 3:1–9). In addition, Jude referred to apocryphal sources as well as to the apostle Peter (vv. 9,14–15).

GENRE AND STRUCTURE

The epistle of Jude is so short that some have called it more of a "postcard" than a letter. Nevertheless, it includes most of the usual structure of a New Testament epistle: salutation, blessing, body, benediction, and "amen." The one element noticeably lacking is final greetings. Perhaps this is due to Jude's intention to send it to a general or universal readership.

Jude refers to **seven examples** from the Old Testament to **describe apostasy**: (1) Israel in the wilderness (v. 5), (2) fallen angels (v. 6), (3) Sodom and Gomorrah (v. 7), (4) Cain (v. 11), (5) Balaam (v. 11), (6) Korah (v. 11), and (7) those targeted by Enoch's preaching (v. 14). The specific sins thus illustrated include unbelief, rebellion, sexual perversion, murder, greed, and usurpation of authority. The seventh example (Enoch) is used to quote a truth concerning the certainty of God's judgment on sinners and apostates. Enoch warned of coming judgment, and God sent the flood.

Jude's style shows a preference for **triads** (groups of three): (1) He introduces himself as Jude, slave of Jesus Christ, brother of James. (2) He describes his readers as called, loved (or sanctified), and kept (v. 1). (3) He blesses them with mercy, peace, and love (v. 2). (4) He states that the apostates defile the flesh, despise authority, and blaspheme glorious beings. (5) In v. 11, he cites three men as examples of apostasy: Cain, Balaam, and Korah. (6) He mentions all three Persons of the Trinity as having a part in the growth and protection of the believer (vv. 20–21).

Jude is also one of the few books of the Bible that quote from **noncanonical** or **apocryphal** literature. He quotes from both the *Assumption of Moses* (v. 9) and the

Bab Edh Dhr, believed by many archaeologists to be ancient Sodom and Gomorrah.

Book of Enoch (vv. 14–15). These two writings are not part of the Old Testament canon. Rather they are pseudepigraphical writings of Judaism dating from the intertestamental period. The fact that Jude quotes them does not mean he accepted everything written in them as truth but rather that what he did quote was true and therefore repeatable in an inspired epistle. Perhaps Jude or one of the apostles had heard from Jesus Himself that these particular statements from the intertestamental writings were true. Though the *Book of Enoch* was a recent work to Jude's time, it may have included a genuine tradition concerning Enoch.

Outline

I. Contending for the Faith (Jude 1–4)
II. Condemnation of the Ungodly (Jude 5–19)
III. Call to Believers (Jude 20–25)

MESSAGE

I. Contending for the Faith (Jude 1–4)

Jude introduces himself as a slave (or bond servant) of Jesus and the brother of James—probably the half brother of Jesus. His reference to James probably shows that his brother had become far more widely known among the churches than Jude. The author states that his readers are "called," "loved" (or sanctified), and "kept" (preserved, v. 1). Jude then shows that the purpose of his epistle is twofold: (1) an **appeal** to believers to contend for sound doctrine; and (2) a **warning** against infiltrators who are ungodly, false teachers.

II. Condemnation of the Ungodly (Jude 5–19)

The major part of the epistle emphasizes the judgment of the **ungodly apostates**. First, God will judge sin and unbelief. This is illustrated first by God's judgment on unbelieving Israelites during their wilderness wandering; second, by God's judgment on fallen angels; and third, by God's judgment on Sodom and Gomorrah for their sexual immorality and perversion (vv. 5–7).

Next, Jude graphically describes the sin of the **godless infiltrators**. They are unreasoning and rebellious in character, rejecting proper authority and acting like irrational animals. They have imitated the sins of Cain, Balaam, and Korah. In their actions they are unfruitful and ungodly. *Enoch's prophecy* concerning the certainty of God's judgment on sinners will come true on them. Their motives are based on lust and the desire to gain advantage over people (vv. 8–16). Then Jude reminds his readers of the apostolic prophecy concerning the coming of mockers and false teachers, who would be full of sensual lust and worldly desires (vv. 17–19).

Dead, fallen tree.

III. Call to Believers (Jude 20–25)

Jude then appeals to believers to **build themselves up** in the faith, to keep themselves in the love of God, and to have mercy on those who doubt. He appears to distinguish three kinds of people who are headed for judgment but still reachable: (1) Some who "doubt" should be shown mercy. (2) Others can be saved as though by "snatching them from the fire." (3) A third group should be shown mercy "with fear"—cautiously. (Jude uses a metaphor depicting great vigilance or wariness in dealing with such people.) Thus, he provides a practical pattern of effective ministry to those in error.

The **benediction** emphasizes God's keeping power and sovereignty. God is able to protect believers from "stumbling" (falling into the evil of the apostates) and cause them to be blameless at the presence of Christ at His glorious return.

CONCLUSION

Why did Jude use such strong language in condemning the infiltrating false teachers? One reason is the evil, insidious, intentional nature of the **apostasy**. These false teachers were using every malicious and deceptive means possible to gain spiritual and doctrinal control of unsuspecting believers in Christ. Another reason is that Peter and Paul had already predicted this kind of apostasy (2 Peter 2; 1 Timothy 4; 2 Timothy 3), and now that it had arrived full blown in the churches, Jude knew that even stronger warnings were needed. The existence of genuine Christianity as a viable propagator of the truth and grace of Jesus Christ hung in the balance.

Study Questions

1. What does Jude mean by the "faith that was delivered to the saints once for all" (v. 3)?
2. How should believers "contend" or fight for this faith? Give some practical methods.
3. To whom do you think the epistle of Jude was originally sent?
4. Do you think Jude's statement about angels who sinned is a reference to some particular event mentioned in the Old Testament? If so, which one?

For Further Reading

Coder, S. Maxwell. *Jude: The Acts of the Apostates*. Everyman's Bible Commentary. Chicago: Moody, 1967.

Davids, Peter H. *The Letters of 2 Peter and Jude*. PNTC. Grand Rapids: Eerdmans, 2006.

Green, Gene L. *Jude and 2 Peter*. BECNT. Grand Rapids: Baker, 2008.

Green, Michael. *2 Peter and Jude*. TNTC. Rev. ed. Grand Rapids: Eerdmans, 1987.

Chapter 31

REVELATION
The King Is Coming

The book of Revelation is the greatest book of **apocalyptic literature** ever written. It captivates our attention, stirs our imagination, and points to our glorious future destiny. The reader is swept away into another time and place as the panorama of the future unfolds in a series of seven visions in lucid detail and symbolic pictures. This final book of the biblical record is the capstone of divine revelation. In this unique book of New Testament prophecy, the curtain is removed, and the future is revealed for all to see.

The **biblical title** of the book is the "revelation of Jesus Christ" (1:1). The Greek title in the original is based on the word *apokalypsis*. Thus, it is often referred to as the Apocalypse, meaning the "unveiling." Accepted as inspired Scripture from the earliest times of the Christian era, the book nonetheless has been vigorously debated in regard to its authorship, date, and proper method of interpretation.[1]

Key Facts	
Author:	John
Recipient:	Churches of Asia Minor
Where Written:	Island of Patmos
Date:	AD 95
Key Word:	Witness (Gk. *marturia*)
Key Verse:	"Therefore write what you have seen, what is, and what will take place after this" (1:19).

AUTHOR

The traditional view of the Christian church has long held that **John the apostle** was the author of the Revelation as well as the Gospel and epistles that bear his name.[2] Opposition to the authorship of John began with Marcion, a second-century heretic, who rejected all the New Testament authors except Paul. The first serious objection was raised by Dionysius of Alexandria in the third century. He argued that the irregularities in the Greek grammar of the Apocalypse stood in marked contrast to the "elegant diction" of the Gospel and epistles of John. Critical scholars have generally followed this same observation suggesting another John (the elder) may have written the book.[3]

The **internal evidence** for the apostle's authorship includes his use of triplets (cf. John 1:1; Rev 2:2), sevenfold arrangements, and the prominent use of terms like "witness," "life," "faith," "light," and "spirit," which appears in his other writings. Only John's Gospel and Revelation refer to Jesus as the "Word" (Gk. *logos*), the Lamb, the "water of life," and "he who overcomes." Both books include an invitation to one who is thirsty (John 7:37; Rev 22:17), and both make extensive use of the preposition *ek* ("out of") and *kai* ("and"), reflecting the Semitic background of the author.[4]

Seven Churches of the Revelation.

The author of the Revelation was certainly **familiar with the Old Testament**. Bruce Metzger noted: "Of the 404 verses that comprise the 22 chapters of the book of Revelation, 278 verses contain one or more allusions to an Old Testament passage."[5] It is obvious the author was a Jewish Christian living in Asia Minor in the first century AD. Metzger concludes: "Certainly from the mid-second century onward the book was widely ascribed to the apostle John, the son of Zebedee."[6]

Two possible explanations for the **irregularities** in the apocalypse have been suggested: (1) John may have used a secretary (*amanuensis*) to record what he said, a view widely held by Greek Orthodox scholars.[7] Some suggest that a different scribe may have assisted him in composing the Gospel and the epistles. (2) John recorded a series of visions received in an ecstatic state.[8] In some instances he used easily identifiable symbols (Lamb, beast, dragon, elders). At other times he seems to be trying to describe the indescribable things he "saw" (flying creatures with a face like a man, hair like a woman, etc.) Since he received this series of visions by direct revelation, he may have felt compelled not to alter his original composition.

RECIPIENTS

John addresses the "seven churches in Asia" (1:4). These were **seven literal churches** that existed in Asia Minor in the first century AD. Ephesus was the largest city in the list and presumably the largest church. Thus it served as a "mother" church to all the others. All seven churches were connected by the local Roman highway in a circular pattern going from Ephesus to Smyrna and Pergamum and turning inland to Thyatira, Sardis, Philadelphia, and Laodicea.[9] The city of Colossae was also in the region near Laodicea in the Lycus Valley. The **Roman province of Asia** was in the western coastlands of Asia Minor (modern Turkey). It had been settled by Greek Hellenists since the days of Alexander the Great. Prior to the Jewish revolt against Rome (AD 66–70), many Jewish Christians moved into this area that had earlier been evangelized by the apostle Paul (Acts 19).

In Revelation 2–3 **individual "epistles"** are written to the seven churches of Asia Minor by Christ Himself. The general condition of these churches is described as wealthy, prosperous, lukewarm, tolerant of heresy, and having lost their first love. This hardly describes the newly founded churches of the 50s and 60s AD. The potential persecution these churches were facing reflects the widespread persecution of Christians under Domitian, the Roman emperor (AD 81–96) at the end of the first century.

Those who first read the Apocalypse, presumably after John's release after Domitian's death in AD 96, were a mixture of **Hellenistic Jewish** and **Gentile Christians** facing the loss of their personal prosperity and the growing threat of persecution from an increasingly hostile Roman government. John indicates that some believers had already been martyred (2:13) and urged the believers at Smyrna to "be faithful until death" (2:10). Much like other first-century believers, John's recipients were facing the constant pressure to conform to their society or face persecution from its leaders.

OCCASION AND DATE

The question of the date of the original composition of the Apocalypse is a matter of **extensive debate**. Some scholars have argued for a date as early as Claudius (AD 41–54) and others as late as Trajan (AD 98–117). Liberal scholars have attempted to date the book as late as possible because of its highly developed Christology which clearly affirms the deity of Christ.[10] On the other hand, preterists insist on dating it before the year 70 because of their insistence that all or most of it was fulfilled in the destruction of Jerusalem.[11]

Most serious scholars propose a date either in the time of **Nero** (AD 64–67) or **Domitian** (AD 95–96) for the original composition. However, those favoring the early date have no external evidence prior to the sixth century (550) and are forced to attempt to rely on supposed internal evidence to support their view. Ironically, those who lived closest to Nero's time did not believe the book was written then. Mark Hitchcock summarizes the **external evidence** in the following chart:[12]

Witnesses for the Domitianic Date (AD 95)	Witnesses for the Neronic Date (AD 64–67)
Hegesippus (150) Irenaeus (180) Victorinus (c. 300) Eusebius (c. 300) Jerome (c. 400) Sulpicius Severus (c. 400) Primasius (c. 540) Orosius (c. 600) Andreas (c. 600) The Acts of John (c. 650) Venerable Bede (c. 700)	Syriac Version of NT (550) Arethas (c. 900) Theophylact (d. 1107)

The **internal evidence** for the late date of Revelation is equally impressive. The condition of the churches of Asia Minor shows all the characteristics of second-generation churches lapsing from their original zeal and enthusiasm. For example, Paul's earlier letter to the church at Ephesus, or his letter to Timothy who was at Ephesus, does not mention the issues raised in Rev 2:1–7. Also, the letter in Revelation does not mention Paul's work in Asia Minor or the three years he spent in Ephesus (AD 52–55), which would have been less than a decade before an early composition of the Apocalypse. Polycarp, writing in 110, indicates the church at Smyrna did not exist during the time of Paul's missionary journeys in the 50s and 60s. In regard to the church at Laodicea, Paul mentions them three times in his Colossian letter (2:1; 4:13,16) in a positive light in about AD 60–62. It hardly seems conceivable that the

Laodiceans lapsed so quickly that the letter in Rev 3:16–22 had nothing good with which to commend them if it was written in AD 64–67.

All things considered, both internal and external evidence lean strongly in favor of a date of **AD 95–96** for the composition of Revelation by John while he was in exile on the island of Patmos in the Aegean Sea, some 40 miles off the coast from Ephesus. The fact that Domitian was known for exiling political dissidents, whereas Nero executed them, lends even more support to the later date, as does the fact that Domitian was the first Roman emperor to insist that he be worshipped as deity throughout the entire empire.[13]

Overview of Patmos, the island in the Mediterranean Sea where John received the Revelation of Jesus Christ.

GENRE AND STRUCTURE

John tells us what he "heard" and "saw" in descriptive **symbolic language**. Some of his symbols are drawn from the Old Testament (e.g., Lion of Judah, song of Moses, tree of life, Lamb of God). Some symbols are from the New Testament (e.g., Word of God, Son of Man, bride of Christ), but some of the symbols have no biblical parallel and are unexplained (e.g., scarlet beast, seven thunders, mark of the beast). Other symbols are specifically identified (e.g., seven lamps are seven churches, and the dragon is Satan) or are self-explanatory (e.g., numbers, seals, songs, trumpets). While the Apocalypse is symbolic, the symbols depict real people, things, situations, and events.

Several elements make the Revelation **the most unique book in the Bible**. The basic structure of the book is woven around a series of threes and sevens. The overarching triplet (1:19) reveals past, present, and future realities.

Past: "What you have seen" (chap. 1)

Present: "What is" (chaps. 2–3)

Future: "What will take place after this" (chaps. 4–22)

The most significant number in Revelation is **seven**. There are seven churches, spirits, stars, lampstands, horns, eyes, angels, seals, trumpets, bowls, thunders, crowns, plagues, mountains, kings, songs, and beatitudes. In addition, there is a sevenfold description of Christ (1:14–16), a sevenfold message to each church (chaps. 2–3), sevenfold praise of the lamb (5:12), sevenfold results of judgment (6:12–14), seven divisions of humanity (6:15), a sevenfold blessing (7:12), a sevenfold triumph (11:19), and seven "new things" (chaps. 21–22).

Other prominent numbers include **12**. There are 12 tribes of Israel, 12 apostles, 12 gates, and 12 foundations of the New Jerusalem, 24 elders (a double 12), and multiples of 12: each of the 12 tribes contains 12,000 people, making a total of 144,000 (12 x 12,000), and the wall of the New Jerusalem measures 144 cubits (12 x 12).

The purpose of the Revelation is to **reveal the future**. Everything in the book points to the second coming of Christ. The risen, glorified Savior who appears to John on Patmos is the same person who returns with His triumphant Church at the end of the book. The One who walks among the candlesticks (churches) as Lord of the Church and our heavenly high priest is the same One who will take His bride to reign with Him in His millennial kingdom on earth.

Outline

I. Preface: Vision of the Coming King (Revelation 1)

II. Proclamation: Letters to the Seven Churches (Revelation 2–3)
   A. Ephesus: Preoccupied Church (Revelation 2:1–7)
   B. Smyrna: Persecuted Church (Revelation 2:8–11)
   C. Pergamum: Political Church (Revelation 2:12–17)
   D. Thyatira: Prosperous Church (Revelation 2:18–29)
   E. Sardis: Powerless Church (Revelation 3:1–6)
   F. Philadelphia: Persevering Church (Revelation 3:7–13)
   G. Laodicea: Putrid Church (Revelation 3:14–22)

III. Problem: Seven-Sealed Scroll (Revelation 4–5)

IV. Process: Seven Seals and Seven Trumpets (Revelation 6–11)

V. Players: Seven Key Figures in the Eschatological Drama (Revelation 12–13)

VI. Plagues: Seven Bowl Judgments (Revelation 14–19)

VII. Postscript: Millennium and Eternal City (Revelation 20–22)

MESSAGE

I. Preface: Vision of the Coming King (Revelation 1)[14]

The opening chapter serves as an introduction to the entire book. It is the revelation (Gk. *apokalypsis*, "unveiling") of Jesus Christ through His angel to His servant John (1:1). John, in turn, is told to record all he saw in the vision and send it to the seven churches in Asia Minor (1:2,4). Jesus is depicted as the "faithful witness" (Gk. *marturia*) who reveals future events that will "quickly take place" (1:1), emphasizing the **suddenness** with which they will eventually transpire (cf. 2:16; 3:11; 11:14; 22:7,12,20).

Tradition claims that John came to Ephesus to oversee the church in the year 66. Now nearly 30 years later, the aged disciple has been arrested for refusing to worship the emperor and exiled to the **island of Patmos** in circa AD 90, during the reign of Domitian. Alone and abandoned on a Sunday morning ("the Lord's day," 1:10), he heard a voice "like a trumpet" (1:10), and turning to see who was speaking to him, he saw "One like the Son of Man," dressed like the high priest of heaven (v. 13).

The description of the **glorified Savior** (1:13–16) follows a sevenfold pattern, which is later repeated in the letters to the churches (chaps. 2–3):

1. Hair: white as snow
2. Eyes: like flames of fire
3. Feet: burnished bronze
4. Voice: sound of cascading waters
5. Right hand: held seven stars
6. Mouth: sharp double-edged sword
7. Face: shining like the sun

The appearance of the heavenly intruder is not only unique; it is supernatural. The grandeur of this description points to the majesty, purity, and authority of the coming king. The "sword of His mouth" is His only weapon, in contrast to the bow of the Antichrist (6:2). He who spoke the world into existence at the moment of creation will use the "sword" of His spoken word to conquer the world at His return (19:15). In the meantime, **the Savior commissions John** to record: (1) "what you have seen" (past); (2) "what is" (present); (3) "what will take place after this" (future; 1:19).

II. Proclamation: Letters to the Seven Churches (Revelation 2–3)

Before the Apocalypse pronounces a message of judgment on the unbelieving world, it first calls the churches to repentance. In these letters the Lord of the church speaks lovingly but firmly to the churches in words of both commendation and condemnation.[15] The message to each church follows the same **sevenfold pattern**:

1. Commission: "To the angel of the church "
2. Character: "The One who . . . says this"
3. Commendation: "I know your works "

4. Condemnation: "But I have this against you "
5. Correction: "Repent . . . turn . . . change"
6. Call: "He who has an ear, let him hear"
7. Challenge: "To him who overcomes"

A. Ephesus: Preoccupied Church (Revelation 2:1–7)

Ephesus, to whom Paul's letter to the Ephesians was written, was one of the outstanding churches of the first century. Paul, Timothy, John, Apollos, and Aquila and Priscilla were all there in the apostolic era. This was a privileged church indeed! Yet, as time wore on, they had begun to lose their first priority and became **preoccupied** with other things. Commended for their good works, they were challenged to regain their "first love" and serve the Lord with renewed passion.

B. Smyrna: Persecuted Church (Revelation 2:8–11)

There were no words of condemnation or correction for the **persecuted** believers at Smyrna, a city that prided itself on its emperor worship. The name of the city came from the aroma of a perfume made there by crushing the resin of a small thorn bush. It was an apt description of the fragrance of the many martyrs who gave their lives there for the cause of Christ, including John's own disciple Polycarp who was burned at the stake in the year 156.

The theater on the Acropolis of Pergamum.

C. Pergamum: Political Church (Revelation 2:12–17)

The massive Roman fortress sat on the acropolis at Pergamum on the Mediterranean coast. It also became the site of the first temple in the area dedicated to the Caesar cult, erected in honor of Augustus in 29 BC. The citizens of Pergamum worshipped power. The Roman army was headquartered there, and the temple of Zeus, the god of power, dominated the city "where Satan's throne is" (2:13). There was no distinction in Pergamum between religion and politics, and the believers were often caught in the temptation of **political correctness** that often led to spiritual compromise.

D. Thyatira: Prosperous Church (Revelation 2:18–29)

The longest letter was written to the church in the smallest town. Thyatira was known for its clothing industry: weaving, dyeing, and sewing were major sources of income, especially for women. The town was dominated by trade guilds, which required religious participation and were dominated by **powerful and prosperous women**. It is no surprise then that a prosperous woman, symbolically called "Jezebel," functioned as a false teacher in the church and tolerated false doctrine.

The Roman gymnasium complex at Sardis. In the foreground are the remains of a basilica style building eventually converted for use as a synagogue.

E. Sardis: Powerless Church (Revelation 3:1–6)

Sardis was an old city. It had formerly been the capital of the region under the Persians, was destroyed by the Greeks, and rebuilt by the Romans. The church, like the city, was dying, and **only a few believers** were left (3:14). The Lord challenged them with five staccato imperatives: Wake up! Strengthen! Remember! Obey! Repent!

F. Philadelphia: Persevering Church (Revelation 3:7–13)

Known as the "gateway to the East," Philadelphia sat in a lush valley in the heart of Asia Minor, near the pass into the Timolous Mountains. It was literally the "open door" between East and West. The church **persevered** with "limited strength" (3:8) and was commended for their endurance and promised to be kept "from" (Gk. *ek*) the "hour of testing" (tribulation) that would eventually come on the whole world (3:10).

G. Laodicea: Putrid Church (Revelation 3:14–22)

In contrast to the open door at Philadelphia, Laodicea was the church of the closed door at which the Lord of the church is pictured knocking (3:20). It is also described as **putrid** and **lukewarm**, despite its material prosperity.

In these letters to the seven churches, we have our Lord's personal encouragement to keep the faith, endure persecution, remain zealous, and seize the opportunity to spread the gospel. Since each letter urges the reader to heed what the Spirit says to all the "churches," we today must also take these admonitions to heart.

III. Problem: Seven-Sealed Scroll (Revelation 4–5)

The scene shifts dramatically at this point. "After this" (4:1) indicates **sequential movement**. This is the key turning point in the Apocalypse. John is summoned into the throne room of heaven and views everything from this point on from a heavenly perspective. The "vision of heaven" (vv. 4–5) turns the reader's attention from earth to heaven and from time to eternity. It introduces the problem of the seven-sealed scroll and the dramatic solution in the appearance of the Lamb.

Archaeological remains of an early church located at Laodicea in Turkey.

John was **called up to heaven**. "Come up here," the word commands, "and I will show you what must take place after this" (4:1). Immediately, John found himself in heaven, transfixed by the glory of God seated on the throne of the universe. His description of the scene emphasizes the inaccessibility of the throne, which is separated by lightning bolts, peals of thunder, angelic creatures, and a sea of glass (4:2–7). In addition, John sees 24 elders, robed in white, representing the church in heaven. Interestingly, other than the symbol of the elders, the church is not pictured in chaps. 14–18, until the marriage of the Lamb and her triumphant return with Christ, her warrior husband in 19:11–16.

The **problem** that emerges in these chapters is **twofold**: (1) no one can cross the "sea of glass," and (2) no one was found "worthy" (Gk. *axios*) to open the seven seals on the scroll in the hand of the Father. The angelic creatures (*seraphim*; cf. Isa 6:2–3) flew about the throne announcing the thrice holiness of the triune God. The interaction of the words "worthy" (*axios*) and "holy" (*hagios*) are clearly evident in the Greek text. Only one who is "holy" is "worthy" to approach the throne of God, take the scroll, open the seals, pronounce its judgments, and bring the kingdom of heaven to earth.

Suddenly, the **Lamb** (Christ) appears seated in the throne, coequal with the Father, and the problem is solved. He takes the scroll, and all the elders and angelic creatures fall down in worship, proclaiming "worthy is the Lamb" (5:9–10). The chapter virtually shouts to the readers of **the deity of Christ**. The symbol of the Lamb, taken from John's Gospel (1:29), is used 28 times in the Apocalypse to define the atoning work of Christ who is depicted in the book as Savior, Priest, Lord, and King.

Greek Highlight

Worthy. Greek ἄξιος **(axios).** The adjective *axios* describes something that is of **comparable value** or worth to something else (*comparable, worth*), or something that is appropriate to a particular person or activity (*corresponding to, deserving of*). In the NT, *axios* occurs several times in reference to those receiving a punishment of death (i.e., the punishment corresponds to the crime: Luke 23:15,41; Acts 23:29; 25:11,25; 26:31; Rom 1:32). In the Gospels *axios* occasionally describes truths about salvation and discipleship (Matt 3:8; 10:37–38; Luke 12:48), and Paul does the same in Rom 8:18 (the related verb *axioo* occurs in 2 Thess 1:11; 1 Tim 5:17; and the adverb *axios* occurs in Eph 4:1; Phil 1:27; Col 1:10; 1 Thess 2:12). In Revelation, the redeemed are found *worthy* of their reward (Rev 3:4); God is *worthy* of glory, honor, and power (Rev 4:11); and the Lamb is *worthy* of **worship** as well (Rev 5:2,4,9,12). Thus, in anticipation of this grandiose reality of their soon-returning King, all believers should "walk *worthy*" of their profound position in Christ (Eph 4:1) as joint heirs with Him (Rom 8:17) while always remembering that Christ alone is worthy of hyper-exaltation above all things (Phil 2:9). Thus, the Lamb (Christ) is *worthy* of our worship (Rev 5:12).

IV. Process: Seven Seals and Seven Trumpets (Revelation 6–11)

The process of **divine judgment** is unleashed by the opening of the seven seals. This results in a series of catastrophic events that express the "wrath of the Lamb" (6:16). Pretribulationalists believe the rapture of the church (1 Thess 4:13–17) takes place prior to these judgments since the Church, the bride of Christ, is the object of His love and not His wrath (cf. Eph 5:22–32; 1 Thess 5:9).

John watched and records as Christ (the Lamb) opens the seven seals and releases their judgments. The first four seals release **the four horsemen of the apocalypse** and a wave of wars on earth. Seals five and six reveal matters in the heavens (martyrs and cosmic disasters), and the seventh seal results in the sounding of the seven trumpet judgments (chaps. 8–9).

The seven sealed judgments are as follows:

1. White Horse: War (6:1–20)
2. Red Horse: Bloodshed (6:3–4)
3. Black Horse: Famine (6:5–6)
4. Pale Horse: Death (6:7–8)
5. Martyrs: "How Long?" (6:9–11)
6. Heavens Shaken: "Great Day of Wrath" (6:12–17)
7. Seven Trumpets: Silence, Then Disaster (8:1–3)

The imagery of colored angelic riders on horses can also be found in Zech 1:8–11. Galloping across the horizon, the four horsemen appear suddenly, riding forth in silence, successively releasing the human instruments of vengeance to execute their divinely appointed task. Though these judgments are providential, they are executed by human agencies. Armies are marching, men are fighting, and the world is at war. They are led by the rider on the white horse, **the imposter** with a bow, not a sword. This is not Christ, as some suppose, but the Antichrist who plunges the world into chaos in the last days.

Between seals six and seven, the seventh chapter serves as an **interlude** revealing a host of people saved out of the "great tribulation" (7:14). They include the 144,000 from the 12 tribes of Israel (7:4–8) and an innumerable host of Gentiles (7:9). Finally, the seventh seal is opened (8:1), followed by a period of silence, broken by the sending of the **seven trumpets of judgment** (8:7–21; 11:15–19):

1. Rain of Fire: Vegetation Burned (8:7)
2. Fireball: Oceans Polluted (8:8–9)
3. Falling Star: Rivers Polluted (8:10–11)
4. Sun Darkened: Air Pollution (8:12–13)
5. Demonic Plagues: Torment (9:1–12)
6. Great Army: 200 Million (9:13–21)
7. Divine Wrath: Heaven Opened (11:15–19)

The devastation predicted by the trumpet judgments was unknown and unfathomable in the ancient world but is certainly a potential reality in our world today. These prophecies portray a global conflagration so vast that **one-third of the planet** is affected. One gets the impression that the revelator watched this destruction in utter amazement.

Another **interlude** occurs in chaps. 10–11 with the sounding of the seven thunders, which John was told not to record (10:4). The appearance of the two witnesses (Gk. *marturia*) follows whose preaching mission ends after three and a half years (42 months or 1,260 days) with their martyrdom, resurrection, and rapture into heaven (11:1–12). These events are followed by the sounding of the seventh trumpet, the opening of heaven, and the revealing of the ark of the covenant (11:15–19).

V. Players: Seven Key Figures in the Eschatological Drama (Revelation 12–13)

Right in the middle of the Apocalypse, chaps. 12–13 reveal seven symbolic "signs" that give the reader a sketch of the hidden forces and worldly powers behind the great climax of history. The author now defines the **major players** of the apocalyptic pageant as he reveals the lifelong struggle between God and Satan that will come to its ultimate finish in the closing chapters (chaps. 14–20) of the Revelation.

The seven symbolic players on the end times' scorecard are as follows:

1. Woman: Israel, Mother of the Messiah (12:1–2)
2. Dragon: Satan, the Old Serpent, the Devil (12:3–4,9)
3. Male Child: Jesus Christ Ascended to Heaven (12:2,5)
4. Michael: Archangel Who Battles Satan (12:7–12)
5. Remnant: Seed of the Woman (12:17)
6. Beast of the Sea: Antichrist (13:1–10)
7. Beast of the Earth: False Prophet (12:11–18)

Many mistakenly identify the woman (12:1–2) as the Church, but this woman is depicted as the "mother" of Christ, not the "bride" of Christ. Her symbols (sun, moon, stars) are taken from Gen 37:9, which refer to the family of Jacob (Israel). The beast of the sea is consistently referred to as the "beast" throughout the rest of the book, whereas the beast of the earth is later called the "false prophet" (19:20; 20:10). The "beast" (Antichrist) is pictured as a political ruler, whereas the false prophet is a

The Valley of Jezreel as viewed from the top of the Megiddo tel.

religious leader who deceives unbelievers into taking the "mark of the beast" (13:16–18).

VI. Plagues: Seven Bowl Judgments (Revelation 14–19)

Following the typical pattern of the Apocalypse, chap. 14 serves as an overview of the events that follow in chaps. 15–19. The chapter opens with the 144,000 on Mount Zion (14:1–5) and proceeds to the proclamation of the three angels (14:6–13), followed by the reaping and harvesting of the earth (14:14–20). Chapter 15 introduces the **bowl judgments** that follow in chap. 16. As each angel pours out his goblet (KJV "vial") from the great bowl of God's wrath (cf. Isa 51:17), the intensified judgments impact the entire world. The human race has gone beyond the point of no return, and it is too late to turn back.

The seven-bowl judgments are basically upon the same objects as the trumpet judgments but with **greater intensity**. Identified as the "seven last plagues" (15:1), the bowls are as follows:

1. On the Earth: Malignant Sores (16:2)
2. Into the Sea: Oceans Polluted (16:3)
3. Into the Rivers: Rivers Polluted (16:4)
4. Upon the Sun: Scorching Heat (16:8–9)
5. Throne of the Beast: Darkness and Pain (16:10–11)
6. River Euphrates: Kings of the East (16:12–16)
7. Into the Air: "It Is Done" (16:17–21)

The judgment of the sixth bowl results in the unsaved nations of the world under the leadership of the beast gathering their armies to the "great day of God" at **the battle of Armageddon** (16:14–16). The stage would now be set for the final confrontation between Christ and Antichrist. Chapters 17–18 describe the fall of Babylon (called "Mystery Babylon"), the kingdom of the beast. This, is turn, sets the stage for the nineteenth chapter, which opens with four hallelujahs of praise, followed by the **marriage of the Lamb** in heaven. The fact that the Church, the bride, is pictured in heaven with Christ indicates the rapture (1 Thess 4:13–17) must have taken place earlier before the tribulation judgments.

The great **climax of the book** comes in Rev 19:11–16 as Jesus Christ, the "Faithful and True" rider on the white horse rides out of heaven with His bride, the Church, robed in white from the wedding (19:8), at His side (19:14). The true King of kings and Lord of lords speaks and with the "sword of his mouth" slays the rebel army and casts the beast and the false prophet alive into the lake of fire (19:20).

VII. Postscript: Millennium and Eternal City (Revelation 20–22)

The book of Revelation ends with a dramatic postscript, which describes the millennium (1,000 years) in which Satan is bound in the abyss and Christ and His saints rule the world with a "rod of iron" (19:15 NKJV; 20:1–6). As ideal as this era will be, it is not heaven but an **earthly kingdom**. After the 1,000 years, Satan is released and attempts a final revolt of unbelievers who were born during the millennial years (20:7–10). Satan is finally cast into the lake of fire, and the great white throne judgment follows, which results in all the lost of all time being cast into the lake of fire, which is the "second death" (20:11–15).

The final chapters of Revelation (chaps. 21–22) describe the ultimate prophetic vision of the eternal state which includes **seven new things**: new heaven (21:1), new earth (21:1), new Jerusalem (21:2), new world order (21:5), new temple (21:22), new light (21:23), and new paradise (22:1–5). We are immediately swept away into the grandeur of the eternal city where all the redeemed of all time will live in peace and harmony forever. Sin, rebellion, sorrow, sickness, pain, and death are eliminated. It is paradise regained. The tree of life is there (22:2). Even more importantly, God is there, and we will "see His face" (22:4).

The Revelation ends with **an invitation** as the Spirit and the Bride say, "Come!" (22:17) and Jesus assures, "Yes, I am coming quickly" (v. 20). John adds the final "Amen! Come, Lord Jesus!" (22:20) and the closing benediction: "The grace of our Lord Jesus be with you all. Amen" (22:21 NKJV).

Study Questions

1. In what way does Jesus reveal the future to John in the Revelation?
2. How do the letters to the seven churches speak to us today?
3. What is the significance of the seven seals, trumpets, and bowls?
4. Why does the Revelation depict Christ as a Lamb?
5. What actually occurs at Armageddon when Jesus returns?
6. What does the promise of the new Jerusalem (eternal city) mean to you personally?

For Further Reading

Easley, Kendell. *Revelation*. HNTC. Nashville: B&H, 1998.

Hindson, Edward. *Revelation: Unlocking the Future*. Chattanooga, TN: AMG, 2002.

Morris, Leon. *The Revelation of St. John*. TNTC. Grand Rapids: Eerdmans, 1977.

Mounce, Robert. *The Book of Revelation*. NICNT. Grand Rapids: Eerdmans, 1977.

Thomas, Robert. *Revelation 1–7* and *Revelation 8–22: An Exegetical Commentary*. Chicago: Moody, 1992.

Walvoord, John. *The Revelation of Jesus Christ*. Chicago: Moody, 1966.

ENDNOTES

1. For details see Donald Guthrie, *New Testament Introduction* (Downers Grove, IL: IVP, 1990), 929–62.

2. See Robert Mounce, *The Book of Revelation*, NICNT (Grand Rapids: Eerdmans, 1977), 27–39. He notes the apostolic authorship of John was held by Papias (130), Justin Martyr (135), Irenaeus (180), Clement of Alexandria (200), Tertullian (210), and Origen (250).

3. Cf. C. B. Caird, *A Commentary of the Revelation of St. John* (New York: Harper & Row, 1966), 1–7; R. H. Charles, *A Critical and Exegetical Commentary on the Revelation of St. John* (Edinburgh: T&T Clark, 1920), cxvii–clix.

4. The book of Revelation has more than 1,200 "ands" (*kai*), more than any other book in the New Testament. They often form a series of *kaimeter* patterns linking lists and numbers.

5. Bruce Metzger, *Breaking the Code: Understanding the Book of Revelation* (Nashville: Abingdon, 1993), 13.

6. Ibid. For alternative theories see Donald Guthrie, *New Testament Introduction* (Downers Grove, IL: IVP Academic, 1990), 945–48.

7. See Otto Meinardus, *St. John of Patmos* (Athens: Lyeabettus, 1979), 1–22.

8. William Hendriksen, *More than Conquerors* (Grand Rapids: Eerdmans, 1962), 12–15.

9. William Ramsay, *The Letters to the Seven Churches of Asia* (New York: Armstrong, 1904), 190–92.

10. See Mounce, *The Book of Revelation*, NICNT, 31.

11. K. Gentry, *Before Jerusalem Fell: Dating of the Book of Revelation* (Tyler, TX: Institute for Christian Economics, 1989).

12. Mark Hitchcock, "Revelation, Date of," in Timothy LaHaye and Edward Hindson, ed., *Popular Encyclopedia of Bible Prophecy* (Eugene, OR: Harvest House, 2004), 336–39.

13. Metzger, *Breaking the Code*, 13–20.

14. Outline based on Edward Hindson, *Revelation: Unlocking the Future* (Chattanooga, TN: AMG, 2002), xiv.

15. See Edward Meyers, *Letters from the Lord of Heaven* (Joplin, MO: College Press, 1996).

Name Index

Subject Index

Scripture Index

IMAGE CREDITS

All maps are owned by B&H Publishing Group, Nashville, Tennessee.

Arnold, Nancy: p. 290

Biblical Illustrator, Nashville, Tennessee: pp. 128, 190, 214, 225, 253, 259, 264, 321, 329, 332

Biblical Illustrator (James McLemore, photographer): pp. 101, 268

Biblical Illustrator (David Rogers, photographer): pp. 61, 208, 231, 289

Biblical Illustrator (Bob Schatz, photographer): pp. 1, 52, 60, 77, 79, 94, 98, 100, 163, 165, 174, 175, 183, 186, 194, 244 (top), 245 (bottom), 300

Biblical Illustrator (Ken Touchton, photographer): pp. 198, 212

Brisco, Thomas V.: pp. 85, 102, 119, 120, 122, 125, 131, 148, 159, 188, 189, 203, 277, 333, 334

Corel Images: p. 71

Ellis, C. Randolph: pp. 37, 111, 229, 233

Illustrated World of the Bible Library: p. 240

iStock: pp. 138, 292, 296, 313, 323

Langston, Scott: pp. 68, 139, 143, 161

McColgan, John: p. 284

Ritzema, Elliott: p. 303

Scofield Collection, E.C. Dargan Research Library, LifeWay Christian Resources, Nashville, Tennessee: pp. 29, 34, 66, 83, 114, 130, 288

Smith, Marsha A. Ellis: p. 115

Stephens, Bill: pp. 27, 82, 85, 137, 150, 197, 199, 207, 282, 307, 337

Tolar, William B.: pp. 38, 80, 164, 204, 256

Wikipedia Commons, http://en.wikipedia.org: pp. 3 (public domain, University of Michigan, Ann Arbor Library, author unknown), 6 (public domain, Foxe's Book of Martyrs), 8 (public domain), 220 (public domain, Snowdog, photographer), 222 (Philly boy92, photographer), 249 (Wikimedia Commons)

ILLUSTRATIONS AND RECONSTRUCTIONS

Latta, Bill, Latta Art Services, Mt. Juliet, Tennessee: pp. 48, 51, 124, 146, 182, 270